European Culture and the Media

Changing Media – Changing Europe Series Volume 1

Edited by Ib Bondebjerg and Peter Golding

First Published in the UK in 2004 by
Intellect Books, PO Box 862, Bristol BS99 1DE, UK
First Published in the USA in 2004 by
Intellect Books, ISBS, 920 NE 58th Ave. Suite 300, Portland, Oregon 97213-3786, USA

A catalogue record for this book is available from the British Library

ISBN 1-84150-110-7
Cover Design: Gabriel Solomons
Copy Editor: Julie Strudwick

Printed in the UK by 4edge Ltd.

Contents

Foreword

This volume contains the first fruits of a major Programme under the title Changing Media - Changing Europe supported by the European Science Foundation (ESF). The ESF is the European association of national organizations responsible for the support of scientific research. Established in 1974, the Foundation currently has seventy-six Member Organisations (research councils, academies and other national scientific institutions) from twenty-nine countries. This programme is the first to be sponsored by both the Social Sciences and the Humanities Standing Committees of the ESF, and this unique cross-disciplinary organization reflects the very broad and central concerns which have shaped the Programme's work. As co-chairpersons of the Programme it has been our great delight to bring together many of the very best scholars from across the continent, but also across the disciplinary divides which so often fragment our work, to enable stimulating, innovative, and profoundly important debates addressed to understanding some of the most fundamental and critical aspects of contemporary social and cultural life.

The study of the media in Europe forces us to try to understand the major institutions which foster understanding and participation in modern societies. At the same time we have to recognize that these societies themselves are undergoing vital changes, as political associations and alliances, demographic structures, the worlds of work, leisure, domestic life, mobility, education, politics and communications themselves are all undergoing important transformations. Part of that understanding, of course, requires us not to be too readily seduced by the magnitude and brilliance of technological changes into assuming that social changes must comprehensively follow. A study of the changing media in Europe, therefore, is indeed a study of changing Europe. Research on media is closely linked to questions of economic and technological growth and expansion, but also to questions of public policy and the state, and more broadly to social, economic and cultural issues.

To investigate these very large debates the Programme is organised around four key questions. The first deals with the tension between citizenship and consumerism, that is the relation between media, the public sphere and the market; the challenges facing the media, cultural policy and the public service media in Europe. The second area of work focuses on the dichotomy and relation between culture and commerce, and the conflict in media policy caught between cultural aspirations and commercial imperatives. The third question deals with the problems of convergence and fragmentation in relation to the development of media technology on a global and European level. This leads to questions about the concepts of the information society, the network society etc., and to a focus on new media such as the internet and multimedia, and the impact of these new media on society, culture, and our work, education and everyday life. The fourth field of inquiry is concerned with media and cultural identities and the relationship between processes of homogenization and diversity. This explores the role of media in everyday life, questions of gender, ethnicity, lifestyle, social differences, and cultural identities in relation to both media audiences and media content.

In each of the books arising from this exciting Programme we expect readers to learn something new, but above all to be provoked into fresh thinking, understanding and inquiry, about how the media and Europe are both changing in novel, profound, and far reaching ways that bring us to the heart of research and discussion about society and culture in the twenty-first century.

Ib Bondebjerg

Peter Golding

Ib Bondebjerg is Professor at the Department of Film and Media Studies, University of Copenhagen. He is co-director of the ESF-project Changing Media-Changing Europe (2000-2004), and presently also director of the Centre for Media and Democracy in the Network Society, University of Copenhagen (2002-2005). He has published widely on both television, film and other media. Books in English: Television in Scandinavia. History, Politics Aesthetics (1996, co-ed.); Intertextuality & Visual Media (1999, co-ed.); Moving Images, Culture and the Mind (2000, ed.) and The Danish Directors. Dialogues on a Contemporary National Cinema (2001, co-ed.).

Peter Golding is Professor of Sociology and Head of the Department of Social Sciences at Loughborough University, UK. He is an editor of the European Journal of Communication, chair of the European Sociological Association media research network, and co-director of the ESF programme from which this volume derives. He is currently directing research on new approaches to media content analysis and media representations of power.

Ib Bondebjerg and Peter Golding

Introduction

Changing Media - Changing Europe:
Interdisciplinary and Dynamic Research Agenda

In February 2003 The European Commission launched a new web portal *Your Voice in Europe* (http://europa.eu.int/yourvoice), to make it easier for European citizens to make their voice heard in EU-policy making. Internal Market Commissioner Frits Bolkestein commented on the launch of this new site with the words: 'We need to listen closely to the business and citizens who are affected by our policies. By keeping our ear to the ground, we help ensure that our new policy initiatives have a solid basis'. The portal was a continuation of an EU-initiative started in October 2001 as part of the Commission's Interactive Policy Making Initiative (IP/01/519), and in the press release announcing this earlier version of the site the Commission boasts of three million users. This European media initiative is one of many examples of the role of modern technology and media in the shaping of a, new Europe. It is indeed an example of new developments in the political dimension of a changing Europe, where the changes from traditional mass media to new interactive media create new possibilities in trying to solve old problems. It is an example illustrating some of the themes and problems in focus in this book, and in the larger research programme from which the book derives.

The book *European Culture and the Media* reflects and analyses developments in European media currently undergoing fundamental changes, following not just decades of globalization, but also an ever deeper cultural and political integration and expansion of Europe as a political vision and project. The themes in the book, and the research on which it is based, are the result of a large interdisciplinary project launched in January 2000 by the European Science Foundation called *Changing Media - Changing Europe*. The project involves over sixty researchers from eighteen European countries, and involves both the humanities and social sciences. The aim is to develop comparative studies and understanding of the dynamics of European media culture, focusing on trends in the last decade, but with a broader historical perspective as an important context. Even though much energy has been devoted to developing policies on a European level for the audiovisual sector, in particular European television and film, and, as the above mentioned example illustrates, new media and information technology, research on European media cultures must keep in focus a whole range of both old and new media. The convergence of media in Europe, as elsewhere in the world, doesn't mean that older media disappear, but rather that they find a place in a new digital media culture: e-books and electronic newspapers and journals are added to the traditional print forms, web-TV stations try to find a niche but also major TV-stations develop Internet-strategies and profiles. The development of media cultures in Europe is a dynamic process embracing old and new media and often-contradictory social and cultural processes.

This is one of the main reasons for the structure of the research agenda in *Changing Media - Changing Europe*. Each of the four main themes of the programme points to dynamic tensions between opposing trends in the European media cultures. The programme focuses on dynamic *processes,* and furthermore tries to combine both qualitative and quantitative approaches and to integrate 'hard' economic, technological and sociological data with 'soft' issues like language, identity, aesthetics and culture. Each of the four teams, all contributing to this book, thus combines a plurality of dimensions in European media cultures with interdisciplinary approaches and comparative perspectives. The keywords behind the study of changes in Europe are interrelated dynamics such as *Citizenship and Consumerism*, dealing with the transformation of the public agenda and sphere in Europe since 1960 and shifting hierarchies of taste, values and norms; *Culture and Commerce*, dealing with challenges to public service institutions and public support mechanism, political communication and cultural and democratic diversity and plurality; *Convergence-fragmentation*, focusing on the digitalization of communication and the emerging new media culture and network society and how this may influence, for instance, everyday life, education and work; and finally *Homogenization-diversity* focusing on cultural identities in a changing

Europe, influenced by both forces of homogenization and a revitalization of regional, national and multi-cultural identities.

The large questions raised in this collaborative research programme are all dealt with on a general theoretical level and through rich case studies in the chapters following this introduction. In their introductory article Katz and Popescu raise some important questions concerning the control and power of communication in a globalized media culture. They suggest rebalancing the power between communicators and audiences, that is to focus more directly on the mechanisms and rhetorical strategies through which media try to construct their audiences. The focus on active audiences and the diversity of audience interpretation and use of the same kind of media and programmes is still an important aspect of the understanding of the dynamics of a European media culture, with all its different constituent cultures. But to deny the actual power of media and communicators in shaping communities and identities, or the effect of American dominance in Europe, would be to overstate diversity and freedom of reception. Media matters - communication can make a difference and influence our culture and perspectives on reality. This is also the reason why a study of media cultures on a European level is so important: European identities and communities will after all not be constituted as real communities unless trans-national institutions and media become a practical and symbolic reality.

The thematic parts of this book and most of the chapters have their basis in a conference in Copenhagen in April 2002 on *European Media, Cultural Identities and Cultural Politics*. Following another conference in the programme *Changing Media - Changing Europe* on *European Media and Globalization* (August 2000) this conference highlighted cultural processes and transformations in European media and the challenges these create for both cultural politics, media institutions and everyday life. The focus was on cultural identities and media at a European level, in national cultures, and the development towards a multi-cultural network society in a more globalized and digitalized media culture. This is clearly reflected in the three parts, and the internal dialogue between chapters in these thematic blocks. *Media, Globalization and the European Imaginary* focuses on cultural industries and popular culture in a both global and European perspective and seen from both the perspective of communicators and audiences. *Citizenship and Cultural Identities* on the other hand take us into the very construction of European identities through old and new media and the tensions between different levels of cultural identities. Finally *Media Institutions in a Changing Europe* looks at institutional policies and strategies trying to cope with the changing European and global scene, both in terms of media politics, political communication and new and more interactive modes of communication.

Media Cultures in a Changing Europe

Our concern, then, throughout the chapters that make up this book, is to see how the marked changes in the political and social formations of Europe relate to changes in the culture, organization, regulation, and political economy of the main vehicles of symbolic distribution in our society, the mass media. Change in Europe has been rapid since the epochal events of the late 1980s. What began as an economic opportunity, and has gradually been recast as a political 'project' of historic cast, has seen the European Union emerge as a focus of intense debate. The geo-political enlargement of the EU has changed the framework within which we debate questions of national and supra-national identity, and indeed has prompted increasingly intense questions about the nature, reality, and source of such a 'European-ness'. We can consider here two aspects of these questions. First, what are the sources and problems of this supposed emergence of a European dimension to identity? Second, are the media a key factor in such cultural changes as we can detect?

Forging a European identity has become an explicit, if variable, target of EU policy. Since the Copenhagen summit of 1973 placed the ideal on the political agenda, it has been clear that the notion of a European identity had its own mythology (Hall, 2003), and existed as a construct, not only of bureaucratic invention, but of the competing narratives of lived history and experience (Stråth, 2002). The explicit drive to forge such an identity has accelerated since 1980, if only at the mundane administrative level (though each has its rich symbolic extensions) of driving licences, flag, anthem, and such initiatives as the European Cities of Culture Programme (Sassatelli, 2002). These all seek, as demanded by the 1992 Maastricht Treaty, to bring 'the common cultural heritage to the fore'. In initiatives supported by the World Commission on Culture and Development, the Council of Europe has also produced a series of policy documents that aim to define Europe through a common 'European culture' (Cronin, 2002).

What, then, are the elements of this common culture? All accounts perceive a common heritage, in which democracy, Enlightenment values, science, reason, and individualism are infused in a potent brew which has a unique European flavour. To this heady mix is added a strong historical sense of roots in a common Greco-Roman tradition, together with a loose association of these values with something called 'civilization'. Inevitably this conveys a static sense of an immutable core, in which 'we intuitively tend to essentialize culture' in a European 'culture of the mind' (Ifversen, 2002; Delanty, 1995). At one and the same time this account describes and discovers a common European culture, but also prescribes its protection and advancement as a proper and important aspiration of policy. This is more than a political or geographical phenomenon confined to a *kleinEuropa;* it emerges from the deep historic unities identifiable across the wider *grossEuropa*, and is made more possible by the rise of individualism and with it the decline, it is sometimes claimed, of national identities, at least in their familiar forms (Outhwaite, 2000).

Any identity that is publicly and consciously constructed is so formed by contrast against its opposites or 'others'. For much European policy, the need to resist and cope with a global North American culture constructed through language and the entertainment media has provided such a focus. However, increasingly the world of Islam has met this need. Europe has constantly to redraw its mental boundaries, as Mihelj illustrates in this volume. Paradoxically the steady convergence of eastern Europe into the west may be rooted in the closer identification with the 'European cultural zone', the greater enthusiasm for this form of rapid 'modernization' and compelling incentives for integration, to be found more in some sectors of the applicant states than among the populations of a frequently sceptical western Europe (Laitin, 2002). At the same time, what has its roots in the formation of identity by contrast with the 'other' has little difficulty in transmuting into a virulent racism, which readily forgets the inherent hybridity and mutability of European identity. This fluidity, created not least by migrant groups, provides the raw material for the celebration and ritualization of identity which characterize attempts to defend and promote it at European as well as national level (Kohli, 2000). At the extreme, fortress Europe assumes rather than discovers a common European identity which 'is understood to have bequeathed an indelible and distinct moral, cultural and political legacy upon Europe and Europeans' (Fink, 2002, p. 121).

There are, of course, many other difficulties in grasping this protean myth of a European culture or identity. The elements so readily discovered in such a formation - western, Christian, rational, modern, democratic, and so on, are, precisely because evoked by reference to abstract universalistic principles, impossible to render concretely in historic or geographical specifics (Soysal, 2002). There is also a discernible contradiction in the policy arena within Europe among the emerging panoply of European institutions and pan-national agencies. The European Community is intensely conscious of its role in fostering a defensive counter to the global hegemony of north American language and culture in both new technologies and the cultural industries. At the same time it has kept a wary eye on periods of Japanese economic expansion in the information and digital sectors. Such work requires an assertive buttressing of economic liberalization and support for the market, with a sharp focus on the private sector. This has underpinned a sequence of initiatives - the Delors white paper in 1993, the Bangemann report in 1994 and so on (Servaes, 2002). The growing obsession with the need to encourage Europe's emergence as the world's first information society has enhanced such rhetoric, in the drive to 'make the European Union the most competitive and dynamic knowledge-based economy with improved employment and social cohesion by 2010' (European Commission, 2002). This ambition , it is asserted, can only be met by the market, as 'Most services are provided by the market. Developing services needs significant investment, most of it from the private sector...' (European Commission, 2002.). The cultural inclinations (for example to be found in much of the public declarations of the European Council) can seem at odds with the economic and industrial policies and imperatives of the Community.

Where, then, do the changing media sit in this complex picture? Three factors are of interest here in our attempt to capture changing media cultures. First is the problematic role and prospects of pubic service broadcasting (PSB). In most European societies such hybrid and unique forms - variably independent of the state but also of the market - have been the corner stones of broadcasting development in the second half of the twentieth century. As Jakubowicz' chapter explains, this role is increasingly precarious. Williams gives as examples 'In Denmark the Liberal-Conservative government plans to privatise TV2; in Portugal the centre-right government plans to close the second public service channel, RTP 2. In Italy, Silvio Berlusconi tightens his grip over RAI through the appointment of his supporters to key positions in RAI 1 and 2' (Williams, 2002). In early 2003 in the UK, home to the archetypal PSB organization, the BBC, the relevant minister announced a 'wide-ranging review' of the BBC as part of the government's preparations for review of the BBC's role and finance which are due for statutory renewal in 2006. In a new environment of digital multiplicity and entertainment-led information systems can such structures be defended or renewed?

The second factor of interest is the failure of a European cultural space to emerge within the media. While newspapers are unfailingly national or local in form and content, broadcasting is hospitably international, but largely through accommodation to the market power of the major US corporations. As de Bens and de Smaele demonstrate, the average proportion of non-national European television shown in prime time across Europe is 14.9%, while the figure for national programmes is 26.5%, and for US imports it is 56.8% (De Bens & De Smaele, 2001). Again we see the contradictions in policy. The Transfrontier Television Directive ties itself in knots in attempting to reconcile the rights of national broadcasters and of local legislation and tradition with the establishment of a continent-wide 'imaginative communicative space', finally arriving at the tortuous requirement that the Directive is 'binding for all member states, but its implementation is left to the discretion of national governments' (Bek, 2003).

It is sometimes argued that the growing popularity of European based entertainment formats, not least in new areas of reality television or 'junk TV' can offer European audiences the common experiences and enthusiasms that form the elements of a single culture. Whether *Big Brother* and its like can carry this historic burden remains to be seen, but plainly many such ritualistic European encounters

- in the Eurovision song contest, in soccer, in *Jeux Sans Frontières* - remain bastions of nationalistic stereotypes and presumptions as much as vehicles for cross national hybridity. The globalization of formats, however, is much more susceptible to the tyrannical cultural force of the major US players. It is certainly true that Europe has its own growing conglomerate media sector; the Vivendi's and Bertelsmann's are powerful operators, and not withstanding the occasional collapse of a Kirch or ITV Digital, American dominance is far from total. Despite the 'Europeanization' of some US groups, though their involvement is such initiatives as AOL Time-Warner's new theme park in Madrid, the general picture is of 'a handful of powerful global media groups taking control of the expanding media and leisure market spanning film, television, book publishing, music, new online media, theme parks, sport, the print media and even the theatre' (Williams, op. cit.).

This is, then, a uniquely opportune moment to assess the changing media cultures across Europe as they shift in form and impact against a backdrop of a continent whose cultural policies and very identity are protean, erratic, contested, and dynamic. These changes and uncertainties are a challenge for analysis and research, to which our contributors have energetically and courageously risen.

Globalization, Identity, and Media

As already indicated, these dynamics and problems related to a changing European media culture are dealt with from three different but intimately connected perspectives. In the first part of the book the focus is on different aspects of popular culture in a European and cultural perspective. In an interesting case study of the development of the originally Danish but now global toy industry Lego, Stig Hjarvard shows how the mediatization of the toys is an important part of the globalization and commercialization processes. His analysis of this particular case, however, also has a more general perspective on the global network economy and the important sector of cultural consumption and entertainment. The article on the one hand offers a detailed study of this historical development from a national company to a global media industry, but on the other hand also introduces general concepts of mediatization, imaginarization, narrativization and virtualization as strategies for developing cultural identities and consumer products. The dynamic between a global media power and a more local-national cultural context is also in focus in Kirsten Drotner's article on audience responses to Disney media products. The paper is part of a larger European study of Disney in Europe and reports on the images and attitudes towards Disney among Danish children and their parents. The specific focus of the article is again related to larger questions of cultural identities, homogenization and diversity in the readings of global media products. The article presents a bottom up perspective on globalization and the whole of media in mundane discourses. Roberta Pearson and Máire Messenger

Davies in their empirical reception study of Shakespeare and the American TV-series *Star Trek* also offer a bottom up perspective on audiences and products normally placed at either end of a traditional taste hierarchy. But in this study of how audiences react to classical European and American popular culture, Pearson and Messenger question too crude oppositions between European high culture and American mass culture and 'dumbing down', and they discuss broader issues of popular imagination and popular culture in the cinema and on television. Finally, Daniel Biltereyst analyzes the highly debated forms of reality-TV in general, as a new popular form of factual entertainment, and in relation to concrete data on the debate and reception of reality-TV in Belgium. The concepts of media panics and moral panics, that have a long tradition in European media research, are used to shed light on this new media phenomenon. In his discussion descriptive, sociological perspectives meet with aspects of a more normative media theory.

In the second part, *Citizenship and Cultural Identities*, questions of citizenship and cultural identity are addressed. Uricchio uses an examination of peer-to-peer networking to assess how the new technologies can radically disrupt our sense of community and identity, not least our affinity with the nation-state. Participatory cultures of the kind he describes and examines pose important questions for both analysis and policy. Schrøeder takes this question deep into analysis of the construction of European identity, by applying cluster and Q-analysis in a combination of quantitative and qualitative methodologies to assess how citizens culturally negotiate national and European identity. Mihelj provides a thorough analysis of Slovenian coverage of Bosnian refugees in order to construct a persuasive and intriguing argument about the formation of cultural boundaries at the edges of Europe. In examining the 'discourse of peripheral nationalism' she is able to provide an understanding of the role of the media, not just in fostering xenophobia, but in providing the symbols and rhetoric from which people are able to understand their place and that of their environment in a shifting European cultural landscape. Ludes offers a test case of such provision in an empirical assessment of a pivotal moment in the construction of a trans-national Europe, namely the introduction of the Euro. As he explains, money has its cultural meanings as well as its material actuality, and, like the coins themselves, this event had a national and a European aspect.

In the last and third part of the book, *Media Institutions in a Changing Europe*, more institutional and policy-oriented aspects of the European media culture are addressed. Karol Jakubowicz in his article takes us through the main phases of a European policy on public service broadcasting. He situates the EU policy in a longer historical development from the early, 'emerging media policy' of European nation states, the more traditional 'public service phase' up till the 1970s and into the 'new paradigm of media policy' facing the challenges of globalization and media convergence. His main conclusion on the EU policy on public service is that it has been more reactive than proactive, and that one of the problems with the EU policy is further that they have generally not taken a culturalist point of view on public service broadcasting. Taisto Hujanen's article extends the discussions and perspectives laid down in Jakubowicz' more general article through a case study of the transformation of the Finnish public service channels after 2000 as digitalization became the key word. Through a case study of one of the Finnish main channels YLE, Hujanen shows how traditional public service strategies are renewed and transformed as YLE moves from a more generalist programme schedule to production for a more profiled digital multiplex of channels. The article raises important questions about the role of public service in a future European media context. In Mazzoleni's article another important aspect of European media culture is raised: the development of political communication and democracy in circumstances of media concentration either on a national or more global scale. Berlusconi's Italy may seem to be an extreme case in a European context, generally characterized by more indirect links between media and political power. But as Mazzoleni clearly demonstrates, the strategies and policies and the power play of Berlusconi as both a media tycoon and political figure reflect broader perspectives in European politics, where media management and control become more and more important elements of political communication.

It is clear that both Europe and its culture(s) are changing, and that the media are a central set of organizations and institutions at the heart of these changes. The following chapters offer a range of insights, ideas, and challenges for thinking about and understanding these social and cultural changes as we struggle not only to analyze and understand, but also to live in changing cultures in a changing Europe.

References

Bek, M.Gencel (2003) European Union Communication Policies and Harmonization. Paper prepared as ESF Young Scholar, and delivered at European Sociological Association meeting, Bremen, 25 January 2003.

Cronin, A. (2002) 'Consumer Rights/Cultural Rights: a new politics of European belonging'. European Journal of Cultural Studies. 5(3), pp. 307-323.

De Bens, E., & De Smaele, H. (2001) 'The Inflow of American Television Fiction on European Broadcasting Channels Revisited'. European Journal of Communication. 16(1), pp. 51-76.

Delanty, G. (1995) Inventing Europe - Idea, Identity, Reality. London: Macmillan.

European Commission. (2002) e-Europe: An Information Society for All (9289437820). Luxembourg: European Communities.

Fink, J. (2002) 'Europe's Cold Shoulder: Migration and the Constraints of Welfare in Fortress Europe'. Soundings. (21), pp. 119-132.

Hall, S. (2003) 'In but not of Europe' - Europe and its Myths. Soundings. (22), pp. 57-69.

Ifversen, J. (2002) 'Europe and European Culture - A Conceptual Analysis'. European Societies. 4(1), pp. 1-26.

Kohli, M. (2000) 'The Battlegrounds of European Identity'. European Societies. 2(2), pp. 113-137.

Laitin, D. D. (2002) 'Culture and National Identity: "The East" and European Integration'. West European Politics. 25(2), pp. 55-80.

Outhwaite, W. (2000) 'Towards a European Civil Society?' Soundings. (16), pp. 131-143.

Sassatelli, M. (2002) 'Imagined Europe: The Shaping of a European Cultural Identity through EU Cultural Policy'. European Journal of Social Theory. 5(4), pp. 435-451.

Servaes, J. (2002) 'The European Information Society: Much Ado about Nothing?' Gazette. 64(5), pp. 433-447.

Soysal, Y. N. (2002) 'Locating Europe'. European Societies. 4(3), pp. 265-284.

Stråth, B. (2002) 'A European Identity: To the Historical Limits of a Concept'. European Journal of Social Theory. 5(4), pp. 387-401.

Williams, G. (2002) European Media Ownership: Threats on the Landscape. A Survey of Who Owns What in Europe (on-line report). Brussels: European Federation of Journalists.

Elihu Katz is Trustee Professor at the Annenberg School for
Communication at the University of Pennsylvania and Professor
Emeritus of Sociology and Communication at the Hebrew University
of Jerusalem. His recent books include Media Events: The Live
Broadcasting of History (co-author with Daniel Dayan; Harvard
1992), and Canonic Texts in Media Research: AreThere Any,
Should There Be, How About These? (co-editor with John D. Peters
Tamar Liebes and Avril Orloff; Polity Press, 2003). He was
awarded the UNESCO-Canada McLuhan Prize, the Israel Prize and
honorary degrees from the Universities of Ghent, Haifa, Montreal
and Paris. He was founding director of Israel Television, and served
as long-time consultant on social research to the BBC.

Mihaela Popescu is a Doctoral Candidate at the Annenberg School
for Communication, University of Pennsylvania.

Elihu Katz and Mihaela Popescu

Supplementation: On Communicator Control of the Conditions of Reception

'New Media/New Europe' conceals a paradox. The new media are media of
segmentation and individuation while the new Europe cries out for media of
unification. Unification was the achievement of the era of mass communication
beginning with the newspaper (Tarde, 1901; Anderson, 1983), followed - all the
more effectively - by classical broadcasting (Cardiff and Scannell, 1987). These
were the media of national unification, and might have served European unity well
if they were not being undermined by the new media of divisiveness - the satellite,
the cable, the internet and the cellphone.

This chapter offers some consolation. On the eve of this new era, we want to argue
that the effect of broadcasting - including the effect on social integration - was not
as automatic as we tend to think. The 'wise communicator' did not rely only on the
broadcast message itself, or on the scope of its diffusion, or on the power of
technology, but invested additional effort to ensure that the message would be
'read' as intended. By now, it is a commonplace observation that most messages are
not distributed at random but are targeted, implicitly or explicitly, to marked
audiences. We will argue that this targeting is not just an epiphenomenon of the
new media technology, but has always been present, even in the one-hundred-and-

fifty years of classic mass communication.

In doing so, we are trying to recalculate the balance of power between senders and receivers, arguing that the time has come to return some of the power that 'reception theory' has taken from communicators and given to audiences. We are not, however, calling for 'return to a theory of powerful effects.' Rather, we are arguing that communicators have restricted audience autonomy by gaining control of those contexts, relations and identities that will reinforce the 'dominant' reading.

The Argument

This argument came to life while reading John Peters' brilliant *Speaking Into the Air* (1999). Peters offers us two competing models of communication - the Socratic model of dialogue, and the Jesus model of broadcasting. The dialogic formula is a well-tailored effort to influence a carefully selected alter, clinically so to speak, i.e. in a manner that is perfectly calibrated to the receiver's reactions and resistances. No overhearers are allowed, because the message might be misinterpreted. For the same reason, it would be better not to write the message down, lest it fall into the wrong hands. The broadcast model is attributed to Jesus, whose messages were cast as widely as possible, fall where they may, in an all-embracing gesture of universalism and equal access. Peters' argument is that broadcasting is an altruistic gesture, a generous reaching out, and less occupied with effectiveness.

This assertion led us to wonder whether other broadcasters - in the generic sense of senders of messages to an anonymous and atomized multitude - surrender their messages so readily. Do they really abandon all hope of influencing the decoding and reception? One wonders even about Jesus who is perfectly aware that there are special people who 'have ears to hear,' and that some of these hearers were given a share in relaying the message and perhaps giving it organizational form (Matthew 28:19-20).

We are alluding here to the general category that Lazarsfeld and Merton (1948) called 'supplementation,' arguing that a message has a better chance of diffusion and acceptance if it enlists others to carry it forward and/or if the receivers are appropriately situated and primed. Lazarsfeld and Merton refer to the listening groups who gathered to hear Father Coughlin's rabid radio talks prior to World War II, but it is equally true of the Rabbi of Lubavitch whose associates organized speaker-phone listening posts around the world, or to evangelists who, not content simply to count the people who raise their hands for Christ, refer these penitents to the church nearest their homes. Nor is it different from Lang and Lang's (Lang & Lang, 1990) discovery that the posthumous reputation, and price, of an artist is a function of whether her name and work were given into the hands of a faithful spokesperson. In short, we are arguing not that the two-step flow of communication works - provided that it supports the message and its source - but that communicators, even altruistic ones, are as smart as we are. Or are they? Do they know about the second step? Do they try to co-opt it? What other things do they do to enhance the reception of their message? To say it another way, we are asking whether the International Olympics Committee, or the networks that broadcast the Olympics or the Superbowl, have not actively intervened in the construction of living-room fans (Real, 1977; Rothenbuhler, 1988).

What Broadcasters Know

That communicators are concerned about the situation in which their messages are received, is documented by Paddy Scannell in several places (1996; 2000). He refers, for example, to the nervous reaction of the Royal Family to the BBC's early proposals to produce live broadcasts of royal occasions, first on radio, then on television. To the initial proposal in 1923, the Family said no, arguing that listeners who happened on the transmission of the Wedding while in a public house 'might not even take their hats off.' On another occasion in 1953, when the Royals were reluctantly agreeing to allow television into the Abbey for the Coronation, the BBC protested that the newsreel cameras were being given a better vantage-point than the TV cameras to the more ritualistic, more intimate, moments of the ceremony. The official reply was that the newsreels had agreed to submit their film for possible editing, and more important for our purposes, that the decorum of the viewers in a cinema would surely be appropriate.[1] But 'what can we expect of television viewers in their homes?' they worried. In other words, they feared that home viewers of the solemn ceremony might view the event in their underwear, so to speak.

To take a related example from the coverage of the Royal Wedding in 1953, we know that the American networks sent their anchors to broadcast from London for a whole week in advance, in order to rehearse their audiences in the symbols, the route of march, the Church service, etc. in anticipation of the roles they would be expected to take as awe-inspired 'witnesses' to the event. In effect, they were preparing their audience to dress up and seat themselves properly on the day, as Members of the Wedding. *Mutatis mutandis*, consider Victor Klemperer's (1998) diary for 11 November 1933, at the crucial moment of the plebiscite. 'During the thirteenth hour,' he writes, quoting the radio announcer, '"Hitler will come to the workers." The language of the Gospels exactly,' Klemperer notes, 'the Redeemer comes to the poor.'

The basic problem of modern broadcasters - sources and transmitters - is the separation, in space, between themselves and their audiences. This compounds the problem of one-to-many. In Jesus' time, there were many but they were present physically; in the era of broadcasting, the problem of many is compounded by the problem of non-presence. Then, as we have just seen, there is the further problem of 'home,' that is, not just that the audience is at a distance, but that it is typically (not always) dispersed in an infinite number of nuclear cells. As a footnote, we should recall that there was a moment when German TV was being designed for reception in the streets, not in homes (Uricchio, 1989), and this was true for a time in Italy as well. Communal reception used to be the norm in Indian villages - maybe still is - for economic reasons, but the communal assembly was also thought to be reinforcing of developmental communications.

But since broadcasting has moved us all inside, we must face up to the question of whether broadcasters are able to 'situate' home viewers in arrangements that are conducive to reception of their messages-as-intended. In a word, can broadcasters rearrange the furniture to suit their messages? Do they even try? Scannell tells us that they do try. Quoting the first Head of BBC Talks, Scannell (2000, p. 10) reports that 'she realized two things: First, that the unknown audience should not be thought of as a mass but as a constellation of individuals, with individual interests, needs, tastes and opinions... Second, that the design of talk for absent listeners should take into account the context within which listening took place. (She) realized that the broadcaster must consider where listeners were situated as they listened, and adapt what was said to those circumstances.'

Scannell is pessimistic. Citing interviews conducted with listeners to the 1937 coronation of George VI, 'What shows up quite clearly,' says Scannell, 'is the impossibility, as the Dean of Westminster foresaw, of controlling the behaviour of listeners to a solemn, sacred event. They could listen, if they wished, in pubs with their hats on or in their bath with nothing on, for that matter.' In spite of his awe for the powers of radio, Klemperer was similarly surprised, observing audience behaviour at the Long Distance Lorry Drivers' Restaurant near Leipzig (11 September 1933) 'The customers all came and went,' he notes, 'taking their leave with "Heil Hitler." But no one was listening, I could barely understand the broadcast because a couple of people were playing cards, striking the table with loud thumps, talking very loudly. It was quieter at other tables. One man was writing a postcard, one was writing in his order book, one was reading the newspaper. And landlady and waitress are talking to each other or to the card players. Truly, not one of a dozen people paid attention to the radio for even a single second, it could just as well have been transmitting silence or a foxtrot from Leipzig'. Are we wrong, then, in thinking that they can surmount such obstacles? That's what this chapter is about.

What Researchers Know

Before returning to what broadcasters do to supplement their message, let's reconsider what *we* know, in communication research, about enhancing the likelihood that a message will be received as intended. A good place to start is Michael Schudson's (1989) 'How Culture Works' which lists five mechanisms for assuring the success of a piece of culture - whether a speech, a person, a message, a ritual, an advertisement, or an idea - where success is measured (implicitly) in terms of salience, longevity, and so on. Using a rhetorical device of his own, Schudson calls attention to the five 'r''s of 1) retrievability, or providing easy access at a low price; 2) rhetoric, in which he includes the compatibility between messages and medium; 3) resonance, which refers to the compatibility between message and receiver's values and concerns; 4) institutional retention, whereby a piece of culture is incorporated in a textbook or a holiday or a prayer; and 5) resolution, or what might be called 'instructions for use,' that engage the society in active response.

Schudson is speaking not as an advice-giver but as an observer of what works. As in the case of 'supplementation,' if the communicator gets to these mechanisms before the audience does, he can press what he has learned into the service of the message, rather than stand by, idly, waiting for the receiver to misunderstand or to decode oppositionally, or ignore. Applying his idea of *pseudo-gemeinschaft*, Beniger (1986) asserts that broadcasters *do* get there first and have been there for a long time, citing, as an example, the calculated use of the personalized rhetoric of sincerity and authenticity, as in Merton's (1946) Kate Smith. In other words - in yet another restatement of our hypothesis - we are suggesting, with Beniger, that broadcasters strive to incorporate dialogic elements to tailor their broadcasts.

In his famous paper 'Encoding/Decoding', Hall (1980) expresses the same idea in different words - namely, that audiences are not free to 'decode' a text as they want, but restrained in their decoding by the normative and performative rules according to which the text is constructed. This is the job of broadcasting.[2]

Researchers know quite a lot more, something which we will repeatedly illustrate as we move along. Specifically, we will attempt to devise a (preliminary) typology of ways in which communicators try to shepherd their messages in order to increase their likelihood of success. That is, we will try to take a step beyond Beniger, Schudson and Hall in cataloguing examples of 'supplementation' which include, but are by no means not limited, to rhetorical devices.

A Typology of Supplementation

We think that there are two kinds of communicative intervention, which we call Constructing and Exploiting, and a number of targets of these interventions, which we call 'space,' 'time,' 'frame,' 'identity,' 'trust,' 'practice,' 'feedback,' and 'feedforward.' These targets seem to collapse into four major categories of control - of the context (space, time and cognitive frames), of roles and relations (identity and trust), of action or implementation (practice), and of reaction (feedback and feedforward).

Communicator Control of the Conditions of Reception

		Constructing	Exploiting
Control Context	Place	1	2
	Time	3	4
	Frame	5	6
Control Relations	Identity	7	8
	Trust	9	10
Control Action	Practice	11	12
Control Reaction	Feedback	13	14
	Feedforward	15	16

By *constructing*, we mean that the communicator tries to constrain the audience to enter a space (real or virtual), a time, a frame of reference, a role, a routine which reinforce the intent of the communicator. By *exploiting*, we mean that the communicator tries to take advantage of pre-existing spaces, times, cognitive frames, roles, routines, etc. Manipulations of space, time and frames refer to the situational contexts of reception; identity refers to a role which is induced in the receiver, trust refers to the relationship proposed between sender and receiver; practice refers to habitual action; feedback alludes to reactions, intended or not, transmitted by receiver to sender; and feedforward implicates the receiver in transmitting a message to others. Notice that these are echoes of elements in the dialogic process, something that we would find quite familiar in a laying-on of hands - that is, a ceremony of ordination, for example. If you will bear with us, we would like to invite you to walk through these boxes, which, for the time being, may serve as a reservoir for sorting ideas rather than as a responsible statement.

1. When the communicator attempts to create an environment that will help assure the proper reception of his/her message, we call this constructing space. Constructions may be made of bricks and mortar, but they also may be made of words and symbols - what Austin (1962) calls performatives. God telling Moses that he is standing on Holy Ground, in case he hadn't noticed that the bush was burning, is such a symbolic construction, designed to enhance the message. So is the gathering at the foot of Mt. Sinai, the thunder and the lightning, and the injunction to keep away from the opposite gender for three days. God knows how to do these things, or used to.

In keeping with media events, consider the contrast between Memorial Day ceremonies in Israel which are broadcast from the enclosure of the Wailing Wall, and Independence Day ceremonies - on the very next day, broadcast from the top of Mt. Herzl, the one to underline the familistic togetherness of the depths, the other to advertise civic openness and outward-orientation (Handelman and Katz, 1990). There can be no doubt that these loci influence those in actual attendance. But can television deliver its audience to these places? Is there a theory to suggest that broadcasters can accomplish this?[3] Cinema theory says yes. And media research is increasingly attentive to the different ways in which audiences write themselves into the script,[4] and there is even some experimentation to prove it (Messaris, 1992; McQuarrie & Mick, 1999). Normative theories that portray public opinion as supportive of a message - as in the spiral of silence (Noelle-Neumann, 1984) or in health-information campaigns (Hornik, 2002) have this quality of constructing (or exploiting) an environment of true or false consciousness.

Space may also be constructed by controlling decorum, as in keeping tourists out when the church service is in progress, or proscribing the reading of sacred texts in the toilet. Farrakhan's 'Million Man March' took on its meaning by excluding women, just as the Florida ballot box intimidated or misled potential voters who would likely have cast their votes for Gore. Thus, there are constructions - physical or symbolic - that reinforce messages for those who are admitted, by keeping others out.

2. Exploiting spaces is cheaper than constructing them. Wiebe's (1951) early paper called 'Merchandising Commodities and Citizenship on Television' clarifies the distinction between constructing and exploiting. In merchandising commodities, says Wiebe, when a toothpaste company manages to motivate viewers, it directs them to the proverbial 'corner drug store' where one and all are welcomed, politely treated, etc. This is true for the physician as well, who can direct his patient to a pharmacy to translate his message into supervised practice. However, says Wiebe, if the conditions for action require construction - as when a documentary programme on street crime urges neighbours to organize in order to take turns supervising their children on the street - the message may often fail in implementation - not for lack of motivation, but because of the difficulty associated with the recommended construction of space.

To take another excursion, consider the Ayatollah Khoumeni who regularly sent home audiocassettes from his exile in Paris. These, in turn, were rushed to the mosques and bazaars of Teheran, the 'safe spaces' (Gamson, 1995) which supplemented the message, and which served as the launching pads of the revolution against the Shah. Such places are not only safe; they offer legitimation for a message. In this sense, a museum authenticates a work of art, and thereby allows the artist-communicator to retain control over his/her claim (Benjamin, 1969).

Communicators may also exploit the social contexts in which media are typically consumed (Freidson, 1953). Thus, the radio, nowadays, finds people alone in their cars, and advertisers exploit that association to capture an audience. A male potency clinic in Israel does this very successfully. Some downtown clothing stores advertise on the backs of buses in order to pinpoint the driver inching along behind. Billboards also exploit this approach to 'captive audiences.' Television programmers used to know that the family room was their territory, for better and for worse; now family members are viewing in their own rooms (Livingstone & Bovill, 2001). And, of course, Internet programmers know that their clients are alone. Print is typically consumed alone and was used as the preferred medium, for a while, for the instructional part of family planning messages in developing countries (Berelson & Freeman, 1964; Bogue, 1990).

Thus, the home as a locus of reception is compatible and incompatible with certain kinds of messages. With respect to the larger question, however, of who benefits from the infinite dispersal of the home audiences, critical theorists such as Gerbner and Gross (1976) would have us consider the possibility that the powers that be enjoy the idea of us staying at home, where it's safe, and keeping our noses out of their politics and policing. Robert Putnam's (1995) theory of bowling alone follows Gerbner closely, on this point, without the conspiratorial twist.

3. Media events are a prime example of *constructing time*. That broadcasters have the power to declare time out - to say that society should hold its breath, that there is nothing more important to do than go home and view television - is incredible. Putting it otherwise, broadcasters have been given the right to declare a holiday, i.e. to interrupt the cycle of life and of routine broadcasting so as to lead us to commune with a shared value, to make ritual gestures, and to be aware that every other in the community is doing the same thing at the same time. Thus did the nation - and sometimes the world - stand still at the moment of the Coronation of Elizabeth, the moon-landing, the Kennedy funeral, the Challenger disaster (Dayan & Katz, 1992). Stated otherwise, television is proposing a holiday to celebrate an event which it has constructed from the raw material of another event (Scannell, 1996), thereby assuring that the re-presentation will be properly received, collectively remembered, and (following Schudson) institutionally retained (Hobsbawm & Ranger, 1983) (Mosse, 1975). You also know, of course, that the Superbowl and the rituals of Superbowl Day are inventions of television (Real, 1977; Schwartz, 1992).

Another budding example of media construction of time is the expansion of the weekend. Newspaper supplements on Fridays now invite us to anticipate the coming weekend, and to enter the liminal mode twenty-four hours earlier than we used to.

4. Apart from constructing time, broadcasters *exploit time*; they adapt their messages to institutionalized time. Soap operas target women in the afternoon, and sports programming waits for men to come home (Beitrose, 1980). Adult programming - says the law - waits until children are asleep, and horror movies wait until after midnight. Broadcasters know that people in Midwest America eat dinner an hour earlier, and that Sunday morning is a resonant time for religion, culture, and political pundits. Late night has a new aura in recent years (Melbin, 1978).

A different example of exploiting time is to ride on the coat tails of the calendar. Thus, the aura of Thanksgiving makes it easier to get media attention for appeals for the needy or the homeless; holiday time is pressed into the service of the message, and appeals are more effective therefore (Hilgartner & Bosk, 1988).

5. Constructing *cognitive frames* - that is, inviting conceptual associations that are compatible with desired decodings - also provides context. The burgeoning research literature on priming and framing offers a host of examples of how this is done. When the wrapping of the cheddar cheese asks, 'Have you had your calcium today?', the communicator is trying to head off the opposing association with high cholesterol. To frame 11 September as 'war' or 'Pearl Harbor' rather than 'terror' or 'Oklahoma City' evokes quite different kinds of understandings (Zelizer, 2002). Anwar Sadat was making the same sort of move when he invoked the Bible to suggest a 'brothers' frame for the present-day conflict between Jacob and Esau (Liebes-Plesner, 1984). Discussing visual framing, the art historian, Ernst Gombrich (in (McLuhan, 1964), declares that cubism is 'the most radical attempt to stamp out ambiguity and to enforce one reading of the picture - that of man-made construction...'

6. *Exploiting extant frames* to introduce an innovation - as in incorporating a known brand of cellphone in a futuristic movie - is to invite cognitive association between the product and its context. Modern political strategies play heavily on a candidate's ability to appropriate frames and intertextual references to popular culture, such as movie themes, and use them to 'sell' the candidate to a group of constituents (Andersen, 2000). For example, when Ronald Reagan alluded to his cowboy-movie days, he was trying to predispose his audience to sympathetic decodings by exploiting a (happily) shared frame. Bob Dole, a candidate in the 1996 presidential campaign, made a show of going to the cinema to see *Independence Day*; he is reported to have said to a group of supporters, at the end of the movie: 'Bring your family. You'll be proud of it. Diversity. America. Leadership' - thus exploiting the patriotic frames in which the movie is cast.[5]

7. Communicators have the power to tell us who we are. 'Interpellation' (Althusser, 1971) or 'altercasting' are terms for what we are here calling *constructing identity*. Public broadcasting, let's say, wishes to evoke our identity as citizens; so do media events. Commercial broadcasters, on the other hand, wish to address us as consumers. In another of his Royal examples, Scannell (1996) argues that BBC and ITV coverage of the Queen's traditional opening of Parliament - the first time that television cameras were admitted - differed as between the two British channels. The BBC evoked the relationship between Queen and loyal *subjects*, whereas the younger, commercially sponsored channel evoked the relationship between parliament and *citizens*. Beginning the day's broadcasting with readings from the Koran or the Bible or the national anthem serves similar functions.

In the OJ trial and the impeachment hearings, we were a jury; we were mourners at the Kennedy funeral; we are voters at the presidential debates. Wittingly or not, we assume these roles that are proposed to us performatively (Austin, 1962) and situate ourselves to deal 'properly' with the message that follows. Of course, we may reject these roles, and read oppositionally, or turn to another channel. But do we?

The most potent form of altercasting is the often-overlooked power of language to create shared identities. The powerful effects of the book, the newspaper, radio, and television were not in changing people's attitudes, but in the 'imagined communities' (Anderson, 1983; Tarde, 1901) that arose in response to being addressed in the national language. We are repeatedly reminded of this fact in discussions of European community, which shows no signs, or so we think, of surrendering linguistic autonomies. For all of its success, CNN is not about to create a global community, because it has no real cultural constituency; indeed CNN is about to launch its Arabic-speaking channel. If the nation-state is declining in importance it is not because of global broadcasting, but because multi-culturalism and its associated multi-channelism is pulling it apart from within. In this connection, one recalls the recurrent effort - repeatedly frustrated - to find one common language for mankind, perhaps. (Steiner, 1975; Eco, 1995)

8. Specialty channels aim at *exploiting identities* as well as constructing them. MTV programming signals to teenagers (Nash, 1999) even across linguistic differences. Women's magazines know how to 'profile' women in terms of age, class and life style, presumably as each group would like to see itself represented. Indeed, the media have long since been sorting the audience demographically, tailoring genres to demographics and selling these packages to advertisers. This is narrowcasting in its truest sense. Rather than competing for very large audiences by means of generalized altercasting and supplementation, the new media technologies specialize in niche communication. As Turow (1997) puts it, 'for the past decades,

their goal as mass marketers was *not* to reach everyone in the same way at the same time.'

9. Turow goes on to develop the idea that these marketers and their publications 'added claims that (they possessed) special relationships' to these segmented audiences. Such claims echo Beniger's (1987) *pseudo-gemeinschaft* which we here translate as *constructing trust*. Through techniques of flattery, in-group allusions, and altruistic gestures, communicators try to fraternize with their audiences. As Horton and Wohl (1956, p. 220) noticed long ago, 'The publicity campaigns built around successful performers continually emphasize the sympathetic image which, it is hoped, the audience is perceiving and developing. The audience, in its turn, is expected to contribute to the illusion by believing in it, and by rewarding the personae's "sincerity" with "loyalty."' The same principle applies to the cultivation of 'brand loyalty' or to karaoke singing. Karaoke emcees, as Drew shows us, rely on their social skills and ability to project trust in order to draw individual patrons to the stage and assure the quality of the karaoke experience. (Drew, 2001, pp. 92-94)

This is by no means a new phenomenon; it was not born with the technology of affixing personalized salutations to mass-marketed letters of solicitation. Pharmaceutical companies had been doing such things long before (Coleman et al., 1966). Gabriel Tarde (1901) pointed out long ago how newspapers and their readers choose each other, almost romantically, on the basis of various cues of compatibility.

10. One hardly need add that *trust can be exploited*; that is the definition of a con game. But exploiting trust can be more innocent. This would be the case, for example, if a peace activist or war-advocate bolsters an argument by reference to a public opinion poll, he/she is exploiting the presumption that the hearers trust in science. The same logic applies to the use of stars to endorse a commercial product. America's favorite songstress of World War II also became America's most successful salesperson of War Bonds by projecting her sincerity and altruism (Merton, 1946; Simonson, 2002).

11. The media also know how to hold and influence audiences by *constructing their practices*. For one thing, they can foster addiction through genres such as cliffhanger serials - whether *The Bold and The Beautiful* or *West Wing*, which induce you to return tomorrow or next week. Newspapers do this, too, in what Tuchman (1978) calls 'continuing stories,' or sometimes by just plain addiction to newspaper reading (Elliott, 1980). Lazarsfeld and Merton (1948) warned, long ago, that this sort of narcotizing may be dysfunctional for politics, when devout readers and viewers mistake their news addiction for political participation.

Critical theorists, as already noted, might say that this is the point itself. Narcotizing may supplement the unspoken message that we WANT you to stay inside, and out of politics, in the same way that Habermas' representational public sphere (Habermas, 1989) wants to dazzle you into blind admiration, or that fascism wants you to be swept away in ceremony (Benjamin, 1968). In each of these, the critical theorist would see supplementation as enhancing not of an explicit message but of a hidden one.[6]

Constructing practice refers to the how of message reception. The doctor's instructions to take the medicine with food or that it should be administered under medical supervision is an attempt to enhance the effectiveness of the 'message' by intervening in the how and the where. Consider the analogy that 'the Torah scroll must be read in the presence of at least ten men.'

Instructions for use need not be separated from the text. They may be embedded in the message itself. Thus, perspective in painting directs our decoding, just as the size of type or the initials 'PG' or 'XX' signals to adults that the book or the movie is or is not intended for children.

Another example from a recent paper by Blondheim and Blum-Kulka (2001) suggests that the practice of studying the Talmud in pairs - which is normative in talmudic academies to this day - is an implicit dictate of the text itself, which is a record of disputations among duelling sages. Similarly, Blondheim's analysis of the Haggadah - the widely known text of the Passover seder - leads him to conclude that it is not intended as prayer, not even as story, but as a ritual agenda for a kind of town meeting. In such cases, the communicator is clearly urging conditions of reception that will stimulate the kind of conversation that Schudson calls 'resolution.' (Schudson, 1989) One might add that the Haggadah even assigns disputational roles to the seder participants (Wise son, Wicked son, etc.) to strengthen the idea that everybody has a part to play. Altogether, ritual practices serve as shrines for messages. Yerushalmi (1982), for example, proposes that holiday practices serve as repositories of collective memory.

12. More to the point, perhaps, is that broadcasters obviously *exploit practices*. Once again, it is not big news that soap operas are timed and geared to the identities of housewives, but it is also geared to their practices. The role conflicts of the housewife, the constant interruptions, and the cycle of minor crises that beset her all parallel the soap opera narrative, says Modleski (1982). That is, the discourse is the histoire.

New York City taxicabs provide a different sort of fit between practice and message. Taking a seat in a New York City cab activates a recorded message from some celebrity reminding passengers to fasten their seat belts. Altogether theory gives strong support to the effectiveness of introjecting relevant messages at the point of practice, like skywriting ads for suntan lotion in the sky over the beach.

13. *Feedback* belongs in this list as *construction* and exploitation. It is perhaps the most obvious of the mechanisms used by broadcasters to assess the diffusion and effectiveness of their message, and it is no wonder that there is constant innovation in the field of TV ratings. We have reached the point of knowing who is in the room when the set is on, what was seen, and, most important, what was bought by these viewers at the supermarket. Here, however, we wish to emphasize that such feedback often enters into the construction of the message. Moreover, fabricated feedback is often inserted into the sound track of a situation comedy, serving to 'coach the audience' at home in how to react to the programme (Horton and Wohl, 1956, p. 219).

Nowadays, on-line shopping services construct feedback by stimulating potential buyers with information concerning what others 'like them' have bought under similar circumstances.

The success of focus-group methodology, if one can call it that, is the surprise of feedback research, both formative and evaluative. From our perspective, it is another illustration of how communicators try to direct and control their influence.

14. Apart from these formal and intended behaviours, we are exuding reactions all of the time, and there are a lot of observers trying to exploit our feedback. We are overheard, so to speak, by agencies of surveillance working for the King or the Dictator, or even for the democratic republic. Darnton's (2000) story of how the police followed an anti-royalist ditty from cafe to cafe is an example. But a famous first reference to such exploitation comes from the classic Horkheimer and Adorno (1947; see also Peters, 2003) to the effect that the Culture Industry recycles feedback, to fine-tune its products. The latest wrinkle in this technique is the focus group.

15. *Constructing feedforward* has to do with enlisting mechanisms to reinforce the message after it has been released. This brings us full-circle to the apostles, the salesman, the retail store, the local health officer, the parish priest, the teacher, the public-relations agency, and so on. One kind of 'gatekeeper' who has been enlisted repeatedly is the disc jockey as Frith (1996) and Hirsch (1972) have shown. School children, for example, have had a share in getting their parents to quit smoking (Hornik, 2002).

16. More informally, one can try to enlist and *exploit* pre-existing networks of interpersonal communication to advance the cause. When the idea of opinion leaders was first broached by Lazarsfeld (1944), it attracted the attention of *Time*

Magazine, which tried to discover who they were and how to co-opt them. Merton's (1949) study of 'local and cosmopolitan influentials' was an attempt to do just that.

Another example of exploiting feedforward is the classic strategy association with Alcoholics Anonymous whereby the most recent convert to the cause is enlisted to initiate the a yet-newer member, thus encouraging the spokesman to convince him/herself, at least!

Caveats and Conclusions

Let's stop here, and try to generalize.

1.   To make our argument, we have tried to demonstrate - albeit only illustratively - that broadcasters are not as spendthrift and scatter-brained as might be thought (even if communications research would suggest that they are, given their poor record of effectiveness). We have suggested, therefore, that it is worth looking into the steps that are taken - intentionally or not - to create conditions of reception that are conducive to message effectiveness, that is, to the increase the likelihood that the decoding should coincide with the encoding (Hall, 1980).

2.   To advance our argument, theoretically at least, we have drawn on elements associated with the effectiveness of dialogue in order to construct a scheme that might direct us where to look. The scheme suggests that broadcasters might try to create or exploit conditions of reception that augment or supplement their messages by controlling the loci, times and reference-frames of reception; by inducing or relating to appropriate identities, roles, and practices; and by enlisting the partnership of receivers in fine-tuning the message and passing it on.

3.   The best we could do, obviously, was to illustrate the workings of these categories without being able to establish the extent to which they are employed or the degree of their success. As it turns out, our illustrations are largely familiar ones, coming, as they do, from mainline communications research as well as marketing and advertising research, cinema theory, framing theory, network theory, and elsewhere.[7] It is for this reason that the illustrations seem like a procession of déjà vu, to which we plead guilty. It is only their juxtaposition that justifies what we have done.

4.   We are aware of problems with the scheme: i) It is clear, first of all, that the examples might better have been profiled than pigeon-holed, in the sense that genres such as soap opera, or media events, or Hollywood cinema draw on an assortment of our categories. Take media events, for example. These live, pre-

planned ceremonies stop time, declare holidays, return us home, turn the home into a public space, convert the living room into a sanctuary, and put a halo on the television set, advise us to view together with others, offer us identities, rehearse us in roles, cue our immediate responses, and sometimes ask us to do something more after the broadcast is over. ii) We are also aware that we have not attempted to distinguish among the source of a message, the proponent of the message or the channel or medium through which the message is transmitted. In this chapter, we treat all of these - singly and in combination - as 'communicators' of the original message. We do, however, treat secondary media when they are enlisted to 'supplement' the original transmission. iii) We are also aware that we have jumbled together attempts to control reception discursively (i.e. *inside* the message) from attempts to supplement the message, to shepherd it from *outside*, so to speak, after it has been unleashed. iv) Note, too, that not all our examples are taken from the realm of broadcasting; we have drawn also on communications of other kinds. v) And, of course, our emphasis on the tactics of encoding and supplementation without lingering on the question of effectiveness.

5. In sum, what we have tried to do is to initiate reconsideration of the concept of broadcasting as it nears the end of its career. Our guiding idea is that broadcasting could not work without the active cooperation of its audiences. That is why the early behaviourist and critical theories seemed wrong. It is what led to theories of the active viewer whose uses and interpretations reflect voluntaristic responses that are, typically and curiously, the dominant ones - but also to alternative and oppositional responses (Hall, 1980).[8] What we are suggesting is that the ability of communicators to induce such dominant uses and readings may be underestimated. In a word, we are proposing to refocus attention on the ability of communicators to intervene in situations of reception, not by talking more loudly or carrying a big stick, but by more subtle dialogic and cognitive means (Beniger & Gusek, 1995). It is in this sense that we want to suggest that supplementation and narrowcasting not only speak of the past and of the future, but of the era of broadcasting as well.

Notes

1   Livingstone (2002) laments the absence of credible ethnographies of audiences attending the performing arts. She cites the history of rowdyism among theatre goers, and lower-class mayhem at certain cinemas.

2   'In speaking of dominant meanings, then, we are not talking about a one-sided process which governs how all events will be signified. It consists of the 'work' required to enforce, win plausibility for and command as legitimate a decoding of the event within the limit of dominant definitions in which it has been connotatively signified.' (Hall, 1980) See Gurevitch and Scannell

(2003) for evidence that Hall's paper is no less about manipulated encoding than about the polysemic decoding that has so widely been adopted by reception theory.

3   Dayan and Katz (1992) argue that 'the experience of not being there' may be equal in power to the experience of 'being there,' but that the experiences are different. Consider also the position of the Catholic Church, which does not give 'credit' for attendance at a mass via television, except for shut-ins.

4   Beginning attempts at identifying types of 'involvement' have been made by McLuhan (see (Meyrowitz, 2003)). Also see (Dayan, 1999; Houston, 1984; Horton,Wohl, 1956).

5   (Menand, 1996), quoted in (Andersen, 2000) at p. 250.

6   This is a step towards solution of the puzzle, alluded to earlier, of when and whether the viewer is more vulnerable - at home, or in public. See also (Katz & Dayan, 2003).

7   How visual artists and literary texts address implied readers and guide interpretation (when they wish to) is another approach that deserves mention here, even though we are, yet again, not quite qualified for the task. See Eco (1994) and Baxandall (1985), for example.

8   The idea that genres are 'contracts' between audiences and producers deserves more attention because it suggests that dominant readings are, in effect, 'agreements between willing members of both sides' (Cawelti, 1976; Dayan & Katz, 1992). In more extreme form, it relates to the argument that mass communication is society talking to itself, which, however, smothers the idea of hegemony.

References

Althusser, L. (1998 [c1971]) 'Ideology and Ideological State Apparatuses'. In J. Storey (Ed.), Cultural Theory and Popular Culture. Athens: University of Georgia Press, pp. 153-164.

Andersen, R. (2000) 'The Commercial Politics of the 1996 US Presidential Campaign'. In R. Andersen & L. Strate (Eds.), Critical Studies in Media Commercialism. Oxford; New York: Oxford University Press, pp. 250-263.

Anderson, B. R. (1983) Imagined Communities: Reflections on the Origin and Spread of Nationalism. London: Verso.

Austin, J. L. (1965 [c1962]) How to do Things with Words. New York: Oxford University Press.

Baxandall, M. (1985) Patterns of Intention: On the Historical Explanation of Pictures. New Haven: Yale University Press.

Beitrose, H. (1980) Monday Night Football. Unpublished manuscript, Institute for Communication Research, Stanford.

Beniger, J. R. (1986) The Control Revolution: Technological and Economic Origins of the Information Society. Cambridge, Mass.: Harvard University Press.

Beniger, J. R. (1987) 'Personalization of Mass-media and the Growth of Pseudo-Community'. Communication Research. 14(3), pp. 352-371.

Beniger, J. R., & Gusek, J. A. (1995) 'The Cognitive Revolution in Public Opinion and Communication Research'. In T. L. Glasser & C. T. Salmon (Eds.), Public Opinion and the Communication of Consent. New York: Guilford Press, pp. 217-248.

Benjamin, W. (1969) 'The Work of Art in the Age of Mechanical Reproduction'. In H. Arendt (Ed.), Illuminations. New York: Schocken, pp. 217-243.

Berelson, B., & Freeman, R. (1964) 'A Study in Fertility Control'. Scientific American. 210(5), pp. 29-37.

Blondheim, M., & Blum-Kulka, S. (2001) 'Literacy, Orality, Television: Mediation and Authenticity in Jewish Conversational Arguing'. 1-2000 C.E. Communication Review. 4(4), pp. 511-540.

Bogue, D. (1990) 'Family-planning and Population-Control: The Challenges of a Successful Movement'. Contemporary Sociology. 19(5), pp. 711-713.

Cardiff, D., & Scannell, P. (1987) 'Broadcasting and National Unity'. In J. Curran & A. Smith & P. Wingate (Eds.), Impact and Influences: Essays on Media Power in the Twentieth Century. London: Methuen.

Cawelti, J. G. (1976) Adventure, Mystery, and Romance: Formula Stories as Art and Popular Culture. Chicago: Chicago University Press.

Coleman, J. C., Katz, E., & Menzel, H. (1966) Medical Innovation: A Diffusion Study. Indianapolis: Bobbs-Merrill.

Darnton, R. (2000) 'An Early Information Society: News and the Media in Eighteenth-Century Paris'. The American Historical Review. 105(1), pp. 1-35.

Dayan, D. (1999 [c1974]) 'The Tutor Code of Classical Cinema'. In L. Braudy & M. Cohen (Eds.), Film Theory and Criticism. New York; Oxford: Oxford University Press, pp. 118-129.

Dayan, D., & Katz, E. (1992) Media Events: The Live Broadcasting of History. Cambridge, Mass.: Harvard University Press.

Drew, R. (2001) Karaoke Nights: An Ethnographic Rhapsody. Walnut Creek, CA: AltaMira Press.

Eco, U. (1994) The Limits of Interpretation. Bloomington: Indiana University Press.

Eco, U. (1995) The Search for the Perfect Language. Oxford, UK; Cambridge, Mass.: Blackwell.

Elliott, P. R. (1980) 'Press Performance as Political Ritual'. Sociological Review Monograph. pp. 141-177.

Freidson, E. (1953) 'The Relation of the Social Situation of Contact to the Media in Mass Communication'. Public Opinion Quarterly. 17(2), pp. 230-238.

Frith, S. (1996) 'Entertainment'. In J. Curran & M. Gurevitch (Eds.), Mass Media and Society. New York: Arnold, pp. 160-176.

Gamson, W. (1995) Safe Spaces and Social Movement. Paper presented at the Department of Sociology Colloquia Series, Northwestern University.

Gerbner, G., & Gross, L. (1976) 'Living with Television: The Violence Profile'. Journal of Communication. 26(2), pp. 172-199.

Gurevitch, M., & Scannell, P. (2003) 'Canonization Achieved? Stuart Hall's Encoding/decoding'. In E. Katz & J. D. Peters & T. Liebes & A. Orloff (Eds.), Canonic Texts in Media Research: Are there any? Should there be? How about these? Cambridge, UK; Malden, MA: Blackwell Publishers, pp. 231-247.

Habermas, J. (1989) The Structural Transformation of the Public Sphere: An Inquiry into a Category of Bourgeois Society. Cambridge, Mass.: MIT Press.

Hall, S. (1980). Encoding/decoding, Culture, Media, Language: Working Papers in Cultural Studies, 1972-1979. London: Hutchinson, pp. 128-138.

Handelman, D., & Katz, E. (1990) 'State Ceremonies of Israel: Remembrance Day and Independence Day'. In D. Handelman (Ed.), Models and Mirrors: Towards an Anthropology of Public Events. Cambridge; New York: Cambridge University Press, pp. 191-233.

Hilgartner, S., & Bosk, C. L. (1988) 'The Rise and Fall of Social Problems: A public Arena Model'. American Journal of Sociology. 94(1), pp. 53-78.

Hirsch, P. M. (1991 [c1972]) 'Processing Fads and Fashions. An Organization-Set Analysis of

Cultural Industry Systems'. In C. Mukerji & M. Schudson (Eds.), Rethinking Popular Culture. Contemporary Perspectives in Cultural Studies. Berkeley, Calif.: University of California Press, pp. 313-334.

Hobsbawm, E., & Ranger, T. (1983) The Invention of Tradition. Cambridge; New York: Cambridge University Press.

Horkheimer, M., & Adorno, T. W. (1972 [c1947]) Dialectic of Enlightenment. New York: Herder and Herder.

Hornik, R. C. (Ed.). (2002) Public Health Communication: Evidence for Behaviour Change. Mahwah, NJ: Laurence Erlbaum.

Horton, D., & Wohl, R. (1956) 'Mass Communication and Para-Social Interaction: Observations on Intimacy at a Distance'. Psychiatry. 19(3), pp. 215-229.

Houston, B. (1984) 'Viewing Television: The Metapsychology of Endless Consumption'. Quarterly Review of Film Studies. 9(3), pp. 183-195.

Katz, E., & Dayan, D. (2003) 'The Audience is a Crowd, the Crowd is a Public: Latter-Day Thoughts on Lang and Lang's 'MacArthur Day in Chicago''. In E. Katz & J. D. Peters & T. Liebes & A. Orloff (Eds.), Canonic Texts in Media Research: Are There Any? Should There be? How About These? Cambridge, UK; Malden, MA: Blackwell Publishers, pp. 121-136.

Klemperer, V. (1998) I Will Bear Witness: A Diary of the Nazi Years (Vol. 1). New York: Random House.

Lang, G. E., & Lang, K. (1990) Etched in Memory: The Building and Survival of Artistic Reputation. Chapel Hill: University of North Carolina Press.

Lazarsfeld, P. F. (1944) The People's Choice: How the Voter Makes up his Mind in a Presidential Campaign. New York: Duell, Sloan and Pearce.

Lazarsfeld, P. F., & Merton, R. K. (1964, c1948) 'Mass Communication, Popular Taste, and Organized Social Action'. In L. Bryson (Ed.), The Communication of Ideas. New York: Cooper Square Publishers, pp. 95-118.

Liebes-Plesner, T. (1984) Shades of Meaning in President Sadat's Knesset Speech. Semiotica.

Livingstone, S. (2002 (in print)) 'The Changing Nature of Audiences: From the Mass Audience to the Interactive Media User'. In A. N. Valdivia (Ed.), Blackwell Companion to Media Studies. Oxford, UK: Blackwell.

Livingstone, S., & Bovill, M. (2001) 'Bedroom Culture and the Privatization of Media Use'. In S. Livingstone & M. Bovill (Eds.), Children and Their Changing Media Environment: A European Comparative Study. Mahwah, NJ: Lawrence Erlbaum Associates, pp. 179-200.

McLuhan, M. (1994 [c1964]) Understanding Media: The Extension of Man. Cambridge, MA: MIT Press.

McQuarrie, E. F., & Mick, D. G. (1999) 'Visual Rhetoric in Advertising: Text-Interpretive, Experimental, and Reader-Response Analysis'. Journal of Consumer Research. 26(1), pp. 37-54.

Melbin, M. (1978) 'Night as Frontier'. American Journal of Sociology. 43(1), pp. 3-22.

Menand, L. (1996) New York Review of Books, 19 September, pp. 4, 6.

Merton, R. K. (1946) Mass Persuasion, the Social Psychology of a War Bond Drive. New York: Harper.

Merton, R. K. (1949) 'Patterns of Influence: A Study of Interpersonal Influence and Communication Behaviour in a Local Community'. In P. F. Lazarsfeld & F. N. Stanton (Eds.), Communication Research. 1948-1949. New York: Harper, pp. 180-219.

Messaris, P. (1992) 'Visual Manipulation: Visual Means of Affecting Responses to Images'. Communication. 13(3), pp. 181-195.

Meyrowitz, J. (2003) 'Canonic Anti-Text: Marshall McLuhan's 'Understanding Media''. In E. Katz & J. D. Peters & T. Liebes & A. Orloff (Eds.), Canonic Texts in Media Research: Are there any? Should there be? How about These? Cambridge, UK; Malden, MA: Blackwell Publishers, pp. 191-212.

Modleski, T. (1982) Loving with a Vengeance: Mass-Produced Fantasies for Women. Hamden, Conn.: Archon Books.

Mosse, G. L. (1975) The Nationalization of the Masses: Political Symbolism and Mass Movements in Germany from the Napoleonic Wars Through the Third Reich. New York: H. Fertig.

Nash, M. (1999) ''Beavis is Just Confused': Ideologies, Intertexts, Audiences'. Velvet Light Trap. 43, pp. 4-22.

Noelle-Neumann, E. (1984) The Spiral of Silence: Public Opinion, our Social Skin. Chicago: University of Chicago Press.

Peters, J. D. (1999) Speaking into the Air: A History of the Idea of Communication. Chicago: University of Chicago Press.

Peters, J. D. (2003). 'The Subtlety of Horkheimer and Adorno: Reading 'The Culture Industry''. In E. Katz & J. D. Peters & T. Liebes & A. Orloff (Eds.), Canonic Texts in Media Research: Are there any? Should there be? How about These? Cambridge, UK; Malden, MA: Blackwell Publishers, pp. 58-73.

Putnam, R. D. (1995) 'Tuning in, Tuning out: The Strange Disappearance of Social Capital in America'. Political Science and Politics. 28, pp. 664-683.

Real, M. (1982 [c1977]) 'The Superbowl: Mythic Spectacle'. In H. Newcomb (Ed.), Television: The Critical View. New York: Oxford University Press, pp. 190-203.

Rothenbuhler, E. (1988) 'The Living Room Celebration of the Olympic Games'. Journal of Communication. 38(4), pp. 61-81.

Scannell, P. (1996) Eventfulness, Radio, Television, and Modern Life: A Phenomenological Approach. Cambridge: Blackwell, pp. 75-92.

Scannell, P. (2000) 'For-anyone-as-someone structures'. Media, Culture & Society. 22(1), pp. 5-24.

Schudson, M. (1989) 'How Culture Works: Perspectives from Media Studies on the Efficacy of Symbols'. Theory and Society. 18(2), pp. 153-180.

Schwartz, D. (1992) Social Construction of Photographic Meaning. Paper presented at the Second Amsterdam Conference on Visual Sociology & Anthropology, University of Amsterdam.

Simonson, P. (2002) Introduction to Robert K. Merton, Mass Persuasion: The Social Psychology of a War Bond Drive [Republication, with new introduction, of 1946 text]. New York: Howard Fertig Publishers.

Steiner, G. (1975) After Babel: Aspects of Language and Translation. New York: Oxford University Press.

Tarde, G. D. (1901) L'opinion et la foule. Paris: Alcan.

Tuchman, G. (1978) Making News: A Study in the Construction of Reality. New York: Free Press.

Turow, J. (1997) Breaking up America: Advertisers and the New Media World. Chicago: University of Chicago Press.

Uricchio, W. (1989) 'Rituals of Reception, Patterns of Neglect: Nazi Television and its Postwar Representation'. Wide Angle. 11(1), pp. 48-66.

Wiebe, H. D. (1951) 'Merchandising Commodities and Citizenship on Television'. Public Opinion Quarterly. 15, pp. 679-691.

Yerushalmi, Y. H. (1982) Zakhor, Jewish History and Jewish Memory. Seattle: University of Washington Press.

Zelizer, B. (2002) 'Photography, Journalism, and Trauma'. In B. Zelizer & S. Allan (Eds.), Journalism after September 11. London; New York: Routledge.

Part A: Media, Globalisation and the European Imaginary

In this first part of the book our authors focus on different aspects of popular culture in a European and cultural perspective. Their interest is in how audiences are responding to and managing the shifting landscape of an increasingly globalised culture available to them through the media. Stig Hjarvard shows how the mediatization of toys is an important part of the globalization and commercialization processes. Toys are not just to be played with; they convey and mediate important meanings for their users. The article on the one hand offers a detailed study of this historical development from a national company to a global media industry, but on the other hand also introduces general concepts of mediatization, imaginarization, narrativization and virtualization as strategies for developing cultural identities and consumer products. Roberta Pearson and Máire Messenger Davies in their empirical reception study of Shakespeare and the American TV-series *Star Trek* offer an empirical investigation into audience responses to products normally placed at either end of a traditional taste hierarchy. But in this study of how audiences react to classical European and American popular culture, Pearson and Messenger question too crude oppositions between European high culture and American mass culture and 'dumbing down', and they discuss broader issues of popular imagination and popular culture in the cinema and on television. The dynamic between a global media power and a more local-national cultural context is also in focus in Kirsten Drotner's article on audience responses to Disney media products. The specific focus of the article is again related to larger questions of cultural identities, homogenisation and diversity in the readings of global media products. The article presents a bottom-up perspective on globalisation and the whole of media in mundane discourses. Finally, Daniel Biltereyst analyses the highly debated forms of 'Reality-TV' in general, as a new popular form of factual entertainment, and in relation to concrete data on the debate and reception of reality-TV in Belgium. The concepts of media panics and moral panics that have a long tradition in European media research are used to shed light on this new media phenomenon. In his discussion descriptive, sociological perspectives meet with aspects of a more normative media theory.

Stig Hjarvard, Ph.D., is Professor at the Department of Film & Media Studies, University of Copenhagen. He is also head of the National Research School for Media, Communication and Journalism: www.fmkj.dk. His research areas include the sociology and history of journalism, the aesthetics of news and factual genres, globalization and the media, the history of Eurovision, the relationship between mediated and interpersonal communication, the mediatization of toys. Recent books include Tv-nyheder I konkurrence (TV news in competition) (Frederiksberg: Samfundslitteratur, 1999); News in a Globalized Society (editor and contributor, Gothenburg: Nordicom, 2001); and Media in a Globalized Society, (editor and contributor, Copenhagen: Museum Tusculanum Press, in press).

Stig Hjarvard

From Bricks to Bytes: The Mediatization of a Global Toy Industry

Introduction

Half a century ago, kid's toys were made of *solid* materials: wood, iron, plastic etc. To play was synonymous with physical activity. Kid's toys often resembled the material inventory of the adult world: they were miniatures of mother's and father's real worlds. Girls played with small copies of the inventory of the household, in particular clothes, kitchen utensils, and baby accessories. Boys played with building tools or artifacts from the modern world: ships, cars, trains, guns, airplanes etc.

Today, toys are increasingly of an *immaterial* nature. This is particularly the case with software for computer and video games, but other toys increasingly involve immaterial aspects like role-playing, programming etc. Play has become synonymous with mental activity: imagining, planning, simulating, reacting, communicating etc. Physical activity is, to a limited extent, still a necessary part of playing, but the manipulation of objects no longer involves the same concrete senso-motoric action. Objects are visual representations on a screen and they are manipulated through a media interface: the mouse, the joystick, game pad etc. Kid's toys seldom resemble the inventory of their mother's and father's world. Instead, they are very often part of a fantasy world, situated in a distant past or future, a faraway galaxy, or a supernatural environment. The actors inhabiting these imagined universes are seldom of a realistic nature; on the contrary they often possess superhuman strength, power, wealth, or beauty, or they are only partly human: half machine - half man, half animal - half woman, half zombie - half human etc.

This chapter puts forward the hypothesis that this gradual move from solid to immaterial toys can be conceptualized as a *mediatization* of toys. Through a case study of the history of the Danish toy manufacturer LEGO, it discerns three different aspects of this process of mediatization: imaginarization, narrativization, and virtualization. The process of mediatization is certainly not limited to the world of toys and play. On the contrary, it is to be considered a core element in current social, economic and cultural transformations, and, as such, a key feature of the current move towards a global network society. Mediatization goes hand in hand with both globalization and commercialization. The 'logic' of mediatization applies to a whole range of social institutions: politics, economics, sex, culture - and, among others, to the play world of children and its cultural artifacts; toys.

Media and Information in the Global Network Economy

In his analysis of the global network society, Manuel Castells (1996) emphasizes the crucial role of information technology for the development of what he calls an 'informational economy'. The social and economic dependency on information and information processing is not new - most societies' economies have relied on information. However, what is definitively new in the economy of the network society is the key role attributed to information. Society becomes 'a specific form of social organization in which information generation, processing, and transmission become the fundamental sources of productivity and power' (Castells, 1996, p. 21).

Communication media are responsible for this generation, processing and transmission of information and as such they facilitate the greater degree of interdependency, the extension of social networks, action at a distance etc. that characterize the global network society. Paraphrasing Marshall McLuhan's notion of the '*Gutenberg Galaxy*', Castells (2001) talks about the emergence of the '*Internet Galaxy*'. As the printing press paved the way for a social and political revolution, so will the Internet - as a kind of generalized media platform - promote a whole new social infrastructure. Thus, media are not only channels of interaction, but mould the ways in which the interaction takes place. Communication and media structures will play the same role as natural and physical infrastructures have played in the past. Just as towns were founded along rivers and coasts, the 'nodes' and 'hubs' of the network society will be founded adjacent to vital centres of communication. As a consequence, the positions of individual actors in this new communicative infrastructure will be decisive for their ability to manoeuvre in a global society: Access to the media and the conditions attached to their use, the areas of the world connected by them, and to what ends - factors like these will be the sources of power and influence.

Manuel Castells calls this new communication infrastructure a *'culture of real virtuality'* (Castells, 1996). By this he means that the virtual world is not merely a simulation or 'pseudo world', but is in fact a social reality. He points out that previously distinct media are converging, melding into a multimedia system that soon will be able 'to embrace and integrate all forms of expression, as well as the diversity of interests, values and imaginations, including the expression of social conflicts' (Castells, 1996, p. 374). This global media system creates a new reality, where visibility becomes crucial to social actors: Whether or not something is real and can be of consequence depends on its presence in the global communication structure. Lack of visibility means exclusion from the social reality that is the product of media's representation.

Cathedrals of Consumption

Manuel Castells focuses in particular on the role of information technology in production and distribution in the last decades of the twentieth century, but a similar and related development has taken place in *consumption* as well. George Ritzer (1999) has drawn attention to the fact that the means of consumption have been revolutionized. In particular in highly developed industrial countries, the consumption of goods has accelerated and the way in which goods are consumed has been industrialized, rationalized, and informatized. A highly visible result of this development is the advent of 'cathedrals of consumption', as Ritzer labels them. Such places of pilgrimage for excessive consumption come in many different forms: theme parks like Disneyland and LEGOLAND; enormous shopping centres or malls that house everything from special shops, restaurants, supermarkets, to entertainment centres (Tivoli, cinemas, casinos etc.), 'megastores' for specific product lines (e.g. music, electronics, books) and global chains for specific products or services (Burger King, Planet Hollywood, Seven Eleven).

The revolution in consumption has paved the way for a 'hyper consumption', in which a steady growing amount of consumer goods has to be sold and consumed within an ever-shorter time cycle. The industrialization and technologization of consumption have spread to many social areas, including social institutions that previously were located outside the consumer market. Museums and sport stadiums, for instance, have gradually become more and more involved in the sale and consumption of consumer goods. The advance of electronic - mediated - methods of credit and payment, in particular the credit card, has worked as a lever for the spread and intensification of consumption (Ritzer, 1995).

In continuation of Max Weber's analysis of the industrial revolution, George Ritzer draws attention to the fact that industrialization of consumption implies an extreme *rationalization* of work processes related to consumption and the appearance and characteristic of products (taste, functionality etc.). In order to make hyper consumption possible, all aspects related to consumption must be thoroughly rationalized. Rationalization implies a constant tension between *enchantment* and *disenchantment*. The cathedrals of consumption are an attempt to create an enchantment through consumption. In highly developed industrialized societies, competition in the market place can no longer be based on the simple utility value, instead, commodities must be furnished with symbolic qualities that endow purchase and usage with an extra quality. A commodity must display a visible difference compared to others in order to prompt a purchase, and the social environment of consumption should be pleasant, entertaining, and, at best, an 'event'.

The cathedrals of consumption are created to endow purchase and consumption with these qualities; as Ritzer describes it: 'Although at one time enchantment stemmed from human wizards or magicians, it now stems from the wizardry of modern robotics and computerized technology. Ultimately, it is the technology of the modern cruise, the Las Vegas casino, and Disney World that astounds us, not the humans who happens to work in these settings or the things they do' (Ritzer, 1999, p. 102).

The drawback of rationalization is that it can just as well provoke disenchantment. For children, Disneyland and LEGOLAND may from a distance appear as magic kingdoms, but the actual experience may just as well be the opposite: endless lines, standardized and calculated experiences, uniform products, personnel that repeat meaningless sentences and behaviour etc. The result is disenchantment, a disappointment of not meeting the unique characteristic of magic: the magnificent, the exceptional, the unforeseen. In order to avoid such consumer dissatisfaction, the consumption industry continuously develops larger and more spectacular symbolic environments for consumption, not least with the use of information technology and media culture.

Media in the Entertainment Economy

From an economic point of view Michael Wolf (1999) has - not unlike Ritzer - drawn attention to the increased role of entertainment in the globalized economy. The entertainment industry itself continues to grow and entertainment components are added to products and services from other sectors of the economy. Service sectors like the bank business, that, until few years ago were considered the antithesis of entertainment, have now added a certain amount of entertainment. Not only should it be easier to make a banking transaction through credit cards and new media, it should also be a pleasure. Young customers get personalized credit cards with motifs from youth culture; advertising emphasizes the ease and joy of netbanking, loyal customers get bonus offers with luxury items, certain bank services, like the 'millionaire account', resemble a lottery. The use of media stars and brand names from the entertainment industry provides ordinary consumer goods and services with a higher attention value. The result is a growing symbiosis between the entertainment industry and industry in general, in which industrial brands and entertainment stars merge into each other: 'Brands and stars have become the same thing. [...] In the emerging world economy, where entertainment and the laws of the entertainment business infuse more and more of the rest of the world of commerce and culture, successful business needs star brands to bring consumers through the door' (Wolf, 1999, p. 28).

Not least, companies that want to penetrate new markets quickly as part of a global marketing strategy, often make use of media symbols to enable a level of recognition among customers that would otherwise be extremely expensive and difficult to achieve. However, such a strategy does also entail dangers. Once a company has attached itself to the entertainment industry, it is difficult to turn back. The company must continuously renew the entertainment component and not only the product, otherwise, the consumer will get disappointed and choose another product. As a consequence, still more companies become dependent on the ups and downs of the entertainment sector: 'Businesses that were traditionally less volatile are now subject to the entertainment business cycle. They are dealing with the same audience realities that every producer has sweated over and prayed since the creation of the chorus line'. (Wolf, 1999, p. 56).

In a globalized economy both production and consumption has increasingly become dependent upon information and media technology, and the symbolic content and entertainment function of the media gain a foothold in more and more types of ordinary consumer products. Whether this is described as the arrival of an informational economy (Castells), a break-through for an entertainment economy (Wolf), or a revolution of consumption through enchantment (Ritzer), a common thread runs through all of these analyses: the growing importance of media and communication technologies. These diverse, but related tendencies can be described as a *mediatization* of economy and culture. It is my hypothesis that globalization and commercialization entail an increased mediatization, both at a material, economic level and at a symbolic, cultural level.

Mediatization
Mediatization as a concept denotes that the media influence social institutions in ways that exceed the simple fact that all institutions rely increasingly on mediated information and communication. The concept has so far not been properly

defined, but it has been used frequently (together with similar meanings) in studies of political communication (Amnå, 1999; Altheide and Snow, 1988). Mazzoleni and Schulz (2002) suggest that the core meaning of mediatization is the 'problematic concomitants or consequences of the development of the mass media'. In the case of politics, this implies that 'Mediatized politics is considered to have lost its autonomy, to have become dependent, in its central functions, on mass media and continuously shaped by interactions with mass media' (Mazzoleni and Schulz, 2002, p. 2).

The notion, that mediatization makes institutions dependent on media in their core functions is an obvious element of the mediatization process. However, it is misleading a priori, i.e. as a defining characteristic, to suggest that this dependency is problematic in itself. At worst such a definition would entail a normative perspective of permanent decline, interpreting all new dependencies on media as one further step down the road of political and social deterioration. Habermas' normative account of the decline of the public sphere and the rise of a mediated publicity culture serves as a paradigmatic example of such deep-rooted skepticism towards (mass) media (Habermas, 1989).

As Schudson (1978, 1997), among others, has rightly demonstrated, much social analysis of mediated politics and mediated social interaction in general is based on the assumption that non-mediated, e.g. face-to-face communication, is inherently better and more democratic, and tends to ignore the fact that democratic ideals, both historically and presently, are heavily influenced by the communication practices that media have made possible. Furthermore, criticism of mediatization often fail to acknowledge the fact that it is very hard to imagine a democratic polity and culture in highly advanced and complex societies without the intervention of media. Instead of considering mediated communication as a less valuable substitute for non-mediated forms of communication, it is heuristically more productive to suggest that mediatization implies both a partial substitution of existing forms of social interaction, and an expansion of the existing repertoire of communication that also changes the condition of face-to-face communication (Hjarvard, 2002). Following this, I will suggest a non-normative definition of mediatization that leaves the question of social improvement or deterioration to empirical research, rather as an inherent theoretical premise.

My *working definition* of mediatization is as follows: Mediatization implies a process through which core elements of a social or cultural activity (like work, leisure, play etc.) assume media form. By media is understood a technology that allows transfer of or interaction with a symbolic content across time or space. A social or cultural activity can assume media form in two different ways, of which the first is the strongest form of mediatization; the second is a weaker form of mediatization:

1. The social or cultural activity itself assumes media form, after which it must be performed through interaction with a medium. A rather simple example of this is the development of chess computer programmes that transfer the chess playing activity between two people to a mediated environment. A more complex example is home banking that allows all types of financial activities (payments, loans, currency exchanges, market information and analysis etc.) to be carried out through mediated interaction with computers via the Internet.

2. The symbolic content and structure of the social and cultural activity is influenced by media environments that they gradually become more dependent upon and interconnected with. A simple example is the use of well-known media figures in the marketing of non-media products like burgers from McDonald's. A visit to McDonald's becomes not only a particular dining experience but also a meeting with and a way of collecting media figures from media created symbolic environments (films, cartoons etc.). A more complex example is the development of intertextual discourses through which media discourses gain access to, and intertwines with, discourses in society in general. For instance, the Danes' knowledge about the USA is to a large degree influenced by media discourses (fictional as well as factual), and as a result, both political and non-political discussions among Danes about the USA are interwoven with mediated images of the USA.

Mediatization will often involve both of these aspects. For instance, the mediatization of political communication in society involves both the transfer of political communication from non-mediated settings (meetings, rallies etc.) to media environments (press meetings, TV talk shows) and the influence of media logics, symbols etc. on non-mediated forms of political communications (e.g. TV transmission of political speeches (Jamieson, 1988)).

Mediatization is a social phenomenon that originates from the interplay between many social processes, including globalization and commercialization. The argument put forward here is not that globalization and commercialization are the only factors that stimulate mediatization, but that they play key roles as levers of mediatization. The reasons why globalization furthers mediatization are manifold: the media are the key technology for the extension and spread of social activities across the globe; media stars and brands are well-known across the globe and thus valuable symbols for companies that want to expand globally etc. Mediatization as a concept and a social process is not synonymous with commercialization, but in actual social practice they are often experienced as two sides of the same coin. Mediatization is an important way in which social and cultural activities can be subsumed to a commodity form and through this, be exploited for commercial purposes. The development and spread of digital media technologies is very much a result of the commercial potential of these technologies. They allow a much more advanced control of both sales and consumption (which in the media are very often one simultaneous process, like movie viewing) as with, for instance, video-on-demand, pay-per-view etc. The synergy thus created between media industries and industries in general favour not only the non-media industry. As non-media industries assimilate media components, the media environment as a whole gains even further momentum.

Co-operation Between Media and Toy Industry

In an American context, mediatization of toys is not a new phenomenon. Running the risk of oversimplifying the history, it began in the 1950s with the increased popularity of television for children, not least cartoons. From the 1960s onwards (Cross, 1997; Englehardt, 1986; Kline, 1993) children's programmes were a regular and growing part of American television and subsequently, advertising began to address the target group, the children. This paved the way for the cooperation between advertising agencies, television programmers and toy manufacturers. Together they developed an economic circuit that proved economically beneficial for all. Toys were marketed not only in advertising, but in television programming as well. Half hour cartoon series provided the toys with characterization and narratives, and thus stimulated sales, and the purchase and subsequent play with toys worked similarly as an incentive to watch the television programmes.

From the late 1960s this economic circuit between advertisers, television and toy manufacturers had acquired such momentum in the USA that it provoked reactions. American Public Services broadcasting (PBS) launched Sesame Street as a quality and educational alternative to the commercial supply and different civic groups tried to lobby for restrictions on commercial exploitation of children's television. However, the Reaganism of the 1980s meant a victory for the commercial actors that worked for a synergy between broadcasting and the toy industry. During the Reagan era television deregulation meant commercialization of children's television and it became the most important channel of communication between the toy industry and its consumers, the children. Concurrently with the deregulation of broadcasting in most other parts of the world during the 1980s and 1990s (in Europe, Asia, Russia etc.), this cooperation between television and toy industry has spread to many other countries.

The combination of television and the toy industry created a boom in toy sales, but at the same time it influenced the symbolic content and structure of the toy. Television advertising and cartoons are particularly well suited to promote toys that contain (or simply are) fictional characters. In particular, it was television's ability to characterize and narrativize fictional figures that made these toys attractive. The synergy between toy and television industry fostered an endless stream of toy figures and personalities, each with their own fictional universe and accessories: Barbie and Ken, He-Man, My Little Pony, Ninja Turtles, Pokemon etc.

Television has been crucial for this initial development but other media have played a role in the evolving synergy between media and the toy industry: cartoon magazines, film, music etc. During the last decade it is primarily the computer and the Internet that have come to play an increasingly prominent role. With the computer and the Internet there has been a decisive transformation in the relation between media and toy. The toy increasingly becomes computer based (like computer games and similar software) or intelligent, as for instance dolls with microchips that allow them to talk and move and respond to certain stimuli. As such, it is no longer the case that the media only work as advertisements for the toys. *The media have become toys, and toys have become media*, making the synergy between toy and media industries not only more complex but also more intensive.

During the last decade, the toy industry has put a lot of marbles into the media business. Media based or media related products are, apart from being a potentially lucrative market in its own right, also a way of ensuring a higher and speedier rate of product renewal by the consumer. When a consumer buys a piece of media entertainment hardware, the ground is prepared for a regular renewal of the software. In order to legitimize the initial expenditure, the consumer will be willing to expand and renew his or her repertoire of software entertainment products.

The move of the toy industry into the media sector must, however, also be considered in relation to a new trend (indeed, an alarming trend from the point of view of the toy industry) in the consumer behaviour of children and young people. It is the so-called 'KGOY' phenomenon: Kids Getting Older Younger. Today, children become youngsters at an earlier age, and subsequently the age range in which children ask for children's toy is shrinking. Instead, both children and young people demand traditional consumer goods at an earlier age, in particular clothes and media products (mobile phones, computers, television, CD-players etc.). As a consequence, the customer base for the traditional toy manufacturers is diminishing and they have to sell more within a shorter time frame to keep businesses running. The move into the media sector is a way to compensate for this change in youngsters' behaviour. By moving from toys to media they not only respond to a change in consumer behaviour in their target group, but they also gradually get prepared for a general move into the media entertainment business as such.

LEGO as a Global Media Industry

Compared to the general international trend in the toy industry LEGO was rather late in adjusting itself to the increased competition in the toy and entertainment industry, and its move into the media industry came even later. This was due to several factors. Although it has been an important international company for many years now, the LEGO Company has a rather conservative and centralized management structure. It is a family owned company that all through the post-war period has emphasized that growth should be financed by its own earnings and development should be based on its own ideas and values. Its origin in a provincial part of Denmark (Billund, Jutland) with a Christian culture has left its imprint on both company and work force and still accounts for the high degree of control exercised through the headquarters in Billund (Byskov, 1997; Cortzen, 1996; Hansen, 1997).

Another reason for the late adjustment to changes in the global toy market has to do with the outlook and self-conception of the LEGO Company. Through the years LEGO has - contrary to competitors like Hasbro and Mattel - not understood itself as an all-round toy manufacturer. Instead, LEGO considered itself as a manufacturer of *construction toys* - and not anything else. Within its own niche, construction toys, LEGO had managed - due to a planned and robust growth strategy - to become the market leader in the 1970s and, because of this, did not consider the other major toy companies as direct competitors. It was not until the 1990s that a change in LEGO's self-conception occurred, and subsequently a different interpretation of the market and competition took shape. The crucial change occurred when the company abandoned the idea that the product, the LEGO brick, was the core activity and key to LEGO's image. Instead, the core of the LEGO-image was reinterpreted as a *value inherent in the LEGO bricks*, but applicable to other kinds of toys and types of play: quality of play. By virtue of this conceptual change, the way was paved for the production of many other, and quite different, types of toys and products.

Due to this development, the competition scenario changed: Earlier on, LEGO would primarily defend its position as market leader against piracy products and newcomers to the construction toy market. Now, LEGO was in fierce competition with, in principle, all other major toy manufacturers, among which there were several actors much bigger than LEGO. In concordance with this transition, LEGO put forward an ambitious aim for the coming years: LEGO should become the most well known brand in the world among families with children. It should not necessarily become the greatest selling or biggest in an economic sense, but its symbolic power, the brand name, should be the strongest among its target group.

In order to achieve this goal LEGO had to expand rapidly on a global scale and its brand name is now marketed in relation to many different kinds of products. Thus, the company now consists of several divisions that are in principle equal: LEGO play materials (bricks etc.), LEGO Media (computer games, magazines etc.),

LEGOLAND Parks (amusement parks in Denmark, USA, England, Germany), LEGO Dacta (educational material) and LEGO Lifestyle (clothes, watches etc.).

This global strategy has been accompanied by a mediatization of the LEGO products. This mediatization has not, however, been part of a unified strategy, at least not from the outset. Several divisions in LEGO have at different moments been involved in the development of media related products and at times there has been competition and disagreement between divisions, so that development has taken different and not necessarily mutually supportive directions. As such, the actual historical and empirical process of mediatization has not been a linear one. However, in order to provide an overview, it is possible to distinguish between four different steps in the recent mediatization of the LEGO product. It must be emphasized, though, that these steps represent a logical-analytical construction rather than a strict historical-temporal development. Each step reflects a certain interpretation of media and what they can be used for in the LEGO products:

1. Media as *information channels*. Apart from advertising, which has almost always been used by LEGO, media initially gained a foothold as an alternative way of providing building instructions and product information. Instead of paper, manuals are provided on CD-Rom or in Magazines. This begins in 1997.

2. Media as an *additional and supportive* activity. Media products become a minor part of the product line. The first real PC game is introduced in 1997 and more follows, but they are not well integrated into the overall product line and they primarily serve as an additional and subordinated activity. This conception of media reflects a simple imitative strategy: new media companies have great success in selling computer games to LEGO's core consumers: boys. Consequently, LEGO must also have such items in its product line.

3. Media as an *integrated* activity. Media based products move into the centre of the company's activity and they are treated on an equal footing with non-media products. Computer games and media characters become part of almost every product line. Intelligent bricks are developed that allow for information based play, e.g. the LEGO MindStorms products.

4. Media as *spearhead and image promoter*. Even though media products quantitatively (in numbers and earnings) are still a minor part of the company's activity, they play a prominent role in the marketing of both products and brand name. In particular the computer and the Internet are important for the renewal of LEGO's image. The traditional image of being a company producing rather old-fashioned toys like construction bricks, i.e. toys of the parents' generation rather than the toys of today's children, is being

recast through the use of media. By associating the bricks with digital media, the LEGO bricks can be projected as a toy of the future - and not as a toy of the past.

These logical steps describe the progressive mediatization of LEGO's product line and the accompanying re-branding of LEGO. They do not, however, provide an understanding of the impact of mediatization on the actual toys, the LEGO bricks. In order to develop a deeper understanding of what mediatization implies for the structure and content of the toys themselves and what kind of play mediatized toys subsequently promote, it is necessary to develop analytical concepts that can guide a more thorough examination of the changes in toys. In the following analysis I will distinguish between three different - although interconnected - aspects of mediatization: imaginarization, narrativization, and virtualization. I will define these three aspects as follows:

• *Imaginarization*. A process through which the symbolic content of the toy, instead of referring to the existing reality, comes to refer to an imagined world.

• *Narrativization*. A process through which the bricks, due to their physical design, marketing, or accompanying text, motivate a play with narrative qualities.

• *Virtualization*. A process through which the bricks lose their physical and tactile sensuous form and become represented in virtual universes.

Imaginarization
LEGO's core product, the LEGO brick, was introduced in 1955 with the name 'LEGO system of play'. Earlier on, the LEGO Company had produced many different types of toys in both wood and plastic, but at the beginning of the 1950s it was decided to concentrate development efforts on one singular product, the LEGO brick. During the first two decades, LEGO bricks were first and foremost considered to stimulate construction play, in which models of the physical inventory of the modern world were built: houses, trains, roads, cars, airplanes etc. Gradually, the system became more differentiated, with still more specialized bricks that allowed for a more detailed representation of the real world. In the same process, the bricks became differentiated in relation to age, with bigger Duplo bricks for small children and Technic bricks for young people, providing better opportunities for technical refinements. The LEGO bricks boxes were gradually organized according to different thematic universes like city, railroad, space etc.

Similar to other toy products, the LEGO bricks gradually changed during the 1970s and 1980s. The thematic universes assumed a still more imaginary character, and bricks were less to be used for building models of the real world and more to be used to create fantasy worlds inhabited by pirates, Indians, knights, space explorers etc., inspired by already existing fictional worlds circulated not least through popular mass media. These imaginary universes did not replace the traditional real world universes, but they became ever more prominent. At the same time, the real world universes went through a process by which the dramatic and high-tech inventory of the modern world came to the fore; advanced police and rescue material, spaceships etc. As this imaginarization gradually advances, the supply of LEGO brick boxes become organized according to the same genres and sub genres that are known from media fiction, and in particular the genres that are preferred by LEGO's primary target group, boys aged five to sixteen years: adventure genre (knights, pirates, Indians, explorers) and action genre (racer, police, fire brigade, space) etc. LEGO series specially aimed at girls gradually emerge, and here we find the typical fictional genres for girls: doll's house universes that thematize family life and emotional relations between parents and children for the youngest girls and a Barbie/youth soap-universe for older girls, in which exclusive leisure activities make up the dominant play activity (horse riding, surfing, skiing, fashion etc.). In accordance with LEGO's educational and responsible image, some fictional genres and narrative components are missing: violence is strongly downscaled and sexual themes are completely absent.

At the end of the 1980s media genres have already become important principles for the differentiation of the thematic universes of LEGO bricks. The development in the 1990s is characterized by a further evolution in this direction (variation and differentiation of genre elements) and an approximation to specific fantasy worlds that circulate in the media. Some of LEGO's thematic universes are very similar to well-known fictional films. The LEGO adventurer Johnny Thunder who in the interwar period explores pyramids, flies in a balloon etc. has strong allusions to the Steven Spielberg's *Indiana Jones* movies. The Duplo brick series 'Little forest friends' has many similarities to the fictional universe of the Smurfs. This tendency was perhaps most evident in the Johnny Thunder series that featured dinosaur hunting on a tropical island; the similarity to the *Jurassic Park* narratives are rather obvious. However, these universes are not licensed and they do also display differences in terms of names and details.

LEGO's much more expansive global strategy from the late 1990s caused LEGO to buy media characters on a licensing basis. In 1998 LEGO reached an agreement with Disney that allowed LEGO to use characters from the Mickey Mouse and Winnie the Pooh universes. In the same year, an agreement was signed with Lucas Entertainment on the *Star Wars* series. Licensing continues to be an important feature and in 2000 LEGO made a deal with Warner Brothers about the *Harry Potter* movie, allowing LEGO to make *Harry Potter* brick universes. In the same year a contract was signed with HIT Entertainment PLC to make Duplo bricks in connection with the popular English television series for children *Bob the Builder*.

As a result, the LEGO brick packages are not only organized thematically according to different fictional genres and imaginary universes, but they are increasingly *imitations of specific* fictional universes already promoted - and owned - by the media industry: the world of *Star Wars*, Disney, *Harry Potter*, Spider Man etc. The licensing agreements are, from one point of view, a traditional example of cross-branding, in which two brands (e.g. *Star Wars* and LEGO) join forces in order to get a wider reach than each of them could get by themselves. However, as should be obvious from the abovementioned, this kind of licensing agreement has a stronger impact on the product than the mere association of the product with yet another brand. The brands (*Bob the Builder*, *Harry Potter* etc.) become the important content of the toys, transforming both the imagery of the bricks and the character of the play.

In 2000 an agreement was made with Steven Spielberg about the development of a complete LEGO film production play set; 'LEGO MovieMaker'. This includes a small film camera, video-editing software and bricks to build a complete film studio and different scenes. In the accompanying advertising material are examples of productions that children can make with this product. The examples are different imitations and partly parodies of scenes from the *Jurassic Park* movies. LEGO has also produced a whole range of additional packages in this MovieMaker series in order to produce many different movie scenes. With this product LEGO has not just created one more product that thrives on fictional stories from the media, the rationale of the play has become imaginarized; the very purpose of the play with the toy is to produce fictional universes in which narratives unfold. As such, it represents a *second order* mediatization: the media are used as play and the purpose of the play is to produce media stories.

Narrativization

In the 1970s and 1980s the different LEGO brick boxes were organized in thematic universes, but they were not provided with narratives. In this sense the thematic universes were completely open-ended; it was left to the children to develop stories in relation to the play with the bricks. The construction work itself was in a very simple sense narrativized, because the instruction manuals provided a detailed scripting of the building process. As such, there was a clear difference as regards degree of liberties in the construction work on the one side, and in the subsequent play with the models on the other. The instruction manual prescribed in detail how each brick was to be used, and in which order, to reach the final result. But when the model was ready to use, there were practically no suggestions or instructions for the subsequent play.

One of the difficulties in creating play narratives has been the LEGO figures' small size, rigid movements and general lack of personal character traits. In order to create a narrative it is necessary to have actors with specified narrative roles (the protagonist, the antagonist, the good, the evil, the assistant etc.) that designate a series of conflicts that are to be solved, and through a set of personal or social character traits (strength, wisdom, boldness, specific skills etc.), some possible narrative developments and solutions are suggested. However, some important developments in the characterization of LEGO figures have taken place during the 1990s: the figures have become more differentiated and certain figures have been given names and act as protagonists in the different thematic universes.

The small size of the LEGO figures has made it particularly important to circulate narratives (characters, storylines etc.) through other media. LEGO has not only relied on the licensing aspect, but has tried to develop a whole environment for distribution of narratives about the LEGO characters: e.g. in the sales catalogues, magazines, computer games, television programmes, and theme parks. The LEGO catalogues increasingly show very short cartoons with LEGO figures in dramatic narrative situations. In 1998 LEGO began to cooperate with the English division of the Egmont Group in order to create a LEGO Magazine for children. The result, 'LEGO Adventures', was first launched in Britain and Germany in 1999. The magazine was a failure in Germany, but subsequently has been introduced in Poland, the Czech Republic, Russia and Spain. The Magazine contains cartoon-like stories (a combination of drawings and photos) in which the LEGO figures and characters are developed in relation to the different thematic universes.

The launch of computer and video games from the late 1990s has also helped to develop characterization and these media furthermore contain developed story lines that can be used as inspiration for the play with physical LEGO figures. In 2000 LEGO created a special unit for TV production that will produce children's programmes for television, Internet and film. This audiovisual production will most likely encourage a further narrativization of the LEGO environment. LEGO's most ambitious project in terms of developing its own narratives has been the Bionicle series. The Bionicle universe consists of a number of figures bigger than the usual LEGO men and women. Each figure has its own story and specified character traits and the Bionicle universe has its own story as well. The genesis of the Bionicle world and the stories about the individual figures are distributed through several media platforms; as computer games, as music CD's, as collecting cards, on Internet sites, and of course as LEGO bricks. As a temporary culmination of this multimedia engagement, LEGO signed an agreement in 2002 with Miramax Films in order to produce a blockbuster movie about the Bionicle story, to be released in 2004. As LEGO gains experience in the media industry, it tries to narrativize it products in two ways; by buying other media narratives to support a rapid expansion in sales and new markets and by developing its own narratives to be branded as unique LEGO stories.

Virtualization

By virtue of imaginarization and narrativization, LEGO bricks are increasingly to be used to build and enact fantasy worlds taken more or less directly from the media's symbolic universes. In addition, mediatization also implies a virtualization, in which the bricks and the construction work lose their physical-sensory qualities in favour of a symbolic representation and interaction. This is most obviously the case with LEGO's computer and video games in which physical bricks are replaced by a symbolic representation, and the play with the bricks (to the extent that it is the bricks that are played with in these games) is performed by manipulation of joystick, mouse and keyboard.

The relationship between the computer and video games and the physical brick universes are rather complicated. On the one hand, there is a clear iconographic connection between bricks and games because the fictional world of the games appears as brick-made universes. Furthermore, there is also a thematic and narrative connection between some of the games and the brick universes, so these games can be considered game versions of the brick universe as for instance the games relating to the LEGO Rock Raiders or LEGO Knights' Kingdom series. On the other hand, the different LEGO games are to some extent built upon existing computer games genres (racing, adventure, chess, simulation/strategy etc.) and make use of these genres' design of game play, conflicts, solutions etc., thus, some of the games are to a large extent a LEGO version of a computer chess or simulation game. The special LEGO brick iconography is used in both physical and virtual worlds but the actual play and interaction in the computer and video games are in some respects disconnected from the LEGO bricks and are in some cases (apart from the iconography) hardly distinguishable from other games.

The connection between computer and bricks is much closer and more developed in the LEGO CyberMaster and LEGO MindStorms products that allow computer manipulation of physical bricks. To some extent the key play component of these toy products is the construction of models with Technic LEGO bricks, but this traditional activity has been extended with the possibility of operating the models by remote control and programming the models to act in specific ways and to respond to different stimuli (pressure, temperature, light etc.). They are a sort of intelligent toy in which the interplay between physical modelling and intelligent control provides a new kind of environment for play. In this case there is no virtualization of the physical bricks - they continue to play a very important role. Instead, another kind of virtualization takes place, in the sense that the actions performed during the play undergo a process of abstraction and formalization. Instead of just moving LEGO models around with the hand and pretending that these movements are part of a narrative (fight, pursuit etc.), the course of events is pre-programmed on a computer as an abstract and logical sequence. As a consequence, the play is to some extent de-narrativized in favour of an experimental playing with causes and effects in an abstract-symbolic environment via the programming language of the LEGO software. Whereas the computer games seem to provide a successful integration of the narrative and virtual components, LEGO has not, so far at least, managed to create a successful integration of narrative qualities with intelligent bricks.

Finally, the Internet has opened up the possibility for another kind of virtualization, the creation of virtual LEGO communities. LEGO has recently made a strong commitment to the Internet part of its activities in order to develop the LEGO Club. As a member of the club you not only acquire information but can also discuss and exchange construction ideas with other LEGO enthusiasts and participate in competitions, both virtually and in the real world. Similar to other toy and entertainment products providers, LEGO has developed its Internet medium into both a virtual shop where you can order and buy LEGO products and an entertainment platform in itself; among other things, you can play LEGO games directly on the Internet.

From Engineering to Adventure

As has been demonstrated, LEGO has undergone a profound change during the last decade. The bricks have been subject to a process of imaginarization, through which most of the products are organized according to the general genres and thematic universes of the media, in some cases even imitate specific imaginary universes from the media. A second order imaginarization has developed: to play is to use media to produce new fictional stories. LEGO toys increasingly invite play in which storytelling is the crucial activity and narratives about the play are promoted through a whole range of media platforms. Through digital media, bricks have not only become virtualized by moving 'into' the media as in the case of LEGO computer games, media have also become 'materialized', when computer technology gets implanted in bricks and physical objects become intelligent.

In terms of production, sales, image making and iconography, the bricks have not lost their importance. On the contrary, without them LEGO would experience both rapid financial disaster and a severe blow to its image. However, the fact that the physical bricks are still around does not make the process of mediatization less consequential or important. The bricks may still be around, but they are profoundly different from the bricks of earlier days. The physical bricks have been circumscribed by the imaginary world of the media industry and the physical bricks of today's LEGO are only one manifestation of the brick icon that circulates on all sorts of media platforms in all kinds of imaginary worlds and narratives.

One important consequence of mediatization of the toy industry is that it brings the children into closer contact with the consumer culture of the adult world. Toys have always been part of the consumer culture in the sense that toys are products to be bought and consumed and the possession of toys has been used by children to display a certain life style and identity. Mediatization pushes the toys - and the children - even further into a consumer culture, because the content of the play becomes invested with consumer values. In the early years, LEGO was dedicated to construction toys and the inherent values of the play were taken from the world of engineering. The hero of the early LEGO bricks was the engineer who constructed the buildings and machines of the modern world. Through play with the LEGO bricks, the child itself could become a small engineer who created replicas of the material wonders of the industrial society. As mediatization progressed, heroes and values stemming from the media industry's repertoire of adventurous heroes gradually replaced the engineer. LEGO's new heroes are seldom occupied with the slow, laborious work of construction, but are much more devoted to fast action in exotic places far from civilization and increasingly engaged in different kinds of violent - yet morally legitimate! - destruction.

This development resembles in many ways the changes Leo Lowenthal reported in his study of biographies of famous people in popular magazines in the first part of the twentieth century (Lowenthal, 1961). In the early years of the twentieth century, magazines portrayed prominent people in industry, political leaders and famous scientists and the biographies were preoccupied with their achievements in the social sphere of work. Half a century later, these 'idols of production', as Lowenthal labels them, have been supplanted by a new class of heroes; the 'idols of consumption'. The new idols have not earned their fame through hard work, intelligence or political leadership, but have reached their fame through exposure in the media. What interests the media is not the Hollywood stars' education, knowledge or working life, but their leisure activities and private affairs. They are heroes due to their experiences in the sphere of consumption. This change is also useful as a general conceptual distinction between different historical phases in the cultural values of toys.

The LEGO Company and its products have been at the centre of this study, but the trend towards mediatization applies to the toy industry in general. The major toy manufacturers like Hasbro and Mattel have also moved closer to the media business in similar ways. As a consequence, today's toy store is filled, not only with teddy bears, bricks and dolls, but increasingly computer games, media merchandising and intelligent toys (James, 2000). The old animal pets and dolls are similarly changing; increasingly they are battery driven with built-in computer chips that allow them not only to move, but also to talk and respond to different kinds of stimuli; touch, sound etc. Today, even the soft toy is programmed by software.

The changes do not only take place in the toy industry and toy stores. Media companies market their products to ever-younger age groups. In particular the market for 'tweens', i.e. those who are between the age of children and 'real' teenagers, has become an important media market. The 'tweens' play with mobile phones, CD-players, television, Internet, computer games etc. just as much as they used to play with the old Wild West fort or the doll's house. For these youngsters, media companies like Nokia, Microsoft, Sony, Electronic Arts etc. are as much toy manufacturers as Mattel, LEGO and Hasbro used to be - although this age group doesn't like the connotations of the word 'toy'. It has become childish to play with toys - and attractive to play with media. If the toy industry wants to play along, it must adapt to these changes in lifestyles and behaviour. Toys have been mediatized, and the development of LEGO is in many ways emblematic of this process and its associated changes: the synergy between the toy manufacturers, the media industry, and the high-tech industrial economy as a whole, the globalization of production and consumption, the dematerialization of cultural artifacts. In short, the history of LEGO reflects the social and cultural transformation of bricks to bytes.

References

Altheide, D. L. and Snow, R. P. (1988) 'Towards a Theory of Mediation', in Anderson (Ed.), Communication Yearbook 11. Newbury Park, CA: Sage.

Amnå, Erik (Ed.) (1999) Politikkens medialisering, Demokratiutredningens forskarvolym III, SOU 1999: 126, Stockholm.

Byskov, Søren (1997) Tro, håb og legetøj: landsbyfolk og industrieventyr i Billund 1920-1980, Overgaard Bøger.

Castells, Manuel (1996) The Rise of the Network Society, The Information Age: Economy, Society and Culture, Volume I, Oxford: Blackwell.

Castells, Manuel (2001) The Internet Galaxy. Reflections on the Internet, Business, and Society, Oxford: Oxford University Press.

Cortzen, Jan (1996) LEGO manden - historien om Godtfred Kirk Christiansen, København: Børsen.

Cross, Gary (1997) Kids' Stuff. Toys and the Changing World of American Childhood, Cambridge, Mass.: Harvard University Press.

Engelhardt, Tom (1986) 'The Shortcake Strategy', in Gitlin, Todd (Ed.), Watching Television. New York: Pantheon.

Habermas, Jürgen (1989) The Structural Transformation of the Public Sphere, Oxford: Polity Press.

Hansen, Ole Steen (1997) LEGO og Godtfred Kirk Christiansen, Store Virksomhedssuccesser, Frederiksberg: Bogfabrikken.

Hjarvard, Stig (2002) 'Simulated Conversations. The Simulation of Interpersonal Communication in Electronic Media', Northern Lights. Vol. 1, Copenhagen: Museum Tusculanum Press.

http://www.lego.com/eng/bionicle/

http://www.lego.com/eng/info/history/

http://www.lego.com/eng/info/press/pressreleases.asp

James, Jennie (2000) 'Tumult in Toyland', in Time. 11 December 2000.

Jamieson, K. H. (1988) Eloquence in an Electronic Age. The Transformation of Political Speechmaking, Oxford: Oxford University Press.

Kline, Stephen (1993) Out of the Garden. Toys, TV, and Children's Culture in the Age of Marketing, London & New York: Verso.

LEGO (1982) 50 år i leg, Billund: LEGO.

LEGO Catalogues and advertising material from 1955 to present.

Lowenthal, Leo (1961) 'The Triumph of Mass Idols', in Literature, Popular Culture and Society. Englewood Cliff, N. J.: Prentice-Hall.

Mazzoleni, Gianpietro and Winfried Schulz, (2002) Keyword: Mediatization, www.lboro.ac.uk/research/changing.media/noticeboard

Ritzer, George (1995) Expressing America. A Critique of the Global Credit Card Society. Thousand Oaks: Pine Forge Press.

Ritzer, George (1999) Enchanting a Disenchanted World. Revolutionizing the Means of Consumption. Thousand Oaks: Pine Forge Press.

Schudson, Michael (1978) 'The Ideal of Conversation in the Study of Mass Media', Communication Research. 5(3), July 1978.

Schudson, Michael (1997) 'Why Conversation is not the Soul of Democracy', in Critical Studies in Mass Communication. No. 14.

Wolf, Michael J. (1999) The Entertainment Economy. London: Penguin.

Máire Messenger Davies is Professor and Chair in Media Studies and Director of the Centre for Media Research in the School of Media and Performing Arts at The University of Ulster. Her B.A. was in English at Trinity College Dublin, and then after a first career as a journalist, she gained her Ph.D. at the psychology department of the University of East London, studying how viewers learn from television. In 1993 she was an Annenberg Scholar at the Annenberg School for Communication, University of Pennsylvania, researching Media Literacy, She has written several books and articles on popular culture and its audiences. Her most recent is Dear BBC: Children, Television Storytelling and the Public Sphere (Cambridge University Press, 2001). She is a media consultant for the British Psychological Society, and a Fellow of the Royal Society of Arts.

Roberta E. Pearson is Professor of Film Studies and Director of the Institute of Film Studies in the School of American and Canadian Studies at the University of Nottingham. She is the author, co-author, and co-editor of numerous books and articles, the most pertinent to this volume's contribution being the edited collection Cult Television (University of Minnesota Press, 2004). She and Maire Messenger Davies are currently writing Small Screen, Big Universe: Star Trek as Television (University of California Press, under contract).

Máire Messenger Davies and Roberta E. Pearson

To Boldly Bestride the World like a Colossus: Shakespeare, *Star Trek* and the European TV Market

But the poet of them all
Who will start 'em simply ravin'
Is the poet people call
The Bard of Stratford on Avon. (Porter, 1948)

Shakespeare was one of the first producers of popular, inexpensive versions of deluxe forms of entertainment. (Yachnin, 2001, p. 39)

'Popular, inexpensive versions of deluxe forms of entertainment' is an almost made-to-measure definition of episodic television drama, and provides a useful thematic framework for this chapter. The commonalities between Shakespeare, the popular dramatist of aristocratic and courtly dilemmas, who sprang from provincial English origins in Warwickshire to be court playwright and eventually 'man of the millennium', and *Star Trek*, a failed, quirky science fiction TV series of the 1960s, with its grand televised narrative of a utopian future, which became the most profitable television franchise ever, constitute our broad theme. We develop this theme in two ways: firstly, within a general discussion about the nature of the relationship between American television and its European and global markets, and secondly, through an analysis of audience responses acquired through opportunistic surveys of cultural consumers at two cultural events: the *Star Trek* exhibit at London's Science Museum on 9 and 10 April 2001 (522 people), and the Bath Shakespeare Festival, 3-17 March 2001 (898 people).

American Film and Television: the Cultural 'Colossus'

In 2000 the European Audiovisual Observatory reported that Europe's deficit in the balance of audiovisual trade with North America amounted to 8.2 billion dollars, an increase of more than fourteen per cent from 1999. North American revenues in Europe had been steadily increasing and European revenues in North America steadily declining since 1998 (European Audiovisual Observatory, 2000). In that same year, the Observatory's André Lang authored a preface to the annual report of the Eurofictions project stating that indicators such as 'market shares, global volume of fiction and films imported as well as those diffused through television, monies received by American distributors in the European market' show 'that the American [film] industry not only remains economically dominant at a global level but that it continues to expand its market share and its revenue within the European market' (Buonanno, 2000, xi). Although the American film industry has benefited from overseas revenues since the first decade of the twentieth century, it was in the century's last decade that these began to equal or even exceed domestic ones.

But the increased deficit reported by the European Audiovisual Observatory in 2000 was 'due basically to the growth in television receipts achieved by the Majors [studios] which grew by twenty-one per cent' (European Audiovisual Observatory, 2000). This increase testified to the spread of the American model of commercial television across Western Europe. Based on 1991 figures, Els De Bens, Mary Kelly and Marit Bakke reported that 'the new European commercial channels had stimulated imports of American TV fiction', with significant increases in the three years between 1988 and 1991. According to them, '[t]he European broadcasting industry is highly dependent on the USA for its film and series imports. While the production of films and series is growing in the USA, the production of feature films and TV drama has declined in Europe' (De Bens, Kelly and Bakke, 1992, pp. 96, 99). Four years later, 'sixty per cent and on some channels ninety-five per cent of drama (films and TV series) shown in Europe was of American origin' (van Hemel, 1996, p. 89). Historical trends would predict a further increase in the percentage of American drama on European television screens, since, as Dennis McQuail tells us, 'at each stage of European expansion it has been the role of America to supply essential but missing components to the European television industry' and American content will be needed to fill the 'the many new transmission hours' resulting from the proliferation of cable and satellite channels (McQuail, 1996, pp. 112-113).

The above figures confirm the gloomiest imaginings of the vulgar cultural imperialists. The American media 'bestride the narrow world like a Colossus' and have just as much sway over the global masses as Caesar had over the Roman plebs. But this is a rather reductionist political economist argument. While Hollywood exports hundreds of hours of film and television, the two media should not be conflated. American film dominates European screens and undeniably has deleterious consequences for local production; even if indigenous producers can fund their films, they have difficulty getting them exhibited, since the American studios have a controlling interest in many exhibition chains. European filmgoers are offered a steady diet of American cinema; the possible behavioural or ideological effects of this remain debatable but the right to see one's own culture projected on the big screen should not be subject to debate. In contrast to film industries, we argue, national television industries in Europe continue to thrive, attempting to address the needs of their varied and respective populaces.

The sheer percentage of American programming on international television screens tells one story; the scheduling, ratings and reception of specific American programmes may tell another. In Europe, says Milly Buonanno, editor of the *Eurofictions* volumes, 'While the entire day is international/American, prime-time is national/European' in terms of the national origins of the programming content (Buonanno, 2000, p. 24). The scheduling of American programmes, often materials to which the broadcasters already own the rights, during the daytime and late night hours cuts production costs, enabling expenditure on original programmes during prime-time (Buonanno, 2000). As of 2000, among the five major European Union countries included in Buonanno's study (France, Germany, Italy, Spain and the United Kingdom) only in Italy did American programmes predominate in prime-time (forty-three per cent domestic to fifty-one per cent American). In France, Germany, Spain and the United Kingdom, the percentage of prime-time domestic programming was respectively seventy-five per cent, fifty-six per cent, fifty-one per cent and fifty-one per cent (European Audiovisual Observatory, 2001).[1]

In Britain, American television drama appeals to a distinct audience, is scheduled only on the minority terrestrial channels (BBC2 and Channel 4) and even there does not number among the best-rated programmes. Industry analyst Albert Moran said in 1995:

> *American dominance of key territorial broadcasters around the world is dropping. In the peak 6pm to 11pm slots, it is very difficult now to get a major American series to work on the main channels here - BBC1 or the ITV Network. So big hit, syndicated shows like The X Files, Emergency Room and NYPD Blue are actually working as cults here on Channel 4 and BBC2 with a half or even a third of the audience reach that they would get in comparable markets (Moran, 1998, citing 1995 interview with himself).*

Even Channel 4, together with BBC2 one of the two terrestrial channels mandated to appeal to 'minority tastes', schedules American programmes differently from domestic ones. Said Janey Walker, Managing Editor for Commissioning:

> *With some of the series we acquire from the States they go out [in the States] at eight o'clock or nine o'clock. We don't have that option here because we want to be showing history documentaries or some other more serious programming at eight or nine o'clock (Right to Reply, Channel 4, 10 November 2000, quoted in Hill and Calcutt, 2001).*

A study conducted by Antony Palmer, a master's degree candidate at Cardiff University, confirms that in Britain American programmes appear primarily on minority channels and outside prime-time (Palmer, 2002). Palmer used *The Radio Times*, the BBC published television listings, as his database, counting the total number of programme hours and the total number of American programme hours on all five terrestrial channels (BBC1, BBC2, ITV, Channel 4 and Channel 5), the most popular satellite/cable channel (Sky One) and Channel 4's digital channel E4 during an eight-week period from 17 November 2001 to 25 January 2002.[2] In an average week on the terrestrial channels, American programmes amounted to 52.5% in daytime, 17.2% in prime-time and 34.3% in late night. On the two cable/satellite channels, the percentages were 46.2%, 24.9% and 28.9%. In an average week US programmes constituted 3% of BBC1's total broadcast hours; 6.6% of BBC2's; 3.4% of ITV's; 15.5% of Channel 4's; 21.1% of Channel 5's; 81.2% of Sky One's and 23.4% of E4's. The largest percentage of American programming appears on Sky One, owned by Rupert Murdoch's News Corporation, which brands itself as the channel that first brings American programmes to Britain. Across the accumulated prime-time programming hours of the eight-week sample period on the terrestrial channels, BBC1 showed 6.5%

American programmes; ITV none at all; BBC2 35.1%; Channel 4 14.1% and Channel 5 5.2%. At the moment in Britain, the more strictly regulated terrestrial

channels offer their audiences overwhelmingly domestic fare during the prime-time hours.

The foreign reception of specific American programmes has been the subject of a handful of academic studies which tend to undermine the political economists' fears of American cultural and ideological dominance (see Ang, 1985; Liebes and Katz, 1990; Gripsrud, 1995). Far from accepting the American values supposedly implicit in any American media product, international audiences actively interpret the programmes within their own cultural framework. Evidence also tends to show that viewers often prefer their own media products to the American, since the indigenous programmes' familiarity renders them easier to comprehend and closer to the viewers' everyday concerns. For example, Daniel Biltereyst compared the reception by Belgian viewers of an American sitcom and a Flemish (Dutch language) sitcom. He concluded that 'the indigenous drama functioned as a forum for introspection to consider themes of identity and current political, cultural and social issues, while in the responses to the US programme such issues hardly ever arose' (Biltereyst, 1990, p. 489). Joseph Straubhaar has shown that many Brazilian viewers remain immune to the lure of global media, particularly as embodied in American programmes: 'Cultural capital, identity and language tend to favour an audience desire for cultural proximity, which leads audiences to prefer local and national productions over those which are globalized and/or American.' (Straubhaar, 2000, p. 212).

Straubhaar's 'cultural proximity' is the flipside of Richard Collins's cultural discount, which refers 'to loss of attractiveness or usefulness that obtains when information is marketed to consumers to whose cultural experience it is alien'. Collins speculates that US cinema and television have achieved success by developing 'programming which reduces "cultural discount"' (Collins, 1990, p. 212). But cultural proximity/discount seems related to demographic variables. In Brazil they vary with social class, which is strongly correlated with the viewing/non-viewing of non-Brazilian programmes. 'Cultural proximity is itself limited by social class stratification. The cultural capital required for wanting to watch many kinds of imported programs tends to be concentrated in the middle and upper classes' (Straubhaar, 2000, p. 212). Conversely, the imported programmes might be said to suffer a high cultural discount among those outside the middle and upper classes. In Britain, by contrast, American media products have historically suffered less from cultural discount among the working classes than among the middle and upper classes. Many working-class cinemagoers in the 1930s and 1940s found US films far more attractive than British films which, if they represented the working class at all, tended to do so as figures of fun. The BBC lost audiences to ITV in the

1950s when the latter showed American programming and adopted American formats and performers (Collins, 1990, p. 212).

But in the UK at the present moment American television is seen by influential elites as superior to British television. The 21 February 2002 issue of *The London Review of Books* came wrapped with promotional material for the upmarket (dare one say elitist?) new BBC4, which Cardiff University master's student Jennifer Callahan suggests 'seems to be positioning itself as an antidote to the popular taste, the Australian and American connotations of digital television, of Murdoch and Hollywood, *Neighbours* and *Dynasty*' (Callahan, 2002). Anyone who has read Bourdieu's *Distinction* (not to mention the BBC's marketing department) would expect a strong overlap between *London Review of Books* readers and potential BBC4 viewers. But the *Review*'s next issue published a sidebar complaining that BBC2 had pre-empted three episodes of *Buffy the Vampire Slayer* in favour of the Olympics. Thomas Jones considers the former better value for money than the latter: 'It's very funny, very clever (and fairly intelligent, too), engrossing, even at times quite affecting.' Jones further comments that BBC2 has reportedly just lost *The Simpsons*, 'the other best thing on television', to Channel 4, which is said to have paid £700,000 per episode for the animated series (Jones, 2002, p. 20). Bourdieu would probably not have predicted that *London Review of Books* readers might be passionate fans of *Buffy the Vampire Slayer* and *The Simpsons*.

Not only journals of relatively restricted circulation embrace American television. The BBC's official television listings magazine, *Radio Times*, recently published an article asking 'Why can't Britain's long-running dramas be more like America's?' Author David Gritten asserted that '[t]he cream of American TV now stands for real quality'. According to Gritten, American television dramas have 'the edge in portraying a broad gamut of human experience' and are 'fast-paced, complex, smart and beautifully written'. By comparison to the American product, British dramas lack 'richness and density' as well as 'the facility to move seamlessly between moments of comedy, high drama, pathos and tragedy.' British television writers can't seem to create the 'indelibly memorable characters whose lives have a dramatic, sometimes even tragic sweep' that inhabit American dramas (Gritten, 2002). On the same day that *The Observer* front page reported that proposed changes in media ownership laws risked further 'Americanization' of British television, the paper's arts section featured an article titled 'Why I Love American TV'. Said Andrew Billen: 'The greatest shows on earth now come from the United States.' (*The Observer*, 28 July 2002, p. 1; *Observer Review*, 28 July 2002, p. 5). Even British television executives now speak of the superior quality of American television. In the James MacTaggart Memorial Lecture at the *Guardian* International Edinburgh Television Festival, 2002, Mark Thompson, chief executive of Channel 4, said:

> *When you're looking for ambitious, complex and above all modern TV, you find your-*
> *self watching not British, but American pieces: Six Feet Under, say, or 24. ... British*
> *television used to be famous for its risk taking. Now we're trailing behind American*
> *television and our viewers (Thompson, 2002, p. 18).*

But American television dramas have a limited appeal for a more general audience:

> *'The West Wing and The Sopranos don't actually win us the highest ratings,' says*
> *June Dromgoole, Channel 4's head of acquisitions. 'We buy them because they*
> *enhance our schedule, and they'll attract a certain section of the British audience.'*
> *Dromgoole calls The West Wing a show for 'youngish, upmarket ABC1 viewers.' So*
> *for an instant dose of quality, buy American (Gritten, 2002, p. 35).*

In the reverse of the situation in the 1950s, American television dramas seem to suffer a heavy cultural discount among a large segment of the British viewing public. Gritten quotes British independent producer Jo Wright. 'People mainly want to see stuff about their own country. I love *The West Wing* and *The Sopranos* but I know people who gave up on them because they didn't quite know what was going on.' And indeed these American programmes never attract as many viewers as a long-running British favourite such as *Casualty*, which can

> *get as high as ten million viewers and never falls below 8.5 million. The West Wing*
> *debuted with 2.5 million but almost half deserted it by the sixth episode. Over three*
> *seasons The Sopranos has struggled to reach an average audience over 1.5 million*
> *(Gritten, 2002).*

The vulgar cultural imperialists might be pleased with these figures; the American media do not automatically win the hearts and minds of the majority. But American television dramas in the UK do seem capable of winning the hearts and minds of elites. In the previous century these elites' forbears often decried American culture as pernicious trash, contrasting it unfavourably with a European culture characterized, in Matthew Arnold's phrase, as 'the best that has been thought and said'. As Richard Maltby has pointed out, this critique of American culture disguised fears that it was 'radically democratic; at a variety of levels, it challenges hierarchies of discrimination, taste and class' (Maltby, 1998, p. 106). But the civilization/barbarism binary continued to structure the terms of debate around the 'Americanization' of European culture as recently as the 1993 controversy over audio-visual products in the last round of negotiations over the GATT treaty, with America advocating inclusion, and some European countries, particularly France, lobbying for exclusion in order to protect their national media industries.

Contributing to the debate about the draft communications bill that would lift restrictions on foreign ownership of British terrestrial television, *The Guardian*'s

Jackie Ashley (2002) contested deregulation in terms of cultural sovereignty:

> *What defines 'Britain'? It's television in part. That's what we talk about. That's what keeps us us. The American media corporations which flood our imaginations through the cinema, the Internet, music and much of television are not yet all powerful, and that matters.*

But in a paradoxical twist on the usual anti-Americanization arguments, Ashley holds responsible not the vulgar masses eager for further vulgarity but those at the top of the social hierarchy.

> *Why don't the politicians get it? Perhaps a strange form of cultural elitism is to blame - West Wingitis. The Washington and Boston-loving 'preppy' boys around Whitehall adore the pinnacle of really good American programming, from ER to The West Wing. But they have little clue of how truly awful the other ninety-eight per cent is, the stuff that surges through the cable and satellite channels here already (Ashley, 2002, p. 16).*

When the *London Review of Books* and *Radio Times* articles described American television drama as refined, cultural and creative they were referring not to the awful ninety-eight per cent but to the really good two per cent, and this two per cent elicits loud praise. These evaluative terms, this discourse of quality, have more often been applied to rarefied high culture than to commercial, popular culture - more often, in other words, to Shakespeare than to *Star Trek*. Now, however, these discourses are becoming more interchangeable across different cultural domains, as our audience research on the differing cultural products - Shakespeare and *Star Trek* - suggest.

Shakespeare and *Star Trek*

Yachnin's definition, quoted above, of Shakespeare's dramas as 'popular, inexpensive versions of deluxe forms of entertainment' occurs in a discussion about the ways in which Shakespeare has been appropriated and reworked by other authors, such as Cole Porter (a process Yachnin calls 'bardicide'). He suggests how this is possible by drawing on Bakhtin's conception of Shakespeare's 'semantic treasures' - the way in which 'he [Shakespeare] constructed his works not out of inanimate elements, ... but out of forms that were already heavily laden with meaning' (Yachnin, 2001, p. 40).

Our definition of 'Shakespeare' and '*Star Trek*', for the purposes of this chapter, follows this concept in conceiving of 'Shakespeare' and '*Star Trek*', not in terms of individual texts, but as franchises - or, in Bakhtin's terms, works 'constructed out of forms ... already heavily laden with meaning' (Bakhtin, 1986, p. 5, quoted in Yachnin, 2001, p. 40). These works, in their turn, have generated further cargoes of meaning through constant performance and usage, and in their various manifestations, over extensive time and space. This freight of meaning both permits and derives from the reproduction and circulation of 'Shakespeare' and '*Star Trek*' in a huge variety of forms of cultural capital - plays, printed books, live performances, merchandise, films, TV programmes, websites and the ever-changing common currency of language - which includes, in the case of *Star Trek*, a vast, unofficial wealth of published and unpublished fan activity.

Shakespeare occupies a central position in British national identity: he is the national poet and the Man of the Millennium whose plays are a compulsory part of the educational curriculum and whose contemporary relevance is constantly debated in the media. Shakespeare has also been a European figure since at least the eighteenth century, when the Germans enthusiastically embraced the poet as '*unser Shakespeare*' and produced the first foreign-language translation. Shakespeare has been successfully exported not only to Europe but also around the world. A reproduction of the Globe stands in Tokyo as well as in Bankside and summer Shakespeare festivals take place in Verona as well as in London. In 2001 in the United States, '"more than 1.1 million people saw Shakespeare plays at fifty-two outdoor theatres" the Institute of Outdoor Drama reported' (CNN website, 2002). Shakespeare is an icon for poetic genius not only in Britain and the rest of Europe, but across the globe; the Shakespeare brand has been established, marketed and relaunched over centuries. Branding and franchising are two key components of success in the global market (McChesney, 1998, p. 34). *Star Trek* is among the most successful of American media exports. Originally pitched by its creator, Gene Roddenberry, to the American networks as 'wagon train to the stars' the programme drew heavily upon the American myth of manifest destiny, as apparent in the famous phrase 'the final frontier'. Some would argue that the programme was then and continues to be a purveyor of American imperialist values and that it projects the *pax Americana* onto the galaxy.[3]

Conversely, others would argue that the *Star Trek* series have numbered among the most progressive of American television programmes. Wrote Donna Minkowitz in *The Nation*: 'People who don't watch *Star Trek* are probably unaware that its vision of our future is socialistic, anti-imperialist and passionately committed to expanding the list of sentient life-forms who are judged to have rights and acknowledged to be persons.' Minkowitz continues: 'And in the sphere of race the show has been bold, exploring racial self-hatred, exploitation and cultural imperialism more acutely than almost any realistic series' (Minkowitz, 2002) But since the *Star Trek* franchise belongs to global media giant Paramount-Viacom, it can easily be made to fit the nightmare scenario of the vulgar cultural imperialists: American capitalist values efficiently distributed round the globe by a huge American corporation. The five *Star Trek* television series, ten feature films and related merchandise (novels, magazines, action figures, mugs, T-shirts and so forth) constitute a significant and important percentage of Paramount-Viacom's annual income. Kerry McCluggage, Chairman of Paramount Pictures Television, told us that for Paramount, to lose the *Star Trek* franchise would be 'like losing an arm, or maybe even an arm and a leg' (Personal interview, 2002).

While *Star Trek* has achieved its greatest overseas success in the United Kingdom and Germany, the original series has been marketed worldwide, from Abu Dhabi to Zimbabwe, and its younger siblings are on their way to equivalent worldwide penetration. In the United Kingdom, in 1999, *Star Trek: The Next Generation* (aired on BBC2 and Sky One) ranked as high as number five among American series and stayed among the top fifteen American series each month. It was what the industry calls 'appointment television', out-delivering its lead-out programme by as much as fifty per cent (based on share). In October 1999, *Star Trek: Voyager* ranked as the seventh highest rated American series among individuals 4+ (Mellon, 2001). In 1999, both *Star Trek*s maintained audience interest despite having been on British television for several years.

We have argued that the Shakespeare and *Star Trek* franchises are both simultaneously national and international. The latter's explicit Shakespearean aspirations also link the two: no commercial television programme has ever so consistently referenced Shakespeare over so many years. Casting long-time Shakespearean actor Patrick Stewart as Captain Jean-Luc Picard in *The Next Generation* formed the most direct connection between the two franchises. The actor has himself commented upon their similarity.

> *All the time I spent sitting around on the thrones of England as various Shakespearean kings was nothing but a preparation for sitting in the captain's chair on the Enterprise. There is something larger than life about the series - Star Trek's dialogue isn't like ordinary dialogue. It doesn't sound like Hill Street Blues or Thirtysomething. You can turn on the television and without looking at the picture, you'll always know you're listening to Star Trek (Oliver, 2000).*

The epic tone of some of the dialogue and plots renders *Star Trek* Shakespearean, but so do the numerous episode titles and quotations from the plays, as well as the actual enactment of scenes by regular and guest casts. Many academics have commented on *Star Trek*'s Shakespearean connections and the academic science fiction journal *Extrapolation* devoted an entire special issue to the topic.[4] *Star Trek*'s Shakespeare obsession is just part of the series' valorization of European high culture. The original series (aired in the US from 1966 to 1969) made frequent allusions to European culture as attested to by episode titles such as *Who Mourns for Adonais*[5] and *Plato's Stepchildren*. *The Next Generation* is replete with such allusions, while *Voyager* to some extent continues the tradition, as when Captain Janeway (Kate Mulgrew) seeks advice from a holographic Leonardo da

Vinci. In this version of the future, the canon and high culture forms seem definitely to have triumphed in the 'culture wars' of the late twentieth and early twenty-first centuries. *Star Trek* rests on a bedrock of Western humanism.

In the rest of this chapter, looking at the data we obtained from our two groups of cultural consumers, we want to suggest that *Star Trek* is also Shakespearean in terms of some of the ways in which it is received and characterized by audiences. As such, the franchise is activating values and responses which educated European audiences have been trained to valorize, partly through their studies of authors like Shakespeare.

An Audience Study of Shakespeare and *Star Trek*: Methods and Procedures

From our audience evidence (discussed below), as well as from industry evidence about the flow and reception of American TV exports (discussed above), we want to argue that a simplistic cultural imperialist model (American low culture overwhelming and overshadowing European high culture) does not accurately describe American television and its global markets generally, nor the case of *Star Trek* in particular. Nor does such a model reveal what the 'cargoes of meanings' are for different groups or individual cultural consumers of various products. Our evidence provisionally suggests that our two different audiences, one in London for a 'low' commodity, *Star Trek*, and the other in Bath for a 'high' commodity, live Shakespearean performance, were, in a number of important ways, rather similar. This was particularly the case in terms of some of their demographic characteristics. It was also the case - from a Bakhtinian point of view - in terms of the reasons people gave for attending the event, and for 'liking' the product - their 'loads of meaning'.

We believe that any scholarly attempt to explain the behaviour of cultural consumers must find ways of consulting these people directly in order to allow them, as far as possible, to speak for themselves. The first challenge in any empirical study is to reach them, and we have been fortunate in obtaining two large opportunistically-acquired samples at the Science Museum and the Bath Shakespeare Festival. The institutions were willing to co-operate since they, too, need answers to the questions: who comes to this venue, and why? In the case of the Bath Shakespeare Festival, we were co-operating with a colleague, Professor John Tulloch, who was carrying out research for a book on the theatrical event and the everyday. We took the opportunity to add some questions of our own to his questionnaire to the Bath theatregoers. In the case of the *Star Trek: Federation Science* exhibit at the Science Museum, we were interested in gaining access to *Star Trek* enthusiasts (or at least those willing to visit a special exhibition about the show) for a book on *Star Trek* as television.

The basic research question for the two groups at the two venues was simple and twofold: who is here, and why? Underlying these questions were issues of taste, class, transnational influences, cultural proximity and discount and aesthetics. Hence, within the two basic questions, were further questions:

1. Are the two groups - both enthusiasts, in that they are specially self-selected for a cultural event featuring a particular named cultural phenomenon, or 'franchise' - demographically different because of the differing origins of the two franchises (the one 'high' and European, the other 'low' and popular American)?

2. Are the two groups similar or different in the reasons they give for being at the event?

3. If similar, or different, what can we deduce from these characteristics about taste and demographic groups in relation to our broader questions about class, taste and European/American cultural circulation?

Our method was concerned to elicit not responses to particular texts, but people's reasons for being attracted to the franchise as a whole - to 'Shakespeare' rather than to *Hamlet*; to '*Star Trek*' rather than to *Star Trek: Insurrection*. Rather than asking people how they interpreted a particular episode or performance of a play, as would a more 'conventional' reception study, we asked the reason for choosing Shakespeare and *Star Trek* in the first place. When people choose to consume cultural texts, they are doing so in terms of the cultural values into which they have been socialized, partly as a result of demographic factors, including nationality - the 'loads of meaning' that they carry. We also differ from other scholars by relating the consumption of one franchise (in itself a wider concept than a text, or a TV series) to more general patterns of cultural consumption.

Research on public, commercial, cultural experiences cannot be entirely controlled by the researcher in terms of selecting samples and controlling their composition. In choosing to study a theatre audience, there are certain factors that cannot be predicted - and some that can. We know that theatre audiences are mainly middle-class, and that museum visitors during half-term holidays are almost bound to be preponderantly people with children. We also know from our conversations with them that staff at the Science Museum and at the Theatre Royal in Bath are aware of the social narrowness of their appeal and want to broaden it.

Demographically, with some exceptions particularly with regard to age profile, our two samples are similarly white, reasonably well off and well educated. The samples were comparable in terms of middle-classness, and with regard to levels of education, but not comparable in terms of sex and age - there were many more women than men in the theatre sample and a higher proportion of younger people in the *Star Trek* sample. The two groups could be characterized as middle-class patrons of cultural institutions bent on cultural improvement either for themselves, their children or their students.

At the Bath Shakespeare Festival a short, 20-25 item questionnaire requiring firstly demographic information, secondly information about why people were at the Festival and thirdly other sorts of cultural experience, was given to all visitors at several venues, either directly or by leaving them on seats in the theatres, and collecting them afterwards. The response rate, based on comparisons with the box office returns, was around fifty per cent. At the Science Museum, researchers stood by the entrance to the exhibit on two days and handed questionnaires to everyone who came in; these, too, consisted of a demographic section; a section on responses to *Star Trek* and a section about other cultural behaviours. The response rate at the Science Museum was between eighty per cent and ninety per cent, since it was virtually impossible for visitors to avoid being handed the questionnaire, and nearly all were filled in.

There are many ways that these data could be presented. For this chapter we have chosen to focus on findings which address concerns about the relationship between American culture (as exemplified by responses to *Star Trek*) and European culture (as exemplified by responses to Shakespeare). Given that the two audience groups were - fortuitously - fairly similar demographically, particularly in terms of their educational levels (we did not have income comparisons), we wanted to see whether differences, or similarities, would emerge:

1. in terms of other kinds of cultural experiences the two groups might enjoy;

2. in terms of the reasons they gave for liking the franchise and wanting to go to a special event related to it.

It could be hypothesized that the *Star Trek* group might prefer American television, or have more populist tastes and cultural behaviours generally than the Shakespeare group. We might also hypothesize that the Shakespeare group would be likely to mention the importance of Shakespeare as part of our national heritage, and perhaps to be more likely than the *Star Trek* group to enjoy the sorts of films and television shows which reflected British preferences and identities.

The Audiences and Media Profiles: Quantitative Analysis

The tables below show a comparison between the two groups in terms of:

1. Frequency of theatre going;

2. Top ten favourite TV shows; and

3. Most recently seen films.

Table 1. Frequency of theatregoing: *Star Trek* and Shakespeare samples.

Frequency of attendance at theatre	*Star Trek* group	Shakespeare group
	Per cent	Per cent
Once a month or more	16.5	39.3
About once in three months	31.6	34.4
Once a year	24.5	13.6
Less than once a year	16.5	6.6

Table 1. shows that, as might be expected, the Shakespeare group had a higher proportion of frequent theatre goers, but the 'once in three months' groups are broadly similar, with around a third of the sample in each. There are more (16.5%) very infrequent theatregoers in the *Star Trek* group than in the Shakespeare group (6.6%), but both groups could be described as reasonably regular theatregoers.

Table 2. Top ten most recently seen films: *Star Trek* group.

What was the last film you saw at the cinema?	Number of People	Percentage of Whole Sample
Miss Congeniality	25	4.8
Chocolat	21	4.0
Crouching Tiger…	21	4.0
Gladiator	15	2.9
Billy Elliot	14	2.7
The Emperor's New Groove	14	2.7
What Women Want	12	2.3
Hannibal	12	2.3
The Grinch	11	2.1
Save the Last Dance	10	1.9
Not Entered	172	33.0

There were ninety-two different responses to this question; therefore only the top ten most common responses are shown.

Table 3. Top ten most recently seen films: Shakespeare group.

What was the last film you saw at a cinema?	Number of People	Percentage of Sample
Billy Elliot	95	10.6
Hannibal	56	6.2
Crouching Tiger…	55	6.1
Chocolat	53	5.9
What Women Want	45	5.0
Castaway	32	3.6
Traffic	24	2.7
Chicken Run	23	2.6
Gladiator	22	2.4
Shakespeare in Love	20	2.2
Not Entered	167	18.6

There were a total of 142 different responses to this question and only the top ten are shown. The fact that the most popular film accounts for only ten per cent of all responses demonstrates this variety. Apart from *Shakespeare in Love*, other Shakespeare-related films included *Hamlet* (two people), *Henry V* and *Henry VI* (both with one mention each).

Tables 2. and 3. show that six films are common to both lists: one British (*Billy Elliott*); one US/UK co-production (*Chocolat*); one US/Hong Kong/China/Taiwan co-production (*Crouching Tiger, Hidden Dragon*) and three rather diverse American - *Hannibal*, *Gladiator* and *What Women Want*. In the *Star Trek* group, the non-common four films mentioned are all American. In the Shakespeare group, one non-common film (*Castaway*) is American; two (*Chicken Run* and *Shakespeare in Love*) are British, made with American money; and the fifth - *Traffic* - is American, but based on a classic piece of British television, made for Channel 4 in 1989, *Traffik*. Again, there is some commonality of taste between the two groups here, with the slight possibility in the Shakespeare group, of a bias towards British-made films - or at least those with British themes.

Table 4. Top ten favourite TV programmes, *Star Trek* group.

Which three television programmes do you watch regularly?	Number of People
The Simpsons	66
Friends	60
Buffy the Vampire Slayer	56
X Files	27
Stargate	27
ER	26
EastEnders	25
Frasier	17
Babylon 5	15
Neighbours	14
No Programmes Named	212

Respondents were asked to name their three favourite television shows other than *Star Trek*. This produced a wide variety of responses; there were 310 different programmes mentioned as favourite one, 271 as favourite two and 232 as favourite three. The table above shows the ten most popular programmes and the number of people who cited them, regardless of whether they mentioned them first, second or third.

Table 5. Top ten television programmes, Shakespeare group.

Which three television programmes do you watch regularly?	Number of People
News	220
EastEnders	141
Friends	97
Neighbours	79
ER	57
The Simpsons	51
Hollyoaks	49
Time Team	48
University Challenge	44
Frasier	38
No programmes named	228

Respondents were asked to name three programmes that they watched regularly. This produced a wide variety of responses; there were 107 different programmes mentioned as favourite one, 146 as favourite two and 143 as favourite three. The table above shows the ten most popular programmes and the number of people who cited them, regardless of whether they mentioned them first, second or third.

Tables 4 and 5 show that six TV shows are common to both lists, though in different positions in the 'league': *The Simpsons, Friends, ER, EastEnders, Frasier and Neighbours*. Of these, four are American (*The Simpsons, Friends, ER* and *Frasier*) and have all been called 'high quality', one is an Australian soap (*Neighbours*) and the others British. None of the four non-common shows in the Shakespeare group are American: the *News, University Challenge, Time Team* and *Hollyoaks* are all British. In the *Star Trek* group, the four non-common shows are all sci-fi genre programmes, and all American (*Buffy, The X Files, Stargate* and *Babylon 5*). The Australian *Farscape*, with eleven votes, just missed the top ten. Thus the major difference between the two groups is the taste for news and factual programmes (home-grown) in the Shakespeare group, contrasted with the strong genre tastes of the *Star Trek* group - tastes which currently are primarily met by American programming. The differences here certainly seem more to do with genre than with anything else. However, cultural pessimists might bewail the absence of serious factual programming (a genre which is often domestically-produced) in the 'mass' tastes of the visitors to the Science Museum. The News and *Time Team* each got ten votes and just missed the top ten list.

In general, the distributions of favourite TV shows were extremely scattered, with around 300 different programmes being mentioned by each sample. The same is true of the films: nearly 100 titles were mentioned by each group, with the majority only having one mention. More remains to be learned from an analysis of what all these individual titles were, what genres they belonged to, what countries of origin they had, and what kinds of individuals mentioned them, and whether there were differences between the individuals in the two groups; all this data is available in the database from the studies. Like other studies of this kind (see Messenger Davies and Pearson, in press) this spread of responses illustrates the diversity and unpredictability of individual audience tastes.

Qualitative Analysis: the 'Quality Humanist' Groups

The reasons people gave for having an interest in *Star Trek* and Shakespeare were post coded, and resulted in nineteen different categories for *Star Trek* and twenty-two for Shakespeare. Some patterns emerged from this analysis. Aside from those who were 'indifferent' or who said they didn't like the show (they were just at the museum with the family), entertainment was the most frequently mentioned reason (9.2%) for liking *Star Trek*. Similarly highly valued (9.0%) was 'quality of the text' - for instance comments such as '[t]he stories/writing is good, is well acted, characters are complex but believable' from a woman in the seventeen to twenty-five-year-old age group, earning less than £10,000 a year, who particularly valued *Voyager* and its female captain, Kathryn Janeway, her favourite character. The next highest was 'vision of the future' (7.7%). For example, a woman between twenty-six and thirty-five said: 'I love *Star Trek* because it portrays a world in the future that I believe in and it has given me the opportunity to meet wonderful people who lately became very good friends.' This woman was one of the few of our respondents who bought merchandise and accessed *Star Trek* material on the Internet 'very often'. But even she, obviously a dedicated fan, who had seen all the films, and watched all the three 'new' series 'very often', did not attend conventions. She was our only respondent who actually belonged to a fan club. This group were not 'fans' in the more specialized sense of those discussed by Tulloch and Jenkins (1995) - however, they could be characterized as 'enthusiasts' and, in their taste for critical evaluative language, as connoisseurs of the franchise.

In the Shakespeare group, language was the most important value, with 10.2% mentioning either poetry or language. As with *Star Trek*, 'quality of the work' was the next most frequent reason (12.9%) - and the language used was also very similar to that of the *Star Trek* connoisseurs, for instance: 'I appreciate the humour and wit', from a teenager (eleven to sixteen age group). References to aspects of national heritage (as might be expected in the case of Shakespeare) and anti-American sentiment (as might be expected in the case of *Star Trek*) were rare. 'English heritage' was referred to by twenty-one people (2.3%) in the Shakespeare group. For example an A-level student, a male in the seventeen to twenty-five age group, visiting the festival from outside Bath, valued Shakespeare as 'part of British culture'; another male respondent, in the fifty-six to sixty-five age group, also talked about 'heritage and culture' as a reason for liking the Bard. Only two people (0.4%) in the *Star Trek* group expressed concern about the fact that *Star Trek* was overly American. A young female in the eighteen to twenty-five age group said: 'The storylines were sometimes cool, though often too smug and American cultural imperialistic for my liking.' A woman in the thirty-six to forty-five age group, a heavy consumer of all the *Star Trek* series and films, with the original series being her favourite, also acknowledged concerns about American hegemony: 'Consistent universe, possibly, if America-centric.'

Many people in both groups sometimes used what we term 'transcendental' language, that is, making large claims for the universal application, cultural value and psychological relevance over time of the two 'franchises'. For example, a male aged twenty-six to thirty-five in the *Star Trek* group, earning £10-15K, gave his reasons for liking *Star Trek* as '[e]xploration, adventure, humanity. The vision of a peaceful earth. Childhood memories.' Similar language was used by a female school student in the eleven to sixteen year old age group, at the Bath Shakespeare

Festival, to justify her liking of Shakespeare: 'His insight into human life is hauntingly true. The emotions are still the same today.' References to textual quality constitute another common discourse in both groups. For instance, a woman in the thirty-six to forty-five age group at the *Star Trek* exhibition, earning over £40K, explained her attraction to the franchise thus: 'Classic adventure stories. Well-drawn characters. Fascinating technology.' Similarly, at the Bath Festival, a male aged over sixty-five, educated to postgraduate level, talking about Shakespeare: 'Wide range of subjects. Marvellous language. Good roles for actors and actresses. Great complex characters.' 'Language and poetry' was a prevalent reason in the Shakespeare group, but similar proportions of compliments were paid in the *Star Trek* group to the formal, 'poetic' aspects of the visual technology and special effects. Leaving aside references to technology or poetic forms, many of the comments would be almost interchangeable between the two groups. *Star Trek* and Shakespeare were talked about as similar kinds of cultural products.

We post coded these individual reasons under a grouped heading of 'humanistic/qualitative' and created a sub-group from the main sample of all the individuals who had given such humanistic/qualitative responses. There were 119 people in the sub group of the *Star Trek* group (22.8% of the 522 respondents) and 108 such people in the Shakespeare subgroup (12% of the 898 respondents). The smaller proportion in the Shakespeare subgroup reflects the fact that many people (unlike those at the *Star Trek* exhibition) gave 'studying' as a reason for being interested in Shakespeare and for being at the Shakespeare Festival. The *Star Trek* and Shakespeare breakdowns of age and education (see Tables 6 and 8 below) show a higher proportion of children in the *Star Trek* group (it was half term and many were visiting the Science Museum with their parents) and a higher proportion of students in the Shakespeare group - where they were asked to identify themselves as students (unlike the *Star Trek* group): 18.7% of the Shakespeare group said they were studying at present or in further education.

Demographics of the Two Audience Groups
The tables below show the demographic breakdowns of both the *Star Trek* group and the Shakespeare group, and of their respective 'humanistic/quality' subgroups.

Table 6. AGE: Breakdown according to age, of visitors to the *Star Trek* Exhibition and their qualitative subgroup, and visitors to the Bath Shakespeare Festival and their qualitative subgroup.

Age group	Whole sample: ST, Science Museum (522 people) (per cent of group)	'Quality' subgroup, ST, Science Museum (119 people) (per cent of group)	Whole sample, WS, Bath Festival (898 people) (per cent of group)	'Quality' subgroup, WS, Bath Festival (108 people) (per cent of group)
0-10	5.9	2.5	0.2	0
11-16	20.9	17.6	18.2	16.7
17-25	12.8	12.6	15.7	18.5
26-35	16.5	21.8	4.6	7.4
36-45	29.3	34.5	6.1	8.3
46-55	10	9.2	14.8	15.7
56-65	1.7	0	15.5	13.0
65+	2.3	1.7	17.8	14.8

Table 6. shows:

• Demographically, neither of the 'quality' sub-groups is particularly different from the main groups. The distributions across ages are fairly similar both in each main sample and in the 'humanistic' sub-group.

• There is a much greater proportion of young adults (56.3% of 17-35 year olds) in the whole *Star Trek* group than there is in the Shakespeare group (20.3% of 17-35s). This partly reflects the high proportion of young families visiting the Science Museum, during the daytime.

• There is a much higher proportion of older people (33.3% over 56) in the Shakespeare main sample than in the *Star Trek* main sample (only 4% in the 56+ groups). This imbalance is even greater in the filtered groups with 27.8% in the 56+ groups in the Shakespeare group and 1.7 - two people altogether - in the *Star Trek* group. This obviously reflects the fact that Shakespeare has been around a lot longer than *Star Trek*, and many people over fifty-five would be familiar with him, but not with the TV series.

In terms of the future of the two franchises, *Star Trek* looks healthier in its ability to attract younger consumers. The older demographics of the theatre group might be of concern, not only to the theatre management, but also in terms of the long-term future of European elite forms of entertainment, such as live theatre - even with such a relatively popular draw as Shakespeare. To the extent that 'the performer' was one of the main reasons given for being at the festival (Simon

Russell Beale as Hamlet), more attention should perhaps be given to using popular and well-known performers as a way of attracting younger audiences.[6]

Table 7. SEX: Breakdown according to sex, of visitors to the *Star Trek* Exhibition and its qualitative subgroup, and visitors to the Bath Shakespeare Festival and its qualitative subgroup.

	Whole sample: ST, Science Museum (522 people)	'Quality' subgroup, ST, Science Museum (119 people)	Whole sample, WS, Bath Festival (898 people)	'Quality' subgroup, WS, Bath Festival (108 people)
Male	51.3	52.1	28.7	33.3
Female	48.1	47.9	61.4	55.6

NB: Where these figures do not add up to 100, this is because some people did not answer.

Table 7. shows that the distribution of male and female was much more evenly balanced in the *Star Trek* groups than in the Shakespeare groups, which were almost 2:1 female to male. This may again reflect whole family outings to the Science Museum, but as in the case of gender, it ought to be a cause of concern to cultural providers that whole families, including the men, do not see the Shakespeare Festival (or perhaps other live theatre) as an appropriate outing.

Table 8. EDUCATION: Breakdown according to education, of visitors to the *Star Trek* Exhibition and their qualitative subgroup, and visitors to the Bath Shakespeare Festival and their qualitative subgroup.

EDUCATION	Whole sample: ST, Science Museum (522 people)	'Quality' subgroup, ST, Science Museum (119 people)	Whole sample, WS, Bath Festival (898 people)	'Quality' subgroup, WS, Bath Festival (108 people)
Up to 16	31.2	23.5	15.8	12.0
Up to 18	13.8	12.6	5.9	5.6
Student at present			13.5	14.8
Up to FE			5.2	3.7
Up to HE	26.4	32.8	19.4	21.3
PG (master)	3.4	1.7	6.7	9.3
PG (profl.)	12.3	17.6	18.3	18.5
PG (Doctor)	3.8	4.2	3.7	4.6

- The proportions of people educated up to Higher Education (degree) level are high in all groups but higher in both the *Star Trek* groups. The Shakespeare groups included more 'students at present' because this category was included on the questionnaire.

- The *Star Trek* and Shakespeare groups with doctorates are virtually identical across the board.

- There is a higher proportion of Post Graduate professionals in the *Star Trek* quality sub-group than in the main sample, whereas these are almost identical in the Shakespeare groups (main and subgroup). More people have Masters degrees in the latter group.

- In general, not only are the two main samples similarly highly educated, but both the *Star Trek* aficionados (who might have been expected to belong to the absurder end of 'Trekkiedom' according to stereotype) and the Shakespeare aficionados are equally highly educated.

With regard to income, there are no figures for the Shakespeare group, so no tables are given. Within the *Star Trek* main group, the largest concentration was in the £40,000 plus group - twenty-eight per cent of the whole sample. A similar proportion - 26.9% - occurred in the 'quality' subgroup. The next largest group indicated the number of children and dependants in the sample - 15.3% in the main sample saying less than £10,000, and 14.3% in the subgroup.

Summary

The demographic characteristics of the groups (which admittedly are broad and lacking in finer details) indicate firstly that they are comparable in terms of education, and secondly that the 'humanistic/qualitative' groups - the people who used critical, evaluative, transcendental language about their loved 'franchise' - do not look particularly different from the groups as a whole. People of different ages, both genders and different levels of education are found in these subgroups too. The similarities in evaluative discourse between the Shakespeare and *Star Trek* samples may result from their similar educational and class backgrounds; it is likely that the respondents have acquired a similar language of moral and aesthetic evaluation through their education and cultural training. But is their evaluative discourse simply a function of their reading formation? Would they apply this discourse to any text or does the text itself contribute to eliciting the discourse? One might answer this question by asking both our *Star Trek* and our Shakespeare respondents for reactions to a text perceived as extremely 'downmarket', such as *Temptation Island*. We would hypothesize that both groups would then use less complex and elevated language, since we expect that people will deploy the discourses of morality and quality to talk about loved texts and franchises, but not about material they don't like or value. In this they contrast with academics, whose language - it sometimes seems to us - becomes more complex and jargon-ridden the more downmarket and unvalorized the text.

Conclusion

Globalization of culture is often equated with Americanization which is, in turn, often equated with dumbing down, particularly in Europe. We want to suggest that instead of blaming the Yanks for dumbing down, we might now want to blame them for smarting up. If there is cause to worry about Americanization, it may be not because American culture is low, vulgar and cheap but precisely the opposite - and hence more persuasive. *Star Trek*, together with many other American cultural forms, is in some ways (but not all) a form of repackaged European culture. It is an epic picaresque adventure story, based on the American trek West ('Wagon Train to the Stars'), drawing on the ethical traditions of the Enlightenment, which include among their most persuasive expressions the American constitution and the founding documents associated with it. To strike a less elevated note, like Starbucks, *Star Trek* mass-markets European culture and then re-exports it back to its lands of origin to successfully compete with the indigenous form. Does Europe have anything to counter with - is there anything that is as popular and persuasive, but also as long-lived and culturally complex as *Star Trek* - other than Shakespeare? The common culture of elites used to be European high culture; could it now become US quality television?

Notes

1   See also Buonanno, 1999; Buonanno, 1998, and Wieten, Murdock and Dahlgren, 2000.

2   The two weeks between 22 December 2001 and 4 January 2002 were excluded due to atypical holiday programming. Children's television, which tends to be the most international of all genres, was excluded. American programmes repeated during the schedule were each counted; Star Trek appearing each weekday at five and again at eleven on Sky One was counted as ten American programmes.

3   As do, for example, several of the articles in Enterprise Zones: Critical Positions on Star Trek (Harrison et al., 1996).

4   Extrapolation 36(1) (Spring, 1995) includes six essays on Shakespeare in *Star Trek*.

5   'Adonais' is the title of an elegy by Percy Bysshe Shelley in memory of his fellow poet John Keats: 'Who mourns for Adonais? Oh, come forth/Fond wretch! and know thyself and him aright.'

6   For more on this point, see Messenger Davies and Pearson (in press).

References

Ang, I. (1985) Watching Dallas: Soap Opera and the Melodramatic Imagination. London: Methuen.

Ashley, J. (2002) 'Puttnam is Right to Want Broadcasting to Stay British', The Guardian. 31 July, p. 16.

Bakhtin, M. M. (1986) 'Response to a Question from Novy Mir' in Speech Genres and other late essays, trans V. W. McGee, (Eds.) C. Emerson and M. Holquist, Austin TX: University of Texas Press.

Billen, A. (2002) 'Why I Love American TV', The Observer Review. 28 July, p. 5.

Biltereyst, D. (1990) 'Resisting American Hegemony: A Comparative Analysis of the Reception of Domestic and US Fiction', European Journal of Communication. 7(4).

Buonanno, M. (Ed.) (1998) Imaginary Dreamscapes: Television Fiction in Europe. Luton: University of Luton Press.

Buonanno, M. (Ed.) (1999) Shifting Landscapes: Television Fiction in Europe. Luton: University of Luton Press.

Buonanno, M. (Ed.) (2000) Continuity and Change: Television Fiction in Europe. Luton: University of Luton Press.

Callahan, J. (2002) 'BBC4's Cultural Agenda,' paper submitted for Principles and Practices of Media Research, School of Journalism, Media and Cultural Studies, Cardiff University, 11 March, p. 9.

CNN (2002) Report from www.europe.cnn.com/2002/SHOWBIZ/news

Collins, R. (1990) Television: Policy and Culture. London: Unwin Hyman.

De Bens, E., M. Kelly and M. Bakke (1992) 'Television Content: Dallasification of Culture?' in Karen Siune and Wolfgang Truetzschler (Eds.), Dynamics of Media Politics: Broadcast and Electronic Media in Western Europe. London: Sage.

European Audiovisual Observatory (2000) 'Press Release: The Imbalance of Trade in Films and Television Productions,' 9 April. www.obs.coe.int/about/oea/pr/desequilibre.html

European Audiovisual Observatory (2001) 'Press Release; TV Fiction Programming',

Gripsrud, J. (1995) The Dynasty Years: Hollywood Television and Critical Media Studies. London: Routledge.

Gritten, D. (2002) 'Lessons From America,' Radio Times, 23 February-1 March, pp. 33, 35, 36.

Harrison, T., Sarah Projansky, Kent A. Ono and Elyce Rae Helford (Eds.) (1996) Enterprise Zones: Critical Positions on Star Trek. Boulder, CO: Westview Press.

Hill, A., and C. Calcutt (2001) 'Vampire Hunters: the Scheduling and Reception of Buffy the Vampire Slayer and Angel in the UK', Intensities: the Journal of Cult Media. www.cult-media.com/issue1/Ahill.htm

Jones, T., 'Short Cuts' (2002) London Review of Books. 7 March, p. 20.

Liebes, Tamar, and Elihu Katz (1990) The Export of Meaning: Cross-Cultural Readings of Dallas. New York: Oxford University Press.

McChesney, Robert W. (1998) 'Media Convergence and Globalisation', in Daya Kishan Thussu (Ed.) Electronic Empires: Global Media and Local Resistance. London: Edward Arnold.

McQuail, Dennis (1996) 'Transatlantic TV Flow: Another Look at Cultural Cost-accounting', in Van Hemel, A. Hans Mommaas and Cas Smithuijsen (Eds.) (1996) Trading Culture: GATT, European Cultural Policies and the Transatlantic Market. Amsterdam: Boekman Foundation.

Maltby, R. (1998) '"D" for Disgusting: American Culture and English Criticism', in Nowell-Smith, G. and Steven Ricci (1998) Hollywood and Europe: Economics, Culture, National Identity: 1945-95. London: British Film Institute.

Mellon, M. (2001) (Senior Vice-President for Research, Paramount Pictures Television) Powerpoint Presentation on Star Trek's International Sales and Ratings.

Messenger Davies, Máire and Roberta E. Pearson (2002) Interview with Michael Mellon Hollywood, 16 January 2002.

Messenger Davies, Máire and Roberta E. Pearson (in press) 'A Star and His Audiences: Patrick Stewart and Cultural Mobility', in Martin Barker and Thomas Austin (Eds.) Stars of the Nineties. London: Edward Arnold.

Minkowitz, D. (2002) 'Beam Us Back, Scotty!', The Nation. 25 March. www.thenation.com

Moran, Albert (1998) Copycat TV: Globalisation, Program Formats and Cultural Identity. Luton: University of Luton Press.

Nowell-Smith, G. and Steven Ricci (1998) Hollywood and Europe: Economics, Culture, National Identity: 1945-95. London: British Film Institute.

The Observer (2002) 'Blair Boost to Murdoch TV Takeover', 28 July, p. 1.

Oliver, Hilary (2000) 'Picard's New Generation', www.efr.hw.ac.uk/EDC/StarTrek/picard.html

Palmer, A. (2002) 'Invasion USA? American Programmes on British Television', Unpublished master's thesis, School of Journalism, Media and Cultural Studies, Cardiff University.

Pearson, Roberta E., and Máire Messenger Davies, Personal interview with Kerry McCluggage, Chairman, Paramount Pictures, Television, Los Angeles, California, 15 January, 2002.

Porter, Cole (1948) 'Brush Up Your Shakespeare' (song in show Kiss Me Kate). In Gottlieb, R., and Kimball, R. (Eds.), Reading Lyrics. New York: Pantheon Books, 2000.

Straubhaar, J. D. (2000) 'Culture, Language and Social Class in the Globalization of Television', in Wang, G., J. Servaes, and A. Goonasekera (Eds.) The New Communications Landscape: Demystifying Media Globalization. London: Routledge.

Thompson, M. (2002) 'What's Wrong with our TV?', The Guardian. 24 August, p. 18.

Tulloch, John, and Henry Jenkins (1995) Science Fiction Audiences: Watching Doctor Who and Star Trek. London: Routledge.

Van Hemel, A. (1996) 'The Complex Debate on Audiovisual Policy' in Van Hemel, A. Hans Mommaas and Cas Smithuijsen (Eds.) (1996) Trading Culture: GATT, European Cultural Policies and the Transatlantic Market. Amsterdam: Boekman Foundation.

Van Hemel, A. Hans Mommaas and Cas Smithuijsen (Eds.) (1996) Trading Culture: GATT, European Cultural Policies and the Transatlantic Market. Amsterdam: Boekman Foundation.

Wieten, J., G. Murdock and P. Dahlgren (Eds.) (2000) Television Across Europe: A Comparative Introduction. London: Sage.

Yachnin, Paul (2001) '"To Kill a King" The Modern Politics of Bardicide' in Michael Bristol, Kathleen McCluskie and Christopher Holmes (Eds.) Shakespeare and Modern Theatre. London: Routledge.

Kirsten Drotner is dr.phil. and professor at the Department of Literature, Culture and Media Studies, University of Southern Denmark. Her research areas include media history, audience studies, methodology, and youthful media culture, and has written widely in Danish within her research areas. In English, she has (co)authored English Children and Their Magazines, 1751-1945 (Yale UP 1988) and Researching Audiences (Arnold 2003), just as she has contributed to a number of anthologies and scholarly journals such as Media, Culture & Society, European Journal of Communication, Cultural Studies, Theory, Culture & Society and Reseaux. She is founding director of Centre for Child and Youth Media Studies (1994-) and of DREAM (Danish Research Centre on Education and Advanced Media Materials, (2004-).

Kirsten Drotner

Disney Discourses, or Mundane Globalization

'We make the pictures and then let the professors tell us what they mean.'
(Walt Disney, quoted in Schickel, 1985)

The Walt Disney Company is one of the oldest and certainly one of the largest of global media corporations. It is ranked as one of the six so-called 'first-tier' media conglomerates in the world characterised by vertical integration and a complex network of interlocking ownership and management (Herman & McChesney, 1997). Thus, Disney offers unique possibilites of studying media globalization empirically as an economic and institutional phenomenon that reaches much further back than the spectacular cross-border mergers and acquisitions of the last decade. It is equally one of the most highly profiled media brands that most people around the globe know of. Thus, it offers unusual possibilities of studying ways in which audiences articulate how they understand and live with media globalization.

The first approach, the political economy and historical approach, has dominated both academic and popular investigations over the years. With the theme parks and the animation films as prime objects of interest, perspectives have ranged from panegyric praise to ideological critique (e.g. Feild, 1942; Dorfman & Mattelart, 1971/1975; Bryman, 1995). The second approach, the reception or audience approach, has been a stable of the Disney corporation itself since the 1930s when the firm initiated informal studio previews (Ohmer, 1991). But until recently, audience studies on Disney, have received relatively little scholarly attention (Real, 1973; Stone, 1975; May, 1981).

The present chapter is part of attempts to begin to redress that imbalance (Wasko et al., 2001). In wider terms, it is part of a growing body of research (Jensen, 1998; Livingstone & Bovill, 2001) that heeds for example John Tomlinson's (1991) and Marjorie Ferguson's (1992) calls for more empirical grounding of globalization theories while still acknowledging the need for empirical research to be theory-driven. Seen within a European perspective, such an empirical grounding almost invariably resonates with pertinent issues on possible reshufflings of cultural formations and identities in the face of supra-national political and social developments.

The basic argument of the chapter is that what may be termed a 'bottom-up' perspective, inherent in audience studies, may yield insights into contemporary processes of media globalization and convergence that may serve to complement, nuance and possibly question top-down perspectives on those processes. These perspectives, by and large, focus on technological, economic or institutional aspects and often harbour dichotomous notions of cultural change: one is a notion of cultural optimism stressing new possibilities in globalization processes of reaching beyond narrow local and national confines and creating dialogues that enhance mutual expression of, and respect for, multiculturalism and civic rights, thereby ultimately advancing social change (Demers, 1999; Gershon, 1997; McChesney, 1997). The other is a notion of cultural pessimism focusing either on the dangers of social and cultural atomization (also termed Balkanization) or, conversely, on a cultural assimilation to the USA and its economic and cultural standards (Frèches, 1986; Garnham, 1990; Turkle, 1995).

Moreover, what I term a mundane take on these processes conveys a picture that may serve to nuance existing, bottom-up analyses of media globalization. So far, these processes tend to focus on diaspora groups for whom questions of roots and routes emerge with particular poignance (e.g. Gilroy, 1995; Morley & Robins, 1995). While such a focus may seem natural and logical in European countries marked by distinct ethnic groupings and heterogeneous, cultural discourses such as in Britain, a similar focus seems less felicitous and relevant in Northern European countries that traditionally nurture discourses of cultural and national homogeneity. Limiting bottom-up studies of media globalization to distinct (ethnic) groupings in these countries easily obscures the socio-cultural diversities and differences found within groupings that are discursively defined as mainstream or perceived as being part of a homogeneous national identity. The unfortunate and unintended result is that less conspicuous groups are left at the margins of intellectual interest and concept-building. Therefore, we need to be as vigilant in searching for divergencies in identity formations and cultural articulations within seemingly mundane processes and entities as we are with diaspora cultures and other groups of visible and often self-defined otherness (see also Drotner, 2001a).

The present chapter draws on the first major audience study on children's articulations and appropriations of the Disney universe (Drotner, 2003). Based on in-depth interviews made in 2000 with forty-eight Danish children (age bands six to seven years, and eleven to twelve years) and their parents, I will address the following questions: How do children articulate their definitions of and associations with Disney? What are the relations between juvenile and adult (parental) definitions? How do these articulations resonate with wider issues on the formation of European cultural identities?

A bottom-up perspective on media globalization offers a way in which we may begin to understand it as more mundane socio-cultural processes. And a comparison of adult and juvenile discourses on Disney offers a way in which we may begin to understand changes in the meanings ascribed to these processes as they are framed within a European context.

Past and Present in the European Disney Universe

The Walt Disney Company has been instrumental in reframing people's understanding of media globalization around the world. Since the mid-1980s, the corporation has dramatically intensified its global reach following the revamping of its economy, production and organisation from 1984 on when the the Bass Brothers Enterprises gained control of the company under a new leadership, the 'Team Disney', with CEO Michael Eisner as primary spokesman. Spurred by international deregulation of the media sector and the concomitant growth in satellite, cable and internet communication, the company has diversified its businesses and intensified its corporate branding through the 1990s. In 1990, Walt Disney International was founded as a centralised branch coordinating all overseas activities. Since the mid-nineties, international revenues have grown by twenty-four per cent and today about twenty per cent of the company's revenue comes from international sources, including US exports (Wasko et al., 2001, p. 63). Still, Eisner, in the corporation's annual report for 1999, observed that the US inhabitants make up five per cent of the world's population but account for eighty per cent of the company's revenues, and he envisioned Europe to be a prime area of expansion:

If we can drive the per capita spending levels for Disney merchandise to just 80 per cent of US levels in only five countries - England, Italy, Germany, France and Japan

- then we would generate an additional $2 billion in annual revenue (quoted in Westcott, 2002, p. 76).

Today, the Walt Disney Company is the world's second-largest entertainment corporation by revenue: in the fiscal year 2000-01 it earned $25.4 billion (24.03 billion EUR) while AOL-Time Warner topped the list with a revenue of $36.2 billion (34.2 billion EUR) (Feilitzen & Carlsson, 2002, p. 247). The takeover in 2001 of Rupert Murdoch's Fox Family Worldwide, which controls Fox Kids Europe, further consolidates this position. And unlike AOL-Time Warner, Disney is much more than a media corporation; it encompasses a wide range of activities of which the most important are media networks, parks and resorts, consumer products, studio entertainment and internet communication. Nearly all of these acivities are united by the branding of distinct Disney characters which makes for vertical and horizontal integration and for cross-selling and promotion to a degree that 'Disney synergy' is the coveted aim of many global firms (Wasko et al., 2001, p. 71).

Within this complex Disney universe, Europe holds a particular position. Disney films, cartoons and merchandise were exported to Europe from the late 1920s on, while in for example Australia and Asia, Disney is a much more recent phenomenon (Nightingale, 2001; Yoshimi, 2001). In the USA, Disney since the 1950s is centrally associated with television and family theme parks: in 1954, the weekly series *Disneyland* appeared on the ABC TV-network, and one year later the first theme park, Disneyworld, opened in Anaheim, California. But in many European countries and regions, Disney until the early 1990s meant print media that children enjoyed on an individual, weekly basis to which was added a sprinkling of ritual family visits to the cinema to watch the latest animation film.[1] Since then, the combined processes of intensified media globalization, commodification and convergence have been catalysts in fundamental changes in output as well as contexts of use in Europe.

The Disney Channel was introduced in Britain (and Asia) in 1995, followed one year later by Fox Kids Network, then owned by Murdoch (the first child-oriented thematic TV channel, Nickelodeon, started in 1979). In 2001, these three companies account for thirty children's channels in Europe as follows: Fox Kids 11, Cartoon Network 8 (owned by AOL-Time Warner), Disney Channel 6, and Nickelodeon 5, the most popular of them. All rely on new output from their US studios or on archive programming (Westcott, 2002, p. 71). In addition to the themed channels, Disney animation features on terrestrial channels that still make up the majority of European children's viewing time. For example, nine out of ten Danish three to seven year-olds and eight out ten eight to twelve year-olds watching television on Friday nights, tune in to the weekly show *Disney sjov (Disney Fun)* broadcast at 7 p.m. on the public-service channel DR1 (*Danmarks Radio* channel one) (Danish Broadcasting Corporation Media Research, 2002).

Since the late 1980s, Disney has intensified its international video releases and closely monitors cycles of re-releases of their animation film library. In the mid-nineties, the company held a comfortable sixty per cent of the family video market in many European countries through Buena Vista Home Entertainment, Disney's international distributor of home videos and interactive businesses (Wasko, 2001, p. 64). The combined developments in television and video distribution has helped boost merchandise sales so that today Disney has an ubiquitous presence in Europe at nearly all times and locales and in all media - from satellite and cable television, video discs and CD-ROMs to music casettes and computer games. As CEO Michael Eisner pronounced in 1998: 'It doesn't matter whether it comes in by cable, or telephone lines, computer or satellite. Everyone's going to have to deal with Disney' (quoted in Wasko, 2001, p. 222).

In addition to the daily Disney, the opening in 1992 of EuroDisney placed the Disney theme park somewhat closer to European families. The Walt Disney Company cut a profitable deal with the French government in negotiations over the park: forty-nine per cent of the ownership is Disney, the land was bought at 1971 prices, the company secured preferential interest rates and the French built a fast train connection to the site. The construction of the park follows the American model with Adventureland, Tomorrowland (which in Euro Disney becomes Discoveryland), Fantasyland and Frontierland, in addition to which comes a Main street and a Sleeping Beauty Castle. But, initially, Euro Disney fell far short of their American models in popularity.

EuroDisney materialised at a time when the effects of deregulating the European media markets surfaced in political and cultural debate. In 1989, the EEC inaugurated its Television Directive (based on the 1984 policy paper, Television without Frontiers) in an attempt to create a pan-European audiovisual space by standardizing television production and distribution and minimizing national regulation. Conversely, in the 1993 negotiations at GATT (General Agreement of Tariffs and Trade) France succcessfully pushed to define culture and audiovisual media not as a commodity but as a common good and hence exempt from the agreement and open to national content quotas (article 14). Thus in Europe, Disney's corporate strategy in the 1990s to consolidate its global position through acquisitions, mergers and joint ventures, and its material and symbolic manifestation of this strategy in the formation of EuroDisney, plays into wider struggles over definitions of European (mediated) culture and national identities *vis-à-vis* cultural globalization that is widely perceived as Americanization.

These struggles were evident in the initial debate over the construction of the theme park. The French theatre director Ariane Mnouchkine called EuroDisney a 'cultural Chernobyl' while others talked about 'the American nightmare' (Guyot, 2001, p. 127). These public sentiments were intensified by the economic losses that the park generated in its first years of existence. Only after Disney in 1994 agreed to forgo £220 million (325.6 EUR) of revenue and royalties for five years and put up extra credit did the tide begin to turn. According to the British sociologist Alan Bryman, the real incentive for Disney's sudden generosity is to counter the association of the brand name with finance rather than fantasy in the public eye (Bryman, 1995, pp. 79-80). EuroDisney was renamed Disneyland Paris in 1994, and backed by intensive promotion campaigns in a range of European countries, the park made a profit for the first time in 1996. In 2002, it was renamed, yet again, as Disneyland Resort Paris. Irrespective of its name, the theme park has been the final element in bringing the European Disney universe close to its American counterpart in production and distribution terms.

Studying Disney Audiences

According to the Walt Disney Company's business chronicler, Douglas Gomery, the sustained success of the corporation rests on its revenues from the family theme parks (Gomery, 1994, p. 86). Still, Disney as a concept is nearly always constructed as being connected to children, either real ones or the child in all of us. But, surprising as it may seem, until my own recent study (Drotner, 2003) there has been no major academic, empirical analysis of the Disney universe as seen from a juvenile perspective. The few existing scholarly studies of people's appropriations and uses of the Disney universe all have young adults, indeed university students, as informants. This does not invalidate or diminish the research results as long as the researchers are aware of the specificities of their sample. But it does imply that the results invariably reflect informants' past experiences with Disney rather than their present engagements with the company and its products.

As a participant in the latest of these studies - a comparative audience study encompassing eighteen countries around the world (Wasko et al., 2001) - I was intrigued by the differences in audiences' Disney universes even within Europe: in Britain and France, adult informants primarily associate Disney with animated film (Guyot, 2001; Buckingham, 2001), while in the Nordic countries, Disney is overwhelmingly associated with weekly comics (Muhr, 1998; Drotner, 2001b; Hagen 2001). Conversely, the national profiles in the study testify to the recent homogenization in contemporary Disney output following the unification of production and distribution described above: an ubiquitous daily presence of televised Disney, Disney videos topping home market sales, Disney stores in major cities, and an ever-increasing plethora of merchandise for young and old.

A natural question to ask is simply: How do children growing up today appropriate Disney? This question set me going, and in the following I focus on the ways in which children lay claim to particular definitions of Disney. This focus is chosen because it operates as an analytical eye opener to the informants' discursive negotiations of the complex Disney universe. I compare the juvenile perspective with that of their parents, who represent the 'past' in reception terms, so as to chart the changing audience perceptions. These changes are perspectivized in terms of the informants' discussions of Disneyland Resort Paris in order to specify how Disney refracts articulations of supra-national, perhaps even European, identities.

'They Put Cartoons into our Heads': The Duality of Disney

All children in our study know what Disney is. Their answers differ, but they all readily provide one. Their associations with the word Disney may be divided into two closely connected dimensions, Disney as an aesthetic symbol and Disney as a material object.

Int: What is Disney really?

Anne (Age 7): It's animated figures and ... I can't quite explain (laughs).

Int: That's O.K. Animated figures.

Anne: It can be in pictures, or ... on video and stuff ... And then on Friday night ... well, after the news, then there is Disney Fun (Disney Sjov) ... And this morning I also saw Disney Fun.

Like Anne, nearly all children immediately mention that Disney equals animated film or characters. But as the quote also indicates, Disney is equally a concept attributed to a weekly TV-programme shown on DR1.

Taking the aesthetic dimension first, it is worth noting that Anne, like many other children, giggle or laugh when being asked to mention what they think Disney is. Other questions create less mirth, and one may take the informants' reactions as an indication that they find the question a bit silly, even if they go along with offering an answer. Apparently, the word Disney is so obvious as to be self-evident. To children in both age bands, Disney is a generic term for animated film, it is the aesthetic standard by which all similar output is measured, defined and understood.

Liv (Age 11): (Disney) is animated figures and stuff like that. You know, fun figures. Cartoons and so on ... the well-known ... the well-known figures (giggles).

Int: Yes. What well-known ones do you have in mind?

Liv: Well, Donald Duck, of course, and ... Mickey Mouse ... and then Goofy and so on

... (laughs) all sorts. And ... what's his name? The one with the long ears? The rabbit, you know.

Int: Who do you mean?

Liv: Uhm, Bugs Bunny ... and a lot of others (laughs).

Bugs Bunny, perhaps the most well-known of Warner Brothers' animated figures, is wrongly labelled Disney by Liv, and her mistake is quite symptomatic of the generic aesthetic status the children atttibute to Disney.[2] We have no examples of characters or films made by Disney defined by our informants as belonging to other brands. Within a bottom-up perspective on globalization, this generic definition of Disney animation is an indication of what may be termed an aesthetic homogenization of reception. It is not that the informants do not recognise other styles of animation, nor is it an indication that they dislike other styles. But these will invariably be held up against the Disney standard as a kind of universal norm.

Also, in production terms, this aesthetic normsetting of Disney is evident in much recent output. In Denmark, one of the primary producers of animated films in Europe (Andersen, 1997, p. 166), one may see a clear change in animation style since the 1970s towards a more cuddly Disney-aesthetic (rounded shapes, big eyes) - even within the style of a single animator such as Flemming Quist Møller, one of the founding fathers of Danish animated films. While his early animations such as *Benny's Bathtub* (*Benny's badekar*) (1971) is in line with a modernist, minimalist aesthetic, the protagonist in *Jungle Jack* (*Jungledyret Hugo*) (1993) obeys the Disney look - what the British historian David Forgacs terms 'the cutifying of Disney products'. (Forgacs, 1992, p. 363).

This aesthetic unification may be compared with the production development that has taken place through the 1990s in Europe. In 1990, one third of the world's animation films were produced in Europe, while in 1996 it was just under two thirds. The growth has been spurred by Cartoon Forum, the highly successful network for animators, producers and investors, which by 1997 had received 1.5 billion DKK (202 million EUR) under the European Union's MEDIA programme (Bjørnvig, 1997, p. 4). However, as Disney consolidated its longstanding position as animator number one, this dramatic development in European output was not matched by a similar stimulation of aesthetic diversification.

As for the other dimension in children's associations, Disney as a material object, the weekly TV show *Disney Fun* is regularly referred to. Its prominence in informants' discourses signals that Disney is an encompassing term, a 'package' that is more than particular characters or single stories. As seven-year-old Maria aptly comments when being asked to explain what she means by animated film: 'It may also appear in *Disney Fun*. That's why it is called Disney, you know'. Particularly for younger children the Friday night show is one of their first indicators of a temporal week cycle by which other activities are coordinated.[3]

Next to TV, informants connect Disney's material dimension with the VCR. As is well-known, one of Team Disney's immediate means of generating increased revenue when they started revamping the firm in 1984 was to video release the company's animated feature library. This strategy not only created immediate and enormous profits (more than $100 million (€ 95 million) in 1986 alone according to Gomery, 1994, p. 81), it also facilitated cross-marketing and cross-branding to an unprecedented degree.

Seen within a Danish context, this development really starts in 1989, when Buena Vista Home Entertainment brings out the first Disney video casette for sale in Denmark (*Alice in Wonderland*). And while Disney cartoons in the cinemas are seen by an average of 500.000 people (equalling ten per cent of the population) by the late 1990s, Danish households with children aged three to ten may claim an average, yearly, purchase of four Disney videos that are watched thirty-four times on average (Bach, 1997). The result is seen with our informants who all have a number of video casettes. These are mostly bought by their parents, are often placed in the children's room if they have one, and are referred to as 'mine'. In this way, young informants' repeated watching of Disney videos serves as an important catalyst for an individualization of juvenile media culture and as a lever in children's training of informal media literacies (Drotner, 2003, pp. 94-95, 122-23).

Interestingly, none of the children mention computer games when first identifying the Disney concept, even if they have some and like using them. Nor is there much mention of the weekly comic *Donald Duck*, which since 1949 has been a stable feature of Disney reception in Denmark, as we shall see in our analyses of parents' associations below. These 'omissions' may indicate a hierarchy of media entries in which television and the VCR are the primary routes into a Disney universe that also encompasses other media and, not least, merchandise.

Raymond Williams (and later James Carey) have made seminal contributions to media theory by defining mediated communication as, at once, symbolic processes engendering meaning for people and as material technologies transporting messages between senders and receivers (Williams, 1976; Carey, 1992). Our young informants' joint definition of Disney as being both a generic name for animated aesthetics and a particular form of media output makes it clear that Carey and others have provided more than fundamental theoretical concepts. Their concepts equally operate as enabling, taken-for-granted tools in handling everyday media practices.

Irrespective of age, what unites the two dimensions for children is an overarching association of Disney as provider of both a symbolic and physical frame for fun, joy, entertainment. Anja, aged eleven, makes the connection clear:

> *(Disney) is cartoons. And it is ... I don't know if they also make them in real film [sic] ... And then it is adventure ... and they are fun to watch and so on. I think they are total fun (helt vildt sjove).*

Ultimately, children find the link between Disney and fun so strong because it is seen as directed at them: Disney is for me. Seven-year-old Søren sums up his take on the connection like this:

> *Søren: (Disney) is something you think of and ... something you think is fun and for kids.*

> *Int: What does Disney make?*

> *Søren: They put cartoons into our heads and stuff ... so I think Disney is fine.*

Precisely the 'for-me-ness' of Disney is an important basis of Disney's global success with children when viewed from a bottom-up perspective. The unprecedented unification and global coordination of Disney's marketing is offset by the intention to localize the contexts of reception. The company's marketing strategy of the 1990s is expressed by a Disney official thus: 'For all children, the Disney characters are local characters and this is very important. They always speak local languages ... The Disney strategy is to ''think global, act local''' (quoted in Wilson, 1996, p. 40). Our young informants have taken the aspect of localization one step further. They see Disney characters not as national or local but as individual. While they articulate this for-me-ness as a reason for liking Disney, our informants equally lay claim to it as a mark of differentiation between early and middle childhood.

'I Used to Like the Old Ones Better': Age Distinctions Among Children

Children in the age band six to seven belong to the primary users of Disney. Most of them cannot read, and the Disney corporation provides dubbed versions of videos, TV animation and computer games even for relatively small language communities such as the Danish. Moreover, Disney's extensive merchandising buys into young children's play and consumer culture, as is witnessed by the company's ten-year contract with McDonald's, signed in 1996, giving the fast-food chain exclusive global rights to promote Disney products in its restaurants.

For the youngest children, the Disney package contains pictures. They are inclusive in their use and make no clear distinctions between animation broadcast on television or watched on a VCR casette (Anne's quote above). More importantly, they make no clear distinctions between the symbolic and material aspects of Disney. They will define their VCR-casette with *101 Dalmatians* as a Disney casette because they know the story from *Disney Fun* on television. Other forms of practical Disney deduction include Jonah, age six, who counts the number of children and adults on the covers of his VCR casettes. If children outnumber adults, he defines the casette as Disney: it is visually marked as being a kid's video, as being for him. Others note that logos have a common style on certain casettes, they have 'the Disney sign' (a picture of the protagonist within a geometrical figure) and so they deduct that these casettes must all be Disney.

Children in the age band eleven to twelve include more products in their definitions of Disney and they regularly mention merchandise. They are well aware that Disney is more than animation, as is seen in eleven-year-old Line's answer:

> *(Disney) is animated film and so on. But sometimes they also make film, real film, I mean, and, well … they also do cartoons on telly and Disney Fun and all that sort of thing, they bring out.*

Line here attempts to draw distinctions between different kinds of Disney output: she calls live-action releases 'real film', she uses the term cartoons (*tegneserier*) about TV animation which she distinguishes from the word animated film (*tegnefilm*) - an apparent attempt to single out cinema features from TV and VCR animation. Such descriptions may be analysed as ways in which older children try to categorize and hence make sense of the complex Disney universe. In addition, many older children are clearly at pains to discursively construct themselves as being discerning users of Disney, if not necessarily connoisseurs. Cecilie, aged twelve, explains:

> *Int: Can you tell me what Disney is?*
>
> *Cecilie: Okay (original phrase), they make both - they make animated film, that's how they started, I think. And now they also make some computer films [sic], and I think they also make ordinary feature films (spillefilm) … And, ahm, the guy Disney, he is dead. And I don't quite know just how many animated films they make; but I think they have a kind of yearly film (årsfilm) or something, where Lion King and Pocahontas and Snow White were the first, I think. When I was small, I used to like the old ones better, now I like the new ones the best.*

Cecilie makes clear that she possesses an insight into Disney's diverse production output and has a fair knowledge about the company's history. Her definition imperceptively turns into taste evaluation, and, in the process, Cecilie creates a vantage point from which she may express distance, at least to some of the Disney output. Like many older children, and unlike the younger age group, she distinguishes between 'material Disney', the producer of a range of products, and 'symbolic Disney', maker of films whose quality she is in a position to evaluate as a mature pre-teenager.

So, two aspects stand out when comparing the two age bands of children. First, the young informants conflate product and producer, or, more precisely, they find such a distinction irrelevant. The older informants, on the other hand, profess a knowledge about that distinction, thus creating a space for invoking judgements of taste. Second, the young children are inclusive in their media uses. They immerse themselves into the Disney universe as *their* universe, while the older ones voice a certain distance. This distance emerges as remarks that Disney is no longer for them, and, more often, as distaste for particular narrative or stylistic aspects. It should be noted, however, that no informant expresses an outright dislike for Disney *per se* as producer of fun and entertainment.

Political economists may well put these age differences down to the Disney company's effective strategies in directly marketing their products to ever younger age groups and thus nurture young children as perhaps the last separate consumer group after having targeted the teenagers, the gay, and the grey gold. This may well be right. Developmental psychologists may with equal insight explain the age differences found in my analysis as a result of cognitive maturation: older children simply posses better skills than young ones in patterning and categorizing their experiences. This may well be right, too. What my focus on cultural discourses may add to these pictures is a frame of analysis, highlighting that people, even young ones, through their media practices continuously articulate positions within an increasingly complex and global media culture and through that positioning make sense of their place in the world. This place is defined in individual terms and autonomy is closely associated with being consumers of Disney fare. Let us turn to look at how the adult Disney audiences juggle those issues.

'You would go on dreaming': Parental Separations

Given our research design where we interview children and their parents it is to be expected that our adult informants express their associations with Disney in relation to their own children. Indeed, this is what we find. Two basic strategies stand out in this positioning process. The first may be termed a strategy of temporal separation: parents compare Disney in their own childhood with what they see today with their own children. The second strategy may be termed a strategy of spatial separation: parents make clear distinctions between 'symbolic' Disney and 'material' Disney, Disney as trusted provider of quality entertainment, and Disney as a commercial exploiter on a global scale.

When being asked about their immediate associations to the Disney concept, most parents start speaking about their own childhood. Karen says:

> Karen: I don't know if there was anything of Disney then (during my childhood) other than the Donald Duck comics.
>
> Int: What about film?
>
> Karen: Well, we didn't watch much television either, and there wasn't much Disney on telly; I can't even remember if I went to the cinema to see any Disney productions. Maybe at Christmas-time, maybe I went to see the Christmas show; but it was really just once a year, if anything.

Like Karen, most parents when speaking about their memories of Disney, focus on the weekly comic *Donald Duck*, published since 1949 by Egmont H. Petersen, now The Egmont Group, which is the world's leading publisher of Disney print media. In terms of sales, the comic had its heyday in Denmark in the 1970s, when many of our adult informants were children, but the Nordic countries still top the international list of Disney comic consumption (Christiansen, 1998).[4] Following the weekly exploits of Donald, his nephews Huey, Dewey and Louie, Scrooge McDuck, Gyro Geerloose and other inhabitants of Duckburg for many parents is associated with an introduction to the magic of reading. Little text, many pictures and a limited number of characters together made the comic an obvious starting point for breaking the code of spelling. A few women refer coyly to their husbands' continued reading of the so-called *Jumbo Books* (1968), 254-page monthlies featuring many Carl Barks classics and one of the topselling booktitles in the country (Drotner, 2001b). Among our young informants, a few note, with some dismay, that their fathers (no mothers here) have banned them from reading their collection of vintage weeklies, 'until I am old enough to handle them properly' as Michael, eleven remarks.

Unlike the situation in many European countries, and in stark contrast to the USA, Danish parents favour the figure Donald Duck, not Mickey Mouse (Disney being nicknamed the Mouse House in the USA). When asked about her immediate associations to the word Disney, Susan, a woman in her early thirties and with a short eduction, says:

> Susan: Donald Duck (giggles). Donald Duck first of all, I think ... and he is a laugh.
>
> Int: Why precisely Donald, do you think?

Susan: Yes, why Donald Duck. Because he is one of the old characters in Disney ... Pluto is too; but Donald he ... uhm, always gets into trouble one way or another. That's what I like to see. You know, we have many books with Donald Duck; and even if Minnie and Pluto and Goofy and all the others say: 'Shouldn't you do it this way?' Then no, he shall not do it this way, and it always ends up wrong.

This siding with the anti-hero (or under-duck?) dominates adult Danes' appropriation of Disney. As analysed in detail in the Danish profile of the global, comparative study on Disney audiences, many Danes domesticate Donald to the extent that they apply his character as a basis for constructing a particular Danishness (Drotner, 2001b). Through this process of domestication, the complexity of global media culture is not only reduced and hence made comprehensible, it is equally linked to constructions of national identity. This process resonates with findings from other European profiles in the comparative study. Thus, French informants deplore Disney's simplification of Victor Hugo's *Hunchback of Notre Dame*, while Greek informants see Disney's *Herkules* as a sorry dumbing down of their national myth (Guyot, 2001; Kaitatzi-Whitlock & Terzis, 2001). Interestingly, no informants comment on Disney's treatment of other icons of European cultural heritage, thus testifying to the way in which Disney narratives serve as a backdrop to the articulation of national, rather than supra-national, or European, identities.

In the present study, and very likely due to our research design, what stands out in parents' defintion of Disney narratives is not so much a particular construction of national identity as a particular construction of childhood - the parents' own and, by implication, that of their children. This is seen with Karen above and it is clearly spelled out by Vibeke, a well-educated woman in her thirties:

Vibeke (Thinking of Disney): I think of ... Christmas time. What I remember from Christmas was the Christmas (show), they broadcast on telly. And it was ... what we saw were snippets of something, and you would go on dreaming, if only you could see a whole programme, that would simply be ... or a whole film with Bambi. It wasn't so common, so it was kind of (special). Today kids get everything on a silver platter, don't they (giggles). Today, I mean.

Together with the weekly comics, the Christmas shows on television top the list of parents' memories of Disney. Since the 1960s, the Danish Broadcasting Corporation, a monopoly public-service channel until 1988, has brought out a yearly *Disney's Christmas Show*, first on Christmas Day and since 1992 on Christmas Eve. Every year the show offers the same shorts plus a trailer for an upcoming cinema release, and in, for example, Sweden and Norway the shows have become institutionalised as part of the Christmas ritual (Muhr, 1998; Hagen, 2001).[5] As is evident with Vibeke, many adult Danes endow the Disney Christmas shows with an aura that rivals the sacredness of Bethlehem - several of our adult informants describe the shows as 'divine' and 'unforgettable'.[6]

Through their own childhood memories, parents in our study construct an image of Disney as something sparse, special and ritualized - either the small, weekly ritual of comic-reading or the big ritual of watching the Christmas shows. This cultural scarcity is interpreted as a catalyst for stretching one's imagination ('you would go on dreaming'), both of which are framed as positive elements of childhood against which the life of today's child is found sorely wanting ('kids get everything on a silver platter').

Parents' repeated celebration of their own childhood Disney, their more or less self-conscious invocation of past pleasures, in a very basic sense are enactments of loss. As I see it, this concept is absolutely fundamental to an understanding of Disney's continued popularity and global appeal: as a modern conception of childhood is globalized, so the psychological and cultural foundations are laid for an ever-increasing number of adult narratives invoking a loss of innocence. It is in order here to bring to mind Walter Benjamin, who in his *Passagen Werk* has made one of the first, and still one of the most perceptive, analyses of loss as a driving force behind adults' continuous and contradictory preoccupation with childhood in modernity (Benjamin, 1983; see also Buck-Morss, 1989).

In several cases, the comparison between childhood then and now permeates into an evaluation of (dwindling) quality. Jette, a woman in her late forties with a short eduction, says that the word Disney reminds her of:

Jette: Cute ... fun figures, isn't it?

Int: Mmm (supportive).

Jette: They were at least when I was a child ... Since then, it has changed of course. Today, they are not quite ... well, there are both cute and more nasty figures.

For Jette, as for many other parents in our study, the word 'nasty' alludes to violence, a concept which carries unanimous, negative connotations. In their discussions, adult informants routinely express their preference for the 'old' Disney characters and films to the more recent ones. Through this comparison, they draw up an opposition between a more authentic and untainted past and an artificial and a troubled present. But despite this opposition, they will routinely 'defend' Disney as in a quality league of its own when compared with other animation output for children today. Peter makes this distinction:

Peter: (Disney) is quality film and quality narratives.

Int: Compared to other output?

Peter: Yes, compared to Cartoon Network and so on - we had that for a while. Strange, violent cartoons ... that are irritatingly bad, and bad pictures. So, Disney is much more quality-like.

Similar to older children, our adult informants, in speaking about Disney, express continuous taste evaluations. When they discuss Disney narratives and style, what I term 'symbolic Disney', they construct themselves as cultural connoisseurs of Disney lore which they find very good. Fathers, in particular, are at pains to focus on the technical professionalism of the films. Morten remarks:

As for the films at least, they are very well made, very professional, worth seeing not only for kids but for childlike minds like me. I love to watch cartoons and Disney films.

Particularly among younger parents, several informants seem to be practising post-modernists in that they express their liking of Disney films as an indication of their catholic taste.

The widespread parental definition of Disney as quality, despite preference for the 'old' output, needs further analytical contextualisation. Danish parents in general express uncertainty in relation to their children's media uses. Since they do not feel in a position to judge the substance, and hence the quality, of most youthful media fare, they mostly regulate their children's use of time and money: computer games are a prime example of the former, mobile phones of the latter (Drotner, 2001c). Disney is an exception to this rule: our adult informants express trust in their own judgement of taste based on their own childhood memories. Their pronouncement of Disney as quality thus hides a more gloomy tale of insecurity when it comes to their children's media culture in general.

Still, irrespective of age, there are limits to parents' praise of Disney. They all recognise that there is more to Disney than half-hour TV-shows on Friday nights. And many spontaneously and early on in the interviews pronounce their criticism of what they take to be a too blatant branding of the corporation. How do they reconcile these views with their professed preference for the Disney output? They don't. But they apply what above I termed a strategy of spatial separation. This strategy seems to be a means of tackling what many of them encounter as an acute dilemma. One mother, Rita, expresses it this way:

I really associate (Disney) with quality. And then I associate it with good business. Lots of money, you see, and the USA, and this American type of culture where every-thing is either black or white, evil or good [...] But I still think it is quality. Most of it.

I think it is O.K. I think, well Disney is O.K. I can handle that, can't I? It's a commercial business, but then again, I also think they bring out something good.

Articulating oneself as a cultural connoisseur of Disney seems important for many parents as an indication of concern for their children's (cultural) welfare (and, for the younger parents as an indication of their own libertarian outlook on life). But this cultural insight equally seems to include a certain acknowledgement of Disney as a global media player, which many parents equate with the US. So, our adult informants attempt to separate 'symbolic' and 'material' Disney, Disney as quality output, good narratives, safe entertainment, and Disney as ubiquitous commodity, merchandise, and American fast food in more ways than one.

This strategy of spatial separation substantiates findings from the comparative reception study on global Disney audiences. Here, too, respondents tend to 'compartmentalize Disney the business from Disney as entertainment' (Phillips, 2001, p. 48). What the present study adds, through its focus on discursive practices and its possibilities of comparing adult and juvenile articulations, is to highlight ways in which different age groups create practical strategies and lay claim to particular social positions in handling processes of media globalization. Moreover, these strategies surface with particular clarity as the handling of supra-national identity positions when informants speak about Disneyland Resort Paris.

European Multiculturalism the Disney Way

With Disney being part of everyday life for most European children, little is left of Disney being associated with particular events, even spectacular rituals. The domestication of Disney's global culture seems inversely proportional to its sustained exotic flavour. Still, its family theme parks seem to capture some of this allure even today, particularly for older children and parents.

Many young children do not know of Disneyland Paris (as most people still call it) or any other of the Disney theme parks. Those who do, associate it with other 'lands' of fun and entertainment such as Legoland, or Bonbon-land, named after a well known Danish candy company. All of the older children have heard of Disneyland Paris, mainly from television and trailers to their video casettes and DVDs, and nearly all of them describe the theme parks in Europe and the US as concrete places of longing. Anja, aged twelve, and raised in a single-parent family where money constraints are an issue, expresses this longing when she says: 'I don't think I may go (to Disneyland) - only perhaps'. Other children her age make distinctions between the original parks in the US and the latecomers whose position remain vague to some. Twelve-year-old Amanda professes:

There is certainly one (park) in England, I think. And then there is one in America somewhere. And it is perhaps the right one, I think. There are certainly two, and one is the wrong one, and the other the right one.

While older children combine the geographical place of Disney theme parks with a general longing for exotic spaces of entertaining experiences, adult informants are more specific. In their descriptions of the theme parks, they clearly define them in terms of supra-national, cultural meeting grounds, and their evaulation of these meeting-grounds are closely related to educational background. Most parents with little education express concern with the parks because they are too far away. To them, discomfort with physical distance and cost override the enjoyment ascribed to the parks' cultural spaces of entertainment and consumption. Pia, aged thirty, has the following solution to the perceived problem:

Pia: I think they should build a Disneyland in each country.

Int: Yes.

Pia: Then they would be damned easier to get to.

Int: (Laughs).

Pia: I would like to visit Disneyland, but it's - far to go.

Int: Yes.

Pia: Just to see Disneyland.

Int: Do you think it would be possible (to have a park) also in Denmark?

Pia: I am sure! For if they built a Disneyland - well, the only thing that would not have to be dumped would be the Tivoli (Garden) in Copenhagen. But Bonbon-land and Legoland and all the other 'lands' they could easily (close down).

Pia expresses her wish to retain the ritual associated with a visit to a Disney theme park but in so doing she seeks to domesticate the supra-national ramifications of the parks. Conversely, well-educated parents define the Disney theme parks as prime possibilites to explore the cultural diversities of Europe. Vibeke and Jens, academics in their late thirties, express their two family visits to Disneyland Paris like this:

Vikeke: There is something international about it - it is great fun staying at such a hotel with the kids, you see, where there are many people from all over Europe; you get a hint of something other than being Danish, right (laughs).

Jens: Yes, and one may add that it is quite special that Disney (is) in France - the French usually promote their own language and so on and so on. But then suddenly, this American stuff becomes something valuable.

Well-educated parents regard a visit to Disneyland Paris as a welcome family ritual and an exercise in European multicultualism.[7] It is not American corporate consumerism that surfaces in these accounts, rather it is cultural diversity refracted as lifestyle. These cosmopolitans lay claim to a definition of European identity as individual, cultural choice while excluding political difference or economic inequality. Perhaps ironically, it is the consumption of the global Disney brand that seems a unifying framework for their defintion of Europeanness, not the real diversities to be explored around the continent.

Irrespective of education and social background, parents, in their discussion on Disney's theme parks, repeat their strategies of temporal and spatial separation as already discussed. Or, more precisely, they conflate the two strategies: by labelling the family theme parks supra-national meeting grounds, parents persist in associating Disney with an exotic ritual in space if not in time. And by associating Disneyland Paris with European multiculturalism they bring the exotic within the reach of reality - even to the point of domesticating global media as intimate culture. These results bring a new dimension to Philip Schlesinger's cogent remark that 'to try to communicate on a European plane is first and foremost to acknowledge the fact of considerable diversity' (Schlesinger, 1993, p. 6).

Now you see it, now you don't: Mundane Disney Discourses

The global reach and ubiquitous presence of Disney products make few people uninformed about or unaffected by the brand. And because Disney for so long has been associated with children's culture, nearly all ages have met with one or more of the brand's narratives, characters or merchandise. The study of Danish Disney audiences indicates that age plays a major role in handling the complex Disney universe. Our youngest informants immediately appropriate the childlike in the universe and take it as an indication that Disney is for them. They domesticate Disney by focusing upon the aspects most closely asociated with their own social and cultural position. Older children and adults both acknowledge the complexities of Disney, and for both groups this acknowledgement sets in motion processes of separation (symbolic vs. material Disney), partial incorporation or domestication (the symbolic dimension) and taste evaluation.

Parents are most explicit in their taste pronouncements, a result that may partially be explained as an enactment of cultural power *vis-à-vis* the researcher. In a more general sense and following Bourdieu, we may see the age variation on taste found in the study as an indication that we are all born with what Bourdieu terms a 'barbaric', inclusive taste but some end up with a more consecrated taste than others. Disney is clearly a complex subject for adults in making taste distinctions: the company has been around for so long and hence enjoys the aura that befalls much popular culture when it comes of age (Drotner, 1999); it holds a tremendous and unquestioned position in adults' own lives and hence cannot be written off as yet another silly/dangerous/incomprehensible fad. And it has an ubiquitous presence as a range of successful American products with global reach. By downplaying or writing off the material dimension of the Disney universe, parents open a space in which they may not only articulate taste, but in which they may equally, and with no less difficulty, lay claim to particular constructions of childhood - and hence set the ramifications of 'the good life'.

Seen from a mundane, bottom-up perspective, Disney's contemporary round-the-clock, round-the-globe presence and its intensified branding runs the risk of losing what audiences traditionally deemed a sacred feature, namely the ritual allure of Disney figures and fantasy. Parents in particular, in an attempt to recapture and re-experience that imagined allure, define the family theme parks in terms of an exotic meeting ground, even if their evaluations differ according to educational background and cultural habitus, to speak with Bourdieu.

By way of conclusion, the analysis offered above, serves to refract the dichotomous picture conveyed by most top-down approaches to media globalization. The complex Disney universe offers a lens through which we may analyse and begin to understand ways in which people in Europe, young and old, seek to tackle media globalization as socio-cultural practices. Ironically, audiences' most distinct pronouncements of a supra-national, European belonging are shaped by one of the most visible US brands in the world.

The author wishes to acknowledge the financial support to this study of the Danish Ministry of Research. Data collection and coding was performed by research assistants Heidi Jørgensen and Nanna Berger Munk, both of whom contributed centrally to my initial phases of analysis.

Notes

1   Disney's close association in the USA with animated films and the family entertainment of theme parks is reflected in the academic studies, most of which are of US origin. Studying Disney from a European perspective offers new empirical insights into the diversity of the Disney universe.

2   In Denmark, Bugs Bunny actually has its own TV slot on Sunday mornings. The name, Bugs Bunny's Sunday Club (Snurre Snups søndagsklub) strictly refers to one character and has not succeeded in branding Bugs Bunny as a Warner character - let alone brand Warner to the same extent as Disney Fun brands the Disney company.

3   A clear indication of the particular position of the weekly TV show Disney Fun is the fact that it invariably creates reactions from concerned parents if the programme is rescheduled because of an important sports' game or similar media event.

4   Today, the Egmont Group, comprising 110 companies in 27 countries, has five areas of production: Egmont Comic Creation (Serieforlaget) which is the largest publisher of comics in Europe; Egmont Books which is the largest publisher of children's books in Europe with a yearly output of over sixty million books; Egmont Magazines publishing thirty magazines in Scandinavia; Egmont Entertainment encompassing videos, computer games, music and, increasingly, on-line services; Nordic Film and TV established in 1992 with the purchase of the world's oldest film company, the Danish-owned Nordic Film (Nordisk Films Compagni). Egmont's turnover in 2001 was 1.141 million EUR (Balleby, 1998, www.egmont.dk).

The Egmont Group is by far the largest licence holder with the Walt Disney Company Nordic A/S, founded in 1960, based in Copenhagen, and directing the corporation's business in Northern Europe. The company takes in ten per cent of the total Disney sales in Europe, not including video casettes and computer games. Disney Nordic sells Disney products for c. 3-3.5 billion Danish kroner per year (c. 0.5 EUR) - again minus video casettes and computer games. Despite its limited population of just over five million, Denmark is the bestselling Disney country in Europe (Mietle, 1997).

Due to a change in management and a stricter obediance to the Walt Disney Company's well-known secrecy, it has not been possible to update the above information, nor the information provided by Christiansen (1998).

5   Also in the 1960s, for a brief spell the Danish Broadcasting Corporation had a weekly show called Disneyland. Again, in the 1980s (1980-1, 1983, 1985-7) the channel featured a weekly show, Så er der tegnefilm (Toon Time) with a mixture of shorts from Disney, Warner, Universal, MGM and Walter Lantz. No parents refer to these weekly shows. But some parents, such as Gerd, who have grown up in the Copenhagen area do recall going to Disney Christmas shows at a particular cinema. Such shows were introduced into the capital in 1932, and the Disney's Christmas Show (five to six short cartoons) was shown almost every year until 1978. In the 1970s and 1980s, when many of our adult informants grew up, only eight feature-length animation films premiered in Denmark.

6   While none of my adult informants frame their memories of the weekly comics and the annual TV shows as an opposition between print media and visual media, as is often the case in public discourse on juvenile media uses (Drotner, 1999), they do distinguish different forms of reception: reading is seen as nurturing a sense of personal autonomy while the Christmas shows represent an inclusiveness of family life.

7   The differences found in adult pronouncements on the Disney theme parks resonate well with

Danes' attitudes to European issues that closely mirror educational background and social position (Gundelach, 2002).

References

Andersen, Jesper (1997) 'Dyrebørn og dukkedrenge: animationsfilmen', pp. 166-93 in Ib Bondebjerg, Jesper Andersen & Peter Schepelern (Eds.). Dansk film, 1972-97. København: Munksgaard Rosinante.

Bach, Charlotte (1997) 'Rappe reklamer skal redde Anders'. Politiken. 28.12.

Balleby, Lene (1998) Interview with the marketing director of the Egmont Group, Søndagsavisen. 14.6: 29.

Benjamin, Walter (1983) Das Passagen-Werk, I-II Frankfurt: Suhrkamp.

Bjørnvig, Bo (1997) 'Et umaetteligt behov' (An Insatiable Need), Weekendavisen..

Bryman, Alan (1995) Disney and His Worlds. London, New York: Routledge.

Buck-Morss, Susan (1989) The Dialectics of Seeing: Walter Benjamin and the Arcades Project Cambridge. MA: MIT Press.

Buckingham, David (2001) 'United Kingdom: Disney Dialectics: Debating the Politics of Children's Media Culture', pp. 269-96 in Janet Wasko et al., (Eds.), Dazzled by Disney: The Global Disney Audiences Project. London: Leicester University Press.

Carey, James (1992) Communication as Culture: Essays on Media and Society. New York: Routledge.

Christiansen, Jesper (1998) Personal interview with the marketing director of Egmont Comic Creation, 26.1.

Danish Broadcasting Media Research (2002) Special survey. Copenhagen: Danish Broadcasting Corporation.

Demers, D. (1999) Global Media: Menace or Messiah? Cresskill, NJ: Hampton Press.

Dorfman, Ariel & Armand Mattelart (1975) How to Read Donald Duck: Imperialist Ideology in the Disney Comic. Tr. David Kunzle. New York: International General.

Drotner, Kirsten (1999) 'Dangerous Media? Panic Discourses and Dilemmas of Modernity', Paedagogica Historica. 35, 3: 593-619.

Drotner, Kirsten (2001a) 'Global Media Through Youthful Eyes', pp. 283-305 in Sonia Livingstone & Moira Bovill (Eds.) Children and their Changing Media Environment: A European Comparative Study. New York: Earlbaum.

Drotner, Kirsten (2001b) 'Denmark: "Donald Seems So Danish": Disney and the Formation of Cultural Identity', pp. 102-20 in Janet Wasko et al. (Eds.), Dazzled by Disney: The Global Disney Audiences Project. London: Leicester University Press.

Drotner, Kirsten (2001c) Medier for fremtiden: born, unge og det nye medielandskab (Media for the Future: Children, Youth and the New Media Landscape) Copenhagen: Høst & Søn.

Drotner, Kirsten (2003) Disney i Danmark: at vokse op med en global mediegigant (Disney in Denmark: Growing Up with a Global Media Giant) Copenhagen: Høst & Søn.

Feild, Robert D. (1942) The Art of Walt Disney. New York: Macmillan Company.

Feilitzen, Cecilia von & Ulla Carlsson (2002) 'Media in the World', pp. 245-55 in (Eds.) Children, Young People and Media Globalisation. The UNESCO International Clearinghouse on Children, Youth and Media Yearbook 2002, Gothenburg: Nordicom.

Ferguson, Marjorie (1992) 'The Mythology about Globalization', European Journal of Communication. 7, pp. 69-93.

Forgacs, David (1992) 'Disney Animation and the Business of Childhood', Screen. 33(4), pp. 361-74.

Frèches, J. (1986) La Guerre des Images. Paris: Denoël.

Garnham, N. (1990) Capitalism and Communication: Global Culture and the Economics of Information. London: Sage.

Gershon, R. A. (1997) The Transnational Media Corporation. Mahwah, NJ: Lawrence Erlbaum.

Gilroy, Paul (1995) The Black Atlantic: Modernity and Double Consciousness. London: Verso.

Gomery, Douglas (1994) 'Disney's Business History: A Reinterpretation', pp. 71-86 in Eric Smoodin (Ed.) Disney Discourse: Producing the Magic Kingdom. New York: Routledge.

Gundelach, Peter (Ed.) (2002) Danskernes værdier, 1981-1999 (Danes' Values, 1981-1999) Copenhagen: Reitzel.

Guyot, Jacques (2001) 'France: Disney in the Land of Cultural Exception', pp. 121-34 in Janet

Wasko et al. (Eds.), Dazzled by Disney: The Global Disney Audiences Project. London: Leicester University Press.

Hagen, Ingunn (2001) 'Norway: Norwegian Memories of the Disney Universe', pp. 222-56 in Janet Wasko et al. (Eds.), Dazzled by Disney: The Global Disney Audiences Project. London: Leicester University Press.

Herman, Edward & Robert McChesney (1997) The Global Media: The New Missionaries of Corporate Capitalism. London: Cassell.

Jensen, Klaus B. (1998) News of the World: World Cultures Look at Television News. London: Routledge.

Kaitatzi-Whitlock, Sophia & George Terzis (2001) 'Greece: Disney's Descent on Greece: the Company is the Message', pp. 135-59 in Janet Wasko et al. (Eds.), Dazzled by Disney: The Global Disney Audiences Project. London: Leicester University Press.

Livingstone, S. & M. Bovill (Eds.) (2001) Children and Their Changing Media Environment: A European Comparative Study. New York, Earlbaum.

May, J. (1981) 'Walt Disney's Interpretation of Children's Literature,' Language Arts. 58(4), pp. 463-72.

McChesney, R. W. (1997) Corporate Media and the Threat to Democracy. New York: Seven Stories Press.

Mietle, Erik (1997) Personal interview with the managing director of the Walt Disney Company Nordic, 28.10.

Morley, David & Kevin Robins (1995) Spaces of Identity: Global Media, Electronic Landscapes and Cultural Boundaries. London: Routledge.

Muhr, Gunilla (1998) 'Disliking Disney: Cultural Imperialism and the Reception of Disney Among Youths in Sweden'. Paper presented at the Nordic Youth Research Symposium, Reykjavik.

Nightingale, Virginia (2001) 'Australia: Disney and the Australian Cultural Imaginary', pp. 65-87 in Janet Ohmer, Susan (1991) 'Measuring Desire: George Gallup and Audience Research in Hollywood,' Journal of Film and Video. 43, pp. 1-2.

Phillips, Mark (2001) 'The Global Disney Audiences Project: Disney Across Cultures', pp. 31-61 in Janet Wasko, Mark Phillips & Eileen R. Meehan (Eds.) (2001) Dazzled by Disney: The Global Disney Audiences Project. London: Leicester University Press.

Real, Michael (1973) Mass-Mediated Culture. Englewood Cliffs, N.J., Prentice Hall.

Schickel, Richard (1985) The Disney Version: The Life, Times, Art and Commerce of Walt Disney. New York: Simon & Schuster.

Schlesinger, Philip (1993) 'Wishful Thinking: Cultural Politics, Media, and Collective Identities in Europe', Journal of Communication. 43(2), pp. 6-17.

Stone, Kay (1975) 'Things Walt Disney Never Told Us', Journal of American Folklore. 88, pp. 42-50.

Tomlinson, John (1991) Cultural Imperialism: A Critical Introduction. Baltimore: The Johns Hopkins University Press.

Turkle, Sherry (1995) Life on the Screen: Identity in the Age of the Internet. New York: Simon & Schuster.

Wasko, Janet (2001) Understanding Disney: The Maunfacture of Fantasy. Cambridge. Polity Press.

Wasko, Janet, Mark Phillips & Eileen R. Meehan (Eds.) (2001) Dazzled by Disney: The Global Disney Audiences Project. London: Leicester University Press.

Westcott, Tim (2002) 'Globalization of Children's TV and Strategies of the 'Big Three'", pp. 69-76 in Cecilia von Feilitzen & Ulla Carlsson (Eds.) Children, Young People and Media Globalisation. The UNESCO International Clearinghouse on Children, Youth and Media Yearbook 2002. Gothenburg: Nordicom.

Williams, Raymond (1976) Communications. Harmondsworth: Penguin. Orig. 1962.

Wilson, Doug (1996) Strategies of the Media Giants. London: Pearson Professional.

www.egmont.dk

Yoshimi, Shunya (2001) 'Japan: America in Japan/Japan in Disneyfication: The Disney Image and the Transformation of "America" in Contemporary Japan', pp. 160-81 in Janet Wasko, et al (Eds.) Dazzled by Disney: The Global Disney Audiences Project. London: Leicester University Press.

Daniel Biltereyst is a professor in film, television and cultural media studies and international communication at the Department of Communication Sciences, Gent University (Belgium). Previously he has been an associate professor at the University of Louvain and a research assistant at the Brussels University. He has published in academic journals (e.g. *Media, Culture & Society, European Journal of Communication*') and readers (including *The Media Book*, *News in a Globalized Society*) on issues dealing with the role of the media as a central forum for public debate and (dis)information. Recently he started a research project on the history of film censorship and controversial audiovisual material as a catalyst for public debate in Belgium (Council for Scientific Research, 2003-6).

Daniel Biltereyst

Media Audiences and the Game of Controversy: On Reality TV, Moral Panic and Controversial Media Stories

Introduction

Since the early 1990s there has been a wide public and academic interest in the explosion and success of new factual television formats associated with reality TV (hereafter: RT). RT has become a widely popular term, referring to various programme types such as docusoaps, reality crime shows, home video programmes, wider human-interest programmes, or even more hybrid programmes such as *Big Brother*, with a mix of real life soap and game show elements. Although RT has become a tendency, a loose meta-genre or a container concept, most viewers and critics share the feeling that it refers to various factual television formats with a high reality claim, stressing the actions and emotions of real people (non-actors), often using a combination of 'authentic' (e.g. police, security or surveillance images) and staged images (e.g. fictionalised reconstructions, post-factum interviews). In this chapter we will not be engaged again in trying to define this hybrid programme category,[1] but rather concentrate on another specific shared feeling among viewers and critics. It deals with the *atmosphere of controversy*, or as French sociologist Dominique Mehl (1994a, p. 104) put it, the 'perfume of scandal' around those programmes.[2]

This atmosphere is not only related to the often-explicit exploration (or from a critical stance, exploitation) of those social and moral issues which touch the spheres of controversy and deviancy, but RT also touches on at least the ideas of a wider moral and media panic. In this chapter we will use these critical sociological concepts in order to understand better why these recent media products have been met by such intense moral outcry and public criticism. The wider debates about 'new' factuality have had, in some cases, many of the characteristics of a media panic (Drotner, 1992) as if a new, scary medium had arrived which threatens middle-class norms and attracts children and young people with vulgarity and a new barbarism. Some RT programmes even became the plaything of a spiralling debate among serious media journalists, fluent intellectuals, worried politicians, all sorts of moral guardians and wider public opinion, ultimately even leading to official action and concrete regulation.

In his monograph on the concept of moral panics, Thompson (1998, p. 139) claims that we have seen an 'increasingly rapid succession of scares in the mass media.' According to Thompson (p. 141) 'certain parts of the mass media have responded to market pressures by competing with each other to present dramatic narratives and spectacles with a strong moral content.' Although he does not explicitly refer to RT as such, it is clear that these programmes fit into the description of similar media strategies in a highly competitive environment. This connection between RT, the exploitation of moral issues in the media and the idea of moral panic has recently been signalled more explicitly by other authors (see for instance Richardson and Meinhof, 1999, p. 126). In this chapter we consider whether the perfume of scandal and controversy around RT is a basic constitutive characteristic of the genre. In order to analyse the phenomenon, we introduce the issue first through the use of concepts such as controversy and deviancy, and secondly through the concepts of moral and media panic. Finally we bring in results from a qualitative audience study on how young people talk about and perceive various types of factual and reality television, including controversial material.

Exploring or Exploiting Controversial Social and Moral Issues?

Issues of Identity Politics, Interpersonal Relations and Society

In its most negative version, criticism of RT tends to portray it as a format with a special interest in harsh, controversial social issues, giving voice to deviant views, creating a platform for eccentric freaks. This extreme argument, which comes close to Dovey's 'Trash TV position' (2000, p. 83), claims that contemporary media operate in a highly competitive, market-led economy and therefore only offer culturally suspect products. This *trash position* is often sustained on the basis of some spectacular, highly publicized shows such as *Rescue 911* or *Big Brother*, or programmes which have been attacked on the basis of fraud in terms of professional deontology or their reality claims. These programmes strongly influenced the public debate about the broader RT genre, operating as media templates in their own turn (Kitzinger, 2000) and limiting a more sensitive discussion on the reality tendency.

In recent years however it has become clear that this position cannot grasp the potential of the wide variety of reality programmes, both as an instrument for social representation and as a forum for new forms of information, participation and debate. There seems to be a growing awareness, even among critics, that 'television's explicit and flexible generic organisation allows it to move in many directions, and to provide many emotional points of contact with the ideas and lifestyles, problems and opportunities, that it is working through' (Ellis, 2000, p. 126). It means that RT in its earlier form has gone through a process of transformation and exerted wider influence on other genres. The stress on everyday life, on strong reality claims, authenticity, intimacy and first person speech has made it possible for RT to shed new light onto various kinds of social and moral issues. We acknowledge three main directions here, namely issues in terms of *identity politics* ('I', manifestation of the self), of *interpersonal relations* ('I and the other'), and of the *relationship between the individual and the wider societal environment* ('I, the other and society') (Biltereyst, 2000).

It is not difficult to relate these issues (treated in RT) to recent important sociological work on contemporary social problems. In his book *The Loss of Happiness in Market Democracy* for instance, Robert Lane (2000) indicates how Western society struggles with a fundamental paradox: despite high material prosperity people more than ever experience personal unhappiness and unease. In his analysis Lane warns of a tragic erosion of solidarity in society, starting with the level of interpersonal and family relations. This lack of warm *interpersonal relationships* and of solidarity in family life is reinforced (especially in the US) by the erosion of basic structures of societal solidarity since the 1980s, as well as by the growing work pressures in contemporary liberal market economies. For Lane it is clear that in a network society people need 'intimacy' and strong relationships based on trust. If this analysis is correct, it is no surprise that contemporary television - from dating programmes, confessional chat shows or *Big Brother* - stress intimacy, the personal voice and interpersonal relations or the cohabiting of various people.

This tendency of explicitly showing intimate (love) relations has often been criticized as voyeurism and exhibitionism, but Mehl (1996) argues that this type of *télévision de l'intimité*, *télé lacrymale* or *télé charité* may be disturbing for the elites because of the irrational discourse being thrown into the public sphere. Those on the defence of intimacy television claim that this type of programme crucially questions the borders between the public and private sphere and the status of expertise and experience. These weaker and shifting boundaries between the public and private ultimately create a more complex public sphere, including a decline of traditional institutions and discourses.

This type of intimacy television can also be easily related to theories on *identity politics*. Manuel Castells (1996, p. 22) defines identity as a complex process whereby an individual defines him/herself and constructs identity meaning on the basis of a 'set of cultural attributes'. In a network society, where media are so prominent, identity construction is more than ever an individual task with many opportunities and possible avenues. Some will experience this as an ultimate proof of liberation. But for others this may be a damaging task, given the absence of the safe haven of family, tradition, neighbourhood and social class. Given the imminent role of media in identity politics, it is only a small step to see various forms of RT as performing forceful, concrete scenarios of identity construction in action, reinforced by its intimacy and everyday life setting (see also Bondebjerg, 2002, pp. 160-1).

Another set of issues deals with how RT explores problems in the relationship between the *individual, societal institutions* and *society in a broader sense*. A striking paradox here is the success of some reality programmes in promoting vox pop and audience participation on the one hand and the crisis of the citizen participation in official politics on the other hand. This explains the intense research on audience discussion programmes (Livingstone & Lunt, 1994), which thematize several concepts of political participation, democracy and civil responsibility. These talk shows seem to perform an open forum where civilized people discuss and try to come to a consensus over important ethical and social issues. According to Mehl (1996, p. 235) this type of vox pop programme formulates an answer to the lack of political participation and direct democracy. Participation is not only present in this type of talk show, but also in the use of voting systems, or the audience power to change the narrative and the course of the game (e.g. in *Big Brother*).

Other aspects are related to how RT actualizes sociological theories on risk and fear in capitalist society (e.g. Beck, 1986). We can draw the connection between the success of reality crime shows on the one hand and the representation of crime and the ecology of fear in neo-liberal society on the other. The latter is illustrated by a long chain of activities and institutions, which operate on the sense of fear, crime and risk - from shopping malls at the outskirts of the city with their own security services, the success of alarm systems and the mobile phone for security, to the abundance of crime and violence on television and film. For Boomkens (1996), reality crime shows are perfect examples of how television operates as a 'fear machine'. Dovey (2000, p. 99) claims that watching reality crime shows combines 'shared expressions of fear and disgust (...) with fearful and protective feelings, making for a TV "family bonding experience". We are able to confirm our own security by looking at those less fortunate. Bill Nichols (1994, p. 55) in his analysis points to fear of social inequality, flexibility and instability as a background for the rise of RT. Nichols (p. 58) claims that RT mainly targets the big middle class, which in a flexible capitalist society continuously feels threatened by a possible social decline.[3]

Trash, Pluralist, Critical and Consumer Culture Positions

All these examples indicate that RT is, in some sense, more than entertainment. Both defenders and critics agree that it openly constructs as well as explores significant issues which go to the heart of how people (can) live with each other in society. Most of these issues are fully part of the sphere of legitimate controversy and rarely actually treat deviancy. However, the controversial nature of RT may be less in *what* than in *how* issues are treated. And here again various positions can be taken up.[4] From a *pluralist position*, RT bears a potential for empowerment, sometimes translated as the forum for new forms of information, participation and debate. In its ideal form this position underlines the potential of RT for opening up an additional independent space where issues can be treated from a bottom-up perspective.

At the other end of the spectrum we can observe various *critical positions,* which claim that RT does not explore, but rather exploits important contemporary social and moral issues. The critical position often stresses the ideological dimension behind how these issues are treated. Nichols (1994, p. 51), for instance argues that, compared to the documentary tradition, RT does not intend to mobilize people or to sharpen their civic sense. The ideas of the liberal pluralist position are seen as mere illusions and as commercial strategies for obtaining wider audiences. The exploitation of the private sphere corresponds with people's tendency to voyeurism, along with the perverse use of symbols of participatory democracy. Television only plays with these ideals of representation, while minority groups are further stigmatized. These programmes pay lip service to democratic ideals, while they use a specific discourse to simulate participation and an authentic voice. Television's forum is highly orchestrated, while real debate is impossible. Patrick Charaudeau and Rodolphe Ghiglione (1997) talk about *une réprésentation fallacieuse* and a *leurre séduisant.*

In accordance with larger positions in terms of media and society (Curran, 1996), the critical position assumes that the media are not only serving commercial purposes, but ultimately function as instruments for social control and ideological reproduction. RT goes along with tendencies of infotainment and tabloidization, leading to more stereotypes and a narrowed knowledge of wider societal issues. Abstract analyses and background information are replaced by a fragmented image with subjective, individual voices. These techniques of subjectivation, fragmentation and personalization ultimately can lead to the implosion of the modern public sphere. These frames hide various other, more intermediate positions, which accept the validity of the fundamental critical approach, while also opening spaces for alternative material. One position, which is closely linked to cultural studies perspectives, can be seen as a *critical consumer culture position*. This position accepts that commercialism often leads to trash, exploitative or socially conservative material. But it at least opens up the possibility that contemporary commercial culture may have the potential for empowerment at some occasion. The arrival of new factual television is mainly a result of commercial strategies and may use the symbols of democracy, but this does not exclude the potential for new forms of public debate, broader representation, or a better access to wider information.

From this perspective there is no need to consider RT as the end of ideals in terms of media and society. According to Bondebjerg (1996), we see the 'creation of a new mixed public sphere, where common knowledge and everyday experience play a much larger role.' The consumer culture in which we live becomes a more nuanced frame of interpretation where democratic potentials are not excluded, notwithstanding the original political-economic motives. In a recent critical overview of RT formats and positions in the debate, Bondebjerg (2002) illustrates how some RT programmes are still informed by, or have clear references to, documentary traditions. Arguing that we have to acknowledge the variety of formats and traditions covered by reality TV genres, Bondebjerg claims that 'from an audience point of view, reality TV covers very different formats and tendencies and cannot just be dismissed as commercial trash-TV' (p. 188). Referring to a Danish and British context, it is interesting how he makes a distinction between the use of RT formats by commercial and public service channels, where the latter more often try to link up with documentary and journalistic traditions. Bondebjerg (1996) argues that 'in spite of this, there is a need for critical perspectives: dramatizing crime, personal problems and social issues in fascinating forms does not necessarily create the basis for public knowledge. There still is a question of balance, relevance and the question of putting things into appropriate perspectives and contexts.'

Provocation, Simulation or Real Moral Panic?
The Intentional Production of Scandals and a Public Discourse of Denouncement

The above discussion claimed that the perfume of scandal and controversy around RT may be linked less to the kind of important social and moral issues treated than to the ways these are (re)presented. As with most news and information programmes, RT operates in the sphere of legitimate controversy, although it uses different means. Dependent on the various (schematic) positions in the debate, there is a different evaluation of reality programmes (in) direct treatment of those controversial issues, their strong reality claims, or their stress on everyday life experiences and on subjectivity. While some see RT as a potential for discussing social issues, others see it as a lure and ideological fraud. We also claimed that the public debate on RT is strongly driven by some eccentric or highly publicized programmes, which tend to become staged media events and even a media template, obscuring the debate.

This leads us to a second step in our analysis, to the *discourses around RT* leading to protest and eventually to scandal and moral panic. An important feeling here is that some reality programmes are engaged in the *intentional* production of a perfume of scandal and controversy. Critics (e.g. Nichols, 1994) claim that reality programmes are highly aware of their exploration of morality and transgressions of norms and values. According to the critics, reality TV and other 'new' factual programmes are not so noble in their discussion of important issues in the public arena, but they should rather be seen as a metaphor for the critical observation that media are driven into commercial goals where crime, scandals and hysteria can create enormous profits (Lull & Hinerman, 1997). Defenders of RT however, claim that this type of programming can only be successful when it appeals to an audience's need to see wider social and moral issues treated in the media. Mehl (1994a, p. 104), for instance, claims that the wave of moralist protest against 'reality shows' in France indicates that these programmes appeal to deeper social phenomena and changes in society, related to changing patterns in power structures of knowledge (Who may speak? What about private, intimate knowledge?). Mehl (1994b) also points to the furious wave of moral protest and indignation, mainly by journalists and intellectuals. This debate reached its peak in France in 2001, when the *Big Brother* derivative *Loft Story* was promoted and broadcast by the commercial channel M6, and caused an unprecedented moral outcry and intellectual hysteria in the national quality press (Kerviel & Psenny, 2001). But there was more. Besides this debate and the faint-hearted public protests by the leading commercial broadcaster TF1 against *Loft Story*, it was amazing that France's regulatory body CSA intervened directly and forced a number of modifications to the programme.[5]

The case history of *Big Brother* shows that in other Western European countries too there have been instances of something like moral panic. The German case is well-known, where arguments about the programme preceded its airing and where public pressure drove regulators in several *Länder* to mandate legal experts to screen the programme content. This indirectly led to the modification of the programme, while the moral outcry from intellectuals, the Church and other 'moral guardians' continued (EBU, 2001; Mikos et al., 2000). What is interesting in the *Big Brother* case, in terms of theories on moral panic and controversy, is that the producers in various countries explicitly looked for and promoted disputes with moral guardians and with regulators in order to get media attention. In Belgium, for instance, months before the launching of the programme, a wide advertising campaign in the press showed ads with quotes from first-rate politicians and well-known critical intellectuals claiming that *Big Brother* was the worst television programme ever to be shown. One advert even quoted the well-respected secretary of the (dominant) Christian-Democratic party, claiming that he will go to court if *Big Brother* violated, even to a small extent, principles of human dignity. This example shows that the programme makers were not only looking for controversy by exploiting social and moral issues (*Big Brother* was after all a very decent programme, as also critics acknowledged later on), but rather played with the idea of a possible moral panic. But the question is to what extent this concept is still useful.

Moral Panic

In his book on moral panics, Kenneth Thompson (1998, p. 140) claims that '(it) is only recently, in the 1990s, that the continuing rapid succession of phenomena commonly described as "moral panics" has begun to force a reappraisal.' Following earlier work on the concept, Thompson (1998, p. 7) refers to the concept as a result or a 'spiral effect produced by the interaction of the media, public opinion, interest groups and the authorities.' In his pioneering work on the confrontations between mods and rockers, Stanley Cohen (1972, p. 9) wrote about how the media were crucial in (re)presenting 'a condition, episode, person or group of persons (...) as a threat to societal values and interests (...) in a stylised and stereotypical fashion.' The electronic and printed media provided the information that fuelled the panic, mainly through a process of stigmatising, thus defining social deviancy (Ben-Yehuda, 1990, p. 103). The mass media did not only exaggerate the scope of events (exaggeration), or defined events as worse than they really were (distortion), they also inferred emotional symbolism and moral values of fear and threat to specific groups ('folk devils'), which were then defined as separated from the majority.

The work of Cohen and of Young on drug takers (1971) demonstrated that the media drew attention to or reflected social problems, as well as actively constructed meaning, by amplifying fear around issues such as crime, sexuality, gender, youth or ethnicity. The ideological nature of the media's use of moral panics became apparent through Hall's et al. (1978) work on mugging. The researchers claimed that the media were whipping up a moral panic around the issue and thus legitimated more intensive policing and punitive measures. Moral panic (and the media's role in stirring it up) became intrinsically linked, not only with conservatism and social control, but also with faked consensus, hegemony and the transmission of a dominant ideology. In this manner, the media are more than mere moral entrepreneurs, but become vehicles for the transmission of ideology, primary definers of consensus, and forces in maintaining social cohesion.

The question however is whether this concept can still be maintained for analysing the public debate around RT. Along with Angela McRobbie (1994) it seems necessary to redefine the moral panic model in a post-modern society. A central idea in McRobbie's criticism of the old model is that moral panics still exist and even show a high rate of turnover, but that, at the same time, all constituents of it has changed radically since the 1980s. She argues that 'the rectangular relationship of positions and processes which held the old model together (the sociologists on behalf of the deviant; the agencies of social control; the media; the moral guardians and experts) has been replaced by a more diverse and more fluid set of institutions, agencies and practices which sometimes interlock' (p. 211).

Various ideas in McRobbie's forceful attempt to redefine the place of the moral panic concept for media and cultural studies may be interesting in understanding the fuss around RT's controversial image. First of all, and in relation to the media, she claims that in a highly competitive environment media often take up the role of moral guardians, becoming the moral voice of the new middle class, alerting them 'to new possibilities for concern and indignation.' McRobbie (p. 202) argues that 'moral panics thus become the norm of journalistic practice', where even quality papers use 'exaggerated, sensational and moralistic headlines.' Given the expansion and amplification of the media in social life, the world of the media can no longer be separated from social reality. Although McRobbie did not refer to RT, she argued that the media in the 1990s provide a forum upon which important social and political issues are 'presented, paraded and transformed, no longer into straightforward moral panics, but rather into a seamless web of narrativized news and media events.' This means that panics are simulated, only rarely taken up and activated, mainly because they are woven into a wider flow or web of news stories and media events.

Secondly, this idea is closely linked to the more complicated and fragmented balance between the media on the one hand and the traditional agents of social control, the 'folk devils' and the moral guardians on the other. As an example McRobbie refers to the impressive growth of various pressure and interest groups, which often succeed in responding to or even countering the stigmatization or demonization of the people they represent. They can produce their own media or try to influence the traditional media representation of (former) folk devils. A standard procedure in this process of de-stigmatization is to give a view upon the everyday life and problems by first hand witnesses. This proliferation of voices in the media, McRobbie argues, has introduced a strong contestation of the traditional moral guardians. And she continues that 'the old days of the clearly defined and highly visible moral panic have been replaced by a much more sophisticated way of representing social and political issues to the public' (pp. 217-8). Contrary to the old moral panic view on society and moral coherence, this also concludes that norms, morality and representation are less stable and belong to a field of contestation and struggle (see also Horsefield, 1997).

A third and final criticism deals with the necessity to bring in and to reconceptualize the audience. Here McRobbie (1994, p. 215) rightly argues that the audience 'in the old moral panic theory played a minor role' and was seen as 'the space of consensus, the space of media manipulation'. The moral panic concept has often been used as a key concept for understanding processes of social control and manipulation, often leading to a quick view upon an easily convinced audience. In this context Horsefield (1997) refers to the whole field of audience reception studies, which 'suggest that the interaction between audiences and mediated messages is much more complex than the media influence theory which underlies the moral panic hypothesis.'

This all seems to make the moral panic concept outdated and inadequate for analysing the role of the media in (re)presenting and discussing moral and social issues in a post-modern society, leading some authors to replace 'the vocabulary of the moral panic with that of representation, discourse and "the other"' (McRobbie, 1994, p. 210). As a summary of this excursion through the moral panic concept, we think that McRobbie's critical reconfiguration of the concept fairly helps to understand RT's controversial nature in various directions. RT as a tendency has been crucial, as authors from a pluralist and 'empowerment' position may argue, in the proliferation of voices from below during the 1990s. It has also been important that using/exploiting stories with a moral panic *angle* as a working practice to attract audiences has led to public criticism of sensationalism and commercialism. The intentional production, or the simulation of, a (possible) moral panic only rarely leads to real moral panics - at least as defined as a spiral effect produced by the interaction of the media, public opinion, interest groups, moral guardians and the authorities. In a post-modern environment, these (potential) moral panic stories are woven into a massive flow of other media stories, events and voices from various horizons. In this context, the chance that they really lead to a momentum of moral outcry is fairly small, at least as a result of specific issues whipped up by the media.

Media Panic

How then are we to explain the moral outcry against specific programmes or against the RT genre as a whole? Here it is necessary to distinguish between moral panic and *media panic*. While in moral panic the media play a role of stirring up a wider debate over a specific social or moral issue, in media panic they become the object, source and (sometimes even) the medium of public consternation (Drotner, 1992). Media panic mainly refers to the historical introduction of a new mass medium and the resulting strong public reactions, sometimes leading to a spiral of fear, threat and (in some cases) regulation or censorship.

Drotner refers to various forms of popular media, such as popular fiction, film, comics, but it may also include a panic over specific genres or cycles of films, books, comics or programmes (see Springhall, 1998). Drotner indicates that the phenomenon is mostly seen as a potential threat to children and the young, and (as an extension) as a possible conflict with enlightenment ideals of human and cultural development. The historical analysis of such panics underlines the strong coherence and repetitiveness of the arguments in the debates. What is interesting in all this and mainly in relation to RT, is, as Drotner (pp. 60-1) rightly claims, that 'media panics do not tell us much about actual media', although they 'tackle central questions about cultural quality, personal development and social change under the rubric of enlightenment.'

It is not so difficult to extend Drotner's analysis to the debate about panic and regulation of RT in some countries. We already indicated how some highly publicized programmes drove this debate, operating as media templates. Again, as in the French case, arguments of quality and civilization were raised, while the young were seen as principal victims of vulgarity. In her 1992 essay, Drotner already indicated that there has been a change in the media panic discourse over the years, where pessimist elitism, paternalist measures and (in some cases) straight censorship (e.g. film in most Western democracies after the First World War) gave space to liberalism, tolerance and 'more optimistic pluralism' (p. 52).

Audiences, Factual Television and Controversial Stories

In this section we will briefly discuss some conclusions of a case study on how young people look at (and learn from) new factual television, including various forms of RT and controversial stories.[6] With this qualitative audience study we primarily wanted to test or confront some crucial issues in the public debate on RT in relation to other factual television, including hard news. Using both interviews and diaries with open questions and specific statements, we wanted to understand how adolescents thought about these 'new' factual programmes. What about their understanding of the different formats and their reality claims? What do they think about the 'new fluidity' across genres (Corner, 1999)? What kind of issues treated by factual television do people talk about? And how do they appreciate the potential information delivered by RT formats with its stress on lay experts, everyday life experiences and the new light that these programmes can bring onto specific issues? What about controversial stories? What about the ethical and deontological questions?

We will only discuss some major results of this study (Van Bauwel & Biltereyst, 2002), but it may be important first to acknowledge that in Flanders both the commercial and public service broadcasters are heavily involved in using reality formats. In recent years, the public television station invested strongly in docusoaps in prime time and includes RT techniques in many of its talk shows, audience discussion and even in its information programmes. Similar trends can be observed on the commercial channels, although they are much more strongly involved in using vox pop in the news as well as in exploiting the more controversial, 'tabloid' genres within RT, such as dating programmes, reality crime shows and big real life soaps (e.g. *Big Brother* and *Temptation Island*). It was no surprise that the latter programmes were often used as the key references in discussions about RT. *Big Brother* in particular has been a major media event in 2000 and again in 2001, when it broke all domestic viewing records and, for months, led to a public debate among politicians, lawyers, intellectuals, programme makers and 'shocked' citizens.

RT as Denouncement and as a Metaphor for Television as Manipulation and Sensationalism

One of the striking results from the diaries and our discussions with recipients was that most of them use RT in a rather negative manner, often as a concept to denounce some overall tendencies in television and society. This was clearly the case for *Big Brother*: this programme was continuously called trash, nonsense and (indeed in a pejorative sense) mere popular culture. Also other forms of RT associated with freak shows, eccentric experiences or openly controversial stories, were larded with words and images usually associated with the 'trash position'. This denouncement included some ambivalence among most receivers: these programmes were very often connected to sensationalism, voyeurism and commercialism on the one hand, but also included entertainment and amusement on the other hand.

This denouncement also included the idea of media manipulation and the deconstruction of RT's reality claims. A quite illustrative statement here comes from a male respondent (B., twenty-one-years-old) who called RT 'rather ridiculous.'

> *Television makers can do with people what they want. 'Jambers' for instance is pure kitsch. He's looking for extreme figures, for instance a guy in a town who's paid for what he tells to the camera. But some people like this programme and find it informative enough while they get a skewed image of reality.*

This critical attitude towards RT, its sensationalism and fake reality claims was far from exceptional and it was often enlarged to a criticism towards television in general. Many recipients talked about manipulation of reality through television. The young people in our study mostly developed a complex, not to say nuanced and critical, attitude towards the reality claims, where they made a clear distinction between fictional and factual programmes. But the latter were also often observed from a mixed perspective. On the one hand, they talked about news, information and reality programmes in a deferential manner, referring to television as a means to get a part of reality, with people of flesh and blood. But on the other hand, they also used a more critical, meta-linguistic frame about factual programmes as constructs of a reality, which have to obey technological procedures and restrictive economic laws. Within the factual category, RT was seen as the worst case scenario or as an invitation to manipulation and the construction of a faked reality:

> *Reality television is not a window to the world. They invite people to have specific reactions. There is always something behind. It is only reality when you don't know that they are filming. (C., female, twenty-two-years-old)*

Generic Distinctions, the Usefulness of Emotion and the Need for Balance
This type of statement clearly echoed critical positions in the public debate, making *Big Brother* the ultimate metaphor for manipulation. However, when discussing other, less openly controversial reality and 'new' factual programmes in more detail, it was clear that the recipients were naturally aware of distinctions between programmes and formats within the RT tendency. Viewers did occasionally refer to leaky genre boundaries.

The respondents talked in a nuanced sense about different reality shows where, for instance, some human-interest programmes were highly appreciated because they made them think about specific issues, which also came up in discussions with other people. A key factor here is emotion, which introduces personalization and the possibility of identification:

> *Some programmes really make me think. I remember a programme with a cancer patient being filmed and interviewed by her sister. This made me think: ooh! This could happen to me! (T., female, twenty-one-years-old)*

It is tentative to see this trinity of emotion, personalization and identification from a critical perspective as a form of trivialization. However, as Elizabeth Bird claimed (1998, p. 39, in a quote from John Tomlinson), personalization can be useful 'in achieving greater imaginative proximity, while the personal can introduce a democratisation of news'. The recipients claimed that emotion may be a gateway for empathy and discussion, but here again, they were often fully aware of the danger of tipping into sensationalism and voyeurism. This nuanced view underlined the general idea that the young recipients *often picked up arguments from various positions in the debate on RT*, from a trash position (e.g. about *Big Brother*) to a critical (e.g. on sensationalism) or a pluralist view on empowerment (e.g. emotion can lead to a better understanding). This can also be illustrated by how they appreciated (but also criticized) other main characteristics of RT such as the use of experiences of lay people, associated with emotion and everyday life experiences. Again people were quite critical in discussing the pro's and con's:

> *Experts know more about it, they analyse things in a neutral manner. Lay testimonies will always be somewhat coloured. But, these testimonies are necessary, mainly because they represent honest emotions. (S., male, fifteen-years-old)*

Most respondents appreciated first person speech and emotions, although this may introduce some dangers of overexposure:

> *I think that testimonies may be somewhat too subjective or personal, or that people are driven by their emotions and feelings... I like to see people talk about what they experienced, because you know that what they think and say is honest. (D., female, twenty-one-years-old)*

Some respondents clearly expressed their ideas about balance in information and in voices on a specific issue:

> *Testimonies are emotional and may not be realistic. The emotional value may obscure the facts and at this moment we need experts who remind us about what really happens. (K., female, nineteen-years-old)*

> *Testimonies are strong in showing what is happening inside people. Experts are more objective. (L., female, twenty-one-years-old)*

> *People know the problems. Experts know also something, but it is often theory. (H., female, nineteen-years-old)*

The Importance of News, the Potential and Conditional Character of RT

Another striking finding was that this fairly young group of television viewers continuously underlined the importance of traditional information programmes. One of the alarming results of many audience studies on news consumption deals with the diminishing attention and attraction of young people for it. We can only speculate about social bias, but most respondents indicated news as the most reliable source of information (although certainly not always free from manipulation):

> *But television does not always provide correct information. It depends on the programme. Soaps for instance are fantasy. The news must be nothing more than reality. They will not invent things, though? (H., male, nineteen-years-old)*

In the diaries people had to indicate a list of stories, social and political issues, which were discussed with friends, colleagues or family members. These lists indicated that most of these stories came from news, rather than from many forms of RT. It was also amazing that the deconstruction of the reality claims of many forms of RT often went hand in hand with a reference to the importance of traditional news and information. This comes close to Bird's analysis (1997) on audiences for tabloids and scandal news, where she indicates that public conversation does not revolve solely around issues of scandal and personality, and not all people avoid hard news. On the contrary, 'people still discuss political issues and complex economic questions', and Bird continues that 'the media do have a crucial role in setting the agenda for public discourse' (p. 119). Bird's analysis, which we would see as a critical version of the consumer culture position, is not so far away from how many respondents in our study think about the balance between traditional news and various RT formats. Although the recipients did not talk in these terms, they were often defending an argument for balance between various forms of factual programmes.

The image of various types of reality programmes was not straightforward, ranging from a trash position to a positive appreciation of the additional informative value of others. According to the recipients much depends upon the general atmosphere and the concrete issues treated. Audiences do not speak in terms of the democratic potentials of some RT, or in terms of an additional forum for information and discussion, for a plurality of views and voices. However, they did argue in more indirect ways for the potential and conditional nature of reality programming:

> *It is true that testimonies of ordinary people must be supplemented by those of experts, in order to get a more objective view on what happens around us. (N., female, twenty-one-years-old)*

It is always easy, and it has become a nearly standard conclusion for qualitative audience studies, to say that viewers are critically involved with media products. However we must acknowledge several weaknesses in the use of diaries, interviews and other qualitative methodologies. It might well be that audiences tend to respond according to traditional taste hierarchies as they are circulated in the public debate. But there are many indications in our data that viewers are actively involved in what television offers as information for their lives, despite what the differences among respondents in terms of cultural capital indicate. The public debate and the media panic around RT did not seem to have influenced their definition, appreciation and use of various forms of reality programmes. However, it seems that they somehow picked up the negative connotation of the overall concept of RT, which they reserve for eccentric and highly publicized formats. But nevertheless people appreciate RT as a wider tendency in as much as the issues presented can touch them emotionally or bring in new practical knowledge. In these cases they search for other generic nouns than RT. An interesting docusoap is then called a 'documentary'.

In a similar manner, the audience was not picking up most claims about RT's potential for theories of the public sphere, not at least in an abstract manner. However, when specific issues are treated in an accessible manner, they very much seem to appreciate strategies such as the use of lay testimonies, new forms of bottom-up knowledge based on everyday life experiences, subjective speech and so on. On all these points, however, we hope to have shown that people also noted a darker side of cheap sensationalism and RT's potential of limiting wider information. They seemed to call into question the idea of balance in types of information (expert versus everyday life experience, top-down versus bottom-up), including the conditional value of RT.

Discussion

This chapter started from the observation that few recent media genres have been more critically received than RT, defined here as a broad container concept, metagenre or a tendency in how television treats specific social and moral issues. In many (European) societies specific RT programmes were seen as troubling and controversial, leading in particular cases to a wide, spiralling debate with (for some authors) all the characteristics of a moral panic. The application of this critical concept to RT was reinforced by the fact that in some countries media regulators were driven to action. The application of the moral panic concept to RT was also somewhat magnified by publicity campaigns of some programmes, which seemingly tried to whip up the debate with intellectuals, politicians, regulators and various groups of moral guardians (e.g. the Church).

In this chapter we've argued that the concept of moral panic may be insufficient to understand the atmosphere of controversy or the 'perfume of scandal' around RT. According to various critics of the concept, it seems that in a post-modern society, with its abundance of voices in different types of media, a fairly narrow view of social coherence and moral stability can no longer be maintained. Media themselves have played a major role in contesting the authority of traditional agents of social control and in questioning values of traditional moral guardians, while other groups gained a clearer voice in the public debate around specific social issues (e.g. gay movement, ethnic movements).

The interpretation of RT's role in this all depends very much on the position that one takes *vis-à-vis* the media and society in general. We've argued that RT as a whole does not herald the end of ideals in terms of media and society, and that in some cases it provides additional information on specific issues. As the audience study indicates, it is clear that people can gain knowledge or learn from how some RT formats (e.g. some human-interest programmes) work upon specific issues in terms of identity politics, interpersonal relations or on issues dealing with the relationship between the individual and society. They offer people concrete scenarios, often applied in an everyday context, with people and their emotions. Although people appreciate concrete programmes and issues, they also make overall distinctions within RT formats, accepting the value of this type of information but still underlining the importance of traditional news for balance and relevance. People were overall fairly critical of specific formats and even applied the overall noun of RT in a rather derogatory manner. People appreciate the potential nature of 'useful' information, although this is often swept aside by sensationalism, game show elements and all that is troubling about this type of programme (e.g. the use of freaks). More abstract theories on the democratic potentials of RT, as often formulated within an empowerment frame (Dovey, 2000), are not useful or applicable for audiences. RT in its most pejorative form only uses the symbols of democracy and stigmatises and may limit a broader representation of some groups and issues.

It is obvious that we should make clear distinctions among genres and programmes, also RT-genres, although this might limit our understanding of generic hybridization in contemporary television (Corner, 1999; Ellis, 2000). RT is also a concrete sociological phenomenon in public debate. The exploitation of stories with a moral panic angle or potential, as well as the attempts to simulate a wider debate for commercial reasons, sometimes causes moral panic against certain types of RT programmes. However, we need more research on the kind of social and moral issues that reality programmes treat, how these themes are related to different national and cultural contexts and how audiences and public discourses react.

It is therefore important to link RT to the history of media panics (Drotner, 1992; Springhall, 1998) and, more broadly, to histories of media censorship, classification and regulation of media representations in Western democracies. Historical research on media panics may come to the conclusion that they are ultimately about central ethical questions, questions of power, and that they may be 'understood as tacit or explicit means of social regulation' (Drotner, 1992, p. 57). Research on the history of film censorship for instance, and by extension all types of research on the regulation of troublesome images, may indicate that censorship is a 'significant social response' (Staiger, 1995, p. 14) and is about the power 'in defining categories of taboos' (p. 15). Recent, more culturalist inspired studies on film censorship and classification, indicate that forms of extreme regulation (e.g. cutting, defining who can speak and what can be represented) must not be seen as just repressive, but also productive and meaningful because they are so explicit in indicating the limitations of representation and in showing pictures that are troubling in a given society.

This link between media panic/censorship and power throws up many questions in relation to who speaks and to the role of who is engaged in public debate on RT.

The case is more problematic for critical media researchers who know about media panics and their link to the role of power in society. This may easily paralyse any participant in contemporary debates on the media. The case is even more difficult with RT and its controversial promotional discourses. In the end, it may be that these public and moral 'crusaders', and not the average members of the audience, are the ones bamboozled by the industry. Their critical attention only supports the industry's promotional search for attention and distinction in the market. The export of RT's promotion to critical opinion pages of quality and other newspapers, may then be the ultimate perversion of reality shows.

Thanks to Sofie Van Bauwel and Philippe Meers for previous work, thoughts and discussions on the joys and angers of reality programmes. Thanks also to the editors and to John Corner for their comments on the original conference paper.

Notes

1   For other definitions, see e.g. Dovey (2000, p. 1), who relates these programmes with the concept of 'first person media', and Kilborn (1994, p. 423).

2   We need to differentiate between scandal and the notion 'perfume of scandal'. Scandals basically deal with actions or events with a clear transgression of certain norms and moral codes, often in relation to sex. Scandals thrive on morality, as well as on public disapproval or denouncement of specific events and actions, and the scandal arises when secrecy is revealed and things made public (see John B. Thompson, 2000). Programmes such as *Big Brother* thrive on transgression of morality and scandal-sensitive events (often sex), but also often lack secrecy and hypocrisy. On the contrary, they often exploit the idea of voluntary participation and openness.

3   See also Langer (1998, pp. 162-4).

4   Dovey (2000, p. 83) talks about three positions: 'Trash TV', 'reality-TV as empowerment' and 'reality-TV as nightmare' position. The second comes close to our pluralist position. For an interesting discussion of these positions, see Bondebjerg (2002).

5   Referring to human dignity and responding to the wide public debate on 'Loft Story', the French regulatory body, the *Conseil Supérieur de l'Audiovisuel*, formulated some general recommendations on the phenomenon of '*télé-réalité*' (La Lettre du CSA nr. 153, July 2002). As a result of this, M6 agreed to diminish the use of alcohol and cigarettes, while the participants were accorded two hours of real intimacy (EBU, 2001).

6   The conclusions are based on data from a reception study where we used both diaries and interviews. In total seventy-nine people between fourteen and twenty-eight-years-old filled in a diary for one week (21 to 26 October 2001), while two waves of interviews (before and after)

were organized. A more detailed account of the study was published in Van Bauwel & Biltereyst (2002).

References

Beck, U. (1986) Risikogesellschaft: auf dem Weg in eine andere Moderne. Frankfurt: Suhrkamp.

Ben-Yehuda, N. (1990) The Politics and Morality of Deviance. New York: State University of NY Press.

Biltereyst, D. (2000) Realiteit en fictie: Tweemaal hetzelfde? Brussels: King Baudouin Foundation.

Bird, E. (1997) 'What a Story!', pp. 99-121 in J. Lull & S. Hinerman (Eds.) Media Scandals. Cambridge: Polity Press.

Bird, E. (1998) 'News we Can Use: An Audience Perspective on the Tabloidisation of News in the United States', Javnost. 5(3), pp. 33-49.

Bondebjerg, I. (1996) 'Public Discourse/Private Fascination: Hybridisation in True-Life-Story Genres', Media, Culture & Society. 18, pp. 27-45.

Bondebjerg, I. (2002) 'The Mediation of Everyday Life. Genre, Discourse, and Spectacle in Reality TV', pp. 159-93 in A. Jerslev (Ed.) Realism and 'Reality' in Film and Media. Northern Lights. Film and Media Studies Yearbook 2002, Copenhagen: Museum Tusculanum Press, University of Copenhagen.

Boomkens, R. (1996) De Angstmachine: over geweld in films, literatuur en popmuziek. Amsterdam: Balie.

Castells, M. (1996) The Rise of the Network Society. Oxford: Blackwell.

Charaudeau, P. & Ghiglione, R. (1997) La parole confisquée. Un genre télévisuel: le talk show. Paris: Dunod.

Cohen, S. (1972) Folk Devils and Moral Panics. London: MacGibbon & Kee.

Corner, J. (1999) 'Documentary. The Transformation of a Social Aesthetic,' pp. 173-184 in J. Gripsrud (Ed.) Television and Common Knowledge. London: Routledge.

Curran, J. (1996) 'Mass Media and Democracy Revisited', in J. Curran & M. Gurevitch (Eds.) Mass Media and Society. London: Arnold.

Dovey, J. (2000) Freakshow. London: Pluto Press.

Drotner, K. (1992) 'Modernity and Media Panics', pp. 42-62 in M. Skovmand & K.Chr. Schroder (Eds.) Media Cultures. Reappraising Transnational Media. London: Routledge.

EBU (2001) 'Big Brother: an International Phenomenon', Diffusion. Quarterly Journal of the EBU, 4, pp. 6-21.

Ellis, J. (2000) Seeing Things. Television in Age of Uncertainty. London: Tauris.

Hall, S., Critcher, Ch., Jefferson, T., Clarke, J. & Roberts, B. (1978) Policing the Crisis. London: Macmillan Press.

Horsefield, P. (1997) 'Moral Panic or Moral Action?', Media International Australia. November 1997, No. 85.

Kerviel, S. & Psenny, D. (2001) 'Loft Story: enquête sur les coulisses de la première émission de télé-réalité', Le Monde, 4 May, p. 10.

Kilborn, R. (1994) 'How Real Can You Get? Recent Developments in "Reality" Television', European Journal of Communication. 9(4), pp. 421-439.

Kitzinger, J. (2000) 'Media Templates: Patterns of Association and the (Re)Construction of Meaning over Time,' Media, Culture & Society. 22(1), pp. 61-84.

Lane, R. (2000) The Loss of Happiness in Market Democracies. New Haven: Yale UP.

Langer, J. (1998) Tabloid Television: Popular Journalism and the 'Other News'. London: Routledge.

Livingstone, S. & Lunt, P. (1994) Talk on Television. Audience Participation and Public Debate. London: Routledge.

Lull, J. & Hinerman, S. (Eds.) (1997) Media Scandals. Cambridge: Polity Press.

McGuigan, J. (1999) Modernity and Post-modern Culture. Buckingham: Open University.

McRobbie, A. (1994) 'The Moral Panic in the Age of the Post-modern Mass Media', pp. 198-219 in A. McRobbie (Ed.) Post-modernism and Popular Culture. London: Routledge.

Mehl, D. (1994a) 'La télévision compassionnelle', Réseaux, 63, pp. 101-22.

Mehl, D. (1994b) 'La 'vie publique privée', Hermès, 13-14, pp. 85-113.

Mehl, D. (1996) La Télévision de l'Intimité. Paris: Seuil.

Mikos, L. et al. (2000) Im Auge der Kamera. Das Fernsehereignis Big Brother. Berlin: Vistas.

Nichols, B. (1994) Blurred boundaries. Questions and Meaning in Contemporary Culture. Bloomington: Indiana UP.

Richardson, K. & Meinhof, U. (1999) Worlds in Common? Television Discourse in a Changing Europe. London: Routledge.

Springhall, J. (1998) Youth, Popular Culture and Moral Panics. London: Macmillan.

Staiger, J. (1995) Bad Women. Regulating Sexuality in Early American Cinema. Minneapolis: University of Minnesota Press.

Thompson, J. B. (2000) Political Scandal. Cambridge: Polity.

Thompson, K. (1998) Moral Panics. New York/London: Routledge.

Van Bauwel, S. & Biltereyst, D. (2002) Veel televisie, veel democratie? Jongeren werpen een kritische blik op het medium televisie, pp. 50-70 in Vanmolkot, R. (Ed.) Publiek/geheim. Ieper: Anno'02.

Young, J. (1971) The Drugtakers. London: Paladin.

Part B: Citizenship and Cultural Identities

As we noted in our introduction, Europe is as much in the mind as on the map. Questions of cultural affinity and the complex and shifting patterns of migration, mobility, and hybridity have all uprooted such set patterns as have ever existed (and most are largely mythical) in the broad and variegated field of European identity. In this part, authors address questions of citizenship and cultural identity. William Uricchio uses an examination of peer-to-peer networking to assess how the new technologies can radically disrupt our sense of community and identity, not least our ties with the nation-state. Participatory cultures of the kind he describes and examines pose important questions for both analysis and policy. Mihelj provides a thorough analysis of Slovenian coverage of Bosnian refugees in order to construct a persuasive and intriguing argument about the formation of cultural boundaries at the edges of Europe. In examining the 'discourse of peripheral nationalism' she is able to provide an understanding of the role of the media, not just in fostering xenophobia, but in providing the symbols and rhetoric from which people are able to understand their place and that of their environment in a shifting European cultural landscape. Schrøeder takes this question deep into analysis of the construction of European identity, by applying cluster and Q-analysis in a combination of quantitative and qualitative methodologies to assess how citizens culturally negotiate national and European identity. Finally, Ludes offers a test case of such provision in an empirical assessment of a pivotal moment in the construction of a trans-national Europe, namely the introduction of the Euro. As he explains, money has its cultural meanings as well as its material actuality, and, like the coins themselves, this event had both a national and a European aspect.

William Uricchio is Professor and acting director of Comparative Media Studies at the Massachusetts Institute of Technology (MIT) in Cambridge, USA, and Professor of Comparative Media History at Utrecht University in the Netherlands. He has held visiting professorships at Stockholm University, the Freie Universität Berlin, and Philips Universität Marburg. His research considers the transformation of media technologies into media practices, in particular, their role in (re-)constructing representation, knowledge and publics. A Guggenheim, Fulbright and Humboldt research fellow, Uricchio has written extensively on both 'old' and new media, popular cultures, and their audiences.

William Uricchio

Cultural Citizenship in the Age of P2P Networks

What do *Napster* (and its successors like *KaZaA* and *Gnutella*), collaborative news networks like *Slashdot* and *Kuro5hin*, and open source operating systems like *Linux* have in common? They are all forms of digital culture that are networked in technology, peer-to-peer in organization, and collaborative in principle. Although they may seem to be on the fringes of the digital scene, their impact on existing media, and with them social power, may well turn out to be disproportionate to their apparent position. Indeed, their implications for how we define certain practices, including the practice of citizenship, and how we participate in cultural production are potentially transformative. These systems might be seen as part of a larger participatory turn in culture, where the users generate the content, evident in such diverse activities as fan fiction production, computer gaming, and club culture. Although the notion of 'participatory culture' is not without its complexities, even at its simplest level of meaning, the concept signals a blurring of the boundaries between the categories of production and consumption, and a subversion of established hierarchies of cultural value and authority. Moreover, certain forms of this cultural turn have already challenged the territorial nation state, shifting the frameworks for authority, control, and citizenly responsibility to entities other than the nation. In the case of aforementioned peer-to-peer (P2P) networks, the implications of this shift range from the reconsideration of how we define and interact with certain cultural texts, to how collaborative communities take form and operate, to how we understand our rights and obligations as citizens - whether in the political, economic, or cultural sphere.

On the level of cultural practice, these particular manifestations of P2P networking have already managed to challenge the dominant meanings and practices associated with journalism, software development, some forms of artistic production, and intellectual property. This challenge stems not so much from a critical discursive posture as from the creation of working alternatives, demonstrations of the advantages of networked collaboration that to some extent 'speak for themselves'. In contrast to the organization of most contemporary cultural industries, these P2P networks thrive in a de-hierarchized, decentralized, and distributed organizational environment and require collectivity and collaboration as a condition of existence. Whether measured in terms of evolutionary advance, or elegance of use of existing infrastructure, or simple economic advantage, these systems are unparalleled by mainstream practices no matter how massive. The music industry has neither computers large enough nor centralized management systems powerful enough to rival *KaZaA* or *Gnutella*'s distributed systems; nor can Microsoft's proprietary and centralized operating system develop with the same speed or responsiveness as open source alternatives such as Linux. Combined with these networks' remarkable ability to find willing participants (within a period of a little more than two years, *Napster* managed to attract nearly thirty million members and *Audiogalaxy* approximately fifty-two million members) these challenges to the status quo (and some extraordinarily powerful corporations) are potentially profound. Moreover, they bring with them a particularly interesting set of implications for the larger social processes bound up in the term 'citizenship'. In extreme cases, they are capable of forcing a conflict between the obligations of cultural citizenship and political citizenship. Yet, if we are to grant credence to the work of theorists such as Pierre Lévy (1997), these developments may well point in the direction of a profound reorganization in social consciousness. And it is here that they may have useful implications for the future of citizenship and civic participation.

I will essentially argue that participation in these P2P collaborative communities constitutes a form of cultural citizenship, and that the terms of this citizenship have the potential to run head to head with established forms of political citizenship. Although I will call upon concepts such as citizenship, community and governance, I do so somewhat reluctantly, aware of their divergent and contested meanings across such different fields as political science, sociology, anthropology, and cultural studies. To be clear, my intention is not to make a technological determinist case for P2P systems (more networks do not necessarily imply more democracy) for, if anything, these instances demonstrate the importance of social construction. Rather, based on my reading of these recent developments, I want to raise some questions about the relationship between notions of citizenship bound up in network culture and those bound up in more banal forms of citizenship (Billig, 1995). And in so doing, I will raise a few questions about the state's current use of the Internet as an instrument in community building and democratic participation.

Media Convergence

The turn towards an enhanced notion of participatory culture has not occurred in a vacuum. One might point to the larger cultural changes in developed Western nations signalled by the appearance in critical discourse of the term 'post-modern'. A descriptor of the weakened state of traditional hierarchies of cultural authority and a testament to the breakdown of the disciplining logics of long-held belief systems (including the modernist commitment to rationality), this cultural turn suggests a wide-ranging set of causal agencies and implications. And while there might appear to be some resonance between the sorts of de-hierarchization implicit in post-modernity and the blurring of the boundaries between cultural producers and consumers and the rise of networked technologies and modes of connection, in fact the situation is not so simple. The deep history of cultural production (folk culture, for example) points to a tradition of dispersed, grass-roots activity at odds with the top-down cultural flows usually associated with industrial (and before it, imperial) culture. This alternate cultural history is highly relevant in thinking through contemporary cultural practice (Williams, 1960 and Thompson, 1968). But second and just as importantly, the challenges posed by post-modern discourse coexist with a material reality that in crucial sectors is more centralized and powerful than ever before. I refer here to those industries involved in the creation and distribution of representation, the media. For all the talk about post-modern diffusion and abandon, certain aspects of capitalist culture - particularly in the media sector - have grown more centralized and all encompassing. The term 'convergence' covers a multitude of meanings, but three in particular are relevant to this development: the convergence of media ownership and production; the convergence of texts across media forms; and the convergence of media audiences, or better said, the ability of audiences to read texts across media forms.

Since the Second World War, global media industries have been in an ongoing process of convergence and consolidation that has been considered by diverse political economists from Herbert Shiller and Nicholas Garnham to Robert McChesney and Ben Bagdikian. Acquisitions and mergers within particular media sectors have helped to produce a race of giants with ever-greater control over the means of production and distribution within particular media industries. Particularly with the period of deregulation that swept the West in the 1980s, the process not only accelerated but also increasingly manifested itself in patterns of cross-media ownership and control. The process of deregulation, although different in particular national contexts, seems generally to have been a response to changes in the organization of global capital, as well as to the proliferation of new technologies in the media sector. So, for example, the past two decades have witnessed an increased reliance on television distribution through satellite and cable infrastructures, the concomitant erosion of old territorial broadcast markets, and a demand for significant investment consistent with the logics of increased competition and market expansion. Whether in the commercial setting of the US or the once state-protected environments that characterized most European nations, the combined impact of deregulation, privatization, and threatened subsidy systems has manifested itself in a frantic search for synergy - from co-productions to cross-investment. Certainly the publishing industry, the film and music industries and some digital industries all have their own structural peculiarities. But the upshot of the past two decades has been a process of convergence within media forms, across media forms, and across national boundaries. Bertelsmann, Sony-Columbia, Time-Warner-CNN-AOL, Disney-ABC, and until recently Vivendi-Universal, have all steadily concentrated their media holdings, dominating the world of content providers to an extent never before seen in human history.

The logics of convergent media ownership have resulted in the production of convergent texts. Economies of production seem best served when a corporation's assets - texts and characters - can migrate across the multiple media forms that it owns, simultaneously promoting its other media iterations of the text and maximizing its return on investments. For example, Warner Bros.' acquisition and development of the trademarked Batman character in print, film, musical, televisual, game, and toy and clothing forms, permitted a text with origins in the comic book medium to circulate throughout its various corporate divisions, both enjoying marketing synergy and garnering efficiently-produced profits (Meehan, 1991 and Wasko, 2001). As Warner Bros., Disney and other media giants well know, trans-media strategies of this kind work best with clearly defined characters or highly reduced narratives capable of articulation, iteration, and commodification in a variety of forms. But they also redefine the terms of audience textual encounters. Just as some media producers have made creative use of the multiple platforms upon which their texts appear, so too have media publics demonstrated increasing sophistication in their readings of texts across media forms. Fans of particular television programmes (*Star Trek*) or popular culture characters (*Spiderman*) or authors (Shakespeare) or literary texts (*Lord of the Rings*) have developed into coherent communities that are built around the cultivation of textual elements, their re-working used as inspiration for the creation of new meanings and a new generation of texts. Moreover, their expertise in reading across textual forms has resulted in their playing an increasingly active role in informing the strategies of the originating media producers (Jenkins, 1992 and Brooker, 2002). Ideal readers of a sort, their tolerances and abilities to shift with texts across media forms suggests *in extremis* the conditions which an average audience should eventually be able to tolerate.

This move towards ever-greater convergence and concentration is being challenged by a discourse of fragmentation and de-hierarchization. It is being confronted by technologically-enabled collaborative networks - a development with its own micro-climate, and thus an environmental factor to be dealt with when thinking about digitally-networked manifestations of participatory culture. But even more important is the sharp contrast between two forms of social organization: the ever-more centralized and hierarchized state of media ownership on one hand, and on the other, the rapid spread of Internet-based participatory network media applications that are by definition de-centralized and de-hierarchized. The recent extremity of both developments and the terms of the conflict are striking, and being played out through a dramatic series of legal and extra-legal battles. In this war, corporate centralism has been remarkably effective in allying itself with the interests of the state, while the opposition has made strong use of network technologies and the spirit of collaborative community. The question - to which we will shortly turn - regards the compelling and contradictory demands made of the political/economic citizen and cultural citizen.

Participatory Culture

Notions of dispersed cultural production and blurred boundaries between cultural 'producers' and 'consumers' are not new. Consider the practices associated with 'folk' culture: 'homespun' narratives and artifacts created, adopted, or reworked by individuals or communities according to their needs. Although industrialization, the processes of social rationalization described by Weber, and an economy based on mass production all formalized the distinctions between producers and consumers, they also provided new opportunities for dispersed cultural production.

The post-war era saw the introduction of photocopy machines and audio and video recorders, enabling the copying, reassembly, and redistribution of existing cultural artifacts, as well as facilitating the production and circulation of new material. The penetration into the consumer market of low-cost video cameras and editing equipment in the decades that followed enabled elaborate productions of music videos, home videos, and public surveillance (the Rodney King video, like the Zapruder film before it), all outside the framework of the media industry. But what marked the emergence of a participatory culture - in contrast to a culture that included a space for creative participation - was the distribution of independently produced content to the wider culture. Public access television stations, programmes such as *America's Funniest Home Videos*, and the news media's increased reliance on 'amateur' video material were certainly testaments to this change, as was the increasingly porous state of the film and music industries. But the proliferation of digital media technologies offered fundamentally new possibilities for distribution (as well as creation) outside of the institutional frameworks of mainstream media.

The situation has been well summarized by Henry Jenkins: 'Patterns of media consumption have been profoundly altered by a succession of new media technologies which enable average citizens to participate in the archiving, annotation, appropriation, transformation, and re-circulation of media content.' (Jenkins, 2003). Countless subcultures and communities have emerged around these practices: fan fiction sites, bloggers, music exchanges, collaborative news networks, and so on. Notable here is the linkage among new technologies and particular social formations, and the resulting production of new cultural practices. Consider the rapid growth of both recorded and performed music based on digital sampling, cutting and mixing. Many hip-hop musicians have dissected existing recorded music, sampling it, quoting it, and transforming it into their own recordings - recordings that are in turn the basis for other participants to subsequently sample, dissect, and construct new meanings. In turn, the 'performance' of recorded music that is the domain of 'DJ culture' is predicated upon the 'live' dissection, manipulation and re-assembly of previously (and usually commercially) recorded music, weaving it into new creative texts (Poschardt, 1998).

Much as with the production of folkloric narratives over the past centuries, there are neither fixed texts nor fixed meanings, but rather a loose assemblage of elements that are re-worked by different individuals for their own purposes, yet still shared by others in the community. Digital technologies have both enabled new forms of production (sampling in particular) and new forms of distribution, bypassing the traditional bottle-necks of centralized, hierarchized culture - such as retail merchandising and radio broadcasting - and enabling musical expressions to be shared within an organically-defined community of fans and available to anyone with an Internet connection. Hebdige (1987) characterizes the consequences of this de-hierarchization of creative and interpretive authority in terms of 'democratic principle' - a broadly political pronouncement to which I will return later.

Video and computer games are also exemplary of this participatory turn. Here, the 'product' is a set of rule protocols with audio-visual enhancement that emerges as a text only through participation ('playing'). Gaming requires the active intervention of its users, and most game platforms permit a near infinity of possible scenarios resulting in unique configurations of the 'text' per encounter. Participation gives the game its specific form, even though the game's defining elements are to some extent engineered by its producers. Yet even here players have intervened, playing with the very protocols upon which the game is based, as if gaming on a meta-level. The engines for games such as *Quake* and *Doom* have been dissected by players, their platforms and rule protocols reworked, and whole new gaming and expressive experiences derived from them - all with the blessings of the games' producers who programmed their products using open code. Indeed, the strength of these on-line games is derived in large part from the creative and collaborative communities that they have spawned and from deliberate company policies of blurring the lines between creators and consumers.

Maxis, the company that produces the *Sims*, encourages the grassroots production and trading of 'skins' (new character identities), props, and architectural structures, even though Maxis is in the business of selling its own version of everything but the code. The *Sims' pater familias*, Will Wright, predicts that ultimately two-thirds of *Sims* content will come from consumers themselves (Jenkins, 2003). While this may not be great for sales of *Sims* accessories, it is fundamental to building a committed and loyal community of collaborators who share in one another's productivity and whose ultimate investment in the *Sims* game universe - and thus the larger interests of Maxis - is intensified. Like the very different gaming universes of *Doom* and *Quake*, the *Sims* has generated a massive community of users; but whereas the former games are web based, the *Sims* is a stand-alone game, making the development of an additional on-line community all the more impressive. The point regarding these games' relationship to participatory culture is twofold: first, the very nature of these gaming experiences demands an explicit level of participation within a variable textual universe; second, the nature of that participation often takes the form of community, with players investing considerable time and resources to develop game elements which are in turn made available to all players free of charge (a logic which we will explore shortly).

On-line communities, are of course, nothing new. Indeed, on-line massively multi-player role-playing games such as *Everquest* and *Lineage*, emerged more or less directly from MUDs and MOOs of the 1980s, and bear a relation to the notion of 'virtual community' discussed by Howard Rheingold (2000) and embodied in the WELL. The range of virtual communities is enormous as a look at the literature or the Internet will affirm, but it is the notion of participation as a *sine qua non* of community structure that I take to be defining in terms of participatory culture. Like MUDs and MOOs, massively multiplayer role-playing games offer compelling examples of experiences whose attraction as games is in direct proportion to the sense of community participation and acts of collaboration generated by hundreds of thousands (and in the case of *Lineage*, millions) of other players. According to analysts, these on-line community-based games represent the future of the industry, with mobile telephony and networked television as the gaming platforms of the near future. In a business whose annual revenues rival those of the Hollywood studios, the computer gaming industry's explicit embrace of consumers as co-producers of product and community is proving to be a good business strategy, a brilliant development tool, and an instrument capable of generating remarkable levels of customer loyalty. But at what point does participation in a community and collaboration in the construction of a cultural system go beyond being 'just a game' or even a new strategy for maximizing profits? Might the term 'cultural citizenship' have relevance to certain forms of participatory culture, and if so, which forms are relevant and what might be the implications?

Cultural Citizenship

Whether viewed as an invented tradition, an imagined community, or a highly contested concept facing trans-national economic, political, and ecological pressures from above and internal identity politics from below, national culture is under siege (Hobsbawm and Ranger, 1984; Appadurai, 1996; and Roche, 2001). Globalization and fragmentation seem only to exacerbate the trend, making it increasingly difficult to see a necessary link between cultural citizenship and our capacity to participate in the reproduction of national culture, whatever it might be (Stevenson, 2001, p. 7). This situation has encouraged some scholars to cut loose the moorings of cultural citizenship from the national culture to which it was once bound. The idea of cultural citizenship is adrift, meaning multiculturalism and identity politics for some, consumerism and taste formations for others; for some it remains analytically bound to the national context, and for others it can only be understood in terms of transnational flows (Delanty, 2002).

With the advent of Internet-based identities and Internet-based communities, focus may have moved further still. The literature suggests any number of ways of thinking about citizenship - flexible, multiple, and conflicting according to the cultural logics of trans-nationality; or nomadic, where culture serves as the *mise-en-scène* through which popular conceptions of local and national citizenship emerge. The complication even on this basic level of conceptualization emerges in part from the speaking position of the analyst in terms of national specificity, disciplinary distinctions, and intellectual. A basic starting point might be to tease out distinctions among forms of citizenship, differentiating them even if heuristically. Theorists such as Castells, Melucci, Appadurai, and Beck have all discussed political, economic, as well as cultural 'flows', 'scapes', and 'dimensions' of citizenship that help to unravel the complex interworkings of this concept. An ongoing Fifth Framework project entitled 'Citizenship and Democratic Legitimacy in the European Union' offers a useful outline of these forms of citizenship (as part of a larger argument which more generally liberates the notion of citizenship from the nation-state). The project:

> ...distinguishes between three different conceptions of citizenship, which are reflective of different conceptions of the EU qua polity. The first is economic citizenship, based on rights associated with the four freedoms, where the citizens are seen as producers, consumers, users, and customers and reflects the notion of the EU as a problem-solving entity. The second is social and cultural citizenship, based on a set of common val-

ues, aimed at establishing a material basis for societal membership, and reflects the notion of the EU as a value-based community. The third is political citizenship, based on a set of common civil and political rights, with the purpose of empowering the citizens to be 'co-authors' of the law, and reflects the notion of the EU as a rights-based post-national union (ARENA, 2002).

This trifurcation with its loosening of the bonds between political and cultural authority and rights, and between the notion of citizenship and the nation-state, strikes me as a useful first step in considering the possibilities of cultural citizenship. Definitions for cultural citizenship abound, and as a starting point, we might consider Renato Rosaldo's work on cultural citizenship and the formation and evolution of Latino communities in Los Angeles, New York City, and San Antonio - work that has been particularly influential in the US. Rosaldo defines the concept as the right to be different (in terms of race, ethnicity, or language) with respect to the norms of the dominant national community, without endangering the right to belong, in the sense of participating in the nation-state's democratic process (Rosaldo, 1994, p. 61). Graham Murdock (1999) agrees that contemporary politics are increasingly centered on the politics of identity - forms of belonging, loyalty, and solidarity. But, citing Alberto Melucci, he states that 'the freedom to belong to an identity, to contribute to its definition or to withdraw from belonging in order to create new meaning' (Murdock, 1999, p. 9) is central to a new political order. The right to belong is not threatened, but Murdock also underscores the right *not* to belong and, moreover, the right to create new meanings, new contexts. Although their frames of reference reflect larger differences between American and European views, both Rosaldo and Murdock share an activist notion of cultural citizenship. Rosaldo notes that, 'since cultural citizenship is about claiming and expanding rights in the community, it goes hand in hand with a micro politics that seeks cultural citizenship in one's plural communities - neighborhoods, workplaces, churches and activist groups.' (Rosaldo, 1994, p. 61). Social change, institutional reform, and the idea of a cultural community built by and for collectives are central to this vision. Murdock's less parochial view maintains the option of belonging to the mainstream by emphasizing public goods over commodities, and it also allows for forms of collective cultural autonomy only hinted at by Rosaldo.

The importance of communities of identity, whether autonomous or not, to a definition of cultural citizenship requires a notion of agency, an understanding of how such communities are formed. Nick Stevenson underscores what I take to be a fundamental element in community formation: participation (Stevenson, 2001, p. 7). The precise nature of this participation has been debated, with some seeing it as being akin to strategies of textual reception (Donald, 2001), and others seeing it as a means of Foucauldian governmentality in which seemingly indirect public processes - sports, radio, film, and arts policies - draw members of society into postindustrial state structures (Miller, 1998). But these two views mirror the standoff between theories of *negotiation* (Fiske, American cultural studies) and *determination* (Althusser, political economy) so familiar from the past twenty years. One can read them as evaluative frames for any participatory act, or one can see in them the minimum required agency for a participatory act (merely observing the passing culture would seem to be enough). I would argue for a more robust sense of participation, akin to the 'claiming and expanding of rights' that can be found in Rosaldo's workplaces, churches, and activist groups. That is to say, cultural citizenship differs from political citizenship in the sense that the latter is acquired as a right of birth, but the former can only be acquired by assertion or action within a particular cultural sphere.

Community, freed from any necessary relationship to the nation-state, and *participation*, in the sense of active, then, are two prerequisites for the enactment of cultural citizenship. The radical potential of cultural citizenship - particularly *vis-à-vis* the nation-state - as a means of expanding rights or creating new meanings has already been suggested. And it is in this context that I want to assert that certain forms of the participatory culture discussed in the previous section in fact constitute sites of cultural citizenship. I refer here particularly to collaborative communities, sites of collective activity that exist thanks only to the creative contributions, sharing, and active participation of their members. Certain manifestations of fan culture, MOOs, MUDs, and massively multi-player role-playing games, would all be examples of communities made up of cultural citizens. Some of these occur face to face within the confines of the territorial nation-state, and others occur 'virtually,' in technologically facilitated networked communities.

Technologies of Diffusion

The contemporary media scene seems to be heading towards a stand-off between massive content industries organized around hierarchized and centralized principles, and quickly-growing de-centralized and distributed collaborative networks; between the requirements of the political citizen and those of the cultural citizen. These collaborative networks offer a fast and cheap means of exchange, and even though they have conceptual roots in older media forms, they bypass many of the difficulties encountered by precedents like circulating libraries and radio relay networks. Moreover, their predication upon user-participation and their cultivation of an active community based upon a notion of mutual exchange and sharing, combine to make a strong case for a notion of cultural citizenship. As a first order of business, we might first ask how might we delineate and define these new peer-to-peer networks? They are of course computer-based, and operate over telephone lines and special cable linkages. But curiously, despite the US Defense Department's initial Cold War vision of ARPANET as a decentralized and therefore effectively bomb-proof network of computing and storage nodes, until the 1990s, most manifestations of the Internet were largely centralized. The growth of the web occurred at a moment when systems tended to be based on single web servers running in expensive and centralized collocation facilities (Minar, 2001). Moreover, the Internet had one basic model of connectivity, the DNS system: machines were assumed to have a fixed IP address, to be on, and to be constantly operating. With the spread of Mosaic around 1994, a new model began to proliferate. Now, computers could be connected to the Internet over a modem with its own IP address. PCs could enter and exit the network frequently and at will, forcing Internet service providers to begin issuing dynamic rather than permanent IP addresses (Shirky, 2003). The situation was complicated by the fact that most PCs had not been designed to be part of the Internet. The introduction of the Pentium chip and upgraded operating systems overcame this limitation, transforming the millions of 'toy-like' home and office PCs into a formidable network by the mid-to-late 1990s. Net-connected PCs are currently estimated to be capable of hosting something like an aggregate ten billion megahertz of processing power and ten thousand terabytes of storage (Shirky, 2003). This is a scale of magnitude that far exceeds anything available to the centralized media industries, and moreover speaks directly to the elegant logic of network culture.

Music File Sharing: KaZaA, Gnutella etc.

Digital music technologies have profoundly changed the way that musical production and distribution are organized. Digital recording and mixing equipment, synthesizers, and sampling technologies, together with CDs, MP3 format, and digital radio as a distribution media, offer new logics of efficiency, fresh creative possibilities, and unforeseen distribution complications. But as important as these changes to the creation and distribution of music have been, digital technologies have also managed to put many of these same devices and capacities into the hands of ordinary consumers. The result has been a dramatic reinforcement of recorded music as a site of participatory activity, bringing to 'garage bands' near professional recording and mixing qualities, and even enabling certain forms of alternative distribution. Home-based musicians can achieve many of the same technical qualities that have heretofore been the exclusive domain of professionals, in some cases upsetting existing hierarchies and demystifying at least some benchmarks of distinction between professional and amateur.

But digital technologies, particularly of the P2P type discussed in this chapter, have done far more. They have radicalized distribution, making massive amounts of recorded music available to anyone with a computer and a modem, and they have done so at next to no cost, requiring neither elaborate digitalization projects nor massive storage facilities. Indeed, P2P applications in the form of music file exchanges such as the ill-fated *Napster* and *Audiogalexy*, together with their more robust siblings *KaZaA*, *Gnutella*, *FreeNet*, *Morpehus*, *Grokster*, and so on, have distributed the labour of sourcing and loading music, as well as of storing and dispersing it. And in the process, they have constructed a community built upon shared tastes, shared labours, and a shared notion of musical culture.

Among *Napster*'s many lessons, several are worth noting in the context of this chapter. Although best known for making vast stores of out-of-print recordings as well as the latest commercial releases available for free downloading, *Napster* (and its clones) was used by many fans to learn more about music and expand musical tastes. This was done in part by sampling unknown tracks, but it was also done by screening for particular taste formations and following their lead. If, for example, one repeatedly came across someone who seemed to share musical interests, one could look more closely at full range of that person's musical holdings, engage in chats, and have a reasonably good chance of learning about other music of probable interest. This process of learning from one another was one of the small 'rewards' that music file sharing systems offered both to users and providers, and it was one of the signs of community that this network displayed.

Another lesson from *Napster* appeared quite visibly in its final weeks. Once most copyrighted music had been blocked from *Napster*'s lists, one could find hundreds of examples of non-commercially produced music ranging from garages in New Jersey to home studios in Bangalore. Forms of music generally absent from American or European radio play lists or record shops such as Hindi techno or Kurdish hip-hop or perfectly competent rock bands suddenly appeared in force. *Napster* facilitated the global distribution of music regardless of its source, and once the commercial noise was removed from its system, the magnitude (both qualitatively and quantitatively) of these normally suppressed alternatives was revealed. The disciplinary control exercised by the recording, broadcast, and retail industries was broken, and in its place, nothing was too esoteric to stand shoulder-to-shoulder with industry hits.

Perhaps the most important lesson that *Napster* and its clones demonstrated, even if implicitly, had to do with pressing the definition of music. Particularly with regard to popular forms of music, one might legitimately question whether music is the product of a creative industry, a commodity, as argued by the RIAA, to be packaged and promoted through a closed circle of advertising, radio play lists, and retail placements. Or one might ask if it is expression, shared pleasure, and a freely circulating part of culture. Without taking the bait of the RIAA with regard to the assertion that the purchase of music equals the maintenance of musical culture, this fundamental question about the status of music, of culture, and their relation to community, was powerfully put by this P2P network. Although the audio-visual industries are currently embarking on an extraordinarily aggressive campaign to maintain their content cartel through their centralized control of software in the face of the threats posed by P2P networks, they are also in a state of near paralysis with regard to the use of new technologies. Setting aside the curious fact that some members of the cartel are also hardware producers (Sony for example), it is increasingly clear that the networked file sharing principle is visible in other technological platforms. The link between mobile telephones and MP3 exchanges has already been demonstrated, and scenarios for television selection and downloading technologies such as next-generation *TiVo* and *Replay* as well as gaming systems such as the next-generation *X-Box* all specifically address the user's ability to download programme content and exchange it with friends.

The film and television industry's response has been to enforce relatively low resolution digital formats until they can figure out a response, and meanwhile, to join with the music industry to both enforce and extend copyright protection, to engage in software encryption, and to push for legally mandated hardware controls. Yet, as previously mentioned in the case of the gaming community, other industries have seen the benefits of cultivating communities of users. Amazon, for example, has used the Internet not only as a medium for book sales, but as a site of exchange of reviews and recommendations, with readers writing and posting critical responses to books, generating ratings, and making recommendations for related reading. Readers effectively speak to one another, and as with file sharing systems, both exchange information and build up a sense of community. These developments, whether Amazon's customer-generated book reviews, or the file sharing practices once central to *Napster* or planned for the future of *TiVo* and the *X-Box*, all speak to a notion of new media that embraces networked communities, shared investment, and bottom-up creation of texts, and as such, constitute a clear 'added value' to more familiar scenarios about the advantages of digitalized production and distribution.

Collaborative News Networks: Kuro5hin, Slashdot etc.

For much of the past two decades, the newspaper world has sponsored research and conferences on the future of their industry in a digital age. Digitalization has wide-ranging implications for the processes of production and distribution. It facilitated a redefinition of markets, encouraging the spread of national newspapers such as *USA Today* and *The New York Times*, and encouraging the development of international papers such as *The Financial Times* and the *Wall Street Journal*. It transformed the nature of physical text production and distribution, reducing the need for certain types of employees and encouraging strategic consolidation. And, by the mid 1990s, Internet access effectively rendered public many of the once closed news channels (the so-called wire services - UPI, AP, Reuters, etc.) that newspapers traditionally relied upon for their reports. The industry's concern focused on this last point, and with it the broader question of how to best deal with the on-line environment. Questions proliferated regarding news presentation in a digital environment, strategies for reader loyalty, new business models, and future technological scenarios. And new questions began to be asked of the relationship of the news media to the public sphere. The newspaper, like local television and radio broadcasts, once helped to bind communities together by providing a common corpus of information and opinion. But on-line news services threatened to intensify the fragmentation already evident in the shift from broadcasting to 'narrowcasting' evident in many markets in the 1980s. The threat was twofold. First, readers might use their computers to read newspapers from outside the local or even national market, weakening the consensual function of the press not to mention its financial underpinnings. A recent example of this was the claim that British on-line newspapers such as the *Guardian Unlimited* or the *Independent* have gained millions of American readers in the wake of the 9/11 attacks, readers in search of sources freed from the nationalist agenda that so dominated the US press. Second, readers might use the capacities of the digital environment to select only those elements of the newspaper of interest to them - an eventuality catered to by some news services which provided the tools for the creation of 'the daily me'. Although marketed as one of the great advantages of on-line news delivery, the notion of a 'customized' newspaper designed for each reader's interests raised concerns about the fate of the common knowledge so essential in the construction of the public sphere and the functioning of democratic governments.

Rather less attention has been directed to the archiving functions possible in many on-line newspaper environments, functions that permit easy consultation with previous news coverage, and which stimulate a developmental and durational notion of public events - and their coverage - rather than the floating 'present' of most print sources. As well, the ease with which readers can 'clip' and e-mail articles of interest to friends, selecting and re-circulating the news, seems to be an under-appreciated dimension of the digital environment. And, if we are to judge by the actions of on-line newspapers, beyond focusing on 'the daily me', relatively few have bothered to investigate and take advantage of the interactive capacities provided by the Internet environment. A recent study of 100 US on-line newspapers indicates that fewer than twenty per cent have forums or chat spaces where readers can express their opinions or exchange views with one another; and fewer than thirty per cent bother to take polls of readers' opinions (Schultz, 1999). Each of these categories recalls the characteristics previously described under the rubric of 'participatory culture.' While the industry as a whole is investing considerable time and energy in thinking through its digital future, the conceptual framework seems decidedly entrenched in the old model of the print medium: a centralized source with a particular vision of the news and a particular house style radiates print as well as digital copies of its views. The reader is free to pick and choose stories of interest, but feedback or the development of a community of readers is not stimulated, nor is a questioning of the assumptions behind the news or journalistic practice.

Slashdot and *Kuro5hin*, the most prominent of a growing number of collaborative news networks, have changed all that. Just as the music file sharing activities of *Napster et al* pushed digitalization's uses well beyond cheaper, easier, and more accessible means of production to the notion of a community, so too does *Slashdot*'s notion of digitalization *vis-à-vis* the dominant thoughts of the newspaper industry (Chan, 2002). First, a few words on what these news sources are and how they operate. Founded in a college dormitory room in Holland, Michigan in the late 1990s as essentially a blogger site, *Slashdot* (appropriately subtitled, *News for Nerds*) culled together reports on computer technology from a variety of news, corporate, and other sources. The site's novelty *vis-à-vis* other early blogger sites was that it invited readers to respond to stories and provide their own links, most of which were in turn posted. *Slashdot* quickly attracted attention and evolved into a reader-written and reader-edited news forum, stabilizing at around a million unique reader-participants per month. Although in the case of *Slashdot* there is an editorial staff charged with ultimate control, in the case of the more radical *Kuro5hin,* editorial evaluation is undertaken by 'jury' of several hundred readers who are selected each week and asked to rate both news stories and the responses they generate. Given that hundreds of stories are vying for the top fourteen or so 'headlines' each day, and that a typical story is capable of generating approximately 1,200 responses (other reports, commentaries, etc.), this rating system is essential in order to give coherence to the mass of available information and opinion. The result is a rich mix of views and sources - some contradictory, some with unexpected connections or insights - regarding any particular issue, combined with the opinions of critics, participants, supporters, etc. of any given issue. Collaborative news networks have challenged the news industry on several fronts. They provide a seemingly viable model of an interest-based news community, one moreover, that makes use of low-cost distributed resources rather than high-cost centralized resources, and one that is largely de-hierarchized in terms of editorial authority and control, again in contrast to the elaborate hierarchies of most news organizations. The collaborative nature of such enterprises far exceeds the abilities of the individual investigative journalist or even journalistic team to research and prepare a story, both in terms of speed of production and the range of scope and resources (*Slashdot* and *Kuro5hin*, for example, although American in orientation, take full advantage of their global members, giving readers near instant access to the same story from Japanese, German, and Australian vantage points).

These examples point to the remarkable economic and newsgathering advantages of collaborative news networks over traditional news organizations. But even more profound implications are to be found in the social domain. *Slashdot, Kuro5hin,* and their clones conceptualize news as community based, as participatory, and as fundamentally social in construction. The community in this case is not necessarily derived from a territorial locality - the domain of the local or national press; and the news generated by this 'virtual' community, while serving its own purposes, may even run counter to the interests of the territorially-based public sphere in the sense that undesired reports and views are circulated. Another implication of socially grounded collaborative news networks regards the status of the journalistic endeavour as objective or near objective. Collaborative news networks by their very nature treat news as a complex process of competing views, data, and evaluative frameworks. Objectivist notions of the news are effectively subverted once different sources can be compared, or once the starting or ending point of an event is resituated, or once the documents upon which the news is based are themselves made available for readers. This redefinition of news and journalists goes to the very heart of long held conventions and professional practices. And it offers a new notion of a news community from a localized group fed more or less the same version of the truth, to a deterritorialized community of collaborators, searching for evidence, struggling for understanding, and debating the construction of the truth.

Linux and Open Source Software

Even Microsoft has begun to attend Linux conferences. The epitome of a hierarchized and centralized corporate software developer, concerned with maintaining its market domination and proprietary product, Microsoft has run head-to-head with Linux, an open source (decentralized, de-hierarchized) network-based provider of the same services. Over the past few years, the governments of Mexico and India have backed the shift of many operations to Linux-based (which is in turn Unix-based) systems; and Industrial Light and Magic shifted over to Linux-backed animation programmes for the appropriately titled *Attack of the Clones: Star Wars, Episode II* in a corporate climate where McDonalds, Shell, Chevron, Pixar, Dreamworks, Salomon Smith Barney, Morgan Stanley, and Credit Suisse First Boston have all recently moved significant parts of their technology infrastructure across to Linux. Perhaps the most notable Linux convert was Amazon, the world's largest online retailer, which last year told Wall Street that it had cut its technology budget by twenty-four per cent, or some $US 17 million per quarter, primarily by moving across to 'free' software (Davidson, 2002).

There are several reasons for this dramatic change. The profit incentive is clear enough, but so are the implications for start-ups or whole economic regions such as the Third World that would otherwise not be able to afford a full range of traditionally commodified software. But an equally compelling reason has to do with the speed with which Linux-based systems can refine themselves. In this regard, open source code has several advantages. First, its developers are spared the significant expenditures of energy that Microsoft and other developers of proprietary software are forced to invest in order to protect key parts of their systems from prying eyes. In the case of open source, the code is freely available and users are encouraged to explore, experiment with, and improve it. Second, Microsoft *et al*'s proprietary stance encourages centralized and hierarchized product development, selected flows of information, and top-down strategies for long term development.

Open source systems by contrast are largely horizontal, with users from different contexts and from around the world making refinements and suggestions based upon insights or needs. Much like collaborative news networks, it is difficult for a centralized operation regardless of its financial resources to compete with this global network of expertise. Moreover, open source software is appealing thanks to its (in computing terms anyway) aesthetics and its status as a community-constructed 'living' computational artifact - an appeal sufficiently altruistic that even engineers with day jobs for competing proprietary developers contribute their time and energy to these community projects. Developments like Linux are also consistent with the logic of a network environment. Computational needs, like the expertise that drives them, are dispersed across thousands of computers. Information is shared, problems are distributed, and massive resources (from human expertise to computing power) are drawn together with very low investment and high yields.

Transgression

As music file sharing networks, collaborative news networks, and open source software developments all demonstrate, a series of fundamental challenges have been mounted to the status quo and even to more recent assumptions regarding digital culture. The very definitions of cultural practices - music, news, software development, and intellectual property - have been put in question by these participatory networks. And the institutional practices behind them have to some extent been subverted, at least that is the claim of the Recording Industry Association of America (RIAA), the Creative Incentive Coalition (CIC), the Motion Picture Association of America (MPAA), and the World Intellectual Property Organization (WIPO), among others. In every case, these challenges have been powered by distributed PCs, bound together by collaborative networks, and given life by participatory communities of users/creators. A blurring of sorts has taken place, not only between producers and consumers as argued above with regard to participatory culture, but with regard to definitions of cultural practices.

Within the context of the territorial nation-state, the definitions of things like commercial music and intellectual property are clear; but in the context of the dispersed collaborative communities of *Gnutella* users, these definitions are far from self-evident. The question, then, particularly at a moment of complex appeals to identity, regards the choice of a framework for cultural citizenship. Those practices that take place in the globally networked on-line communities thus far discussed call upon enactments of cultural citizenship that are defined by high levels of participation. But the act of participation also brings with it a good chance of transgression - for the territorial nation state has long been the definer of regulatory power and the enforcer of legal code - and a strong measure of challenge to the status quo (Reidenberg, 1999). Citizenship in the nation-state, at least with regard to these issues, seems to be more a matter of obeisance to legal restrictions that define participation somewhat dully in terms of consumption, and that increasingly speak for the interests of concentrated media industries. At issue is the definition of culture, and the question of its status as a commodity and/or as a vital force in human creative communities.

How might we understand or even label the activities of citizens in this participatory culture? The investments of time and resources that members of these various participatory/collaborative communities make have variously been described with terms drawn from the existing economic order. 'Generalized Exchange' - best explained through the analogy of helping a stranded motorist not because one expects that person to reciprocate, but in hopes of reciprocation from some other member of the community should help be needed in the future - is one such description (Yamagishi and Cook, 1993), 'Gift Economy' is another (Kollock, 1999). Rooted in Marcel Maus's (1935) work in the mid 1930s, the relevance of the gift economy to Internet interactions has been underscored by Richard Barbrook's (2002) and Bell's (1999) suggestion of the historical involvement of scientists and academics with the net's development. We are accustomed to 'give' papers and take our pleasures in shaping discourse and being cited, rather than in making money with our ideas. Others such as Peter Kollock, have coined new terms such as 'digital goods,' transforming the notion of public goods to the virtual environment. One might even fall back on the Latin meaning of the term 'community' - to give to one another - as a way to inscribe these developments, and with them, the importance of participation to the enactment of cultural citizenship. As these developments continue to take form, one of our tasks will be to develop new language (representation, after all, is power). Another will be to consider the new de-territorialized regulatory systems that will inevitably emerge. I do not here mean the feeble attempts of AOL or Compuserve to crack down on terrorism or child pornography at the behest of the territorial state, but rather something along the lines suggested by David Johnson and David Post in their historical analogy to the development of the eleventh-century *lex mercatoria* ... the 'distinct set of rules that developed with the new, rapid boundary crossing trade of the Middle Ages.' (Johnson and Post, 1997, pp. 646-47).

Until these rules emerge, we are left facing a situation where the terms of participation in certain de-territorialized cultural communities run head to head with the terms of participation in territorialized political communities, where the terms of cultural citizenship run counter to the terms of political citizenship. This sort of conflict has been hinted at in the past. Consider the struggle of the Basque in Franco's Spain, where the terms of Basque cultural citizenship were in direct conflict with the terms of Spanish political citizenship. As in so many cases of territorial struggles for cultural rights, the government feared that the next step would be demands for a reformulation of political citizenship, and so chose to suppress cultural citizenship before things got out of hand. Perhaps this legacy, so much a part of every nation's history, informs the way that national governments have reacted to Internet-based cultural citizenship. In this sense, the virtual and the de-territorialized pose tangible challenges to the long-term autonomy of the real and territorial. We are little more than five years into these new forms of P2P cultural citizenship, and it is far too early to do more than suggest the nature of the impending conflict.

Effect and Affect

Throughout this chapter, I have argued that various instances of networked collaborative communities can be seen as constructions that cultivate, and indeed, depend upon, the practice of cultural citizenship. Before closing, it may be worthwhile to ask what uses can be made of networked technologies by existing political regimes? To what extent can we talk about network-facilitated political citizenship? Are there similarities of strategy with what we have seen of networked cultural citizenship? A nuanced mapping of various governmental initiatives is beyond the scope of this chapter, nevertheless two broad orientations can be distinguished. On one hand, there are initiatives such as UK-Online in the national sphere or ICE.gov (the International Center for Governance) or EDEN (Electronic Democracy European Network) in the trans-national sphere which seek to implement the process of governance either by offering an electronic means of renewing one's driving license or voting, or by offering space and resources to stimulate its promotion. These applications serve the functional ends of the governance process, and might be labelled by the condition they intend: *effect*. On the other hand, there are Internet sites closely allied with national interests that seek to create a virtual national community, a home away from home for the traveller, the migrant worker, or the recent emigrant. Initiatives such as 'virtual Scotland', 'virtual Argentina', and so on, might be considered in terms of the feeling they provoke: *affect* (see Boczkowski, 1999; Miller and Slater, 2000; and Elkins, 1997). In contrast to the more utilitarian or explicitly functionalist applications of sites of the effective variety, the affective sites seek to create, in Raymond Williams' terms, a structure of feeling - a sense of belonging, belief, and participation no matter how removed from the daily ebb and flow of political events.

Together, these twin strategies of affect and effect serve the interests of the state, facilitating the emotional and informational cohesion so important to identity, and contributing to the more mechanical processes of governance by enhancing speed, access and feedback. But these applications might be likened to the use of the Internet by current newspapers - an enhanced source of information, an efficient means of news processing, and a cheap and effective means of distribution. They are all advances on the status quo, and they all reflect the benefits of digitalization. But they fail to make use of the potential of network culture to construct a collaborative community or to redefine the meaning of 'governance' or 'citizenship' in ways that, to continue the analogy, *Kuro5hin* and other collaborative news networks have done for the news.

Graham Murdock offers an interesting argument regarding the challenges posed to citizenship by the 'shared culture of consumption'. He argues that it privileges personal spending over social and political participation, creating shoppers rather than moral communities; and that it equates social difference with variations in choice and style, negating any attempt to conceive of a common good based on negotiation of difference. While it would be too glib to link the emergence of this 'shared culture of consumption' with the decline in electoral activity and political debate evident in several developed nations, it is nevertheless an insight worth considering. Among the four conditions for pursuing 'the unfinished project of citizenship in the era of privatization,' Murdock argues that cultures 'must ensure that the full range of their services remains equally available to all. They must defend their status as public goods and resist their conversion into commodities.' (Murdock, 1999, p. 15). At a moment of unparalleled convergence in our industries of representation, the importance of the Internet-facilitated participatory communities as potential counterweights to cultural monopoly cannot be understated. As the artifacts that constitute culture continue to be trademarked and copyrighted, as news organizations continue their pattern of global mergers, and as our means of processing information risk falling into ever-larger corporate hands, we have evidence of a movement that has embraced these various cultural forms as public goods, and seems committed to making their full range of services 'equally available to all.'

The Latin roots of the term 'community' - of fellowship, of sharing - run counter to our economic logic with the same vigour that they apply to our cultural logic. Unfortunately, the heuristic distinctions that I have deployed for this chapter do not apply in the 'real' world; moreover, a long and important tradition of critical thought has explored the inevitable interdependencies of economics and culture. Yet, without seeking to align myself with the utopian euphoria of the 'Californian ideology' of Rheingold, Barlow, Dyson, et al., the P2P communities discussed in this chapter do seem to suggest that something very promising is possible, something that will enable cultural participation outside the framework of commodification. That said, a number of crucial questions remain.

Nevertheless, if we make the link between participatory culture as found in certain P2P communities and cultural citizenship, as this chapter does, several things follow.

First, certain cultural practices (particularly those associated with media industries at their historically most concentrated moment of development) are in the process of being redefined from protected commodities back to everyday culture. Second, the growth of P2P participatory networks seem consistent with a number of other structural changes in fields such as genetics, engineering, and energy as outlined by Pierre Lévy (1997, pp. 39-55) and are likely to have growing impact on how we think about culture. And finally, notions of 'electronic' democracy, citizenship, and governance need to shift from the rather thin models of on-line voting or license applications, to making fuller use of ideas taken from the more robust participatory communities that we can see in the cultural sector. Again, the changes upon which these consequences are based are extremely recent, dating back to transformations in technology that occurred five or so years ago. The challenge is to see what is possible, and to guard against the inevitable attempts to turn these developments back into the tools of the dominant political order. The fact that these developments are de-territorialized and virtual may assist in their survival in the territorial and real world. And the coincidence of an enabling philosophical discourse (post modernity) may add resonance and depth to what is unfolding (or at least it might confuse the enemy!).

Notes

1   Shirky's estimate is based on 100 million of the net's 300 million PCs, each with a 100 Mhz chip and a 100Mb drive.

2   This blurring even extends into the realm of networked culture. As evidenced by Amazon's reliance on open source software and its stimulation of a community of reader-reviewers, the traditional business community has not been slow to explore the possibilities of P2P applications. The adaptation process has sometimes missed the larger point - as Bertelsmann's attempted reworking of Napster suggests. Yet the development of viral marketing strategies testifies to the increasingly insightful use of participatory (but not necessarily P2P) networks in the interests of traditional business ends. Word of BMW's on-line films, featuring the work of directors such as Ang Lee, Guy Ritchie, and John Frankenheimer, and starring an automobile, is sent from person to person rather than being promoted by BMW itself. YaYa's viral campaign is based on the circulation of on-line computer games, elegantly compressed to work smoothly even on 56K modems. The games require certain choices - the selection of Nike sportswear or certain features on a GM car - at which point the player can engage in a skiing competition or car race, in turn sending the results to friends, and thus spreading the advertisement or marketing query on to an ever-larger circle of friends. Such developments demonstrate, as if

such demonstration were needed, that networked technology has no inherent radicalizing or even transgressive qualities.

3   The sense of functionality implied here is quite broad, and could include the persuasive use of the Internet in the sense of political advertising or even lobbying. My point is not to offer a refined definition of various functionalities, but rather to point to directions or tendencies in the use of the Internet in the political (and particularly governance) sphere.

References

ARENA [Advanced research on the Europeanization of the Nation-State] (2002)

http://www.arena.uio.no/news/bulletins/CIDELNews.html

Arjun Appadurai (1996) Modernity at Large: Cultural Dimensions of Globalization. Minneapolis: University of Minnesota Press.

Bagdikian, Ben H. (1997) The Media Monopoly. Boston: The Beacon Press.

Barbrook, Richard (2002) 'The High Tech Gift Economy' in First Monday.

Bell, Duran (1991) 'Modes of Exchange: Gift and Commodity' Journal of Socio-Economics. 20(2), pp. 155-167.

Billig, Michael (1995) Banal Nationalism. London: Sage.

Boczkowski, Pablo (1999) 'Mutual Shaping of Users and Technologies in a National Virtual Community' in Journal of Communications. (Spring), pp. 86-108.

Brooker, Will (2002) Using the Force: Creativity, Community and Star Wars Fans. New York: Continuum.

Chan, Anita J. (2002) 'Collaborative News Networks' MSc Thesis, MIT.

Davidson, John (2002) 'Free Spirited Linux is Still Open for Business' Financial Review. 20 February 2002. http://afr.com/specialreports/report1/2002/02/20/FFXL7UF5TXC.html

Delanty, Gerard (2002) 'Two Conceptions of Cultural Citizenship: A Review of Recent Literature on Culture and Citizenship: A Review Essay' in The Global Review of Ethnopolitics. 1(3), pp. 60-66.

Donald, Stephanie Hemelryk (2001) 'History, Entertainment, Education and jiaoyü: A Western

Australian Perspective on Australian Children's Media and Some Chinese Alternatives' in The International Journal of Cultural Studies. 4(3), pp. 279-299.

Elkins, David (1997) 'Globalization, Telecommunication, and Virtual Ethnic Communities' International Political Science Review: RISP. 18(2), pp. 139-153.

Garnham, Nicholas (1986) 'Contribution to a Political Economy of Mass-Communication' pp. 9-32 in Richard Collins, et al., (Eds.), Media, Culture and Society: A Critical Reader. London: Sage.

Hebdige, Dick (1987) Cut and Mix. New York: Routledge.

Hobsbawm, Eric and Terence Ranger (1984) The Invention of Tradition. Cambridge: Cambridge University Press.

Jenkins, Henry (1992) Textual Poachers: Television Fans and Participatory Culture. New York: Routledge.

Jenkins, Henry (2003) 'Interactive Audiences?' pp. 157-170 in Dan Harries, (Ed.), The New Media Book. London: British Film Institute.

Johnson, David and David Post (1997) pp. 644-657 'The Rise of Law on the Global Network' in Brian Kahin and Charles Nesson, Borders in Cyberspace. Cambridge: MIT Press.

Kollock, Peter (1999) 'The Economies of Online Cooperation: gifts and public goods in cyberspace' pp. 220-239 in Marc D. Smith and Peter Kollock, Communities in Cyberspace. London: Routledge.

Lévy, Pierre (1997) Collective Intelligence: Mankind's Emerging World in Cyberspace. Cambridge: Perseus Books.

Maus, Marcel (1935/1969) The Gift. London: Routledge and Keegan Paul.

McChesney, Robert (1999) Rich Media, Poor Democracy: Communications Politics in Dubious Times. New York: The New Press.

Meehan, Eileen. (1991) '"Holy Commodity Fetish, Batman!" The Political Economy of a Commercial Intertext' pp. 47-65 in Roberta Pearson and William Uricchio, (Eds.), The Many Lives of the Batman: Critical Approaches to a Superhero and His Media. New York: Routledge, 1991.

Melucci, Alberto (1989) Nomads of the Present: Social Movements and Individual Needs in Contemporary Society. London: Hutchinson Radius.

Miller, Daniel and Don Slater (2000) The Internet: An Ethnographic Approach. New York: New York University Press.

Miller, Toby (1998) Technologies of Truth: Cultural Citizenship and the Popular Media. Minneapolis: University of Minnesota Press.

Minar, Nelson (2001) Distributed Systems Typologies: Part One. http://www.openP2P.com/pub/a/P2P/2001/12/14topologies_one.html

Murdock, Graham (1999) 'Rights and Representations: public discourse and cultural citizenship' in Jostein Gripsrud, Television and Common Knowledge. London: Routledge.

Poschardt, Ulf (1998) DJ Culture. London: Quartet Books, Ltd.

Rheingold, Howard (2000) The Virtual Community: Homesteading on the Electronic Frontier. Revised Edition. Cambridge: MIT.

Reidenberg, Joel (1999) 'Governing Networks and Rule-Making in Cyberspace' pp. 79-87 in Brian Kahin and Charles Nesson, (Eds.), Borders in Cyberspace: Information Policy and Global Information Infrastructure. Cambridge: MIT Press.

Roche, Maurice (2001) 'Citizenship, Popular Culture, and Europe' pp. 74-98 in Nick Stevenson, (Ed.), Culture and Citizenship. London: Sage.

Rosaldo, Renato (1994) 'Cultural Citizenship in San Jose, California' in PoLAR, 17(2), pp. 57-63.

Schultz, Tanjev (1999) 'Interactive Opinions in Online Journalism: A Content Analysis of 100 Online US Newspapers' in Journal of Computer Mediated Communication. 5(1) http://www.ascusc.org/jcmc/vol5/issue1/schultz.html

Shirky, Clay (2003) 'What Is P2P and What Isn't?' http://www.openP2P.com/pub/a/P2P/11/24/shirky1-whatisP2P.html

Stevenson, Nick, (Ed.) (2001) 'Culture and Citizenship: An Introduction' in Stevenson pp. 1-10, Culture and Citizenship. London: Sage.

Thompson, E. P. (1968) The Making of the English Working Class. Harmondsworth: Penguin.

Wasko, Janet, Mark Phillips & Eileen R. Meehan (2001) Dazzled by Disney? The Global Disney Audiences Project. London: Leicester University Press.

Williams, Raymond (1960) Culture and Society 1780-1950. New York: Columbia.

Yamagishi, Toshio and Karen Cook (1993) 'Generalized Exchange and Social Dilemmas' in *Social Psychology Quarterly*. 56(4), pp. 235-248.

Sabina Mihelj is a member of the junior faculty of the Institutum Studiorum Humanitatis – Ljubljana Graduate School for Humanities. She has participated in a range of research projects dealing with media and culture in Slovenia and the wider region, and is currently in the final year of her doctoral research project. Her major research interests include the role of media in post-Cold-War transformations in Eastern and South Eastern Europe, with a particular emphasis on nationalism and the dissolution of Yugoslavia.

Sabina Mihelj

Negotiating European Identity at the Periphery: Media Coverage of Bosnian Refugees and 'Illegal Migration'

Introduction

Entering the last decade of twentieth century, Europe found itself involved in two logically opposed, yet curiously interlinked processes. To the West of the vanishing iron curtain, nation-states were engaged in establishing a supranational union. Simultaneously, the existing supranational structures positioned to the Eastern and South-Eastern margins of the rising European Community were rapidly disintegrating. Paradoxically enough, the European integration itself was used to legitimize the tearing apart of already existing supranational unions. Throughout the late 1980s and early 1990s, the political elites and the mainstream mass media in Slovenia - the only former Yugoslav republic that survived the violent break-up of the federal state without much scarring - were framing the process of gaining independent statehood in terms of exiting 'the Balkans'[1] and entering 'Europe' (Rupel, 1997; Bakić-Hayden and Hayden, 1992). However, the presence of a growing number of refugees after the outbreak of the war in Bosnia and Herzegovina (Doupona, Verschueren, Žagar, 2001) was a disturbing sign of the fact that 'the Balkans' were not as far as the prevailing rhetorical frame would have it. In order to retain the consistency of this frame, most mass media would employ a number of strategies which effectively put distance between Slovenians and Bosnians, including representing Bosnian refugees as Slovenia's negative mirror image, as an intrusion of 'the Balkans' into 'Europe'.

At the turn of the millennium, having successfully distanced itself from 'the Balkans' and undertaken negotiations for EU membership, Slovenia was -

according to the mass media - endangered by a new 'tide of migration'. This time, the wave did not originate in 'the Balkans', but further away in 'the East', where countless individuals, driven by poverty and oppressive political regimes, decided to search for a better life in 'the West'. From existing analysis one can infer that media representations of both 'Bosnian refugees' in 1992 and 'illegal immigrants' in 2000/2001 activated very similar interpretative frames. Indeed, the object of media representations - 'illegal migrants' - again functioned as a focus point for negotiating Slovenia's own identity, including its relationship to 'Europe'. However, the symbolic mapping underlying media reports on 'illegal migration' revealed an importantly different positioning of Slovenia. Far from being unambiguously positioned on the side of 'Europe', Slovenia was now referred to as the 'rampart' or 'threshold' of the West, caught between the 'proper West' (i.e. the European Union) and the menace of 'the East' (including 'the Balkans'). While representing 'Bosnian refugees' and 'illegal migrants', media in Slovenia were thus also involved in renegotiations of Slovenia's relationships with its neighbouring nations as well as broader regions, including Europe.

One of the main aims of the chapter is to track these changes in Slovenia's symbolic positioning (and identity) by examining the way the issues of 'Bosnian refugees' and 'illegal migration' were framed in mass media representations, as well as to point to the ways in which these changes in framing were coinciding with developments in the political field. The question of how a European space and identity gets moulded by media inside European Union itself was already addressed by various authors (Schlesinger, 1991; Morley and Robins, 1995; Meinhof and Richardson, 1999 to name just a few), while the question of the role of a European identity for countries positioned at the outskirts of EU remained marginal. The present paper is thus also an attempt to fill this gap by providing a case study for Slovenia. In the concluding sections, special attention will be paid to the attribution of responsibility (scapegoating 'the West') connected with the changes in symbolic positioning of Slovenia at the turn of millennia.

Theoretical Underpinnings

The most important theoretical pillar underpinning the chapter consists of the interdisciplinary field usually called symbolic or cultural geography, which finds its main reference in Edward Said's seminal work on *Orientalism* (1978). Said's critique of orientalism was immensely influential in the last two decades; research agendas in many scientific disciplines were redefined with respect to it. Yet, it was also extensively criticized, even severely condemned (Ahmad, 1992). Thus, I am applying the notion of *orientalism* only after rereading it through the lens of subsequent critiques, paying special attention to developments that went against ahistorical and essentialising tendencies and were ramifying the initial conceptual framework in order to account for specific regions, collectives and their histories of changing borders - particularly Eastern Europe, the Balkans, Central Europe and the territory of former Yugoslavia (Wolff, 1994; Todorova, 1997; Bakić-Hayden and Hayden, 1992; Gingrich, 1998).

The understanding of identity adopted in the chapter follows the *actionist perspective* which 'requires us to see collective identity not as a prior condition of collective action but rather as a continually constituted and reconstructed category,' (Schlesinger, 1991, p. 173). Far from being just passive mirrors of this on-going process of constitution and reconstruction, mass media are actively involved in it, contributing to the reality of a given collective by invoking appropriate collective references and recreating the continuity of a the collective over time and across space. Accordingly, the understanding of *nation* adopted in the chapter is not one that sees nations as pre-existing, fixed and bounded realities, nor does it deem nation-states to be a *sine qua non* of social organization. Contrary to that, nation is understood as a phenomenon of recent historical origin (Gellner 1987, 1998; Hobsbawm, 1983), and as an imaginative social construction (Anderson, 1983; Brubaker, 1996) which is undergoing constant change and appropriation and is never fully unitary (Verdery, 1996).

Finally, taking media representations of 'Bosnian refugees' and 'illegal migration' - i.e. two instances of *migration* - as a starting point to discuss the issue of Slovenia's changed positioning and identity was not a random choice. When faced with a new or unexpected phenomena, the role of collective representations, including media representations, is to anchor the phenomenon in something familiar, to integrate it into an existing mental universe (cf. Jodelet, 1991, p. 52). However, migration presents a serious challenge to the existing mental (as well as, necessarily, institutional) universe characteristic of modern societies after the industrial revolution. This universe takes nations to be a *sine qua non* of every social organization, and is based on what L. Malkki (1997) calls *sedentarist metaphysics*. The latter consists of a set of taken-for-granted ways of thinking about identity and territory based on a naturalised identity between people and place and an implicit assumption that the world should be composed of sovereign, spatially discontinuous units. Yet, migrants often seem to disregard the linkages to places assumed to be 'theirs' and want to settle down in another place. Thus, when taking into account migration, the 'world of nations', conceived as a discrete spatial partitioning of populations 'rooted' in territories, becomes a highly inaccurate way of representing the world. Consequently, various institutions engaged in the process of naturalizing the national order of things, including the mass media, have to invent a range of policies and interpretative frames to preserve the integrity of such an order of things.

Media necessarily rely on established repertoires of references shared by their audiences, but also have the choice to *select* and *connect* them into interpretative frameworks with relative freedom, supporting some frames while avoiding others. Or - to apply what some authors dealing with communication inspired by writings by Erving Goffman (especially his *Frame analysis: an essay on the organization of experience*, 1974) see as a potential new paradigm - media necessarily get involved in *framing*. According to Robert M. Entman, to frame is 'to select some aspects of a perceived reality and make them more salient in a communicating text, in such a way as to promote a particular problem definition, causal explanation, moral evaluation, and-or treatment recommendation for the item described' (Entman, 1993, p. 52). Making selected bits of information more *salient* (i.e. more noticeable, meaningful or memorable) enhances the *probability* (yet does not *guarantee*) that receivers will perceive the information, discern the meaning and store it in memory. The probability increases if the frames are provided by those media that are conceived as an authoritative source of information, as well as if the frames interlock with those provided (and possibly quoted in media) by other institutions holding authority in a given society (representatives of the state, science etc.).

Following the broad definition of *collective representation* as 'a mental act by which a subject relates itself to an object', and by which this object acquires meaning for the subject (Jodelet, 1991, p. 37) - but also, we should add, by which both the object and the subject get constituted -, the chapter has two main threads. One is dealing with elements of media representations primarily linked to the *object* ('Bosnian refugees' and 'illegal migrants'), the other focuses on those frames that primarily constitute the *subject/addressee* of these same media representations (mostly, yet not exclusively, Slovenians and/or Slovenia). However, this division is far from being sharp: as will become evident through the exposition of results, constituting the object necessarily involves also constituting the position of the subject (the ideal recipient or addressee).

Research Strategy and Limitations of the Database

In his questioning of xenophobia and racism on television, Jérôme Bourdon argued that '[t]he praiseworthy approach of pointing out 'incidents' and 'excesses' of all kinds - in other words, overt and avowed racism - is bound to be insufficient,' (Bourdon, 1995, p. 23). Following his argument, both the selection of focus periods and media to be analysed as well as the choice of the research strategy was conducted in such a way as to avoid focussing only on most obvious examples of xenophobic or racist treatments of refugees and migrants. The two periods in focus are the year 1992 (March to December), when the peak of migration of war refugees from Bosnia occurred, and the period from September 2000 to May 2001, when 'illegal migration' was on the prime-time agenda. In both cases, key events such as political agreements, public demonstrations etc. were taken as orientation marks for defining the time-slots most suitable for analysis. Yet, in order to include also an analysis of specific trends in media coverage that might have led to the outburst (or silencing) of the 'crisis', the focus periods were extended to include periods before and after the most disputed events.

In accordance with the concept of framing as sketched above, the analysis focuses on specific elements of media texts which are involved in framing, such as naming and labelling, compartmentalizing, archiving and showing. These elements are to be scrutinized as possible indicators of Slovenia's changing positioning *vis-à-vis* Europe. The analysis predominantly involves a comparison along the diachronic axis, i.e. it compares representations of 'Bosnian refugees' in 1992 to representations of 'illegal migration' in 2000-2001. However, the comparison along the diachronic axis is at some points complemented by the comparison along the synchronic axis in order to provide a comparison of different media with regard to the their proximity/distance to mainstream framing.

Among four main television channels in Slovenia, attention was paid to just those two of them that produce daily news programmes: the first channel of *TV Slovenija* (*TVS1*) and *Pop TV*. Out of all television genres, only news programmes were analysed, and among those, bulletins broadcast in prime-time were of highest interest. Among the news programmes of *TVS1*, almost all daily news bulletins were covered, including the prime-time bulletin starting at 7:30 p.m. and the evening news appearing in the 10 p.m. slot, as well as the chronicle of local and regional news broadcast before the prime-time bulletin. For the limited period of the escalation of the crisis (November 2000 to February 2001), the weekly programme *Tednik* (*Weekly*) was also analysed, a news programme with high viewing share and a tabloid character. *Pop TV*, since founded in 1995, did not yet exist when the refugees from Bosnia were in focus. However, in autumn of 2000, when the 'illegal migration crisis' entered the media stage, their daily news bulletin *24ur* (*24 hours*) starting at 7.15 pm was already a well-established and widely watched part of the programme. *Pop TV*'s news bulletin was not covered as extensively as the news programmes broadcast by *TVS1*; it was analysed systematically only in the period from 29 January to 21 February. In the case of print media, all major daily press was covered: the nationwide *Delo* (*Work*) and *Slovenske novice* (*Slovenian News*), the region-centred *Večer* (*Evening*) and the city-centred *Dnevnik* (*Daily*) for both periods, the nationwide *Republika* (*Republic*) and *Slovenec* (*A Slovenian*) just for 1992, since they both ceased to exist in 1996. A selection of periodicals was also taken into account: national ones such as *Mladina* (*Youth*) and *Mag* and regional ones such as *Primorske novice* (*News of the Littoral*). Before looking at the results of the analysis and their interpretation, it is necessary to place all the selected media into the context of changes and continuities in the Slovenian media landscape in the 1990s.

Slovenian Media Landscape Before and After the Dismemberment of Yugoslavia

Contrary to what has happened in some other countries inside the former Eastern block (cf. Giorgi et al., 1995), the largest part of the Slovenian press market is held by a small number of local owners, and is not substantially controlled by large European and American corporations. Three out of four still existing daily newspapers in focus (the nationwide *Delo*, the region-centred *Večer* and the city-centred *Dnevnik*) originate from the period of Yugoslavia. Except for *Slovenske novice*, which took an explicit sensationalist approach to news making and succeeded in attracting a wide enough audience, all three other nationwide dailies formed after 1990 (*Slovenec*, *Republika* and *Jutranjik*) failed. In 2001, companies publishing *Delo*, *Večer*, *Slovenske novice* and *Dnevnik* controlled more that ninety per cent of the daily newspaper market.

The situation regarding television in Slovenia at the turn of the millennium may best be described in terms of a duopoly. In 2001, eighty-one per cent of viewers in Slovenia watched the four main national channels, two public (*TVS1* and *TVS2*) and two commercial ones (*Pop TV* and *Kanal A*). The remaining nineteen per cent watched mainly Austrian, Italian and Croatian programmes (Bašič Hrvatin, 2002, p. 71). As opposed to the press, the developments in the sphere of television in Slovenia are similar to those in Central and Eastern Europe. The real progress of commercial television begun in 1995, when *Pop TV* and *TV3* were introduced. Given its offer of cinema and television hits, the rating of *Pop TV* soon exceeded that of *TVS1*, and also its prime-time news bulletin *24ur,* which attracted the audience by sensational news and life-stories of 'common people', proved to be a serious competitor to the prime-time news bulletin broadcast by *TVS1*. The figures for TVS1 average annual shares of viewing from 1996 to 2001 reveal that prime-time viewing fell from slightly over forty per cent in 1996 to slightly over twenty-five per cent in 2001 (Bašič Hrvatin, 2002, p. 69).

From the point of view of central issues here addressed, it is important to note that the Slovenian media, although formerly functioning in a political formation that integrated many different nations, did not have to imagine their national community from scratch. During the 1960s and 1970s, the political power in Yugoslavia was devolved from the central (federal) organs to the six republics (Bosnia-Herzegovina, Croatia, Macedonia, Montenegro, Serbia and Slovenia) and two autonomous provinces within Serbia (Kosovo and Vojvodina) and their respective branches of the League of Communists of Yugoslavia. At the same time, the media were also decentralized; they were (with the exception of a few pan-Yugoslav media) controlled at the republican level and were increasingly geared for republican audiences (cf. Thompson, 1994, pp. 5-7). What set Slovenian media apart from other Yugoslav media (with the exception of Macedonia) was also the fact that they produced contents only in Slovenian, a language incomprehensible to most of the remaining Yugoslav audiences (Bašič-Hrvatin, 1996, p. 16). Therefore, it should be clear that during the establishment of a fully sovereign state, the Slovenian media did not have to change their ways of reporting, modes of address and ways of imagining the addressee that drastically (cf. Vogrinc, 1996, p 13).

Such an understanding of relationships between media and nations in Yugoslavia partly coincides with the arguments of various scholars dealing with nationalism in Yugoslavia that seem to agree that Yugoslavia never succeeded in becoming a melting pot, moulding previously separate nations into one, Yugoslav nation (Djilas, 1995, p. 85; Banac, 1995, p. 118). Yet, this should not lead to claims that the fall of Yugoslavia was an *inevitable* outcome of either 'ancient hatreds' suppressed during communism or the specific federal structure adopted in 1974. The disintegration was a process requiring specific economic and political interests reinvoking the hatreds as well as appropriated references shared by wider masses, previously inculcated by educational and cultural policies (cf. Wachtel, 1998, pp. 14-18). The mass media was a crucial player in these processes, especially with regard to selection, specific combination, interpretation and strengthening of existing collective references and frames. The analysis presented below unveils some of the references invoked in framing the issues of 'Bosnian refugees' and 'illegal migration' in Slovenian mass media - especially those appertaining to the realm of symbolic geography -, and shows how they were used to make sense of the events, ascribe responsibility and legitimate solutions.

Mapping the Subject and the Object

The symbolic mapping implicit in media representations was unveiled primarily by means of an analysis of labels and phrases appearing in connection to various entities of the symbolic map: individual countries ('Slovenia', 'Croatia', 'Italy', 'Austria' etc.) as well as wider regions ('Europe', 'the Balkans', 'the East', 'the West'). The analysis was predominantly qualitative and consisted of grouping the labels and phrases with regard to their denoted and connoted meanings, taking in account also their position in the chapters and news items (labels and phrases appearing in titles and in topic sentences of news items were regarded as more indicative).

Mapping 'Bosnian Refugees': Exiting 'the Balkans', Entering 'Europe'

In 1992, the symbolic mapping present in media representations of 'Bosnian refugees' included two main, opposing, entities: 'Europe' and 'the Balkans', the first being equated with Western Europe, the second with republics of former Yugoslavia. Most media representations were sharply demarcating Slovenia from 'the Balkans' and placing it into 'Europe', and thus paralleled the developments in the political arena. After gaining international recognition, Bosnian refugees, as well as those Slovenian politicians and intellectuals arguing for a less sharp departure from 'the Balkans' (their views were most often appearing in *Mladina*) were represented as prolongations of 'foreign' ('Balkan') interests. The policy measures aimed at settling the 'refugee problem' supported this frame: refugees were preferably held in centres far from main roads, city centres and tourist attractions, their freedom of movement was restricted and they were not allowed to work. It could thus be argued that the Europeaness of Slovenia was literally negotiated through Bosnian refugees: if Slovenia was to prove its Europeaness, Bosnians had to be kept out of sight and remain complete strangers. Finally, in August 1992, the Slovenian government, claiming that 'all possibilities in the Republic of Slovenia for accommodating and caring for temporary refugees are exhausted' (quoted in Doupona, Verschueren and Žagar, 2001, p. 26), closed the borders to refugees.

This symbolic travel from 'the Balkans' into 'Europe', and the concomitant framing of Bosnians, was supported by developments initiated long before 1992. As already pointed out, press and broadcasting systems in Yugoslavia were, for the most part, increasingly regulated from within the republics from the late 1960s, and they already had their nationally defined imagined communities. However, reports on events happening within the respective republic were regularly complemented by substantial blocs of reports on events from other republics. As far as television news is concerned, in the moments of crisis at the end of the 1980s, this general pattern did not change - the only change appeared on the level of length, since the bulletins grew longer and tended to consist predominantly of Yugoslav news (Vogrinc, 1996, p. 14). Contrary to that, the press was already changing significantly. While Yugoslavia was falling apart in the press, television continued to portray the symbolic universum of a homogeneous state, and it was the last medium to allow opposition speakers on the screen (Bašić Hrvatin, 1996, p. 158). But the really sharp changes - obviously sharper in television than in the press, which is again consistent with developments in Poland, Hungary and Czech Republic (L. Giorgi et al., 1995) - came in 1990/91, in the period marked by the plebiscite for independence (held on 23 December 1990) and the *Declaration of Independence* (adopted by the Slovenian Assembly on 25 June 1991). In this period, the amount of space in the prime-time news bulletin on *TVS1* dedicated to the rest of Yugoslavia was sharply reduced, news from the former fraternal republics categorised as 'foreign news' and preferably reported by *TVS* resident correspondents (Vogrinc, 1996, p. 14). It can be said that from that point on, the relationship between press and television with regard to placing Slovenia onto the symbolic map was reversed. Television took the leading role in drawing Slovenia out of 'the Balkans', while the press was more often representing voices calling for a more active Slovenian attitude towards 'the Balkans', arguing that Slovenia should take advantage of having a better knowledge of this space than most Western European states.

Mapping 'Illegal Migration': Slovenia as the 'Threshold of the West'

At the turn of the millennium, the relative roles played by press and television remained roughly the same: television would foster mainstream arguments, while the press would present a wider range of perspectives. From existing analysis (Žagar, 2001; Kuhar, 2001; Jalušič, 2001) one can infer that mainstream media activated interpretative frames very similar to those appearing in the case of Bosnian refugees. Media, politicians and sometimes even humanitarian organizations (like the Slovenian Red Cross in 1992) alike were using metaphors from the realm of natural phenomena or catastrophes (the refugee tide, swamped over...), describing 'Bosnian refugees' as well as 'illegals' as belonging to a different civilisational and cultural level, observing different behavioural patterns, disrupting the habits of the local population, being potential criminal offenders, bringing tensions etc. In other words, the object of media representations - 'illegal migrants' - again functioned as a focus point for negotiating Slovenia's own identity, including its relationship to 'Europe'. And again, mainstream media reports and prevailing rhetoric used by representatives of the state (first and foremost the police and Ministry of Internal Affairs) supported each other in legitimating the introduction of restrictive measures such as limiting the freedom of movement. Yet, in contrast to media representations of 'Bosnian refugees', media reports on 'illegal migration' revealed an importantly different map - not least because it comprised larger portions of the world and was, in a sense, global - as well as a much more ambiguous positioning of Slovenia *vis-à-vis* Europe.

The main division reiterated the mapping known from the Cold War period, dating back to the Enlightenment: 'the West' was opposed to 'the East' (cf. Wolff, 1994). 'The West' subsumed Europe as conceived in 1992 (as Western Europe or EU) and was usually even equated with it, while 'the Balkans' are seen as one element in the hierarchy of entities constituting 'the East'. Furthermore, 'the Balkans' were no longer conceived simply as an opposite to 'Europe', but were characterized by ambiguity, transition, contradictions, in-betweenness, liminality. As such, these representations fit into the discourse of *balkanism* as identified by Maria Todorova, formed gradually in the course of two centuries and crystallised with the Balkan wars and World War I (Todorova, 1997). It is hardly a surprise that the route along which illegal migrants were coming was persistently represented as the 'Balkan route', connected also with other kinds of illegal trafficking, especially drugs. A further important point is that the recurrent symbol of 'the Balkans' in this mapping was 'Bosnia' and especially Sarajevo airport, represented as the main opening for the influx of illegal migrants. Moreover, journalists rarely forgot to mention that Bosnia, as 'traditionally open to Islam countries', does not have visa requirements for them. Thus, contrary to representations in 1992, Slovenia was no longer pictured as endangered by the influx of 'the Balkans', but by the influx of 'the East' - arriving *through* 'the Balkans'.

The mapping emerging here can partly be conceived in terms of what Milica Bakič Hayden and Robert M. Hayden called a system of *nesting orientalisms*, in which 'there exists a tendency for each region to view cultures and religions to the south and east of it as more conservative and primitive' (Hayden, 1992, p. 4). From this point of view, the hierarchy of 'Bosnian refugees' and 'illegal migrants' can be seen as a prolongation of the political rhetoric that 'since the late 1980s has revolved around constructions that claim a privileged 'European' status for some groups in the country while condemning others as 'Balkan' or 'Byzantine', hence non-European and Other,' (Hayden, 1992, p. 5).

Another suitable concept to account for the above-sketched hierarchy of Oriental Others is the concept of *frontier orientalism* coined by Andre Gingrich. This 'complement to or a variant of orientalism in general' is, in his view, a distinctive feature of folk cultures in (roughly) the southern parts of Central Europe, which made up the central domains of the Habsburg Empire: eastern Austria, Hungary, north-eastern part of Italy and Slovenia. It is a 'folkloristic glorification of decisive local military victories in past times, either against Muslims or together with Muslims, but serving present nationalist purposes, and it places the home country and its population along an adjacent territorial and military borderline which is imbued with a timeless mission,' (Gingrich, 1998, p. 119). Among key structural elements of frontier orientalism as conceptualized by Gingrich, two are of particular relevance to the analysis presented so far: the Good Muslim Oriental (the Bosnian) and the Bad Muslim Oriental (the Turk). The hierarchy established between 'Bosnian refugees' and 'illegal migrants' may be seen as a variation of this dual image of the Other. This thesis is supported also by the overrepresentation of Turks with regard to actual proportions of migrants coming from Turkey (to be discussed in more detail in following sections).

It may well be that what is arising here is a reworking of a definition of Europe to which Islam, rather then Communism, is now seen to supply the Eastern boundary (cf. Schlesinger, 1991, pp. 189-190; Morley and Robins, 1995, p. 80). Yet, it is important to note that in the map underpinning media representations of 'illegal migration' in 2000/2001, Slovenia was no longer positioned unambiguously on the side of Europe. Rather, it shared many qualities otherwise recognised as 'Balkan'. First and foremost, it was consistently represented as a transit point between West and East, a neither-here-nor-there land, caught between two large bodies exerting pressure on it: the West and the East (metaphors and phrases ascribing such a position to Slovenia appeared in almost every article or news item). However, contrary to the discourse of Balkanism as conceptualized by Todorova (1997, p. 15), Slovenia was not represented as the *crossroad* or *bridge* between East and West. Rather, it was referred to as 'the rampart of the West', 'the waiting-room of European Union', the '*cordon sanitaire* of Europe' and the wall which is bound to protect Europe from the tide of migrants coming from the East. This difference can be interpreted as a consequence of the discourse of frontier orientalism intervening into the discourse of Balkanism.

Before proceeding to changes in the attribution of responsibility, appearing together with above described changes in the symbolic positioning of Slovenia, I will first turn to the analysis of a selection of other elements of media representations contributing to the overall mapping as described above.

Positioning the Subject by Constituting the Object

Besides explicit symbolic positioning of Slovenia by using labels referring to geographical units such as 'East', 'West', 'Europe' or 'the Balkans', the above depicted symbolic mappings were supported also by a range of other elements of media representations that are not so obviously linked to geography. In the following sections, I examine four such elements of media representations: naming/labelling and showing the object, compartmentalising and archiving news items.

Naming and Labelling the Object

Names and labels are usually so strongly identified with their referents, so deeply embedded into common sense and thus 'obvious', that their arbitrary nature largely passes by unnoticed. However, names, labels and words in general do not describe independent, pre-existing things; rather - to rephrase the title of John L. Austin's famous book (1962) - words actually *do* things. Of course, not *any* words - for an utterance to acquire a performative power, the authorisation of a legitimate institution which has access to symbolic resources is needed (Bourdieu, 1991, p. 109; cf. Melucci, 1989, for a similar argument on naming). Mass media with nationwide audiences and highest viewing rates or circulation are certainly well equipped to provide such institutional conditions; the words used by them can thus easily achieve the power to *create* things, to bring them into existence (cf. Bourdieu, 1996, p. 19). This power is even greater if the naming they provide is left unchallenged by other, alternative media, and if it is used also by other authoritative institutions in a given society. For the purposes of the present chapter, the frequency of names and labels referring to war refugees from Bosnia and non-registered migrants in all the titles of all articles appearing in the focus periods was analysed. The sample included main titles, subtitles as well as short paragraphs summarising the main points of the article directly below the title. In the case of *TVS1*, the data base consisted of partial transcriptions with brief descriptions of news items appearing from 1990 to 2001 collected in a specialised computer-based archive. The news bulletin *24ur* could not be fully included in the analysis, but the pattern retrieved for the limited period in focus is in tune with the general pattern of changes discerned in other media.

As Igor Ž. Žagar observes, in 2000/2001 the media virtually never used the term 'refugees' when talking about immigrants, regardless of the fact that the use of the term was in accordance with the UN Convention on refugees and the definitions in the Geneva Convention. Rather then 'refugees', migrants were most often labelled as *'ilegalni migranti'* (illegal migrants), *'ilegalci'* (illegals), *'tujci'* (foreigners) or by using the peculiar term *'prebežniki'* (or, most often, *'ilegalni prebežniki'*) (Žagar, 2001, p. 7). The qualitative analysis of these terms gives a good entry point for the discussion of the reasons for the shift in naming which occurred in the 1990s. The noun *'prebežniki'* is derived from the verb *'bežati'*, the same one from which also the Slovene word for refugee is derived (*'begunec'*), and it means 'to run away' or 'to escape'. But an important difference is introduced by the prefix pre-, which implies that the people referred to as *'prebežniki'* did not run away with the intention to come *to* Slovenia and stay *in* the country. Contrary to that, their goal was to flee *through* or *over* Slovenia to reach a place somewhere else. Therefore, already the labelling of the object contributed to the specific mapping of Slovenia described in previous sections: the use of the label *'begunci'* constituted Slovenia as the ultimate final destination of migration, while the label *'prebežniki'* presented it as a transitory space, a space in-between.

Two other frequently used labels - *'ilegalci'* or *'ilegalni migranti'* - carry explicitly negative connotations: they classify the people as criminal offenders, place them out of the safe world regulated by laws (e.g. Slovenia), and do not imply any connection to fleeing from something and/or seeking asylum. Contrary to that, the labels *'azilanti'* and *'prosilci za azil'* (asylum seekers) have a rather neutral denoted meaning. Yet, since journalists were frequently stressing that the asylum was just a *cover up*, *abused* by migrants who did not want to stay in Slovenia but reach one of the Western European countries, the two labels acquired a negative connotation. In print media, this connotation was reflected in the frequent use of quotation marks; the asylum seekers were labelled as 'asylum seekers', i.e. as not real asylum seekers. The possibility of such subtle shifts in the meaning of labels, largely dependent on specific contexts, need to be taken in account when looking at changes in the quantity of different labels over time.

The quantitative analyses of titles in print media revealed a basic shift in labelling which occurred uniformly in *all* press media considered. In 1992, people fleeing from the war in *BiH* were, with hardly any exceptions, named 'refugees', while the migrants in 2000-2001 were most frequently referred to with labels 'foreigners' or *'prebežniki'* (both terms were used in roughly one third of cases), 'illegals' or 'illegal migrants' (in about twenty to twenty-five per cent of cases), and the label 'refugees' appeared in only about fifteen per cent of all cases. The same shift can be discerned also in news items broadcast by *TVS1*. In January 2001, the use of the labels 'illegals' and 'illegal migrants' decreased in favour of the label *'prebežniki'* and 'foreigners'. This, however, was most probably not due to a conscious change of attitude or heightened level of awareness of the power of naming among journalists. Rather, it was a consequence of the fact that due to a concerted action of Non-Governmental Organizations (NGOs), police ceased to be the central authoritative source of information on non-registered migration. Rather, the issue became a top priority on the main political agenda, and the prevailing labels shifted accordingly; the migrants were no longer seen solely in terms of criminal activity and security, but in terms of citizenship and asylum. Again, the media simply followed the labelling used by the main authoritative institution providing information: initially, they would most often turn to the police, while from January on, they would more often turn to the highest representatives of the Ministry of Internal Affairs, as well as to the NGOs. Relying on the police was characteristic especially of television; while television journalists would turn to the police in roughly one third of the cases, press journalists would do so in twenty per cent of the cases.

An additional level of naming that contributes to the constitution of distance between the addressed audience (generally, Slovenians) and respective objects is the use of individual names instead of collective labels (this part of the analysis was made just for *TVS1*). Again, labelling without individual names was much more persistent and widely present in the case of 'illegal migrants' than in the case of 'Bosnian refugees', thus instituting a greater distance between the addressee and 'illegal migrants' than between the addressee and 'Bosnian refugees'. Again, the share of individual names in reports on illegal migration increased in January 2001, parallel to the decrease in the share of labels such as 'illegals' and 'illegal migrants' and thus parallel to the move of the topic of non-registered migration from the realm controlled by the police onto the main political agenda.

Compartmentalising the Object

The way each medium presents its news compartmentalized into a few 'naturally given' thematic fields, sequenced hierarchically in time with the more important usually at the beginning, is another well-known strategy which contributes to the naturalization and objectivation of media representations. The compartmentalization into rubrics was analysed just for daily news bulletins and daily press, since others do not have comparable structures of rubrics.

Roughly, the changes in compartmentalization followed the main shifts regarding the 'refugee problem' in the political field. From April to July of 1992, i.e. in the period of the first major condensation of media attention to 'Bosnian refugees', articles and news items about refugees would mostly appear on pages or inside segments of news bulletins dedicated to 'internal affairs'. In October and November, when refugees again became a hot issue (they would appear as one of the most important topics in campaigns for parliamentary elections), 'internal affairs' was still the prevalent rubric. However, from September 1992 on, articles and news items would very often appear also in rubrics dedicated to education. This was linked to the fact that a separate education system for refugee children was being organised in Slovenia, held in their 'mother tongue' (cf. Doupona Horvat, Verschueren, Žagar, 2000, p. 36). Another rubric into which articles and news items about refugees were more and more frequently put from September on was culture. The unifying trait of articles and news items appearing both under 'culture' as well as 'education' was the reduction of refugees to their culture and/or collective identity. Namely, both education and cultural activities were presented as means of *preserving* their culture/identity. A concomitant aspect of this seemingly tolerant perspective was the neglecting or even repulsion of refugees who did not want to stick to their presumed collective roots and would rather mix indistinguishably with the host society. Thus, one could say that by representing the refugees as culturally different, the media were playing a central role in hindering the integration of refugees into the host society. What is more, the difference between the two collectives was often represented in terms of religion, i.e. Christianity and Islam. Therefore, distancing the subject (as well as the addressee), i.e. Slovenians, from the object, i.e. 'Bosnian refugees', was not just a matter of instituting a difference between two nationalities, but much more a matter of drawing a distinction between different civilizations and, *intera alia*, between 'Europe' and 'the Balkans'.

Throughout 1992, articles and news items about refugees only rarely appeared in crime-related rubrics, although allusions to refugees as potential crime-offenders were appearing quite often. Contrary to that, 'illegal migrants' entered the media stage in a completely different manner, which again coincided with the main approach taken with regard to the issue in the political field. In the initial period of the escalation of 'crisis' (September-November 2000), up to seventy-five per cent of articles and news items about migrants were published as parts of regular police chronicles, and in about eighty per cent of news items journalists turned to the police for information. Such a compartmentalization had similar effects as the use of the labels 'illegals' and 'illegal migrants'; namely it identified migrants as criminal offenders and placed them out of the safe world regulated by laws. Another important difference with regard to media representations of 'Bosnian refugees' was the fact that news about 'illegal migrants' almost never appeared in rubrics dedicated to education and culture. This is an indication that they were less intensively treated with reference to their specific collective identity, but rather simply as foreigners, indistinguishable among each other. This thesis is supported also by the results of analysis of classification used by professional archivists working in archives inside particular publishing and broadcasting institutions.

Archiving the Object

The categorization of articles and news items followed in media archives is crucial for the establishment of long-term, institutional memory. As such, it can be read as another indication of the interpretative framework shared by journalists and editors of a given medium. The analysis took into account the time span from 1990 to 2001, and considered the two largest media archives in Slovenia - the archives of TV Slovenia and archives of the publishing house Delo. Contrary to news items and articles about Bosnian refugees, which were mostly classified under the larger heading of 'Bosnia and Herzegovina' or 'Bosnia', most news items about 'illegal migrants' were not classified with reference to their source country. This can partly be explained by the fact that archivists in 1992 still followed the classifying structure established in the times of Yugoslavia, where each republic had a separate and amply differentiated heading, while rubrics dedicated to other countries were not so well differentiated. A further possible explanatory factor is that 'illegal migrants', as opposed to 'Bosnian refugees', mostly appeared in mixed groups comprising people from different countries, which made a classification according to their source country too time-consuming to be applied.

A counter-argument can be found in an aspect of naming and labelling that was not mentioned in the previous section: the distortions in representation with regard to the source countries and nationalities of migrants involved. Although (in the period in focus) Iranians were by far the most represented nationality in actual statistics provided by border police, the proportion mentioning Turkey and Turks reaches almost the same level as the proportion mentioning Iran and Iranians. Another strong distortion in representation was that the reported numbers of Chinese migrants were four times greater than the actual statistics. What is encountered here can adequately be conceptualised using the distinction of *elaborated and limited codes* (Eco, 1996, pp. 155-157). In the absence of an elaborated code, journalists based their representations on limited codes that were melding very different people together to make them suit those few images of the Other that were long segmented in collective memory in Slovenia. The fact that 'illegal migrants' were perceived as importantly different from Bosnian refugees called for representations referring to more distant Others, and the most suitable ones appeared to be the Turks and the Chinese. However, this does not yet explain why archivists would turn to exactly such a limited code - involving Turks and Chinese - in the first place. In order to provide an answer to this explanation, it is useful to differentiate between the *internal other* (or, to use a term employed by Maria Todorova, *alter ego* - cf. Todorova, 1997, pp. 18-19) and the *external other*. Despite perceived cultural, especially religious differences, 'Bosnian refugees' are still regarded as somehow similar - they appertain to the same, i.e. Slavic race -, and can thus fulfil the role of the internal other. Contrary to that, 'illegal migrants' are perceived as completely different and thus fulfil the role of the external other.

Showing the Object

Amongst all media, television - or, more specifically, television news programmes, - received additional attention in the analysis. Although both press and television used roughly the same ways of constituting the object of representation, television was most influential in terms of the wider population, since it is by far the most important source of information for most Slovenes (Toš et al., 1997). Furthermore, it could be argued that television played a specific role in developing a sense of being placed (as a member of a collective) in space. In common-sense perceptions as well as in many scientific approaches, the *differentia specifica* of television - as compared to other forms of mass media - is deemed to be the presence of visual signs, especially moving images. If we accept the general classification of signs into those crucially linked to time (roughly, audio signs) and those decisively linked to space (roughly, visual signs) (Saussure, 1997, p. 84; Mounin, 1999, p. 36), the importance of television, as well as newspaper photographs, for developing a sense of being placed in space, can hardly be a surprise. What is more, state borders proved to be a much more attractive object of representation for television than for the press: among items on 'illegal migrants', 13.9% of them were dealing with developments at the border, while in the press, only 3.4% of articles were taking borders as the central issue. And among the latter, most were longer reports with photos, which is a further argument in support of the thesis that visual representations play a central role in constituting a sense of being placed into a territory with clearly established borders.

Anchoring is probably the best term to define a series of strategies by means of which the relationship between the sender, the object of representation and recipient gets constituted. Many of them are not common to all media, and I will focus mainly on some of them which are specific for television news: the role of the anchor person (the absence/presence of reporters), the selection of 'spots' where reports are made, the use of objects as symbols of something else (e.g. war or chaos) and the role of the camera's movement.

According to Jože Vogrinc, an important factor in enhancing the imagined distance between Bosnia and Slovenia via television was the absence of a resident correspondent. During the escalation of war in Croatia in 1991, *TVS* relied heavily on its own special reporters from the frontline, as well as resident correspondents. When in spring 1992 the war in Bosnia broke out, *TVS* reversed its previous policy and recalled reporters from Bosnia as well as Kosovo. This withdrawal strongly inflected the discourse of the central news bulletin: because *TVS* 'is not there', because it has no representatives at the heart of the matter, by virtue of its monopoly of representation of Slovene viewers, *Slovenes are not directly involved* (Vogrinc, 1996, p. 15).

Absence of resident correspondents apart, when the war in Bosnia and

Herzegovina escalated, *TVS1* was still following the events regularly and in much detail, which could at least potentially contribute to a stronger solidarity with refugees. Contrary to that, when 'illegal migrants' became a hot issue, a much greater distance separated them from addressees. Reports on 'illegal migrants' only occasionally got coupled with information on the situation in their source countries, which could contribute to the representation of them as refugees and not just plainly 'foreigners' or 'illegals'. Among news items in bulletins on *TVS1* in 1992 dealing (at least partly) with Bosnian refugees, over a third of them appeared as part of reports on actual developments in Bosnia. In comparison to that, only one per cent of news items dealing with illegal migrants in 2000-2001 were explicitly addressing the situation in their source countries. A fact linked to that is that illegal migrants were not commonly used as a *symbol* of war or deteriorating social and economic conditions in their countries. This is another difference with regard to Bosnian refugees, which were consistently represented in such a manner (Bašič Hrvatin, 1996, p. 18).

A further aspect of televisual representations contributing to framing on the visual level is the movement of the camera, connected also with the selection of scenes, including lights and sounds. As Steven Heath argued when writing about narrative space in cinema, what is moving is not simply the camera, but the spectator (Heath, 1996, p. 353). Actually, the movement of the camera is, on the level of visual signs, a functional equivalent of personal pronouns on the level of linguistic signs, and can thus be seen as a visual complement of verbal deixis which constitute the banal nationalism as defined by Michael Billig (1995). Furthermore, by constituting the relationship between object and addressee, the movement of the camera also contributes to the organization of space, its division into 'home' and 'foreign'. When analyzing smaller samples (six items for each 'period of crisis') of news items from this point of view, important differences were recognised between representations of 'Bosnian refugees' and 'illegal migrants'. In the case of the latter, the distance between object and subject/addressee was intensified by the use of sharp oppositions between light and darkness (the latter being associated with 'their', 'foreign' spaces on the other side of 'our' border), and, in some cases - especially in the weekly, yellow-press *Tednik* on *TVS,* by use of music evoking fear. 'Bosnian refugees' would mostly be shot at the border in daylight, from relatively close to. Contrary to that, news items about 'illegal migrants' often included shots of woods and empty, muddy roads in darkness. These were taken from police vehicles during their regular border controls in the night, and when cameras came across migrants, these would frequently be shot from afar. In this way, the movement of the camera also contributed to the constitution of a specific positioning of and relationship between the addressee (Slovenians) and the object ('Bosnian refugees'/'illegal migrants'). By showing 'illegal migrants' consistently in connection with visual signs that carry negative connotations (darkness, mud, emptiness), and in the absence of other explicit explanations, it supported the attribution of responsibility for the situation to 'illegal migrants' themselves. Such a frame of attribution of responsibility was virtually the only one provided by media in the first phase of the 'illegal migration crisis' (September-December 2000). Later, frames attributing responsibility to the Slovenian State or, most often, to 'the West' or 'Europe' complemented it. It is this aspect, connected to the already described changes in symbolic mapping, that will be the focus of the rest of the chapter.

Scapegoating 'the West'

As argued before, media representations of 'illegal migration' in 2000/2001 constituted Slovenia as a land 'in-between', caught between 'the East' and 'the West'. Contrary to the prevalent mapping drawn by media representations of 'Bosnian refugees' in 1992, 'the Balkans' now no longer played the role of the absolute Other, since this position was reserved for 'the East'. Rather, 'the Balkans' now functioned as a despised Alter Ego, i.e. a part of the self which is pictured as negative and neglected. At the same time, however, Europe no longer played the role of a *positive* dominant Ego-image, i.e. a part of the self pictured as worth aspiring to, but was instead acquiring rather negative overtones - while nevertheless keeping the dominant position. Therefore, it is not enough to say that Slovenia, when it came to screening the South and the East, adopted the 'Western gaze' (itself an often essentialized category in texts exploring orientalist and similar discourses, including Said's), since it was an object of that same gaze too. To understand the whole complexity of the mapping, one should look also for manifestations of a specific internalization of and/or repulsion from these same orientalizing and Balkanizing discourses. These internalizations can be explored as elements of a discourse that could be referred to as *occidentalism* and can be further ramified similarly as orientalism (i.e. one can talk about *nesting occidentalism* and *frontier occidentalisms*).

One of the most persistent elements of this discourse as appearing in media representations of 'Bosnian refugees' as well as 'illegal migration' is homogeneity. For example, when comparing Slovenia to other countries, the media would most often talk about 'European' or 'Western' policies towards migration *en bloc*, without pointing to differences between measures employed in specific countries. While from inside of the European Union, media programmes such as *EuroNews* have problems addressing their viewers as Europeans - all deictic references still point to respective national spaces (cf. Meinhof and Richardson, 1999, pp. 75-86), the Slovenian media seem to have no second thoughts when presenting Europe and its inhabitants as a unified entity. This is an argument supporting the thesis that it is not so much 'the West' itself who is producing an imbalanced picture of the world inside which one, homogeneous West is opposed to a range of different Orients (Near East, Middle East, and Far East). Rather, such a map might be a product of various subjects self-conceived as Oriental, who, while trying to 'enter the West', tend to picture it as homogeneous, stretching its borders to include themselves into it, while at the same time also excluding immediate neighbours towards the East and South and thus producing additional hierarchies in representations of the Orient. From this point of view, the tendency to point to 'the West' as the sole source of orientalizing discourses can function as an excuse for one's own exclusivism, shifting the responsibility onto another subject ('the West'). This is, I believe, the backbone of most of the *quid-pro-quo* rhetoric employed in East and Southeast European countries when dealing with migration. By claiming Europe is the one exerting pressure on it to become an effective filter for migration, Slovenia, along with other countries at the margins of EU, is believed to be legitimized to introduce more restrictive regulations and, if necessary, close its southern and eastern borders.

But while the homogeneity of 'the West' or 'Europe' is a feature persisting in media representations of both 'Bosnian refugees' and 'illegal migration', the overall value of this entity changed considerably. Contrary to 1992, when the prevailing connotations connected with Europe were positive, in 2000/2001 the West was presented as ambiguous. This is most clearly evident in print media, where the words 'Europe' and 'the West' regularly appear together with the adjective 'promised' or the phrase 'promised land' put into quotation marks. Since these are a marker of distancing a certain speaker in relation to the statement (they *derealize* what is said), such a use of quotation marks expresses a doubt towards 'Europe' and 'the West'; the positive character of this part of the world is challenged. The main argument appearing alongside such attitudes is that 'the West' no longer keeps to its own standards of democracy and liberalism; when faced with the influx of migrants, they tend to close their borders. With regard to this point, no media in Slovenia is an exception; all of them picture Europe in mixed tones, claiming its liberalism and openness to be a fake.

Parallel to changes in the overall representation of Europe/the West, the character of relationship between Slovenia and Europe/the West was also substantially changed. While in the 1992, Slovenia was predominantly represented as a 'long lost' part of Europe now returning to where it always belonged, in 2000/2001 'the West' was no longer uniformly pictured as an entity Slovenia would like to enter at any cost. 'The West', especially the EU, was now increasingly seen as the prime cause of the 'illegal migration crisis': attracting migrants with its wealth yet denying them entrance upon arrival and forcing countries at its outskirts to perform the role of a *cordon sanitaire*. Inside such a map, Slovenia appeared as an innocent victim of both the wave of migrants, themselves deluded by images of a prosperous West, as well as the pressures of the 'fortress Europe', reluctant to accept the migrants. Only rare journalists - usually those writing for the periodical *Mladina* or individual journalists writing for *Delo* - were countering the prevailing representations and pointing to the fact that Europe is not such an impermeable fortress.

In 2001, after months of gradually increasing, media-supported xenophobia and Euro-scepticism, loosely organised groups of intellectuals, supported by a couple of non-governmental institutions as well as branches of international organizations, managed to challenge the above described mainstream framing of 'illegal migration'. To an extent, they even succeeded to force alternative frames onto both the media and the government. They were demanding a public denunciation of xenophobia and calling for implementation of policy measures that would enable Slovenia to cope with the phenomenon of non-registered migration in accordance with democratic standards, avoiding human rights violations. The public protests, taking place in the capital of Ljubljana in February 2001 coincided with the election of the new ombudsman, a gesture that was meant to represent government's willingness to fulfil the expectations voiced by the protest, and thus its acceptance of alternative frames. However, although rejecting some of the central characteristics of mainstream frames - the normalization of xenophobia and blaming the victims - these developments left the basic mapping unveiled in the paper almost intact, including the attribution of responsibility to 'Europe'. Such a frame was discernible in statements given by the co-organisers of the public manifestation and quoted in news bulletins and press articles, as well as in their publications appearing in the aftermath of the crises (for example Milohnić, 2001).

Moreover, when the 'crisis' was over, mass media soon re-established the same frames of reference. In May 2001, when police again supplied journalists with data on illegal migration, mass media activated similar frames as in early phases of 'illegal migration crisis', with the sole exception that now, the 'crisis' was a matter of the past. This shows that the alternative frames were accepted by mainstream media only when supported already by the central political power structure.

Conclusion: The Recurrence of Peripheral Nationalism?

To summarize, mass media regularly used discourses of Balkanism, orientalism (especially frontier orientalism) and occidentalism, and the discourse of peripheral nationalism to frame the issue of both 'illegal migrants' as well as 'Bosnian refugees'. By selectively invoking certain frames appertaining to the realm of symbolic geography, and therefore by (re)positioning Slovenia with regard to different geographical units and collectives such as 'Europe', 'the Balkans', 'East' and 'West', they also played an important role in shaping the political processes, including the legitimization of xenophobic policies and attitudes. For the most part, they uncritically echoed or supported the frames offered by different authoritative institutions, especially the police and the Ministry of Internal Affairs. This was characteristic especially of television news, while alternative frames would most often appear in the press, especially the non-mainstream print media and those not explicitly conceived as nationwide media.

In media representations of 'Bosnian refugees' in 1992, 'Europe' mostly figured as unambiguously positive, while Slovenia was positioned inside 'Europe' and sharply divided from 'the Balkans'. Contrary to that, the map drawn by media representations of 'illegal migration' in 2000/2001 pictured 'Europe' (equated with EU), as well as 'the West' in general, in ambiguous tones. Slovenia was now positioned on the outskirts of Europe, as a neither-here-nor-there land caught between 'the East' (including 'the Balkans') and 'the West'. As such, it frequently appeared as an innocent victim of requirements imposed by the EU as well as the pressure of migration 'from the East'. The latter was itself explained as a phenomenon provoked by 'the West', which attracted the migrants by claiming to follow liberal standards, yet denying them access when they actually arrive. As a future member, obliged to follow the rules set by 'the West', Slovenia was presumably forced to become a *cordon sanitaire* of 'fortress Europe'.

Arguably, the specific mapping arising in media representations of 'illegal migration' is not an unprecedented novum, but resembles the positioning (and thus identification) of the Slovenian nation at various points in its history. Early Slovenian nationalism as formed in the nineteenth-century - national 'awakening' according to nationalist accounts - is close to the ideal type of *peripheral nationalism*. This is a type of nationalism which, according to the typology of nationalism suggested by Michel Hechter (2000), occurs when a culturally distinctive territory resists incorporation into an expanding state, or attempts to secede and set up its own government. Often this type of nationalism is spurred by the very efforts of another type of nationalism, *state-building nationalism*, which is embodied in the attempts to assimilate or incorporate culturally distinctive territories into one state.[2] Slovenian nationalism developed primarily in opposition to - but also, to a large extent, in alliance with - one such state-building efforts, namely the Habsburg Empire (and later mainly the Austrian part of the Empire). However, although perpetuating an ambiguous relationship towards the Habsburg Empire, the central Other against which Slovenian nation was defined was the Ottoman Empire (and later the Turks). Later, the Slovenian nation was reshaped in opposition to other state-building efforts in the region. On the basis of the analysis presented above it can be argued that a similar logic of defining the national identity - against a dominant Ego-image (not necessarily always pictured as positive) on one hand, and against a despised alter-Ego, i.e. an internal Other, as well as an external Other, on the other hand - is reproduced also in recent media discourses. Among functional equivalents of the Habsburg Empire one can list 'Europe' and 'the West', while 'the Balkans' as well as all the competing nationalisms that developed South of Slovenia, occupy the position of the internal other (the despised alter-Ego), and 'the East' receives a position structurally similar to the Ottoman Empire. Such a mapping of nation can easily be used to support policies that foster multiculturalism, as well as to form a position critical of any of the geographical entities and thus political formations involved, including those playing the role of the dominant Ego-image. However, the mapping can also be selectively activated - as in the case of 'illegal migration' - in order to voice criticism, that is in turn used as an instrument for shifting responsibility and as an excuse for one's own xenophobic attitudes and policies.

As the example of media coverage of 'illegal migration' shows, discourses supporting a negative attitude towards 'the West', especially as a part of the discourse of peripheral nationalism, can easily be reactivated. Therefore, one could expect that when tackling with domestic problems, scapegoating the EU might serve as a ready-made framework for attribution of responsibility in the future as well, especially if the transfer of a part of sovereignty onto the EU will be perceived as a loss rather than gain. Whether and how political actors in Slovenia will return to the discourse of peripheral nationalism upon Slovenia's accession to the EU, defending 'their people' from 'the foreign state', and whether and to what extent mass media will support the same discourse, remains to be seen.

Notes

1   Names, labels and phrases commonly appearing in media are among the aspects of media representations analysed further on in the article. In order to distinguish them from analytical categories introduced later, all such common labels are be cited in quotation marks.

2   Michael Hechter appertains to the range of authors who take distinct cultures (and with this nations) as given, or at least do not deal with the question of how these cultural distinctions were formed in the first place, and thus take an importantly different epistemological position compared to the one chosen in the paper. Therefore, his typology is employed with a reservation; rather than seeing it as a typology of nationalisms developed according to the process of their historical formation, it is taken as a typology of nationalist representations of these processes - representations that are in function of geopolitical structures established at the time of the formation of these narratives themselves.

References

Ahmad, A. (1992) In Theory: Classes, Nations, Literature. London in New York: Verso.

Anderson, B. (1995 [1983]) Imagined Communities. London and New York: Verso.

Austen, J. L. (1962) How to do things with words. Oxford. Oxford University Press.

Bakić-Hayden, M. and Hayden, R. M. (1992) 'Orientalist Variations on the Theme 'Balkans'; Symbolic Geography in Recent Yugoslav Cultural Politics', Slavic Review. 51(1), pp. 1-15.

Banac, I. (1995) 'Nationalism in South-Eastern Europe', in C. A. Kupchan (Ed.) Nationalism and Nationalities in the New Europe. Ithaca and London: Cornell University Press.

Bašič Hrvatin, S. (1996) 'Slovenia and Croatia', in J. Gow, R. Paterson, A. Preston (Eds.) Bosnia by Television. London: British Film Institute.

Bašič Hrvatin, S. (2002) Serving the State or the Public? The Outlook for Public Service Broadcasting in Slovenia. Ljubljana: Peace Institute (Media Watch).

Bašič Hrvatin, S. and Milosavljevič, M. (2001) Media Policy in Slovenia in the 1990s. Regulation, Privatization, Concentration and Commercialization of the Media. Ljubljana: Peace Institute (Media Watch).

Billig, M. (1995) Banal Nationalism. London, Thousand Oaks and New Delhi: Sage.

Bourdieu, Pierre. (1991[1982]) 'Authorized Language: The social conditions for the effectiveness of ritual discourse' in Pierre Bourdieu: Language and Symbolic Power, translated from French by Gino Raymond and Matthew Adamson, Cambridge, Oxford: Polity Press.

Bourdieu, Pierre. (1996) Sur la Télévision. L'émprise du journalisme. Paris: Raisons d'agir.

Bourdon, J. (1995) 'Foreigners on prime time or is television xenophobic?', translated from French by P. Ridel, in C. Franchon and M. H. Vargaftig, European Television and Ethnic Minorities. London: John Libbey & Company Ltd.

Brubaker, R. (1996) 'Rethinking nationhood: nation as institutionalized form, practical category, contingent event', in Nationalism reframed. Nationhood and the National Question in the New Europe. Cambridge, New York, Melburne: Cambridge University Press, pp. 13-22.

Djilas, A. (1995) 'Fear Thy Neighbour: The Breakup of Yugoslavia', in C. A. Kupchan (Ed.) Nationalism and Nationalities in the New Europe. Ithaca and London: Cornell University Press.

Doupona Horvat, M., Verschueren, J. and Žagar, I. Ž. (2001 [1996]) The Pragmatics of Legitimation. The Rhetoric of Refugee Policies in Slovenia. Ljubljana: Peace Institute (Media Watch).

Eco, U. (1996 [1985]) 'How Culture Conditions the Colours we See', translated by M. Blonsky, in P. Cobley (Ed.) The Communication Theory Reader. London and New York: Routledge.

Entman, R. M. (1993) 'Framing: Toward Clarification of a Fractured Paradigm'. Journal of Communication. 43(4), pp. 51-58.

Gellner, Ernst (1987) Nations and Nationalism. Oxford: Basil Blackwell.

Gellner, Ernst (1998) Nationalism. London: Phoenix.

Gingrich, A. (1998) 'Frontier Myths of Orientalism: The Muslim World in Public and Popular Cultures of Central Europe', in B. Baskar and B. Brumen (Eds.), MESS: Mediterranean Ethnological Summer School, Piran-Pirano, Slovenia 1996, Vol. 2. Ljubljana: Inštitut za multikulturne raziskave.

Giorgi, L. and Pohorles, R. J. (1995) The Post-Socialist Media: What power the West? The Changing Media Landscape in Poland, Hungary and Czech Republic. Aldershot, Brookfield USA, Hong Kong, Singapore and Sidney: Avebury.

Goffman, E. (1986 (1974() Frame analysis: an essay on the organization of experience. Boston Notheastern University Press.

Heath, S.1996 [1981]) 'Narrative Space', in P. Cobley (Ed.) The Communication Theory Reader. London and New York: Routledge.

Hechter, M. (2000) Containing Nationalism. Oxford and New York: Oxford University Press.

Hobsbawm, E., Ranger, T. (Eds.) (1983) The Invention of Tradition. New York: Cambridge University Press.

Jalušič, V. (2001) 'Ksenofobija ali samozaščita. O vzpostavljanju nove slovenske državljanske identitete' in B. Petkoviç (Ed.) Poročilo skupine za spremljanje nestrpnosti 01. Ljubljana: Mirovni inšitut (Media Watch).

Jodelet, D. (1991 [1989]) 'Répresentations sociales: un domaine en expansion', in D. Jodelet (Ed.) Les répresentations sociales. Paris: PUF.

Kuhar, R. (2001) 'Zagrabiti in izgnati. Vzorec ksenofobičnega diskurza v Slovenskih novicah', in B. Petković (Ed.) Poročilo skupine za spremljanje nestrpnosti 01. Ljubljana: Mirovni inšitut (Media Watch).

Malkki, L. H. (1997) 'National Geographic: the Rooting of People and the Territorialization of National identity among Scholars and Refugees', in A. Gupta, J. Ferguson (Eds.) Culture, Power, Place. Duke University Press.

Melucci, A. (1989) Nomads of the Present. London: Hutchinson Radius.

Meinhof, U. H. and Richardson, K. (1999) Worlds in Common? Television Discourse in a Changing Europe. London and New York: Routledge.

Milohnić, A. (2001) Evropski vratarji. Migracijske in azilne politike v vzhodni Evropi. Ljubljana: Mirovni inšitut (Politike).

Morley, D. and Robins, K. (1995) Spaces of Identity. Global Media, Electronic Landscapes and Cultural Boundaries. London and New York: Routledge.

Mounin, G. (1999 [1970]) Introduction à la sémiologie. Pariz: Les éditions de minuit.

Rupel, D. (1997) 'Slovenia's Shift from the Balkans to Central Europe', in J. Benderly, E. Kraft (Eds.) Independent Slovenia. Origins, Movements, Prospects. Houndmills, London: Macmillan.

Said, E. (1995 [1978]) Orientalism. London: Penguin Books.

Saussure, F. de (1997 [1916]) Predavanja iz splošnega jezikoslovja, translated by B. Turk. Ljubljana: ISH - Fakulteta za podiplomski humanistični študij (Studia Humanitatis).

Schlesinger, P. (1991) Media, State and Nation. London and New York: Sage.

Thompson, M. (1994) Forging War. The Media in Serbia, Croatia and Bosnia-Herzegovina. Article 19, International Centre against Censorship.

Todorova, M. (1997) Imagining the Balkans. Oxford and New York: Oxford University Press.

Toš, N. et al., (1997) Slovensko javno mnenje 1997/1. Ljubljana: Fakulteta za družbene vede, CJMMK.

Verdery, K. (1996) 'Whither "nation" and "Nationalism"?', in Gopal Balakrishnan (Ed.) Mapping the Nation. London, New York: Verso, pp. 226-234.

Vogrinc, J. (1996) 'Close Distance. Dilemmas in the Presentation of the War in Bosnia in the Daily news Bulletin of TV Slovenia', in J. Gow, R. Paterson, A. Preston (Eds.) Bosnia by Television. London: British Film Institute.

Wachtel, A. B. (1998) Making a Nation, Breaking a Nation. Literature and Cultural Politics in Yugoslavia. Stanford, California: Stanford University Press.

Wolff, L. (1994) Inventing Eastern Europe. The Map of Civilization on the Map of the Enlightenment. Stanford, California: California University Press.

Žagar, I. Ž .(2001) 'Foreword to the 2nd edition', in M. Doupona Horvat, J. Verschueren and I. Ž.

Žagar, I. Ž (2001 [1998]) The Pragmatics of Legitimation. The Rhetoric of Refugee Policies in Slovenia. Ljubljana: Peace Institute (Media Watch).

Kim Christian Schrøder (http://akira.ruc.dk/~kimsc/) is Professor of communication at Roskilde University, Denmark. He is co-author of *The Language of Advertising* (Blackwell, 1985) and *Researching Audiences* (Arnold, 2003), and co-editor of *Media Cultures: Reappraising Transnational Media* (Routledge, 1992). His research has dealt with discourse analysis and reception analysis of advertising and televised serial fiction. He has published widely on the theoretical and methodological aspects of qualitative audience research. His current research deals with political discourses and the media in a combined text/audience perspective.

Kim Christian Schrøder

Mapping European Identities: A Quantitative Approach to the Qualitative Study of National and Supranational Identities

A remarkable story is unfolding in Europe. It is a story well worth telling not only for the political and economic change that is taking place of an unprecedented scope and type, and which goes against the grain of so much history in Europe: Who could have imagined a generation ago, for example, that Europeans would willingly give up their currencies? It is also remarkable for the comparatively slower, and thus more imperceptible, change that is happening in how Europeans feel about their individual nations and how they relate to them. (...) (This) raises fundamental questions about the ability of people voluntarily to acquire new forms of identity with new political institutions. (Robyn, in press)

This quotation from a new book about the changing face of European identities deals with something that is of immense political and cultural importance, something that is affecting us all and will continue to do so in years to come. The movement towards, as well as the resistance against, Europeanization at the levels of the nation and the individual cannot be overestimated.

This chapter contributes to the illumination of these urgent political and cultural issues by reporting on a study in one of the European countries (Denmark) whose population is, somewhat uneasily it appears, taking part in these momentous historical processes, with a comparative side-glance at another country which appears to have related reservations about the overall European project (Great Britain). In doing so, however, the chapter is also driven by an equally important methodological motivation, as it presents and discusses a new approach to the exploration of communication and discourse, which I believe to hold great potential for increasing the explanatory power of research, as it extends the repertoire of methods available to media and communication researchers beyond the classic divide of quantitative versus qualitative.

The 'new' approach that will be demonstrated here is not new in an absolute sense, but it is a method that has undeservedly lived its life at the margins of respectable social research, mostly in social psychology and political science. It is usually referred to as Q-methodology, and uses a particular form of factor analysis for the scientific study of various forms of subjectivity (Stephenson, 1953, 1978; Brown, 1993; Rogers, 1995).

For someone like myself, solidly based by academic upbringing in the qualitative tradition, the Q-methodological approach can be a solution, with some kinds of research issues, to two of the fundamental and related problems that have been the Achilles' heel of qualitative research, even in the self-perception of qualitative researchers: *how to generalize* qualitative findings (Halkier, in press), and *how to compare* them across nations and cultures (Livingstone and Bovill, 2001; Livingstone, 2002). The generalization problem is the primary one: If you cannot, or don't want to (Ang, 1991), generalize your findings - adequately - then you cannot compare them with others. And vice versa: Once you have found a valid way to generalize your findings you can move on to comparing them with others - although (as will be demonstrated below) the comparison will not necessarily be an easy process!

Through the Q study of national and supranational identities in Denmark in the following, I am first going to address the question of qualitative generalization. Then, by drawing on the findings of a similar British study using the same methodology (McCormack, 2003), I am going to discuss the question of cross-national comparison of qualitative comparison.

In some ways Q methodology can be seen as a way of neutralizing the epistemological and methodological division between qualitative and quantitative approaches, and the very fact of its emergence in European media and communication research through this project can perhaps be seen as a symptom of the abandonment of the kind of methodological orthodoxy and polarization that has characterized the field until recently and which is not yet everywhere entirely a thing of the past. The mainstream scholarly climate today, however, is one of methodological cross-fertilization and convergence of the once hostile camps towards peaceful co-existence.

In order to leave as much space as possible here for the presentation of the methodological innovation offered by Q methodology, the reader interested in previous discussions of the epistemological and methodological development away from entrenched dogmatism is referred to other sources (Danermark et al., 2002; Deacon et al., 1999; Schrøder, 1999). Suffice it to say that Q methodology is offered here as the next logical step from the mutual curiosity of methodological difference practised as triangulation (Denzin, 1970; Friessen & Punie, 1998). This buzzword in itself implies a challenging exploration of the precise meaning of the notion 'complementarity of methods' (Jensen, 2002), but without moving beyond the successive use of one method after the other (Bryman, 2001). Q methodology, as I see it, is a method that makes it possible to synthesize qualitative and quantitative methods onto one epistemological platform and into one empirical design for fieldwork in media and communication studies.

Beyond Duality: National and Supranational Identities in Denmark

Denmark and the EU: Short Historical Overview

The relationship between Denmark and the rest of Europe has enjoyed a permanent prominent presence on the public agenda in Denmark for more than thirty years. And the issue has probably been more controversial than in most other countries. This controversiality can largely be ascribed to the structure of the constitutional system, which requires that all issues to do with the giving up of national sovereignty must be decided by the people through a referendum. This constitutional practice has had the effect of polarizing the issue, as six consecutive referenda since 1972 have required the Danes to submit to the curse of duality that follows from perpetually having to decide for or against, first the question of entry into the then Common Market, later the successive stages towards the building of an economic and political European Union, with increased integration between the EU member countries. Except for the 1972 referendum they have all showed a division of opinion with only a slight deviation from a complete equilibrium of those in favour and those against.

In spite of the specific economic and political measures to be voted on (such as the Maastricht Treaty, The Edinburgh Agreement, The Common Currency) all the referenda have had a tendency to develop into general votes of confidence for the EU project as a whole: whether we want our membership to continue at all. This perspective has been kept alive as a real possibility for many citizens, because Danish EU resistance, particularly at the right and left ends of the political spectrum, has succeeded in preserving a strong institutional platform, consisting of several well-organized popular movements across party-lines (The Popular

Movement Against the EU, The June Movement), with an institutional superstructure and the public visibility resulting from having elected members of the European Parliament. The existence of these party-like movements has further had the effect of also, to some extent, forcing the yes/no duality onto the agenda of European Parliamentary elections, with an 'opponent block' consisting of these two movements and the extreme right and left parties pitted against an 'adherent block' of more centrist political parties.

In a sense, Denmark has been the *enfant terrible* of the EU, both because the perennial referenda have caused a permanent uncertainty in the EU institution as a whole about the advancement of the integration process, and because the sometimes negative, sometimes positive outcomes of the referenda have imposed a stop/go effect on the more visionary, increasingly impatient supranationalists in the higher echelons of the EU system.

The present study was conducted in Denmark just after a parliamentary election in November 2001 that caused a swing of the pendulum from a centre/left coalition government to a moderately rightwing coalition government, whose parliamentary majority depends on the support of a more extreme nationalist, anti-immigration, and anti-EU party. This was one year after the latest referendum, in which the Danes rejected the European currency.

Quantitative and Qualitative Studies of Danish EU Sentiment

The most well-known monitoring device following popular opinion about EU affairs in Denmark is the Eurobarometer polls conducted in all member states since 1973, with the declared aim to provide 'an overview of how European citizens feel about the European Union, its policies and institutions' (*Eurobarometer, 56*:1). Another source of insight about EU sentiment has been the Danish contribution to multinational *European Value Survey* that has explored issues of national and European identity (the latter in a fairly peripheral manner), with results that confirm the tendency of the Eurobarometer findings. On the issue of people's feeling of attachment to different geographical entities, this survey finds that the attachment to one's local area is up from forty-seven per cent in 1981 to seventy-seven per cent in 1999, whereas attachment to one's country is down from thirty-six per cent to twenty per cent, and EU attachment remains low with a decrease from three per cent to one per cent in the period (Gundelach, 2002a: 49). Commenting on these figures, Gundelach concludes that nothing appears to indicate that the project of creating a common European identity has been or will be successful in the foreseeable future. The study finds a considerable increase in national pride, with an increase from thirty-three per cent of Danish men in 1981 to forty-nine per cent in 1999 who say they are 'very proud' to be Danish, the figures for women being almost identical (Gundelach, 2002b).

These statistical measurements of opinions and values to do with nation and the EU are valuable indicators of public opinion, especially because they provide comparability when conducted at regular intervals over a long period of time. This is also true of the EU polls carried out at regular intervals by various newspapers and TV stations in order to monitor developments in Danes' attitudes to specific EU issues and to questions to do with immigration and multiculturalism.

However, as Gundelach himself observes, 'questionnaire-based studies of this kind provide a fairly superficial picture, but their strength lies in their representativeness' (Gundelach, 2002b). To this superficiality we may add the limited explanatory power of the survey approach, which originates in the fact that each question produces a statistical mapping of opinion that remains an isolated fragment, one piece of a giant jigsaw puzzle whose pieces will collectively never be able to produce a meaningful picture. This is because in surveys the relationships between each opinion and concrete individuals, and the relationships between the ensemble of opinions held by different individuals, remain obscure.

Qualitative methodologies constitute one way of complementing and providing depth to the 'superficial' picture of survey findings. The European Commission has itself initiated a qualitative study of European citizens' views on the EU, publishing the report *Perceptions of the European Union. A qualitative study of the public's attitudes to and expectations of the European Union in the 15 member states and in 9 candidate countries* in June 2001 (*Perceptions...* 2001).

The objective of the study was to identify and describe for what reasons, and to what extent, people embrace the idea of the European Union, and what fears, reservations and objections they may have to the European project. Focus group discussions were carried out in all member and candidate countries, two in small countries, and four in big countries. In the case of Denmark, two interviews were carried out in a major provincial city. On the theme of 'belonging' it was found that a stark contrast exists between 'the South' and 'the North' of Europe, with the southern populations (i.e. all countries except the UK, the Netherlands, Denmark and Sweden) being strongly aware of the existence of cultural ties between people who may well be very diverse, but who nevertheless share common roots, and who may be an important oppositional force to the dominance of the USA on the world scene. Conversely, in the 'northern' countries, Denmark among them,

> the sense of common historical and cultural ties is much less present in people's minds (...). In these countries there is a deep-seated conviction of the superiority or specificity of the model of society that the country has developed with its own values, and a weak propensity to share with others, who tend to be seen as a threat. (Perceptions: 5)

More specifically on the question of the role of the European Union, these countries (as represented by the four or two focus groups) do not favour the building of a strong, federal Europe, there is rather:

> *a strong distrust of the European Union and a desire to contain its scope for action. It can be seen, rationally and pragmatically, that belonging to the European Union is useful for the economic interests of the country (...), but in all other fields it appears to be more of a threat (...) any harmonization tends to be perceived as a downward harmonization, to the lowest common denominator, or as contrary to the interests of the country. It is these countries that have the most widespread caricatures of the Community being only concerned with pointless, absurd, even freedom-infringing measures (...) a perception of a sprawling, inefficient, spendthrift bureaucracy, and a general suspicion of the existence of illegal benefits and payments, and corruption (Perceptions: 8).*

The strongly negative views about the EU found in this qualitative study can certainly be found in a 'northern' country like Denmark. However, it would seem that many nuances are lost when just two focus groups are taken as representative(s) of 'the Danish view'. As a (Danish) reader, who knows better than this mono-dimensional picture, it is tempting to conclude that the picture painted here is itself a caricature.

There is therefore a great need for a study in Denmark of national and European identity, which avoids the dual pitfalls of quantitative superficiality and unwarranted qualitative generalization. The Q study reported below makes it possible to probe into the diversity of opinions and perceptions within a country, while holding on to the ambition of being able to discern distinct patterns of identity that together characterize the population of a country.

The Q Study of National and European Identities in Denmark Step by Step[1]

The first stage of the Q project consisted in capturing, in a finite number of statements or claims, the essential features of the discursive terrain in question. This may be done through a number of in-depth interviews about the field, through a thorough analysis of the public debate about the issue in the media, or through consulting the scholarly literature about the issue. In this study a combination of such sources was used by the project leader for putting together the so-called P-set of statements for all eight countries involved in the study. Each major discernible position in the discursive terrain was represented through an equal number of statements that express the many-facetted character of the position, so that the set of statements forms a miniature of the discursive terrain being investigated. Twelve statements were chosen to represent the variety of sentiments making up each of three prominent positions on the issue, defined by the researchers' hunches: 'Nationalists' (nation as a core value), 'national pluralists' (some openness towards a union of nations), and 'supra-nationalists' (belief in the vision of a united Europe) (Robyn, in press).

Among the issues covered by the thirty-six statements were some of those used by the Eurobarometer - feeling European and/or Danish, national pride, the perceived benefits of EU membership, the speed of European integration - as well as several other issues relevant for one's sense of identity: globalization, aspects of Danishness, sovereignty, the role of the Danish language, etc. (an excerpt of the P-set is shown in Appendix 1). The statements were originally developed for the French study, and were used in all other participating countries, because standardization was necessary to fulfil the comparative ambition of the cross-national project. Our translations of the original statements were rarely verbatim, as we wanted all wordings to sound unequivocally Danish. In other words, we tried to reach a compromise between, on the one hand, comparability across the national studies, and linguistic genuineness and cultural affinity on the other (for details, see Schrøder & Hansen, in press).

In the second stage, the statement-claims were used in random order as an interview guide for individual, structured qualitative interviews about the issue.

The principle of diversity guided our recruiting of participants, resulting in a near-equal representation of the genders, of high and low educational backgrounds, of young and older adults, and people with metropolitan and more provincial backgrounds. Each statement, printed on a small, numbered card, was read aloud by the interviewer and handed to the participant. It thus served as the input of a dialogical speech event, in which participants were invited to think aloud as they negotiated their stance, with the interviewer facilitating the process by probing in order to clarify the participant's position on each statement in turn. The main difference so far in relation to the typical semi-structured qualitative interview was that the turn taking between interviewer and participant was structured by the obligatory progression through the randomly packed cards. Another difference was the relatively high number of informants (thirty), who took part in the study. The interviews were audiotaped and transcribed.

In the third stage, the participant was asked to place the cards one at a time, as a kind of puzzle game, on to a scalar grid representing a continuum with (in this study) nine positions from Most Agree to Most Disagree. Appendix 2 shows how one participant sorted the thirty-six statement-claims. In practice this occurred immediately after each card had been responded to verbally, and thus overlapped with stage two. Typically participants would explain briefly or at length why they placed a card in a specific slot. The transcripts therefore hold a multitude of reflections about the cultural and political issues articulated on the cards. As the grid was gradually filled with the thirty-six cards, the participant was free to reposition individual cards so that ultimately the grid came to express the participant's meaning universe on the issue.

In relation to a survey questionnaire this is where the crucial difference lies. All the thirty-six statements of the Q study could equally well have been used in a classic survey, but there each answer would in principle be unrelated to all other answers. The effect of placing all thirty-six statements on the grid is that each response becomes related to the thirty-five other responses, so that a *relational map* of the participant's meaning universe is produced.

At the fourth stage, the relational maps of the thirty informants were subjected to computerized factor analysis, which correlates the similarities and differences among the participants' meaning universes, and discovers the patterns of meaning expressed by the participants through their card sorting. The end product is a number of 'factors', which each comprises a grouping of participants whose card sorts were similar, compared with the sorts of other participants. We found four statistically significant factors, each characterized by aggregate card placements that distinguish them from the other factors.

In the fifth stage, the identity profile of the participants making up each factor was interpreted on the basis of the factor scores, which were arranged as a Top-36 from Most Agree to Most Disagree (see Appendix 3 for an excerpt of a factor profile). After extensive interpretive work on the factor scores we found that the four factors could be characterized as Whole-Hearted Europeans, Pragmatic Europeans, Euro-Skeptical Danes, and Danish Danes, comprising thirteen, eleven, seven, and three participants respectively.

A purely qualitative analysis might also have generalized its findings with such a typology of different national identities (for examples of typologies generated through qualitative interpretation, see Stald, 1999; Schrøder et al., 2003, ch.7). The advantage of generalizing the types through computerized factor analysis is simply that the computer is able to handle the enormous amount of data similarities and differences much more reliably than the brain of the human scholar. The validity cost, conversely, lies in the data reduction required in order to distill the complex discursive negotiation of each statement-claim down to one square on the Q grid. Pulling in the opposite direction, however, is the fact that this reduction is carried out subjectively by the participants themselves, not by the interpreting researcher. It is not without justification, therefore, that Q methodology is also called 'the scientific study of subjectivity'.

The factor analysis also shows which participants in each factor grouping are particularly typical. The researcher can therefore, in the sixth stage, go back to the interview transcripts of such typical specimens, in order to put some discursive meat on the analytical skeleton supplied by the factor analysis, regaining some of the thick description that was lost during the statistical operations. The end result of the analysis is therefore both a generalized and a detail-rich profile of the prominent positions in the discursive terrain of national identity. Next we shall take a look at some of the evidence for this claim.

The Q Study of National and European Identities in Denmark: Findings

As stated above, our factor analysis of the participants' card placements resulted in four factors significant at the .01 level. This means that the participants we used in our fieldwork formed into four identity groupings that are statistically significant. This reveals that there are at least four groupings in Danish society when it comes to attitudes to the issues of national/supra-national identity. Although we constructed the set of participants to cast as wide a net as possible into Danish society, it is possible that we would have found more factors by enlarging it. For instance, our sample of participants did not do full justice to the geographical variation between more and less urbanized areas of Denmark, and to some extent over-represented younger individuals with high education.

Although the four types appear at first sight to divide themselves neatly into two superordinate groups of 'Europeans' and 'Danes', there is no indication in the interviews that there is a simple correlation between the 'Europeans' and the 'Danes' of this study and the Yes-sayers and No-sayers, respectively, of the EU referenda of recent years.

We did not systematically ask participants about their voting record in EU referenda, but many volunteered this information, enabling us to say with some confidence that while the first and last groupings do seem to correspond to the duality of the referenda, the two middle groupings consist of people who voted either way, and who may already (i.e. approx. one year after the referendum) have regretted the way they voted. With all thirty participants, their cultural identity is the product of an ongoing signifying process full of ambivalences and contradictions, fluctuating along sections of the continuum from strong nationalism to strong globalism. Here is an example of a participant reflecting on her attitude to Denmark adopting the European currency:

> It's also to some extent this feeling that Denmark should continue to be Denmark, and then something about, well, I somehow do think we should keep our own money, and I just see a kind of charm about, well, our monar..., well, the royal family and all that, but at the same time I sometimes waver a little bit, because obviously I do realize the advantages of it, but nevertheless I cast a clear no-vote last year, I didn't hesitate for a second (...). But things are moving all the time, one has to open the door a little, I would say.

The Q-methodological framework can thus be implemented as a social constructionist approach to the analysis of culture, as it enables the expression of national identity as 'constructed and never fixed; (...) it is constantly reworked from a repertoire of traditions, myths, and representations; (...) it can be employed when it makes political sense' (Robyn, in press). It follows from this that the study's underlying vision of the nation is that of an 'imagined community' (Anderson, 1983).

What Q-analysis does to the potentially confusing picture of ambivalences and contradictions is to 'freeze the picture', and thereby to hold each participant 'accountable' for an analytical positioning of their identity at a particular point in time, and also to claim a relative degree of permanence for this position. The Q study in Denmark froze its thirty participants into four distinguishable cubes:

Whole-hearted Europeans are people who share a very positive attitude to the EU, believing that in today's world one country cannot control its future on its own, and that Denmark has definitely benefited from its EU membership. They distance themselves from any vestige of nationalism: 'I don't feel any of that arch-Danishness, I probably feel more as a European than as a Dane, but I also feel more as a citizen of the world than as a European. (...) It is quite true that globalization is a threat to the Danish national culture, but then I don't have anything against that'. They whole-heartedly embrace the prospect of further European integration and a diminishing role for Danishness, to be complemented by a feeling of also being European: 'Obviously when people start to feel more like Europeans this must work to supersede some of that Danishness. (...) But I don't know if our identity will become 'blurred', rather we will get a feeling of 'We live in Europe *and* we live in Denmark', instead of just 'We live in Denmark'. (...) In some areas we will begin to feel more like Europeans, but in other areas we will begin to feel more Danish.'

Pragmatic Europeans see Europeanization essentially as an inevitable process, which they regard with caution but not without awareness of its benefits - for Denmark: 'I voted for the Euro (...). I am not one hundred per cent aware of exactly what it entails, but it is more, well, I mean we will get the Euro no matter what. In say two years when people come here wanting to pay with Euros then we cannot say 'Sorry, we only accept Danish money', that's a joke, so there's really nothing to discuss here'. With respect to the EU ideal of 'unity in diversity' they give precedence to diversity: 'I don't think that the countries will accept having some kind of president of the EU in the foreseeable future. (...) It will continue to be each country to itself in this respect. A superpower would be like the USA, where he can just say, Bush I mean, 'Send the troops!' and likewise in a lot of other areas. (...) And that's because the European countries are so special somehow, each in itself.' They support increased EU cooperation on condition that our national identity is not jeopardized.

Euro-sceptical Danes are characterized by a general ambivalence of cultural and political identity. They strongly disapprove of the cultural homogenisation effected by the EU, but they also warn against national self-aggrandizement. However, Danish sovereignty should be maintained at all costs. They are sceptical about whether Denmark has really benefited from EU membership, as the reverse negatives and conditional positives in the following statement show: 'If you look at the statistics, then you have to say that *Denmark has at least not been the great loser* in EU affairs. But you have to graduate what you think are the good things about the EU, but economically and in other ways, then I do think that we have had *some benefits* from it' (emphases added). They don't identify with all things Danish, and nor do they believe that our national culture is endangered by cultural Others: 'I think it's okay to say that you're proud to be Danish, because it would be a bit pitiful if you couldn't say that, wouldn't it, but on the other hand I just won't be like those who say 'Denmark for the Danes', you see, there is a clear difference there, I am not so afraid of the aliens, I happen to believe that the aliens who have come here have enriched our culture, but I think that some of the fear is due to lack of knowledge, people don't understand that the Moslem living around the corner he is not dangerous for me just because he prays to whoever he prays to, and I go to church'.

Danish Danes inhabit a staunch Danishness with a distinctive nationalist orientation, a personal, deep-felt Danishness that saturates everyday life. They believe that our historically inherited values are under threat from an unstoppable Europeanization and globalization process: 'That's where I get afraid that in the long run people in our little country will have to ask Brussels for permission to breathe - I know this is a bit exaggerated okay? - and I don't want it to be like that, you see. (...) I'm against the Euro. I am so fond of our little 'Danish kroner'. It would annoy me if we were to lose it, so therefore I don't want the Euro in, that's why it had to go'. They view the external encroachments from a position of fatalism and impotence, a feeling of being culturally corned.

The Contribution of Q-methodology to the Conceptualisation of National and European Identities

The most significant contribution of this Q-methodological study to the ongoing portrayal of the national and European identities of Danish citizens lies in the *complexification* of the otherwise polarized picture of Danish EU sentiment. Looking at the diversity of each participant's differently patterned card placements and their thinking-aloud reflections, the inner discursive landscapes of these thirty individuals are characterized by ambivalent and fluctuating cultural and political identities, which mirror, in many individual minds, the close to fifty-fifty situation at the macro level that has been the outcome of all referenda about Denmark/EU relations over the last thirty years.

At the same time, the methodology used also enables us to distinguish, amidst the flux and diversity of opinions, a *pattern* of four groupings, each consisting of individuals whose identity configurations have enough in common to distinguish them from the other groupings.

But even at this generalized level of orderly groupings, *complexity asserts itself* in the middle of orderliness, as the following selected ranking comparisons show (the table should be read like this: the Whole-hearted Europeans on average ranked Statement #8 in tenth place out of thirty-six, the Pragmatic Europeans ranked it in first place, and so on; the wording of the statements can be seen in Appendix 1):

Statement #	Whole-hearted	Pragmatic	Sceptical	Danish
#8	10	1	25	27
#10	20	2	29	22
#12	22	36	36	36
#13	9	12	16	9
#14	8	19	28	33
#16	13	8	31	30
#17	17	11	6	1
#19	15	2	4	3
#21	19	31	35	25
#32	3	13	17	19

We find the 'expected' linear distribution between the groupings' rankings of #14, 17, and 32, for instance the increasing disagreement that one feels 'closely connected to Europe as such' (#14), and an increasing insistence that Denmark must keep its independence (#17).

In some cases, we find a situation of one group against the other three, as when the Whole-hearted Europeans are considerably less adamant that they do not think of themselves first as Europeans, then as Danes (#12), and less insistent that Europe should let Denmark be Denmark (#19). In other cases we find a neat division between two more pro- and two more anti-European groups, as when the Whole-hearted Europeans and the Pragmatic Europeans tend towards neutrality regarding the possible development of the EU into a superpower, whereas the Euro-Sceptics and the Danish Danes believe that the EU project is super-power oriented (#16).

Complexity also shows itself in some unexpected deviations from the expected pattern, as when the Pragmatic Europeans, against the other three groupings, express strong agreement that the EU is the best way to secure peace and stability for Denmark in the future (#10).

Of equal interest are the issues on which the positions of all four groupings converge. Thus, on #13, there is fairly close agreement that the goal should be a Europe with politically and culturally very different countries, and some agreement that integration between the EU countries should not move faster (#21). On this point the findings of the Q-study corroborate the Eurobarometer poll reported above.

Comparing Apples and Oranges: Applying Q-methodology to the Comparative Study of Identity in Denmark and Great Britain

'Comparative research may be impossible, but it is also necessary', writes Sonia Livingstone in a paper that tries to illuminate the epistemological and practical challenges of doing comparative research across cultures or nations (Livingstone, 2002, p. 16). Considering the increasing number of cross-national projects in media and communication studies (Liebes & Katz, 1990; Jensen, 1998; Livingstone and Bovill, 2001), it appears that necessity is - quite appropriately - gaining the upper hand over impossibility. One can only agree with Livingstone, however, that in conducting cross-cultural research, 'we should resist the ambition, fantasy even, that by this means a complete, comprehensive account can be produced' (Livingstone, 2002, p. 24). Nevertheless, when we do get involved in cross-cultural comparative research we should constantly strive to approximate precisely such a complete and comprehensive account, i.e. to design the study theoretically and methodologically in such a manner as to maximize its explanatory power.

In the case of the eight-nation comparative study of national and supranational identities across Europe, the 'necessity' guiding the project was the desire to understand how the populations and electorates in eight different countries are responding to the same challenges of Europeanization. The national studies were carried out independently of each other, apart from the fact that they all used the same standardized methodology and the same set of interview questions, as described above in connection with the Danish study.

Here I shall undertake a comparison of the Danish and the British findings. It will be rather superficial, due to lack of space and to my lack of access to the full data from the British study. In spite of this superficiality I hope that the comparison will manage to show how the Q methodological approach is able to overcome some of the traditional barriers that have prevented the systematic comparison of qualitative data. As Livingstone says, 'the difficulties in ensuring comparability of measurement tools and in applying standardised forms of analysis' have been met:

by adopting quantitative rather than qualitative methods: certainly, the experience of many involved in cross-national research (has been) that quantitative data are easi-

er to share, and so to compare, than qualitative data. Quantitative data is straightfor-wardly coded and can be analysed statistically by anyone; qualitative research demands interpretation of the data in context, by the researcher who collected the data (...). Similarly, data files of numbers can be collated, circulated and analysed across different countries, while transcripts written in different languages cannot. (Livingstone, 2002, p. 15)

Qualitative researchers have therefore often criticized quantitative cross-national research for imposing a theoretical and methodological universalism, 'at the cost of cultural specificity in failing to recognize the context-dependent nature of meaning' (Livingstone, 2002, p. 15.), and arguing that standardization inevitably means the sacrifice of ecological validity.

Underlying the comparative Q study of European identities is a claim that this method provides a way to share and compare *qualitative* data, or if the argument is accepted that Q methodology is neither qualitative nor quantitative (or both), that the dichotomy is avoided altogether. In these Q studies each country is analysed *in its own terms*, even if this is done through the standardized research vehicle of the P-set (the thirty-six statement-claims). It is precisely the configurability of the P-set according to the individual subjectivities of the participants that guarantees cultural specificity and context-dependent data, manifesting itself in the interview dialogue and in the relational map that each participant constructs for him - or herself. And as argued above, the factor analysis preserves a large amount of the complexity of meaning expressed by the participants. This does not mean that comparison becomes easy, because after all one is attempting to compare apples with oranges.

In Britain McCormack's study found five different types of identity across the spectrum from nationalist to supranationalist: Optimistic Pluralism, Besieged Nationalism, Patriotic[2] Pluralism, Beyond National Identity, and Anti-nationalism. Here follows McCormack's summary descriptions of each of the five factors:

Optimistic Pluralism
Enthusiasm for the EU as a project for peace and stability in Europe.
Respect for the diversity of member states is a strength of the EU project.
Rejection of nationalist sentiments, perceived as 'racist'.
No European attachment - pluralism is it!

Besieged Nationalism
English nationalism, a sense of being under threat.
Explicitly anti-European.

Patriotic Pluralism
Emphasis on diversity as being necessary to the EU project.
Otherwise ambivalent about the pros or cons of European integration.
Strong patriotism.

Beyond National Identity
A rejection of nationalism.
No particular enthusiasm for the EU; other transnational attachments expressed.

Anti-Nationalism
Strong opposition to nationalism.
Strong anti-racism.
Ambivalence about Europeanization and globalization, seen as inevitable processes.

At first sight, the British identity pattern resembles the Danish pattern in an important respect, as both point to the inadequacy of conceptualising attitudes to the EU in simple binary terms: 'While a primary cleavage in attitudes towards the European Union remains between Eurosceptics and Europhiles, such categorization does not adequately describe the range of attitudes that individuals form about this complex political institution' (Haesly, 2001, p. 82, quoted by McCormack, in press). But what else can one say about similarities and differences between the two countries?

It is clear that, even with the generalizations resulting from a standardized research tool like Q methodology, dimensions of comparison don't suggest themselves easily, as we have to match a typology of four (Denmark) with a typology of five (GB). In order to proceed any further we need to take a closer look at the underlying factor configurations and the participants' thinking-aloud reflections.

But first of all we also have to reconceptualize the very notion of 'comparison', taking it out of the realm of quantitative more-or-less comparison, into a more hazy interpretive territory that we may still only be able to deal with metaphorically, because the inadequately theorized nature of comparative research forces us to resort to extensive metaphorical circumlocution, as opposed to a precise scientific nomenclature. Livingstone thus leans on the proverbial metaphor of fruit comparison, as she talks about comparing apples with apples, oranges with apples, and even the possibility of comparison through the lens of a 'fruitology', 'identifying universal dimensions of variation (size, colour, taste, etc. on which each fruit is expected to vary' (Livingstone, 2002, p. 13).

Faced with the identity findings, I can do no better than suggest another extended metaphor that seems to me to better capture the interpretive processes at stake:

that of the quilt. Two quilts are likely to be different in size, number and composition of patches, colour, and texture. They may have many things in common: certain patches may be almost identical, others entirely different; two patches that look different at a first glance may turn out on closer inspection to be quite similar, etc. The sets of identity groupings coming out of the Danish and British Q studies can be regarded as two such quilts.

With these 'identity quilts' comparison is made easier than with conventional qualitative findings, because the typologies originate in the same standardized empirical design. There is no natural or obvious fit between them, but a closer look at the factor configurations appears to warrant the following relationships:

Denmark	Great Britain
Whole-hearted Europeans	Beyond National Identity
Pragmatic Europeans	Optimistic Pluralism
EuroSceptical Danes	Patriotic Pluralism
Danish Danes	Besieged nationalism
	(Anti-nationalism)

What these relationships postulate is that the discursive terrains of national and supranational identities in the two countries are similarly structured, as the defining characteristics of the four groups appear to match each other quite closely.[3] Obviously these relationships would have to be scrutinized more closely, searching the data for variations between pair members. But on the whole it would appear to make sense that the identity patterns of precisely these two 'Eurosceptical' countries correspond in the manner indicated.

The data available to me from the British study makes it possible, however, to also point out some of the shades of meaning that differ between pair members. The nationalist groups shared the feature of feeling 'culturally cornered' (DK) or 'besieged' (GB), but in Britain the nationalist group appears to be driven largely by a post-imperial resentment of Britain's 'fall from greatness', whereas in Denmark the group's nationalism originates in the almost opposite sense of 'Lilliput chauvinism' (Østergaard, 1992, quoted in Jenkins, 1997, p. 157) that manifests itself verbally in fears that 'little Denmark' will be swallowed up by big neighbours.

The supranationally oriented groups differ in their orientation towards Europe or the lack of it. The British group 'Beyond national identity' are ambivalent towards

Europe, disagreeing quite strongly with the 'feeling European' statements in the P-set (#12, #14). The Danish Whole-Hearted Europeans are neutral (#12) or mildly positive (#14) about these attitudes. This difference may reflect the historical circumstance that Denmark has always been closer to Europe, geographically and mentally, while British debates about 'joining Europe' have tended towards a certain insularity and a greater orientation towards North America and the former British empire.

Q-methodology as 'Applied Research'

This brief consideration of the potential for cross-national comparison offered by Q methodology appears to demonstrate that the level of generalization offered by this methodology does not make it into a panacea for the challenges of context-sensitive cross-national comparison. On the other hand, with Q methodology such comparison becomes considerably less messy and amorphous than with traditional qualitative methods.

In terms of 'use value', the study reported here can serve, on the one hand, as an academic contribution to the public understanding of the European issue in the eight countries in which it was carried out. But the generalizing capability of the method, as it materializes in the identity profiles produced, also makes the analysis potentially useful for the various agents on the EU scene in different countries. For instance, campaigns - for or against increased Europeanization - now have concrete groupings of people with complete identity profiles to 'aim for'. They no longer have to rely exclusively on the findings of surveys and polls, with their multitude of representative but superficial and disconnected 'attitudes' to the issues on the EU agenda.

A Q-methodological study can enable campaigners in a specific country to address a multitude of concrete issues on the public agenda more accurately and efficiently, in a manner that does not conflict with other views held by the identity-profiled groups. In order to do that, one might want to devise a more comprehensive Q-study, which related the social groupings discovered more accurately and representatively to the kind of demographic or psychographic parameters that would make the groupings identifiable in the social landscape.

Notes

1 The study was the Danish part of a comparative study of national and supranational identity done in eight European countries, organized by Professor Richard Robyn, Kent State University, Ohio, USA. The findings from all eight studies will be reported in the book, Richard Robyn, (Ed.), The Changing Face of European Identity: An Eight-Nation Q Study of (Supra)National Attachments. Lynne Riener Publishers (in press).

The Danish project was funded by and carried out as a joint study between The Department of Communication, Journalism and Computer Science, Roskilde University (Kim Schrøder), and ACNielsen-AIM, a major market research company in Denmark (Søren Esben Hansen). In addition, the project has benefited from the assistance of Eva Jakobsen, Director of Qualitative Research, and Bo Nielson, Qualitative Researcher, both at ACNielsen-AIM. Analytical assistance has been provided by Richard Robyn and Steven Brown, Kent State University, both experienced Q-method practitioners, who did the statistical analysis of the participants' Q-sorts and the preliminary interpretation of the four factors. Without them, it would not have been possible to do the study. I also wish to thank Professor Mark Popovich, Ball State University, IN, for first introducing me to Q methodology.

2   Following Orwell, McCormack distinguishes between 'patriotism', i.e. "devotion to a particular place and a particular way of life, which one believes to be the best in the world but has no wish to force on other people' (Orwell, 2000, p. 300), and 'nationalism', which is 'inseparable from the desire for power' (ibid.).

3   The fifth British grouping I shall leave aside here, as it is all but dismissed by McCormack as odd, as it is really a 'negatively defined' subgroup of the Besieged Nationalists, with two individuals with otherwise somewhat ambiguous profiles. Methodologically this group indicates that further research is needed in order to fully illuminate the British situation.

Appendix 1

The P-set of statements used in the Danish study (English translation, excerpts)

N= Nationalist sentiment (12)

PL= Pluralist sentiment (12)

SN= Supranational sentiment (12)

1. Our identity as Danes will become more and more blurred if Europeanness is promoted. (N)

8. One day it will become necessary for Denmark to join the Euro (the common European currency). (PL)

10. The European Union is the best way to secure peace and stability for Denmark in the future. (PL)

12. I think of myself first as a European, then as a Dane. (SN)

13. I want a Europe with countries that are as politically and culturally different as they are different geographically. (PL)

14. I feel closely connected to Europe as such. (SN)

16. To create European unity through the EU is not a way to create a European super-power. It is merely a way to create change in Europe. (PL)

17. Denmark must keep its independence while taking part in European cooperation. (N)

19. Europe will be stronger the more it lets Denmark be Denmark, France be France, England be England, each with its customs, traditions and identity. It would be stupid to try to melt them together. (PL)

21. Integration between the EU countries ought to move faster. (SN)

32. On the whole Denmark has benefited from its EU membership. (SN)

Appendix 2

One participant's card sort of the 36 statements

-4	-3	-2	-1	0	+1	+2	+3	+4
				36				
			21	4	30			
		25	34	3	10	2		
12	11	1	33	13	5	19	20	17
23	29	24	22	32	26	18	28	35
8	14	7	16	31	6	9	27	15
- 4	**- 3**	**- 2**	**- 1**	**0**	**+ 1**	**+ 2**	**+ 3**	**+ 4**
Most disagree						Most agree		

Informant # 1, Copenhagen, Female, Bus driver, 42 years of age

Appendix 3

Excerpt of the factor profile of 'Whole-hearted Europeans'

Statement No.		Z-SCORES

TOP SIX (Most agree)

31.	It is possible to be a citizen of a united Europe without all Europeans having to be the same.	2.058
6.	One country cannot control its future on its own.	1.752
32.	On the whole Denmark has benefited from its EU membership.	1.352
33.	In the future Danes must be able to command both Danish and English in order to be able to cope in Europe.	1.308
34.	If the EU works according to the principle of subsidiarity, it is possible to both support a united Europe and to preserve Danishness at the same time.	1.302
36.	There will be better room for national minorities in a united Europe, because a united Europe is more capable of handling such differences.	1.046

BOTTOM SIX (Least agree)

26.	I believe that integration between the EU countries has gone as far as it possibly can.	-1.295
3.	The globe's population can be naturally divided into nations.	-1.349
15.	Danish culture is worth preserving because it has existed for more than a thousand years.	-1.375
5.	I feel that aliens in Denmark dilute our national identity.	-1.484
9.	It would be difficult for my parents if I didn't marry a Dane.	-1.610
7.	Your sense of belonging to your country comes before anything else.	-1.797

Legend:

The top statement for each Factor (Grouping) is the one this grouping most agreed with, the bottom statement the one they least agreed with.

The complete data for the four factors can be seen in the pdf version of the article by Schrøder & Hansen (in press), downloadable from http://akira.ruc.dk/~kimsc/

References

Anderson, B. (1983), Imagined Communities. London: Verso.

Ang, I. (1991) Desperately seeking the audience. London: Routledge.

Brown, S. R. (1993) 'A Primer on Q Methodology'. Operant Subjectivity. 16, pp. 91-138.

Bryman, A. (2001) Social Research Methods. Oxford: Oxford University Press.

Danermark, B., Ekström, M., Jakobsen, L., and Karlsson, S. C. (2002) Explaining Society. Critical Realism in the Social Sciences. London: Routledge.

Deacon, D., Pickering, M., Golding, P., Murdock, G. (1999) Researching Communications. A practical guide to methods in media and cultural analysis. London: Arnold.

Denzin, N. (1970) The Research Act: A theoretical introduction to sociological methods. Englewood Cliffs, NJ: Prentice-Hall.

Eurobarometer 56, Public Opinion in the European Union, The European Commission, April 2002, http://europa.eu.int/comm/public_opinion.

Friessen, V. and Punie, Y. (1998) 'Never Mind the Gap - Integrating Qualitative and Quantitative Methods in ICT User Research: The Case of Busy Households', in R. Silverstone & M. Hartmann (Eds.) 1998, Methodologies for Media and Information Technology Research in Everyday Life. Research Report, The Graduate Research Centre in Culture and Communication, University of Sussex.

Gundelach, P. (Ed.) (2002a) Danskernes Værdier 1981-1999 (The Danes' Values 1981-1999). Copenhagen: Hans Reitzels Forlag.

Gundelach, P. (Ed.) (2002b) 'Danskernes værdier', in Universitetsavisen 4. University of Copenhagen.

Haesly, R. (2001) 'Euroskeptics, Europhiles and Instrumental Europeans: European Attachment in Scotland and Wales.' European Union Politics. 2, pp. 81-102.

Halkier, B. (in press) 'The challenge of qualitative generalizations in communication research', Nordicom Review. 25 (1).

Jenkins, R. (1997) Rethinking ethnicity. Arguments and explorations. London: Sage.

Jensen, K. B. (Ed.) (1998) News of the World. World Cultures Look at Television News. London: Routledge.

Jensen, K. B. (2002) 'The Complementarity of Qualitative and Quantitative Methodologies in Media and Communication Research', in Jensen, K. B. (Ed.), A Handbook of Media and Communication Research. Qualitative and Quantitative Methodologies. London: Routledge.

Liebes, T. and Katz, E. (1990) The Export of Meaning. New York: Oxford University Press.

Livingstone, S. (2002) 'On the challenges of cross-national comparative media research', Paper presented at The Centre for User-Oriented Communication Research, Department of Communication, Journalism and Computer Science, Roskilde University, Denmark, 2 December 2002.

Livingstone, S. and Bovill, M. (Eds.) (2001) Children and their Changing Media Environment: a European Comparative Study. Mahwah, N.J.: Lawrence Erlbaum Associates.

McCormack, U. (in press) 'Being in Europe: Pluralism and patriotism in England and Scotland', in Robyn (in press).

Perceptions of the European Union. A qualitative study of the public's attitudes to and expectations of the European Union in the 15 member states and in 9 candidate countries. The European Commission, June 2001. http://europa.eu.int/comm/public_opinion/quali_en.htm

Orwell, G. (2000) Notes on Nationalism in ESSAYS, London: Penguin Classics.

Østergaard, U. (1992) Europas ansigter: Nationale stater og politiske kulturer i en ny gammel verden, (The faces of Europe: nation states and political cultures in a new old world. My translation). Copenhagen: Rosinante.

Robyn, R. (Ed.) (in press), The Changing Face of European Identity: An Eight-Nation Q Study of (Supra)National Attachments. Lynne Riener Publishers.

Rogers, R. S. (1995) 'Q Methodology'. In Smith, J. A., Harré, R. and Langenhove, L. V. (Eds.), Rethinking Methods in Psychology. London: Sage.

Schrøder, K. C. (1999) 'The Best of Both Worlds? Media Audience Research between Rival Paradigms', in P. Alasuutari, (Ed.), Rethinking the Media Audience. The New Agenda. London: Sage.

Schrøder, K. C. and Hansen, S. E. (in press) 'Beyond Duality. Danes' views on Denmark and the European Union 2001', in Robyn, R. (Ed.). http://akira.ruc.dk/~kimsc/Beyond_Duality.pdf

Schrøder, K. C., Drotner, K., Kline, S. and Murray, C. (2003) Researching Audiences. London: Arnold.

Stald, G. (1999) 'Living with Computers. Young Danes' uses of and thoughts on the uses of computers'. Sekvens 1998, Yearbook of the Department of Film and Media Studies. University of Copenhagen.

Stephenson, W. (1953) The Study of Behavior: Q-technique and Its Methodology. Chicago: University of Chicago Press.

Stephenson, W. (1978) 'Concourse Theory of Communication'. Communication 3. pp. 21-40.

Peter Ludes is Professor of Mass Communication, Integrated Social Sciences, at International University Bremen. Vice Head of the Research Network *'Mass Media and Communication'* of the European Sociological Association. More than one hundred publications, recently on Multimedia and Many Modernities: Key Pictures (with a CD-ROM), Wiesbaden, 2001 and the DVD-ROM 'Medien und Symbole: uropäische MedienBILDung', Siegen 2002. Studies, research and teaching at Brandeis, USA; Newfoundland, Canada; Siegen, Germany; Harvard, USA; Mannheim, Germany. Primary research areas: mass and multimedia communication, visual analyses, intercultural comparisons, sociology of knowledge and culture.

Peter Ludes

EUROvisions? Monetary Union and Communication Puzzles[1]

The introduction of the Euro had been prepared for several decades by generations of politicians, entrepreneurs, unionists, social movements and individual citizens. Major reasons advanced in the 1990s focused on an improvement of the European (Monetary) Union's economies in their competition with the other major global players, mainly the United States (itself strengthened by its economic integration in NAFTA, jointly with Canada and Mexico), Japan and the already emerging Chinese and Indian global market competitors. The chief executive director of the European Central Bank argued that the introduction of the Euro would enhance the European Monetary Union's gross domestic product by roughly one per cent. The Euro-push for the Eurozone's economies is considered as a prerequisite for the specific Western European and Scandinavian welfare systems. Last, but probably not least, the re-unification of Germany in 1990 shifted its balance of power with the other member countries of the European Union too much in favour of the dominance of the German Mark.

There is a chance to see the non-introduction of the Euro in three member countries of the European Union (namely the United Kingdom, Denmark, and Sweden) and the non-participation of the most highly developed European economy in the European Union, Switzerland, as a kind of *'natural experiment.'* Using the introduction of the Euro as an means of economic calculation, comparison and purchase at the beginning of 2002 (as a counting currency it had already been established in January 1999), the following countries have been selected for analysis: Germany, France, and the Netherlands plus the United Kingdom and Switzerland.

Section 1 discusses the 'social meaning of money' and introduces analysis of the major mass media and their focus on the introduction of the Euro as a cultural indicator of national particularities and European commonalities.

In *Section 2,* some media examples and key pictures will be presented for the week of the introduction of the Euro-kit, 14 December (France and the Netherlands) or 17 December (Germany) to 21 December 2001.[2] In addition, the state heads' *Christmas* or *New Year's speeches* will be interpreted as official statements on cultural, economic and political values. In general, this shows that national frames and concerns overshadow European perspectives. Nationally oriented mass media inadequately convey the historically new phase of monetary and economic European Union. *Section 3,* therefore reviews the possibilities of *'EuroVisions'* for the next decade.

The 'Social Meaning of Money' and the Introduction of the Euro as an Indicator of Europeanization

The *'social meaning of money'* (Zelizer, 1994, pp. 12, 18-19 and 27, emphasis added) is neglected in media analyses:

> *The monetization of social life spreads uniformity, precision, and calculation. ...Classic theorists emphasized its instrumental rationality, apparently unlimited capacity to transform products, relationships, and sometimes, even emotions into an abstract and objective numerical equivalent. But money is neither culturally neutral nor socially anonymous. It may well 'corrupt' values and convert social ties into numbers, but values and social relations reciprocally transmute money by investing it with meaning and social patterns.*

As Heinemann clarified in his almost classic *Sociology of Money* from 1969, *money represents abstract structures of expectation, attitudes, prejudices, needs. Money* is a means of communication which *frees and steers the adaptation of behaviour, its co-ordination and integration* - which is highly necessary in functionally differentiated social realms, allowing for the interaction and interdependencies of relatively autonomous institutional entities, transcending and connecting separated actors in time and space. *The use of money is a type of interaction in which each participant influences and is influenced by the other*: this characterizes its fundamental difference from power and domination. Money always is more encompassing in its usage than personal ties and can be transferred to unknown persons and institutions in the future or in other regions or functional realms. According to

Heinemann (1969, p. 150), money offers the opportunity to participate effectively in a rapidly changing world - including a higher degree of empathy. Thereby *money not only is a symbol of social order but also of human thought styles and mentalities.*

Deutschmann (1999) nevertheless recently interpreted money as the blind spot of contemporary sociology, and emphasized the religious nature of capitalism as promising absolute wealth. Von Müller (2001, p. 41) summarized the expectations of the Euro as: enhancement of a homogeneous price system, its facilitation of market decisions by the consumers, its reduction of transaction costs, its deletion of the danger of inner-European speculations in currency changes and its prerequisite for a free trade of work, goods, services, and investments. In these terms *money* definitely transcends present conditions and becomes *a vehicle of our desires, promising to fulfil them.* As Jochen Hörisch (1999) elaborated, money can be interpreted as both successor to bread and wine in the Christian liturgy and as the major means of communication in modern societies, resembling the hostia: Christ's body in the form of a commodity - whereas von Müller emphasizes that the hostia had imitated the form of a coin. Both Hörisch and von Müller, however, agree that *the true meaning of money is credit* - which should not be underestimated in our EuroVisions. The introduction of the Euro already shows *mutual trust* (tested time and again by economic indicators) and a promise to trust each other even more in the future. Money therefore is a *means for transporting and evoking images, shaping social functions and modes of exchange.* The Euro bills show bridges, doors, and windows - ways and views into Utopia, projections and fulfilments beyond any Windows programme used so far.

Mass media coverage of the Euro, however, lags behind the prerequisites of long-term trust. Despite the considerable convergence of living conditions in the European Union, mass media distribution and usage may well differ more fundamentally (cf. our list of major media characteristics of the countries selected here and a few additional ones on www.mediastudies-wel.com/mamaku under the topic of '*Medienkultur*'; see also European Audiovisual Observatory 2000). Given the high variety of topics between print and broadcast media in the European Union (cf. Sievert, 1998; Ludes, 2001), there may be considerable differences in EuroVisions in the general publics and markets of opinions and attentions. The commonalities and dissimilarities of culture - and media-specific foci on various aspects of the introduction of the Euro are tested in the next section.

Dutch, French, German Enthusiasm, British Disdain and Swiss 'Frank'-ness

Television prime-time programmes, the major national popular and quality newspapers, the print newsmagazines, as well as the major web information offerings for each of the Euro-countries selected, plus the UK (with the exception of TV) and Switzerland (with the exception of private television) have been selected for an analysis of their coverage of the introduction of the Euro. (See Ludes, 2002b.)

In general, we can observe French and German enthusiasm surpassed by Dutch willingness to throw away the Guilder and to welcome the Euro. The international news channel of *BBC World News* offers more critical comments on the introduction of the Euro than all other channels combined. It is noteworthy that *BBC World News* referred to a two thirds rejection of the introduction of the Euro in Germany (without giving an exact source), whereas *EuroNews* showed a graphic with sixty-two per cent support for the Euro in Germany (cf. the data by Eurobarometer, http://europa.eu.int/comm/dg10/epo/polls.html).

The German-Swiss public service television programme covered the introduction of the Euro almost as extensively as the French, German or Dutch television programmes; it made efforts to introduce Swiss components, referring to the specific money paper produced in Switzerland, its expertise in safe money and the importance of the Swiss Franc which, however, would be supplemented by some use of the Euro in Swiss travel bureaux, hotels and supermarkets. In general, the public service programmes showed much more on the Euro than the commercial channels.

The Swiss print magazine *Facts*, in its web edition of the 13 December 2001, added some information not taken into consideration in the journals or the television programmes analysed, starting with the so-called best joke on the Euro: 'We would like to inform you that, due to the introduction of the Euro, from 2 January 2002, the Kamasutra position usually known as '69' will now be known as 35.28 ... the Euro exchange rate.' This web page also stated that forty-five of the total of 120 different Euro coins show men, whereas only sixteen of them show females, eight of which are Queen Beatrix of the Netherlands. The Italians have Venus on their ten cent coins. France had introduced all of its school pupils to various aspects of the Euro and the European institutions during 22-29 October 2001- children and pupils in general knew more about it than most of their parents.

The former German Chancellor Helmut Kohl published his commentary on the Euro as a key to the common European house in various European journals (here quoted according to *Le Monde* of the 13 December 2001). He interpreted the Euro as a milestone on a long road towards European unification, an irreversible process because of this common currency, interpreted as the condition of peace and liberty in the twenty-first century. *Money* is considered here, not only as a means of payment, but *as a symbol of political and cultural identity*. The interpretation of the introduction of the Euro, however, can be quite contradictory. Both n-tv.de and facts.ch, for example, saw Germany as sceptical whereas lemonde.fr (17 December

2001) emphasized its big hello in Frankfurt.

The Christmas or New Year's speeches of the heads of state (cf. Eisner, 1991; Mohler, 1989; Gozzi, 1990) show a different picture. The German Chancellor Gerhard Schröder started his New Year's speech saying:

> *All of us will participate in writing history. We are part of a new epoch of which men and women in Europe had dreamt for centuries: Travelling without borders and payment in a common currency - in Euro and cent*

He added, 'the *dream of a common currency can now be touched* and the European Union might become a model for other regions in the world'. (author translation.). In contrast, the President of the Federal Republic of Germany, Johannes Rau, in his Christmas speech on the 24 December of 2001 did not mention the Euro at all, nor did Jacques Chirac, President of the French Republic, Swiss President Kaspar Villiger, Queen Beatrix of the Netherlands and Queen Elizabeth of the United Kingdom.

The Prime Minister of the United Kingdom, in his New Year's message of the 30 December 2001, first and foremost referred to the importance of the public services and the war against terrorism, while also stating that the UK is interested in a strong Europe which cannot be interpreted as contradictory to its special relations with the United States:

> *With so much of our trade and so many of our jobs tied up in businesses with the rest of Europe, it is massively in our interest that the Euro succeeds. ... It remains the government's policy to join the Euro zone, provided that the five economic prerequisites we have laid down are met and the British people give their consent in a referendum.*

Taking the media messages together, it becomes evident that the production, security and shape of the Euro bills and coins constitute the common elements – which are then put into national media contexts: In the Netherlands, children can be shown as representatives for the public, in Portugal (portrayed in Arte), a priest explains the new value of the Euro in contrast to the old currency and he shows a Euronote as if it were the holy cross.

Nevertheless it is also obvious that the prerequisites and achievements considered most important in current social sciences remain invisible in the mass media. Referring to Manuel Castells' theory on the unification of Europe, on globalization, identity and the new type of a European network state (1998, Chapter 5)[3] we may recall his thesis that the unification of Europe is supposed to 'bring to an end the millennial war-making between major European powers' (mainly referred to in Gerhard Schröder's New Year's Eve speech). Whether 'European identity, throughout history, was always constructed against 'the other', 'the barbarians of different kinds and different origins': in other words, the complementarity of inclusion and exclusion,' was hardly discussed in the mass media. That European-wide policies take over national ones is mostly framed in terms of a threat to citizens and sovereignties; 'different levels of integration depending upon countries and issues,' the 'variable geometry' of Europe, however, is hardly taken into account.

Mass Media Shifts and EuroVisions

The 'modalities of mass communication' have undergone an enormous change since the beginning of the twentieth century. The moving image has gained dominance (Boeckmann, 1994; Doelker, 1999; Jarren, 1999; Ludes, 2001; Rose 2001) and fostered the reception of optical-iconic symbol systems. With the interconnection of different symbol systems, forms of presentation and options for interaction between communicators, links of information offerings and e-mails, chat and bulletin board communication, 'a media revolution' began 'at the end of the twentieth century' (Wilke, 2000). These individually combinable modes of communication, their novel and fast interaction and potential obligations break up (fragmentize) traditional forms of media use. Traditionally, messages from professionally organized senders were passively received by dispersed publics in their leisure time. Since the digital multimedia shift at the turn of the millennium, interactive media gain importance. A multitude of new types of different senders (ranging from professional media corporations to self-representations of different institutions and private information offerings) offer their programme modules to individualized users. Moreover, the latter uses the 'multimedia networks' both at work and in their leisure time for informing/entertaining themselves, shopping or other services.

Since its technical realization in 1992, the World Wide Web has joined the already established mass media like the press, movies, and broadcasting at historically unprecedented rates of growth. In 2001, twenty per cent (France), thirty-four per cent (Germany), forty-seven per cent (Switzerland), fifty-five per cent (UK), and fifty-four per cent (the Netherlands) of the population of the investigated countries had online access (www.nua.com/surveys, 18 February 2002). Thus different offerings on the Web need to be interpreted as mass media (Ogan, 1996; Berghaus, 1999). Even more important is the usage of 'multimedia networks' in international and trans-national corporations to coordinate and inform quickly and cost-effectively about production cycles and management decisions (Pavlik, 1998; Pethig, 2000).

With the establishment of the EMU, all goods, services, income, and savings that can be measured in monetary units will be more easily comparable

(Klingemann/Neidhardt, 2000; Ludes, 2000 and 2001). What remains less comparable - throughout national media cultures and national states - are basic patterns of differentiation concerning groups of 'us' and 'them', gaining and defending resources of power, the formation of opinions in media-specific partial publics or expert systems, everyday affective connections within families, couples or friendships. Money requires trust in the system (cf. Luhmann, 1973; Deutschmann, 1995, 1999; Forschungszentrum Karlsruhe, 1998); it recurs in experiences which cannot easily be transferred from national currencies to the Euro. Value-oriented connections and liabilities must therefore support the institutionalization of the Euro (Ludes, 1998 and 2000).

In the twenty-first century, mass media and target group media will play a more important role for collective identities than in the nineteenth and even the twentieth century (Habermas, 1998; Faulstich and Hickethier, 2000, part II). What must be investigated is, according to Habermas, a 'new definition of the media rules'. In view of the shift towards digital production methods all those who organize the distribution of audio-visual products via television, video, and cinema (not only using hardcopies but later on also through satellite transmissions and the World Wide Web) will experience an 'explosion of the demand for audio-visual material.' A special function concerning the preservation and the further development of democracy, moreover, is attributed to the technical media of distribution (cf. Neidhardt, Koopmans and Pfetsch, 2000). Digitally interconnected media of distribution also strengthen the re/presentation or exclusion of topics, symbols and hence group specific or culturally specific sets of knowledge, schemes of relevance, and models of (in-)security or (dis-)orientation (cf., e.g., Modoux, 1998; Ludes, 2002a).

Towards European Media

In the European Monetary Union more than 300 million people, on a day to day basis, already act as Euro-consumers. This role is not yet enlightened by sufficient information on European politics, economy, and culture. From July 2001 to June 2002, in the major German television news for example, the European Union was only covered by 1.3% of items in the *Tagesschau* and less than one per cent in *heute* and the evening news of the major private-commercial television channels. The major newspapers and print magazines allowed for about five per cent of their articles on the European Union. (*Medien Tenor Forschungsbericht* Nr. 124, 15 September 2002, p. 61). Therefore I will conclude with six proposals furthering the emergence of *European media* (rather than only regional or national media in Europe).

1. Public multimedia networks and closed intranets must be coordinated in terms of securing

interoperable technical standards, screen designs, and sign combinations. Functional specialization and complementarity can be shaped according to European necessities.

2. The visual language of TV programmes and WWW content has gained importance at the cost of face-to-face communication and reading. Starting with well-known European key pictures (like the Acropolis or the Eiffel Tower), these perspectives can be made more explicit, adding elements of a European visual language to the various national languages. This vision calls for special energy, given the continuous spread of US-American movies and TV programmes in all European countries. The new digitization, archiving, distribution, and transformation of visual data will contribute to the realization of such a European (audio-) visual vision.

3. Given the more immediate and emotional appeal of pictures, they can also strengthen more pàrasocial interactions between European citizens.

4. There are few economic, political, cultural challenges which are not shaped and transformed by information and communication technologies, presentation formats, and modes for using such information. A stock of common European symbols and arguments (key pictures and key issues) must support European public discourses on a more understandable as well as more visible level.

5. Europe is more than a dialogue of national and regional cultures. And whenever crises arose in the European Union during the past decades, it became clear that any return to national egotism and international conflict weakens all those involved. Similar to the coordination of economic transactions by means of the Euro, a 'European Communication Union' therefore should support some dialogue between the rich heritages of various individual, regional, or national personality structures, habits, and actions.

6. These dialogues call for adequate arenas. Various expert groups are already players in the markets. Market constraints and competitive chances thereby are taken into account. The prerequisites for sustainable regional, national democracies and a commonly supported European democracy require, however, more attention.

In conclusion, the present phase of media in Europe calls for the emergence of new, European Media. They need not cover the same topics or use the same formats, but share similar concerns. Human sentiments, attitudes, and actions have always required media of orientation and communication. The availability, scope, range, and formats of these media continuously shaped social standards, degrees of dis/integration, qualities of life, and identity models. The European Monetary Union confronts more than 300 million people on a day-to-day basis with a monetary-communicative network. But the average standards of living in the member countries studied: salaries, levels of education, housing conditions, social benefits etc. usually do not vary more than relations of one to five, at most seven, between the lowest and the highest national averages. The biggest differences apply to comparisons between Portugal and the Netherlands. Yet, economic advantages do not always coincide with subjective perceptions of standards of living. And criteria such as safety in the neighborhood (low in the U.K.) may be more important than the number of rooms available.

European identity is made up of various national, regional, gender, professional, age group and lifestyle identities. According to Eurobarometer surveys, only a small group of about five to seven per cent identify themselves primarily as Europeans. Yet, in contrast to other parts of the world, 'Europeanness' may appear more prominent. Similar to the development of a new historic type of a European network state, made up of multilevel economic, political, and cultural interdependencies, the traditional notion of identity must be reformulated for a multitude of reference groups within the European Union. One-dimensional Europeanness will hardly emerge as a core identity.

Only the mass media can integrate otherwise highly fragmented markets or publics into more encompassing combinations of these segments for some enduring common knowledge. As we have seen, this media education has barely begun in national terms in the context of introducing the Euro. However, democratic participation requires some common knowledge and possibly a few common value hierarchies and agendas. These provide common means of communication and dis-/orientation for democratic opinion making and decision-taking. Although the majorities of the various member countries hardly long for European social cohesion, some degree of the latter is necessary for European public spaces and the democratic control of trans-national as well as trans-atlantic powers and share-holders.

The member cultures of the European Union share a long tradition of common means of orientation and basic symbols. In contrast to other parts of the world, punctuality and long-term calculations, deferred gratifications and an economic account of time (similar to that of money) prevail. The densely populated (urban) areas of most of Western Europe have enhanced personality traits like personal detachment, situational flexibility in the context of social security systems and free access to all levels of education. A hidden dimension of European identity and cohesion is located in shared fundamental means of dis/orientation, not only concerning time and space, but also activism, rationality, individualism, and European 'Christian' values as universal. With the rise of multimedia-communication and as a (corresponding) deterioration of the significance of personal territorial space, there emerge some new ambiguities and competitive relations between the various types of personal and mediated dis/orientation which undermine elements of identity so far taken for granted.

Those aspects of technological, legal, economic convergence which accompany European standards, work and product regulations and the monetary unification enhance the mobility not only of tourists, but of students, employees, enterprises, and social movements. WWW-information and entertainment offerings will supplement cable and satellite television in integrating symbolically clusters of minorities spread throughout the European Union, for example: Spanish students; automobile workers; software industries or ecological movements from various countries - as well as, last but not least, experts on changing media and changing Europe. The considerable increase in communicative, cognitive, media, educational, professional, and political flexibility and geographical and social mobility will shake and re-shape traditional identities.

Yet, whether these developments will be experienced as an increase in the quality of life, can be doubted. There will arise a high variation of winners and losers, not only between regions and groups but also within individual life times. EuroVisions show both sides of the coin, a national one and a European one, just like the Euro coins.

Notes

1   I am deeply indebted to the University of Siegen which financed this research, the Media Centre of Siegen University (my colleagues Hartmut Simon, Volker Hess, Stephan Schopp, Alfred Schäfer, Harald Becker, and Norbert Greiten) for the recording of the television programmes, and the download of the web offerings and team 3 of CMCE for its discussion of the research design, as well as Tobias Kohler, Michael Hellermann, Hannes Wöhrle and last, not least, Georg Rademacher for their research assistance. The complete account of the media analysed as well as numerous examples, especially forty minutes selection from the TV programmes, are presented and analysed in more detail on my DVD-ROM 'Medien und Symbole: €UROpäische MedienBILDung. Mit zwei Beiträgen zur Medienzivilisierung von Jürgen Zinnecker.' Technik, Gestaltung, Realisation: Medienzentrum der Universität Siegen: info@universi.uni-siegen.de (15 €).

2.   I am deeply indebted to the students of my seminar 'European Monetary Union / European Communication Union' (Winter 2001/02) who - together with me - selected the most pertinent sequences of about 330 hours of the television programmes recorded for further analysis. Barbara Kummler and Vincent da Silva were experts on Switzerland and Germany, Nadja Hoffmann and Maren Königsberg for France, Miriam Fraas for Arte, Britta Rohr for the Netherlands and Hannes Wöhrle and Fabian Gard for the news channels.

3.   Castells (1998, p. 319) is convinced that the unification of Europe will be anchored in the creation of the Euro. The three dominant currencies in the World, the Euro, the US-Dollar, and the Yen, 'will be likely to be packed to each other in the future, thus eliminating national sovereignty for all practical purposes' (Castells 1998, p. 420). Castells (1998, p. 324) also foresees 'the significant shrinkage of the welfare state ... a dramatic increase in inequality, poverty, and social exclusion ... Ultimately, political legitimacy will be undermined since the welfare state is

one of its pillars.' The major actors in these developments consist of a: 'complex, changing geometry of European institutions that combines the control of decision-making by national governments ... the management of common European business, by a competent, if unpopular, Euro-technocracy ... and the symbolic expressions of legitimacy in the European Parliament, the Court of Justice, and the Court of Auditors' (Castells, 1998, p. 340). In these terms, changing Europe comes first and changing media are only a minor part of more dominant economic, political, technological, and cultural forces. As Castells (2000, p. 354) states:

But, unlike the United States, ... most Europeans of the European Union continue to long for a culturally and ethnically homogeneous society, which is now irreversibly gone with the global wind. This schizophrenia between self-image and the new demographic reality of Europe constitutes a key feature of cultural and political dynamics linked to the redefinition of European identity.

Germany as the major economic power, Britain and France as the major military powers are the most important nodes in the network state European Union, a new form of state, which might be considered as characteristic of the Information Age (Castells, 1998, p. 332). Castells' theory points beyond the emphasis in communication studies and political sciences on the transformation of the public sphere, in both of its major expressions as trans-national structures of resonance (Eder and Kantner, 2001) or as similarities of topics and their relevance in combined national and trans-national media (Gerhards, 2001).

Europe changes faster than its media, at least its mass media. Invisible convergences of lifestyles contribute more to its 'relative homogeneity' (Welzel, Inglehart, Klingemann, 2001) than convergence in topics or markets. However, similar media technologies and formats most probably are more important than the aforementioned differences. Meier and Jarren (2001) recently emphasized the additional major shift, accompanying and enforcing the transformations enhanced by the introduction of the Euro: the digitization and increase of multimedia networks leads from a primacy of information to a primacy of selling. This shift cannot be understood by a focus on current developments alone.

References

Beck, Klaus (2000) 'Entgrenzung durch Computernetze? Medienintegration und Mediendifferenzierung an der Schwelle zum 21. Jahrhunder' ('Transcending borders via computer networks? Media integration and media differentiation on the threshold of the 21st century'), in Brosius, Hans-Bernd (Ed.), Kommunikation über Grenzen und Kulturen (Communication across borders and cultures) (Schriftenreihe der Deutschen Gesellschaft für Publizistik- und Kommunikationswissenschaft, Bd. 27), Konstanz, pp. 173-186.

Berghaus, Margot (ed.) (1999) Interaktive Medien - interdisziplinär vernetzt (Interactive media - in interdisciplinary networks) Opladen: Westdeutscher Verlag.

Boeckmann, Klaus (1994) Unser Weltbild aus Zeichen: zur Theorie der Kommunikationsmedien (Our view of the world from signs: on the theory of the communications media), Vienna: Wilhelm Braumüller.

Brettschneider, Frank: 'EU und EURO - die Verantwortung der Medien' ('EU and EURO - the Responsibility of the Media'), in Medien Tenor Forschungsbericht (Research Report on the Tenor of the Media) Nr. 107, April 2001, pp. 42-45.

Castells, Manuel (2000 [1998]) The Information Age. Economy, Society and Culture. Vol. III: End of Millennium. Malden, Massachusetts/Oxford: Blackwells.

Deutschmann, Christoph (1995) 'Geld als soziales Konstrukt. Zur Aktualität von Marx und Simmel' ('Money as a social construct. Concerning the relevance of Marx and Simmel') , in Leviathan. Zeitschrift für Sozialwissenschaft, 15, pp. 376-393.

Deutschmann, Christoph (1999) Die Verheißung des absoluten Reichtums (The Promise of Absolute Wealth), Frankfurt am Main: Taschen.

Doelker, Christian (1999) Ein Bild ist mehr als ein Bild. Visuelle Kompetenz in der Multimediagesellschaft (A picture is more than a picture. Visual competence in the multi-media society) (second revised edition), Stuttgart: Klett Cotta.

Eder, Klaus; Kantner Cathleen (2001) 'Transnationale Resonanzstrukturen in Europa. Eine Kritik der Rede vom Öffentlichkeitsdefizit' ('Transnational structures of resonance in Europe. A critique of the talk about the lack of a public'), in Friedrichs, Jürgen; Mayer, Karl Ulrich; Schluchter, Wolfgang (eds.) Die Europäisierung nationaler Gesellschaften. The Europeanisation of national societies).(Kölner Zeitschrift für Soziologie und Sozialpsychologie. Sonderhefte) (Cologne Journal for Sociology and Social Psychology. Special Issues) Wiesbaden: Westdeutscher Verlag, pp. 306-331.

Eisner, Manuel (1991) Politische Sprache und sozialer Wandel. Eine quantitative und semantische Analyse von Neujahrsleitartikeln in der Schweiz von 1840 bis 1987 (Political Language and Social Change. A quantitative and semantic analysis of New Year leading articles in Switzerland from 1840 to 1987), Zürich: Taschen.

European Commission (1998) Das digitale Zeitalter. Europäische Audiovisuelle Politik. Bericht der hochrangigen Gruppe für audiovisuelle Politik.(The digital age. European audiovisual policy. Report of the high-ranking working group for audiovisual policy) Brussels/Luxemburg.

European Media Institute(1998) 'Media in Europe': The Yearbook of the European Institute for the Media. 1998, Düsseldorf.

European Audiovisual Observatory (2000) Statistical Yearbook. Film, Television, Video, and New Media in Europe. Strassbourg.

European Communication Council Report (1999) Die Internet-Ökonomie. Strategien für die digitale Wirtschaft (The Internet-Economy. Strategies for the digital economy), Berlin/Heidelberg.

European Union (no year) A View from the Top. Top Decision Makers and the European Union. Conducted by EOS Gallup Europe. Report prepared by Jacqueline M. Spence. Wavre.

Faulstich, Werner (2000) Medienkulturen (Media Cultures), Munich, Fink 2000.

Faulstich, Werner and Hickethier, Knut (eds.) (2000) Öffentlichkeit im Wandel. Neue Beiträge zur Begriffsklärung (The Public in the Process of Change. New contributions to the clarification of a concept), Bardowick: Taschen.

Forschungsschwerpunkt Marktprozess und Unternehmensentwicklung: Infrastruktur und Wachstum (Research Focus: Market Process and Enterprise Development: Infrastructure and Growth), in WZB-Mitteilungen, 79 (1998), pp. 28-31.

Forschungszentrum Karlsruhe Technik und Umwelt. Institut für Technikfolgenabschätzung und Systemanalyse (ed.), TA-Datenbank-Nachrichten (TA-Data-Bank News). Heft 2, Jahrgang 7 (Nr2/ Vol 7) (1998) Schwerpunktthema: Elektronisches Geld und Internet-Zahlungssysteme (Special Issue on Electronic Money and Internet Payment Systems), pp. 5-54.

Gerhards, Jürgen (2001) 'Europäisierung von Ökonomie und Politik und die Trägheit der Entstehung einer europäischen Öffentlichkeit' ('Europeanisation of economics and politics and the slowness in the development of a European public'). in Friedrichs, Jürgen; Mayer, Karl Ulrich; Schlucher, Wolfgang (eds), Die Europäisierung nationaler Gesellschaften (The Europeanisation of National Societies). Kölner Zeitschrift für Soziologie und Sozialpsychologie. Sonderhefte. (Cologne Journal for Sociology and Social Psychology. Special Issues)Wiesbaden: Westdeutscher Verlag, pp. 277-305.

Gozzi, Raymond, Jr. (1990) New Words and a Changing American Culture. Columbia: University of Columbia Press.

Habermas, Jürgen (1998) Die postnationale Konstellation. Politische Essays (The post-national constellation of forces. Political essays). Frankfurt am Main Suhrkamp.

Heinemann, Klaus (1969) Grundzüge einer Soziologie des Geldes (The basic features of a sociology of money). Stuttgart: Enke.

Holmes, Diana.and Smith, Alison (eds.) (2000) 100 years of European Cinema. Entertainment or Ideology? Manchester: University Press.

Hörisch, Jochen (1999) Ende der Vorstellung - Die Poesie der Medien (The End of Imagination - The Poetry of the Media). Frankfurt am Main: Suhrkamp.

Humphreys, Peter: 'Das Rundfunksystem Großbritanniens' ('The Broadcasting System in Great Britain'), in Hans-Bredow-Institut: Internationales Handbuch für Hörfunk und Fernsehen 2000/2001 (International Handbook for Radio and Television), (2000), pp. 378-396.

Huntington, Samuel P. (1996) The Clash of Civilizations. New York: Simon & Schuster.

Jarren, Otfried (1999) 'Bilder, Bildanalyse und Bildstrategien in der Mediengesellschaft' ('Images, Image Analysis and Image Strategies in the Media Society'), in Amann, Daniel et al. (eds), Medien lesen. Der Textbegriff in der Medienwissenschaft (Reading the media. The concept of Text in Media Sciences), pp139-152. Zürich.

Klingemann, Hans-Dieter and Neidhardt, Friedhelm (eds) (2000) Zur Zukunft der Demokratie. Herausforderungen im Zeitalter der Globalisierung (On the future of democracy. Challenges in the era of globalisation) WZB-Jahrbuch 2000, Berlin.

Ludes, Peter (1998) Towards a European Information Union, Introductory Paper: European Information Societies and Media Cultures, Siegen, November 1998.

Ludes, Peter (2000) 'Die Notwendigkeit einer europäischen Informationsunion' ('The need for a European Information Union'), in Düllo, Thomas et al. (eds) Kursbuch Kulturwissenschaft, pp. 45-59 Münster/Hamburg/London.

Ludes, Peter (2001) Multimedia und Multi-Moderne: Schlüsselbilder. Buch: Fernsehnachrichten und World Wide Web - Medienzivilisierung in der Europäischen Währungsunion (Multimedia and Multi-Modernity: Key images. Book: Television News and World Wide Web - The civilizing of the media in the European Currency Union). CD-ROM: Schlüsselbilder. Wissenschaft, Politiker und einfache Leute, Wirtschaft, Militär und Medien (Key images. Science, Politicians and Ordinary People, Economy, Military and Media) , Wiesbaden, Westdeutscher Verlag.

Ludes, Peter (2002a) 'Medienbeobachtungen und Medienausblendungen. Zur Anästhesie der Bildschirmmedien' ('Media Observations and Media Fade-Outs. On the Anaesthetics of the Screen Media'), in Peter Gendolla, Peter Ludes and Volker Roloff (eds.), BildschirmMedienTheorien (Screen Media Theories), Munich: Fink, pp. 133-144.

Ludes, Peter (2002b) Medien und Symbole. €uropäische MedienBILDung. Mit zwei Beiträgen zur Medienzivilisierung von Jürgen Zinnecker. Technik, Gestaltung, Realisation (Media and

Symbols: €uropean Media Formation [IMAGE making]. With two contributions on the civilising of the media by Jürgen Zinnecker. Technology, Shaping, Realisation): Medienzentrum der Universität Siegen: info@universi.uni-siegen.de (15 €).

Ludes, Peter. and Werner, Andreas (eds.) (1997) Multimedia-Kommunikation. Theorien, Trends und Praxis (Multimedia Communication. Theories, Trends and Practice), Opladen: Westdeutscher Verlag.

Luhmann, Niklas (1973 [1968].) Vertrauen. Ein Mechanismus der Reduktion sozialer Komplexität (Trust. A Mechanism for reducing social complexity), Stuttgart: Enke.

Medien Tenor Forschungsbericht Nr. 124, vom 15. September 2002 (The Tenor of the Media Research Report No. 124, 15 September 2002), pp. 60-63.

Meier, Werner.and A. Jarren, Ottfried (2001) 'Ökonomisierung und Kommerzialisierung von Medien und Mediensystem. Einleitende Bemerkungen zu einer (notwendigen) Debatte' ('Economisation and Commercialisation of the Media and of Media Systems. Introductory Remarks concerning a [necessary] debate'). In M&K, Vol 2, pp. 145-158.

Meinhof, Ulrike Hanna (2001) 'Auf der Suche nach EuroNews-Land: Satellitenfernsehen und die Konstruktion kultureller Identitäten' ('In Search of Euro-News-Land: Satellite Television and the Construction of Social Identities') in (ed. Brigitta Busch; Brigitte Hipfl; Kevin Robins) Bewegte Identitäten. Medien in transkulturellen Kontexten (Turbulent Identities. Media in Transcultural contexts), Klagenfurt: Drava, pp. 111-127.

Modoux, Alain (1998). Un gigantesque ghetto cybérien menace l'édifice des droits de la personne. Human Rights and the INTERNET et les droits de la personne (Unity for the freedom of expression and democracy A gigangtic cyber-ghetto threatens the edifice of human rights. Human Rights and the INTERNET and human rights), Montreal: UNESCO.

Mohler, Peter. (1989) 'Wertkonflikt und Wertdiffusion? Ein Vergleich von Ergebnissen aus Bevölkerungsumfragen und einer Inhaltsanalyse von Leitartikeln der FAZ' ('Value Conflict and Value Diffusion? A comparison of findings from population surveys and an analysis of the content of leading articles in the Frankfurter Allgemeine Zeitung'), in Kölner Zeitschrift für Soziologie und Sozialpsychologie, 41, 1 (1989), pp. 95-123.

Müller, Achatz von (2001) 'Die Währung von Entenhausen' ('The Currency of Entenhausen'), in Die Zeit No. 1, 27 Dec. 01, pp. 41.

Münch, Richard (1998) Globale Dynamik, lokale Lebenswelten. Der schwierige Weg in die Weltgesellschaft (Global dynamics, local living worlds. The difficult path into world society). Frankfurt am Main: Suhrkamp.

Neidhardt, Friedhelm, Koopmans, Ruud and Pfetsch, Barbara (2000) 'Konstitutionsbedingungen politischer Öffentlichkeit: Der Fall Europa' ('The Constitutive Conditions of a Political Public'), in Die Zukunft der Demokratie. Herausforderungen im Zeitalter der Globalisierung (The future of democracy. Challenges in the age of globalisation): Klingemann, Hans-Dieter/Neidhardt, Friedhelm (eds.) WZB-Jahrbuch 2000, pp. 263-293. Berlin.

Ogan, Christine: (1996) 'The Internet as Mass Medium', in Journal of Communication. 46(1), pp. 39-50.

Pavlik, John V. (1998) New Media Technology. Cultural and Commercial Perspectives, Boston/London/Toronto/Sydney/Tokyo/Singapore: Allyn & Bacon.

Pethig, Rüdiger (2000) 'Technik und Ökonomie im Prozess der Digitalisierung' ('Technology and Economy in the Process of Digitalisation'), in Krewani: Angela (Ed.), Artefakte Artefiktionen. Transformationsprozesse zeitgenössischer Literaturen, Medien, Künste, Architekturen (Artefacts, Artefictions. Transformation processes of contemporary literatures, media, arts and architectures), Heidelberg: Winter, pp. 383-393.

Reenen, Ben van (2000) 'Die niederländische Rundfunklandschaft im Jahr 2000' ('The Dutch Broadcasting Landscape in the year 2000'), in Hans-Bredow-Institut: Internationales Handbuch für Hörfunk und Fernsehen (International Handbook for Radio and Television) 2000/2001, Baden-Baden.

Rose, Gillian (2001) Visual Methodologies. An Introduction to the Interpretation of Visual Materials, London/Thousand Oaks/New Delhi: Sage.

Saxer, Ulrich (Ed.) (1998) 'Medien-Kulturkommunikation. Publizistik' ('Cultural Communication in the Media') Sonderheft (Special Issue) 2/1998, Opladen/Wiesbaden: Westdeutscher Verlag.

Schmidt, Siegfried J (2000) Kalte Faszination. Medien - Kultur - Wissenschaft in der Mediengesellschaft (Cold Fascination. Media - Culture - Science in the Media Society), Weilerswist: Velbrück Wissenschaft.

Sievert, Holger (1998) Europäischer Journalismus. Theorie und Empirie aktueller Medienkommunikation in der Europäischen Union (European Journalism. Theorie and Empirical evidence of current media communication in the European Union), Opladen/Wiesbaden: Westdeutscher Verlag.

Welzel, Christian, Ronald Inglehart and Hans-Dieter Klingemann (2001) 'Human Development as a General Theory of Social Change: A Multi-Level and Cross-Cultural Perspective', in Wissenschaftszentrum Berlin für Sozialforschung Discussion Paper FS III Berlin.

Wilke, Jürgen (2000) Grundzüge der Medien- und Kommunikationsgeschichte. Von den Anfängen bis ins 20. Jahrhundert (Basic Features of the History of the Media and Communication), Köln/Weimar/Wien: Böhlau.

Zelizer, Viviana A. (1994) The Social Meaning of Money. New York: BasicBooks.

Part C: Media Institutions in a Changing Europe

In this third section we look at institutional policies and strategies trying to cope with the changing European and global scene, both in terms of media politics, political communication and new and more interactive modes of communication. Taisto Hujanen's article provides a thorough case study of the transformation of the Finnish public service channels after 2000 as digitalisation became the key word. Hujanen shows how traditional public service strategies are renewed and transformed, and raises important questions about the role of public service in a future European media context. In Mazzoleni's article another important aspect of European media culture is raised: the development of political communication and democracy in circumstances of media concentration either on a national or more global scale. Berlusconi's Italy may seem to be an extreme case in a European context, generally characterized by more indirect links between media and political power. But as Mazzoleni clearly demonstrates, the strategies, policies and the power play of Belusconi as both a media tycoon and political figure reflect broader perspectives in European politics, where media management and control become more and more important elements of political communication. Finally, Karul Jakubowitz provides a broad context for these discussions, and takes us through the main phases of a European policy on public service broadcasting. He situates the EU policy in a longer historical development from the early, 'emerging media policy' of European nation-states, the more traditional 'public service phase' up till the 1970s, and into the 'new paradigm of media policy' facing the challenges of globalisation and media convergence.

Taisto Hujanen (Ph.D. 1986, University of Tampere) is Professor of Electronic Media and Communication in the Department of Journalism and Mass Communication at the University of Tampere. Research interests include public service broadcasting, digitalization of broadcasting and the generic history of broadcast journalism. He served as Guest Editor for a symposium in the *Journal of Radio Studies* (together with Per Jauert) on Scandinavian Radio (1998). A recent book: *The Power of Schedule: Programme Management in the Transformation of Finnish Public Service Television* (University of Tampere Press, 2002). He has also served as co-ordinator of the Nordic network for post-graduate studies in public service and electronic media (1997-99).

Taisto Hujanen

Public Service Strategy in Digital Television: From Schedule to Content

Introduction

The launch of digital terrestrial television (DTT) accelerates the transformation of public service broadcasting organizations from production-oriented cultural institutions to programming-oriented cultural industries. Public service television as unique, original production will be replaced by *public service as a brand*, developed and maintained by strategic programming choices and marketing campaigns. The fight about visibility requires a continuous growth of programme output and, at the same time, broadcasters need to consider their presence in the new technological arena and transmission networks. When responding to these challenges, public service broadcasters can hardly count on additional resources. So, similar to the crisis management of the 1990s, there will be a continuous need for increased cost-effectivity, better management and for a more streamlined programming.

The emerging new identity of public service broadcasters as 'content providers' is grounded on a technological optimism. It is believed that digitalization will create possibilities for more effective use of content resulting in increased cost-effectivity. Following the so-called new media value chain, broadcasters are supposed to concentrate on production and packaging of contents to be distributed by several carriers, functionally separate from broadcasters.[1] The content itself is understood as a joint corporate resource, formatted and versioned for different uses and audience segments, simulcasted, re-cycled and repeated in several parallel networks. As before, a part of the content is of own production in the internal market, but most probably the need for externalization of production will continue and, parallel to that, the search for alliances and co-operation in the external market will be strengthened.

The new identity of 'content providers' re-articulates the traditional relationship between programming and production in European public service broadcasting. If applying Raymond Williams' (1974) known comparison of European and American television, one could say that the European tradition has been dominated by programme making and the American by the construction of flow. In relative terms, the aesthetics of programme making, programmes as individual works of 'art', is constitutive of the European broadcasting tradition. The importance of flow in the American tradition is a consequence of a more competetive television environment. But similarly, because of the new competetive environment of television, the construction of flow started dominating even the approach of the European public broadcasters towards the end of the 1980s.[2] Organizationally, the emphasis on flow resulted in the functional separation of broadcasting and production; in other words, programming operations like scheduling were seen distinct from production of programmes.

The functional separation of broadcasting and production resulted in a power shift, which according to the British TV producer and scholar John Ellis (2000a) made scheduling as the power centre of television. My own research on the transformation of Finnish public service television points to a similar shift, as the public service broadcaster YLE trimmed its organization and practices for intensified competition in the 1990s. One of my interviewees for the study, the then head of programming for TV1, characterised the schedule as a tool for the broadcaster or publisher. He continued talking about separation of broadcasting and production:

> Today, the publisher considers what is the best menu and how to set and market it so charmingly that one wants to receive it. The producer concentrates on making the portions in the best possible way. The schedule is used then to ensure that the portions remain similar: If one orders salad, one gets salad and not meat rolls. (IK18052000)[3]

The above citation represents the schedule as a mediating structure between audiences and production. From the management point of view, the schedule appeared useful in a double sense: It could be used to structure and systematise the broadcasters' relationship with their audiences, but it could also be applied to the control of production.[4] Because of such a nature it had the potential to make the whole chain from production to programmes to audiences operative. This potential is the reason why the emphasis on the schedule became so important in public service television's search for a better management in the new competetive environment of television. The way the schedule connected production and audiences made it promising in the implementation of the so-called audience orientation which public service broadcasters now preferred to present as the basis of their social responsibility and accountability.

The Transfer to Digital: Contrasting Schedule and Content

Below, the schedule-oriented approach of the 1990s is contrasted against the content-oriented strategy of public service broadcasters at the start of the new millenium. The analysis and discussion will make use of the research data which I collected in the autumn 1999 and in 2000 inside the Finnish public service broadcaster's (YLE) two television channels TV1 and TV2. The data consists of interviews with programmers and schedulers of the channels, including the new category of commissioning editors, and with a selection of executive producers. In addition, I have used the records of the decision making and consultative bodies of the channels and collected a series of policy and planning documents. The study as a whole focused on a description and analysis of a management practice which YLE's television division adopted in 1994 and which at first was called audience-oriented management by schedule, later shortened to Management by Schedule (Hujanen, 2002). YLE Television, the new division level of organization was created in order to increase the harmonization between the two separate channels TV1 and TV2. Harmonization was seen necessary if YLE wanted to match the open competition with commercial television introduced by the 1993 channel reform.

Building up Management by Schedule lasted the rest of the 1990s and connected, in this way, directly with the launch of DTT into the new millenium, on the 27 August 2001. By the end of the year 2002, YLE is the only digital operator to have really initiated the new digital channels (about the original structure of the digital multiplexes, see Appendix 1). The retail sale of set-top boxes needed for digital reception was delayed, and the MHP standard boxes (and receivers) which enable the use of the interactive capacity of digital television are not yet widely available. The estimate at the end of 2002 is that some three per cent of households own a set-top box for digital reception. That is why commercial operators have postponed the full-scale launch of their digital services, and a part of the planned services have been cancelled. YLE seems to be convinced that the early bird catches the worm, and this attitude illuminates its digital strategy since the principal decision of the Finnish Government in 1996 to start planning the digitalization of broadcasting.

The introduction of Management by Schedule (MBS) re-articulated the goal-oriented rationality of the old programme planning culture and transformed it to a management practice which aimed at linking the strategic assessment of the immediate and future environment with the present-tense operative action. As a form of strategic management, MBS integrated strategic planning functions with scheduling, commissioning and evaluation (including audience research). This integration is the source of the increased power of the schedule, perceived by all the interviewed managers and producers in this study. The introduction of market logic in transactions between programming operations and production, the introduction of internal/external market, was an essential structural condition for MBS. The practice of Producer Choice was introduced in 1996, and two years later both TV1 and TV2 set up their tailored versions of commissioning. The new commissioning editors for fact and fiction adopted a key role in the implementation of MBS in relation to production. At the same time the idea of commissioning as such symbolised the new corporate culture where programmers and schedulers acted as buyers and producers as sellers; and audiences as customers for the actors of the internal market.

Table 1. below summarises the context and impact of MBS as constructed in YLE's management discourse. In addition, the table contrasts the schedule-oriented strategy of the 1990s with the digital strategy of the new millenium. Many categories of Table 1. have already been commented upon above. At this point, a few comments will be added concerning the contextual change from the 1990s to digitalization. The impact of MBS on YLE's corporate culture will be described in a separate section and, similarly, the two key elements of the digital strategy will be analysed. The latter two aspects refer to the notion of channel profilization and to the re-organization of production in the form of so-called skill centres.

As Table 1. below demonstrates, many contextual aspects of public service television remained constant. These include the saturated economy and the consequent need for cost-effectivity, audience orientation, the search for accountability and the normative basis for operation in the form of public service. In YLE's case, the requirement of public service is based on a special law from 1993 (Law No. 1380/1993) which states that the function of the company is to offer full-service broadcast programming to everyone on equal terms. The formulation of the law ties YLE with what could be called the universal service obligation of broadcasting. The universalism is understood in a broad sense so that it does not only refer to universal access to broadcasting, but covers for example the broad generic range of services (cf. Harrison & Woods, 2001).

Growth of competition and growth of supply belong also to constant contextual features. However, the continuous growth of supply and the consequent intensification of competition is leading to a qualitative change which John Ellis in his recent book (2000b, pp. 162-178) identifies as a change from availability to plenty. The latter notion, television of plenty, refers to the consequences of digitalization which accelerates and multiplies the supply in old and new distribution networks. As pointed out in the beginning, in such an environment branding products becomes a key issue.

Table 1. Construction of public service television in YLE's management discourse: a summary view.

1) Television in the 1990's	2) Digital television
What remained constant?	
Growth of competition	Growth of competition
Growth of supply	Growth of supply
Saturation of economy	Saturation of economy
Cost-effectivity	Cost-effectivity
Audience orientation	Audience orientation
Accountability	Accountability
Public service	Public service
What changed?	
Multi-channel environment	Multiple / multimedia environment
Television	Integrated service entities
Schedule-oriented strategy	Content-oriented strategy
*Management by Schedule	*Management by Content
Channels	Packaging & Branding
*Full service	*Multiplex of channels
* Co-ordinated universalism	* Channel profilization
Programme production	Content production
Schedule-oriented professionalism	* Multi-skill professionalism
* Production as commission	* Cross-commissioning
* System of executive producers	*Skill centres (genre)
* From departments to teams	* Co-production & alliances

The most radical change, however, concerns the interpretation of the operative context of television and of television itself. In the 1990s the operative context was defined as a multi-channel environment (cf. for example Avery, 1993). One should add that such a definition considered broadcast television as a particular form of electronic media, a discrete medium with its own specific characteristics. In YLE's digital strategy, television itself is more secondary and the operative environment is depicted in terms of the new media logic and understood as a multiple/multimedia environment. In this way, television becomes part of 'integrated service entities', and its particular features are re-articulated in terms of packaging and distribution. As a consequence, television production is no longer production of programmes but production of content. These changes correspond to how two British researchers refer to the British context: Television is increasingly defined as a multimedia access technology as opposed to a traditional discrete media form (Sampson & Lugo, 2002).

In the following, the focus will turn at first to the re-articulation of the programming/production relationship in YLE Television as a consequence of MBS. Two key features of the digital strategy, channel profilization and skill centres, will also be analysed and evaluated in terms of continuity and change. The questions to be dealt with are how these aspects of the new content-oriented strategy affect the co-ordinated universalism of the former two-channel structure and how they, once again, re-construct the programming/production relationship in public service television.

The Impact of Management by Schedule

The introduction of Management by Schedule in YLE Television was a part of a major organizational reform in April 1994 which aimed at giving priority to programming and programmes in resource allocation. Broadly speaking, Management by Schedule (MBS) can be understood as an overall label for several major changes in YLE's television operations which all strove for increasing strategic thinking in programming and production as well as for their closer integration with the corporate strategy and economy. Among these major changes, interlinked with MBS, one could list the gradual introduction of Producer Choice by transforming distinct resource departments of the channels into the so-called result units by 1996 and, later, by combining them as joint functions on the division level. This transformation was complemented in 1998 by a system of programme commissioning within channels and with the external independent market. These two reforms symbolize the creation of the internal/external market as a measure to increase the transparency and cost-effectivity of broadcasting.

MBS represented a radical change in the corporate culture of Finnish public service television. The requirement to put programming and programmes at the centre re-constructed the traditional relationship between programming and production. As TV1's internal Working Order defined it, MBS required that the process of programming is kept distinct from production. In terms of organization, this meant that there is a clear division of responsibilities between those who work with programming and those who work with production. As the later adoption of Producer Choice and commissioning shows, the relationship between programming and production was understood as a *contract relation* in which programming was responsible for the definition of goals and resource allocation, and production for delivering the agreed contents.

The new contractual relationship between programming and production is basically a hierarchical relationship between these two worlds - MBS means 'tightly controlled decision-making in terms of the schedule', as pointed out by TV1's head of programming (IK18052000). MBS reduces the editorial independence of the individual producers and emphasises the importance of executive producers as mediators between programming and production, as 'shepherds' (IK18052000.) of the slot-based projects and production teams. The old ideals of journalistic and artistic independence are replaced by the *responsiveness to the schedule*, meaning a professionalism which values team-work and cost-effectivity, a sensitivity to time-tables and to certain kinds of audiences as well as skills to meet standard generic and stylistic requirements (cf. characterisation of MBS in Table 1. above).

The introduction of Producer Choice created a new category of managers who can be called commissioning editors. TV1's commissioning editor for fiction concluded in his interview that commissioning complements MBS and aims at ensuring that the chain from viewers to broadcasters to producers is operative (KK10022000). In production, he says, this approach favours a *slot-oriented competence*, an ability to make programmes for certain audiences and for a particular programme environment, defined by the schedule and the overall channel environment. He emphasises that audiences should act as a measure of the quality control in the commissioning process. But to accomplish this would require, as he says, that the producers would learn to evaluate their ideas in terms of the intended audience. Accordingly, he would like to reduce his own role to the minimum in the evaluation: The *imagined audience* should be the decisive factor, not his opinion. The imagined audience in his formulation is not a result of free imagination, but it should be based on a careful analysis of the audience research data in relation to the particular slots.

Although both TV1 and TV2 adopted Producer Choice and commissioning as aspects of their MBS by the end of the 1990s, each developed their own version of the practices. The different solutions demonstrate that the specific traditions of the channels still influenced the application and practices of the internal market. However, as the cross-commissioning between channels increases, the pressure to standardize the practices will grow and the possibilities of tailoring will diminish. As pointed out by the commissioning editor for fiction at TV1 in his interview (KK10022000.), Producer Choice as a principle remains a necessity that is created by intensified channel competition. For him, Producer Choice represents a *form of creativity* that makes it possible to manage the equation of ever growing output and saturated budgets. He acknowledged that the average price of a programme hour has gone down steadily and will continue to do so in the new digital multiplexes.

The commissioning editors have a powerful role to play in the present application of Producer Choice. From the producers' point of view, their position is particularly important because they represent the most immediate connection with the broadcaster functions of the channels. However, both the interviewed commissioners and the heads of production departments pointed out that the producers continue consulting directly with other people in the management, including the directors of programmes for the channels. It seems that scheduling is one of the areas in which the producers may find that their interests are different from the commissioners. For example, the head of factual programmes at TV2 pointed out that the commissioning editor also represents the independent sector (IS21062000). That is why he felt that he needed to 'by pass' the commissioning editor in matters which concern the scheduling of his productions. About his own role as head of department, he said that through the introduction of commissioning his responsibility is more and more *to act as a seller* and in that sense to represent his own programme area in the internal market.

In the new corporate culture of YLE, audience orientation is considered central not only in the interpretation of YLE's overall social responsibilities but also as a measure of quality in programming and production. *Learning to imply an audience* was seen as a basic requirement of the new production culture. However, as pointed out by TV2's head of planning in her interview, some producers still think that the definition of a target audience for a programme might scare away the rest of the viewers (UK02062000). She thought that such a view represents an approach to programme making which characterised public service television before the channel competition. The point with definitions of target audiences, she said, is not the inclusion or exclusion of certain kind of audiences, but the need for a *co-ordinated action* in a competitive channel environment. The coordinated action refers to the interplay between the various phases and actors of the programming process including the channels, in which the defined target audiences are positioned in a central role as a measure of co-ordination. The result of co-ordination is, as she concludes, more satisfied viewers and, in the end, more satisfied producers. So the producers should realize that a high *viewer satisfaction* is as important a reward as high numbers in the headcounting.

Continuity and Change in YLE's Digital Strategy

The latest interviews of the study, recorded in the late spring and summer 2000, strongly reflect a change of atmosphere inside YLE after the turn of the new millenium. As to the nature of the change, there is an interesting parallel between the Big Channel Reform of 1993 and the challenges of the new millenium, as perceived by the interviewed managers. The Big Channel Reform opened up an explicit competition between YLE and its commercial competitor MTV3, and the consequent adoption of MBS aimed at trimming up YLE Television to manage competition. In summer 2000, after the turn of the millenium, YLE found itself in a similar situation with new and urgent challenges in competition. This time, the challenge was not only one or two more competitors, but rather a whole new television environment based on the launch of so-called *digital television*. Canal Plus started actively marketing a digital satellite service in Finland and a domestic terrestial network for digital television was supposed to be ready for launch in August 2001. The three digital multiplexes were planned to carry some ten new channels in addition to the former four national services (Appendix 1). YLE itself was to master one of the multiplexes and offer, in addition to TV1 and TV2, three new channels as well as a more developed version of teletext, renamed as Super Text TV.

Politically and economically, digitalization has been considered as a part of the Finnish national strategy in the construction of the so-called *information society*. In this sense, YLE's active pursuit of digitalization represents the political will of the government and the parliament. In fact, the government decision that allowed YLE to charge a higher television fee from 2000 was essentially motivated by YLE's important role in the national strategy for digitalization. The increased fee, together with the sale of half of YLE's distribution company (Digita) to a French partner, were supposed to carry YLE over the investment threshold into digitalization.

Despite the higher television fee (note: the fee had remained the same since 1991) and some extra income from the sale of the distribution company, YLE once again found itself in a situation with a number of new obligations and scant possibilities for additional financing. Parallel to this, it became clear that in a few years YLE will lose some ten per cent of its financing as a result of the new law on the communication market that was to be passed before summer 2002.[5] The new law reduced the so-called annual licensing fee of the commercial broadcasters to about a half. In the case of the biggest commercial operator, MTV3, this fee represented about twenty per cent of its annual turn over. The fee is collected by a special govermental office that also administers the collection of television fees, and most of the money is transferred over to YLE.

This sketches the background of the new atmosphere sensed by the interviewed managers in spring and summer 2000. The time was ripe for new radical changes in YLE Television, as the company prepared for the launch of digital television. It seemed that the application of MBS had not succeeded in fully 'harmonizing' the operations of the two traditional television channels, as anticipated by the motivations of the new management practice. The need for harmonization was even more urgent at the start of the new millenium, with a whole multiplex of channels for co-ordination and with many times more competition from outside. In this context, the two traditional television channels of YLE were forced to essentially re-consider their mutual relationship.

The results of the negotiations between TV1 and TV2 were published in June 2000 as the Board of YLE agreed on the so-called YLE Vision 2001-2003, a three-year-plan that was supposed to guide YLE towards the final transfer from analogue to digital transmission. As to television, the vision included two major reforms that were identified as *channel profilization* and as creation of the so-called *skill centres* (in Finnish, *osaamiskeskus*; could also be translated as competence centres). The former represented a re-articulation of the policy of channel co-ordination which used to define the relationship between TV1 and TV2; the latter was a measure to re-organize the channel-based structure of production so that one and the same production machine could serve the whole multiplex of old and new channels. In fact, as a part of the digital vision, these skill centres were supposed to gradually break the old border-lines of various media and to develop practices of cross-media and multimedia production (cf. characterization of content production in Table 1. above).

From Channel Co-ordination to Profilization

Although Management by Schedule clearly succeeded in introducing the schedule-oriented professionalism in production, it failed in the harmonization of the programme flow of the two channels. With reference to the new strategy of profilization, TV2's director of programmes characterized in his interview the earlier efforts for harmonization between TV1 and TV2 as 'excercises' of profilization that always ended in scepticism (JP06092000). Despite these excercises, he concluded, the two channels had become, on the image level, increasingly close to each other. As he thought, such a similarity would have been fatal in the new digital environment and, consequently, it was necessary to agree on basic rules between the old and new channels.

The problems of similarity between TV1 and TV2 dated to YLE's failure in the 1993 channel reform. As TV1 did not succeed in attracting big general audiences in mid-evening, it was also compelled to turn to smaller and more specified audiences. So from the point of view of YLE Television, the result was not two complementary prime-time strategies but two similar and often overlapping strategies. This is the background which towards the end of the 1990's obliged the two channels to search for new measures to coordinate their activities. This resulted in the re-formulation of the former practice of channel co-ordination and led to the adoption of the new programming approach identified above as channel profilization. According to TV2's head of planning, this would mean in prime-time that TV1 and TV2 each more clearly concentrated on their strengths in programming (UK02062000). As she formulated it, the basic idea should be that the channels had a common view of how to maintain a steady *flow of audience* in prime-time - and not for each channel separately but the two channels together.

But why worry if the programmes do well, reach a good number of people, and even make a part of viewers clearly satisfied? Thinking about the internal relationships between YLE's television channels, the answer has certainly something to do with the future of the two traditional channels. Will YLE need *two generalist television channels* in the future? If only programmes matter, why should they be distributed through two rather similar channels? One of TV2's traditional answers to such a question about its existence is that it represents the other Finland, the regions outside the capital area of Helsinki. It has been a successful argument in the former political culture of broadcasting, but in today's more market-oriented environment this branding appears problematic. In a consumer-oriented society like Finland today, 'regional' often has a negative connotation and such an image has been more a burden for TV2 lately. As the director of programmes for TV2 acknowledged in his interview (JP06092000), TV2 has sometimes projected an image of a *juntti* channel (the word juntti refers to a person who is most probably male and a sort of social outcast), when judged in terms of the media-sexy urban twenty-five to forty-five-years-olds.

According to the director of programmes for TV2, the image misrepresents the character of TV2 as a channel which, for him, appeared as pluralistic and diverse as TV1 (ibid.). But as he pointed out, the problem today is more the similarity of the two channels and that is the problem for which the adopted policy of profilization now must try to find a solution. He describes profilization as a process that starts with the definition of a channel's values and ends up with a particular kind of 'channel sound'. The profile, the channel sound, is not a policy declaration, but as he says, it must be recognised by the core audience segments for whom the sound helps to map the channel in relation to other channels.

The division level director of programming at YLE Television confirmed in his interview that the relationship between the two traditional channels is decisive for the future implementation of YLE's digital strategy (HS31082000). He coordinated the negotiations between TV1 and TV2 on profilization and forecasts that the coordinating role of the division will be even more important in the future as the number of channels increases. As a result of profilization, a new practice called *channel commissions* was introduced (2001) to mark the commitment of various channels to fulfil their strategic obligations within the whole of YLE. Thus the contractual relationship, typical in the application of Producer Choice, will also be applied to the operative definitions of the individual channels. All this symbolizes that profilization means the end of old-style channel co-ordination and, as a consequence, even TV1 and TV2 will find it hard to maintain their independence (if there is any left). As a practical reason for more co-ordination between the channels, the director of programming for YLE Television mentioned the option of *simulcasting* (ibid.). In addition to repeats and versioning, the cost-effectivity of the digital multiplex will require that the channels find slots for simulcasting, such as the news on YLE24 and their parallel transmission on TV1 & TV2 at certain times.

In the YLE Vision for 2001-2003, profilization is included among the measures needed to implement a transformation that is called the structural change of the editorial work. About the profilization itself, the vision says that it can be considered successful if the listerners and viewers perceive it. In other words, *audience perception* is, in the last instance, the measure of any channel profile. Next, profilization is presented as a *justification* for YLE to maintain several channels. So in YLE's argumentation, profilization is clearly connected with the need to maintain the company's share of the growing output of radio and television. But if the company is to respond to this need, it should concentrate on developing its services in a more profiled way. Finally, it is supposed that profilization reduces overlaps in programming and production and assists in effectively concentrating the corporate resources.

According to the director of programmes for TV2, the break-through idea of the negotiations about channel profilization was to consider the profiles of the two old channels in terms of all basic *genre areas* (JP06092000). So if one thinks about the two channels in relation to each other and the other channels, they should appear distinct not only in their overall image but also in the part of each major genre field. In Table 2. a more elaborated profilization between the two channels is sketched in terms of the basic channel commissions. The listing is based mainly on a document from YLE Television (dated 1 September 2000) concerning definitions of channel commissions, complemented by a few other working documents from summer 2000.

In the future, YLE's two traditional television channels are supposed to appear clearly distinct in a number of dimensions. But one should emphasise that the channels are not supposed to become specialised channels in terms of content or target audience(s). In other words, the two channels will also remain generalist in their basic orientation in the future. The idea of *universal service*, both in terms of access and of contents, will remain the point of departure for these two channels. This principle is first of all expressed by the owner's (meaning YLE as a whole) overall commission to the channels, which is identical for both channels (see Table 2.). As stated, each channel is expected to offer pluralistic, independent and reliable public service programming. Another similarity is the definition of target audience(s) which is, in both cases, referred to as *big basic audiences*. However, at this point one should notice in addition that each channel is supposed to have, alongside the basic audiences its own focus, segments that are different from the other channel. The third aspect of similarity is the *generic range* of programming. Although profilization at this point emphasises the division of work and focus between the channels, both channels will offer something in all basic genre areas and not only concentrate on a certain type of programming.

The interviewed managers characterize TV1 and TV2 as *full-service* channels. As has been shown earlier, according to the law, YLE's general obligation in terms of public service is to offer full service broadcast programming to the whole nation. All interviewed managers accept the conclusion that full-service channels are also needed in the digital future. For example the then director of programmes for TV1 repeated the conclusions that were included already in TV1's internal interpretation of public service in 1997: Full-service channels are important as forums of interaction between segments of society and culture and, accordingly, as sources of shared experiences and a common social reality (AG27062000). As to television viewing, she believed that even in the time of digital multiplexes a proportion of people prefer to have an *edited view of the world* from one channel; a conclusion which is at a distance from forecasts that television viewing will be more or less individualised.

Table 2. Profilization of TV1 and TV2 in the launch of digital television (YLE Vision 2001-2003)

DIMENSIONS:	TV1	TV2
The Owner's Commission	Pluralistic, independent and reliable public service programming	Pluralistic, independent and reliable public service programming
Basic Obligation	A channel of high demands which by knowledge and narratives structures our time	Easy to come close, a channel for the whole nation by which many segments of audience entertain themselves
Image (Viewers' Commission)	Reliable, attentive, addressing; a well-structured output	Warm, with a sense of humour, unpolished; a well-structured output
Audience Segments	Big basic audiences + a particular focus on: demanding, active young people	Big basic audiences + a particular focus on: entertainment-oriented, children, sport audiences
Goal in the Target Audience	Intensive viewer relationship in several segments, one of the basic channels nationally	Broad satisfaction in basic audiences, one of the basic channels nationally
Central Contents / Profile	Traditional news & current affairs	Regional angle in news & current affairs
	The channel of strong drama	Comedy-oriented fiction
	The channel for documentary and deep journalism	Service, hobby and life-style programmes
	International angle	Domestic angle
	The channel for young people of school-age	Small children's channel
	The basic services of culture and education	Recorded events
	Responsive entertainment, with satire as a special field	Basic entertainment output, with music as special field
	Debating channel	Sports channel
	Transmission of big events	

When looking at the definitions of the basic obligations and goals for the two channels, it seems that profilization aims at making the channels distinct according to a rather traditional division of work between the channels. For example, one should remember that after the catastrophe of the Big Channel Reform in 1993, TV1 strongly emphasised its role as a news and current affairs channel, and that orientation remains central to its future role. A recent comparison of the overall Finnish TV supply in the year 2000 characterised TV1 as an internationally-oriented channel of factual information, with a strong emphasis on news and current affairs (Suomalainen tv-tarjonta 2000; cf. Aslama et al., 2002). TV2 was characterised as a rainbow of different programme types, with much stronger emphasis on sport, movies, foreign fiction and children's programmes compared with TV1 (ibid.).

From Schedule to Content: Production in YLE's Digital Strategy

The traditional connection between the channel and its production has meant that each channel broadly reflects the main areas of its production. Against this background, it is easy to understand that exercises of profilization, if using the expression of TV2's director of programmes, ended in scepticism. If TV1 is supposed to be the channel for documentary and deep journalism, what will happen with TV2's strong tradition of documentaries and current affairs journalism? These are the kinds of questions that once again created a lot of worry and a fighting spirit within the production personnel in the spring 2000, when TV1 and TV2 negotiated the guidelines of profilization. The solution to the problem will be the so-called *skill centres* that will represent the basic generic fields of production and will break the traditional connection between channels and their production.

Although the new skill centres are supposed to break the traditional link between channels and their production, they remain administratively 'a part of some channel', as the YLE Vision for 2001-2003 expresses it. Ideally, the division of the centres between the channels should correspond to their accepted profiles. The functions of the centres in relation to the channels are defined as follows: The skill centre is a *unit for programme production*, while the channels act as *commissioners* and *distributors*. The new structure emphasises the network character of the channels, which has already been an important aspect of both TV1 and TV2 . Since the introduction of the joint television division in 1994 a part of programme production has been organised as joint functions on the division level (News & Current Affairs, Sport, Text TV, Import and Export). Both TV1 and TV2 have also acted as distributors of special Swedish-language programming, produced by FST, the Swedish-language television unit of YLE.

The new logic of organization does not require a link between the channels and the skill centres, and one can forecast that the importance of the link will soon diminish the more the centres start operating on the basis of *cross-commissioning*. As formulated by the YLE Vision, the centres will 'transact' with more than one channel and they will have an operative autonomy. The centres specialize in producing programmes for a certain *genre* area and for specified *slots*. In this way, the characterization of production is tied with the kind of professionalism which above was connected with the consequences of Management by Schedule. The remaining links between channels and units of production reflect the continuity aspect of YLE's organizational reforms. A direct step from channel-based production to a genre-oriented structure would have caused too much insecurity among the personnel and would have risked the implementation of the reform.

In terms of YLE's corporate economy and its resource allocation, the creation of the skill centres means that the re-organised old production machine is also supposed to serve the new digital channels. In the foreseeable future, cross-commissioning will increasingly succeed the traditional media-based lines of production. As hinted by Director General of YLE, Mr. Arne Wessberg, in a recent interview by the personnel magazine of YLE (17 October 2001), the division structure of the organization will be put under scrutiny with the creation of the skill centres. The old divisions follow basically the borderlines of different media and, according to Mr. Wessberg, this structure is now challenged by more *content-oriented management* highlighted by the logic of the skill centres.

By autumn 2001, a major part of the production units in TV1 and TV2 was re-organized into a structure of skill centres. Until now, the centres are mainly based on re-organization of production inside TV1 and TV2, which shows that there is still strong resistance among the personnel to the idea of breaking the traditional borderlines between the channels. One should also remember that the two channels are located in different cities, which certainly affects the logistics of the reform. But already, the rule is that the centres are supposed to serve not only their 'host' channel but also other channels. A couple of major areas of production, news and current affairs plus education and culture, will receive a new host among the new channels of YLE's digital multiplex. *News and Current Affairs* will be located under YLE24, the new 24-hours digital news channel, which started operating August 2001. The channel will act as a skill centre in its particular field of production.

Education and *Culture* were transferred from TV1 to a new digital channel called YLE Teema (YLE Theme) which, in addition, will offer programmes on science. As shown above in relation to profilization (Table 2), culture and education will remain an important part of TV1's orientation in the future. Since March 2002, TV1 and YLE Teema came under a joint director of programmes, so it remains to be seen what will be the final effect of the transfer of education and culture to YLE Teema. *Sport* remains located as a joint function on the division level, and it has de facto acted already as a skill centre in its field. It is, however, uncertain how long the media-based divisions will continue as such, so one can suppose that the location of sport in the organization will soon be put under scrutiny.

In addition to the already separate news and current affairs and sport, the rest of the new skill centres included, by autumn 2001, some ten units whose location followed the generic traditions and focuses of the channels. In weekly programmes, documentaries and drama the two traditional channels continued having parallel production units. In other words, the skill centres represent in many ways continuation of the channel-based structure of production. Considering the earlier discussion on the consequences of Management by Schedule, it seems that YLE's reformers have preferred the *continuation of editorial traditions* instead of a total transfer to a team-based production structure. The adoption of Management by Schedule raised discussion about the role of the old *production departments* which seemed to turn into anomalies in the new more producer-centred culture of production. As interpreted by the interviewed managers, the main functions of the production departments seemed to be social and cultural; the departments represented a sort of 'home base' for varied and changing teams of production. This function will now be taken over by the newly organised skill centres.

Although the skill centres represent the continuation of the editorial traditions of the channels, it is clear that the importance of the channels will be reduced in their future identification. Parallel to that, one can anticipate that the future social and cultural cohesion of these units will be based, if anything, on a more *genre-oriented professionalism*; and secondarily, on a general awareness of being part of a public service broadcasting organization. As designed by the YLE Vision for 2001-2003, the skill centres are supposed to be operatively autonomous, although they remain administratively part of some channel. It seems reasonable to anticipate that cross-commissioning is the basis for the autonomy of the skill centres. In this way, the break-up of the traditional connection between channels and their production machine is supposed to increase the autonomous space of manoeuvring for the production units in the internal market.

In the context of Management by Schedule, the power of the schedule was related to the central role of the channels in the implementation of the corporate strategy. In the eventuality that the skill centres reach their intended autonomy, the question arises whether the channels remain strong enough to guarantee the implementation of the strategic choices in terms of their channel commissions. This question is even more urgent if one takes into account the fact that the channels represent the media-based form of organization. As hinted by the description of the skill centres above, these centres already operate over the traditional borderlines of media and also consider *multimedia production* as an important option. In this sense, it is not surprising that the search for new tools of strategic management is underway within YLE, as demonstrated by the conclusions of the Director General of the company in the interview which was highlighted above.

Judging on the basis of the YLE Vision for 2001-2003, the basic intention of the new content management is as before: to put programmes at the centre. This change is identified by the YLE Vision as 'the re-allocation of resources to programme production'. Already in 2003, the share of programmes and the immediate costs in relation to them should rise to eighty per cent of all costs, the percentage today being around seventy-five per cent. These formulations seem to indicate that the basic intentions of the new content management correspond to the former schedule-oriented management. However, in the same connection of the YLE Vision, the basic function of the corporation is described as *production of content* (in Finnish, *sisällöntuotanto*), a mode slogan typical to a cultural industry approach to the so-called information society. Such an identity represents broadcasters as content providers in a new media value chain in which their relationship with audiences is mediated by several gate-keepers such as owners of distribution networks and manufacturers of technology (EBU Digital Strategy Group, 2001; cf. Küng-Shankleman, 2000, pp. 41-42).

Conclusions

The above contrast between Management by Schedule and YLE's digital strategy is a concrete example of the challenges which European public service broadcasters face on the way to digital convergence. As YLE's case demonstrates, visions about the digital future are turning to concrete actions which can and should be considered in their consequences. As to the impact of YLE's digital strategy, a number of preliminary conclusions can be made which are relevant to discussion about the future of public service broadcasting.

The YLE Vision for 2001-2003 is characterised as a strategy for the transition period from analogue to digital broadcasting. As to television, the original vision in Finland was that digital television will become dominant by 2006, but it seems today that the transition to digital will take much longer. This makes digitalization a risky process, not only economically but also for the reliability and credibility of broadcasters. The current evidence in Finland shows that the insecurities of digitalization have already harmed YLE's reliability, as demonstrated by YLE's audience report for 2001 (Kytömäki & Ruohomaa 2001). The promise of the so-called new digital services has been central in the visioning of the digital future and, in that sense, the first steps in digital television hardly fulfil expectations.

YLE's strategy for transition from analogue to digital emphasizes in many ways more continuity than change. The overall strategic goal is to maintain YLE's position among the major players of the market in the new digital environment. That is why the company has taken a leading role in the launch of digital broadcasting and aims at guaranteeing a strong public service element in the development of the new digital services. YLE's case demonstrates that competition over market share requires once again a clear growth of output in order to guarantee the visibility of public service in the new market conditions. One should keep in mind that the decisions on new digital channels and services were made without any clear guarantee of additional resources; in fact, it seems more probable that YLE will find it hard to retain even the present level of revenues. All this means that *quantity will dominate over quality* in the implementation of the digital strategy and that YLE must continue re-articulating its traditional notions of quality.

The creation of the skill centres represents the solution for how to get more result from one and the same production machine in the conditions of growing output and the saturated corporate economy. There is no doubt that re-organization of production is the most radical element of change in YLE's digital strategy. However, one should notice that there is no hesitation in YLE's strategy as to the need for the inhouse production machine in general. YLE will continue as an 'integrated factory' of programming and production (on this notion, see Küng-Shankleman, 2000, p. 56) in the digital environment, although the share of independent production and co-operative productions will continue growing. For the moment, the share of independent production in YLE Television is about one fifth of domestic supply, but that figure will most probably rise to one quarter before completion of digitalization (Hujanen, 2002, p. 31; cf. Ytreberg, 2002, pp. 292-294).

In terms of packaging, channel profilization represents the key aspect of YLE's digital strategy for television. Instead of two more or less similar channels (TV1 and TV2), YLE will master five channels in its digital multiplex, each with their separate characteristics. Thinking about YLE's tradition of two generalist television channels, the new structure may at first look radically different, but a closer look reveals that the change is much less dramatic. In fact, the basic idea is that in the foreseeable future YLE's two generalist channels remain the core dimension of the company's digital services. Despite their distinct features, they are both supposed to attract as it is said 'big basic audiences' and remain 'basic national channels' (see Table 2. above). They will continue offering a broad range of genres and retain pluralism and diversity of output. All these represent content dimensions which are considered typical to the so-called *universal service obligation* of public service broadcasting (Harrison and Woods, 2001; on the concept, see also Collins et al., 2001 and Tracey, 1998, pp. 26-27).

One can conclude that YLE's continuous emphasis on generalist channels stresses more the vertical diversity within the channels than the overall horizontal diversity of its services. However, it is important to notice that YLE's digital multiplex includes new kinds of channels which can be characterized as specialized (niche) channels. Such channels, like CNN, represent, according to Küng-Shankleman (2000, p. 47), an editorial strategy as distinct from a flow strategy; with the latter characterizing the present generalist channels of the European public service broadcasters and the US networks. It is also worth noticing that in YLE's multiplex the specialized channels which complement the two generalist channels all represent the most traditional areas of public service programming - news and current affairs, culture and education, as well as service for minorities.

In principle, it would have been possible for YLE to select a more radical form of channel profilization and organize its universal service obligation totally along the horizontal dimension of diversity.[6] As the interviews with YLE's managers demonstrated, the problem with such an option is that it encourages the individualization of television viewing that could damage the role of television as a forum of interaction between segments of society and culture and, accordingly, a source of shared experiences and a common social reality. It seems that the YLE management accepts fully the European Broadcasting Union's recent recommendation that public service broadcasters should not weaken their generalist channels, although - as it is said - public choice of media content will be greater in the future and generalist channels will inevitably lose audience (EBU Digital Strategy Group, 2001, p. 5). Universalism and distinctive content remain, according to the EBU, the objective of public service broadcasting in the digital environment.

YLE's channel profilization is a concrete example of how important branding is considered to be, even for public service broadcasters. As the EBU's strategic analysis puts it, viewers and listeners live in a sea of media, and they will need brands as 'islands of trust' (EBU Digital Strategy Group, 2001b, p. 5.). In the EBU's definition, branding is understood as 'the conscious effort to make the viewer and listener remember characteristics they associate with the content, or the content delivering organization' (EBU, 2001b.). Distinct from product-oriented promotion, consumer orientation is typical for branding, as McDowell and Batten point out (1999, p. 14). In this way, branding complements the so-called audience-orientation of public service broadcasters, which in YLE's case became a central element of its management approach towards the end of the 1990s. Audience orientation of branding is explicit in YLE's digital strategy because it posits that channel profilization can be considered successful only if it is watched by audiences.

In the EBU's strategic analysis, branding is also connected with the quantity of output. Visibility is considered part of the success of branding and, consequently, more channels and more platforms are necessary for maintaining visibility (EBU Digital Strategy Group, 2001, p. 6). So also from the point of view of branding, the quantity of output will remain on the strategic agenda of public service broadcasters. According to the EBU (EBU, 2001, p. 6.), the issue of quantity has to be balanced against the cost-effectiveness of media delivery method, platform or channel, and the recources available to provide high quality content for it. But as was noted above in relation to YLE's competition over shares, any such balancing will require continuous re-articulation of the relationship between quantity and quality.

As a whole, YLE's digital strategy aims at retaining the company's role as one of the major players in the market. In the 1990s competitive environment, YLE did not manage to match its main commercial rival MTV3; and, even less to reach the intended share of fifty per cent of viewing figures. However, for the moment, YLE's overall share exceeds that of MTV3 (in 2001: 43.3 per cent for YLE and 39.1 per cent for MTV3). Whether it is realistic or not, the point of the selected strategy is to fight against the marginalization of public service broadcasting. One can wonder whether any other strategic choice was feasible if public service broadcasters want to retain their universal service obligations. Should public service broadcasters concentrate only on what Harrison and Woods (2001, p. 495) call 'worthy' and 'minority'programming, they would run the risk of branding public service as something out of the mainstream and therefore not something most people would want to watch. A marginal public service broadcasting with only small audiences could hardly fulfil the universal service obligations.

The schedule-oriented professionalism of Management by Schedule emphasized *genre competence* as a measure of streamlining production and programme supply. It seems that generic skills are considered even more important in the context of YLE's new orientation towards content production. Generic logic dominates the two key aspects of the digital strategy, channel profilization and creation of skill centres. The break-through during negotiations over channel profilization was based on an idea to consider the similarities and differences of the channels along generic categories of programming. Similarly, the re-organization of production in terms of skill centres took place according to generic distinctions. The risk with such a strategy is that it runs against the continuous increase of generic mix of television which blurs and re-constructs the traditional borders of genre. So if the social cohesion of public service broadcasting organizations should rest on generic skills and orientation, the question is whether that orientation can develop strongly enough to substitute the earlier channel- and media-based cohesion.

Notes

1   The chair of the European Broadcasting Union's digital strategy group Mr. Christian S. Nissen formulates the new media value chain from the point of view of boradcasting as follows: Content - Channel controlling - Gatekeeping - Distribution - Consumption (Nissen, 2002; cf. EBU Digital Strategy Group, 2001).

2   This perception formed the point of departure for the joint study in Nordic countries on scheduling in public service television (see Ytreberg, 2000 and 2002). My own research (Hujanen, 2002) contributes to that study. The growing emphasis on scheduling had been documented by several studies in the 1990s (Søndergaard, 1994; Syvertsen, Hellman, 1999; Ytreberg, 1999).

3   The code refers to the initials of the informant, and to the day, month and year of the interview.

4   This kind of view of schedule as a tool for broadcasters is central in the model of Eastman and Ferguson (1997) which I used as the point of departure for my own research. The model represents programming as a cycle of three elements: scheduling, selection, evaluation.

5   Following the EU Green Paper on Convergence from 1997, the new law aims at technology neutral regulation of broadcasting and telecommunication networks. It combines the former separate laws about radio and television networks and telecommunication market.

6   The British BBC considered the reduction of the genre mix on BBC1 and BBC2 in early 2000. According to Born (2002), after a lot of ciriticism, BBC changed plans and confirmed that they would remain mixed genre channels. BBC's plans were commented upon by a TV columnist in Helsingin Sanomat (26 June 2000), the biggest newspaper in Finland, with a conclusion that BBC will end its public service channels.

Appendix

Digital television (DTT) in Finland as decided by the government in summer 1999: channels, major owners, content, funding, and present status (August 2002)

Channel	Major owners	Content	Funding	Present status
YLE TV 1D	YLE	Parallel to analogic TV1 News & current affairs, domestic drama, international	Television fee	In operation
YLE TV 2D	YLE	Parallel to analogic TV2 "A channel for the whole nation": Entertainment, sport, children, domestic	Television fee	In operation
YLE24	YLE	News & currents affairs (24/7) Topical talk shows, teletext	Television fee	In operation
YLE Teema	YLE	Culture, education, science with added new services Drama, movie classics, classical music	Television fee	In operation
FSTD	YLE	Full service channel in Swedish-language	Television fee	In operation
MTV3D	Alma Media	Parallel to analogic MTV3 Movies, series, domestic drama, news & current affairs, with added new services	Advertising	In operation
City-TV Subtv, Finland plus cable operators	Mainly MTV	Regional news & current affairs, European movies	Advertising	Replaced by a cable channel of MTV Finland
Urheilu-kanava	MTV3 50%, Swellcom 35%, Veikkaus Ltd 10%	Sport events and background, added interactive services like games, betting, entertainment	Advertising	In operation
Wellnet	Wellmedia 26%, Janton 20%, transmissions regional newsp. publishers 33.5%, Edita 13.5 %, plus associations	Housing, consumer economy, health and leisure Community approach	Advertising Pay TV	Only promotion
Nelonen D	Swellcom 86%, TS-company 14%	Parallel to analogic TVFour Movies, series, entertainment, news & current affairs	Advertising	In operation
School Channel	Sanoma-WSOY	School news, education, edutainment in co-operation with WSOY's learning portale	Pay TV	Cancelled
Movie Channel	Sanoma-WSOY	Movies (24/7), in co-operation with Canal+	Pay TV	Cancelled
Canal+	Canal+	Premium movies, sport, enterntainment news, documentary	Pay TV	Cancelled

Note: The government will decide on the vacancies in the multiplexes (due to cancellations) in December 2002.

References

Aslama, Minna & Hellman, Heikki & Sauri, Tuomo (2002) 'Turn on Diversity: Finnish Television Programming in the Verge of the Digital Era', A paper presented for the RIPE@2002 Conference on Broadcasting and Convergence. Helsinki and Tampere (Finland), 17-19 January.

Avery, Robert K. (Ed.) (1993) Public Service Broadcasting in a Multichannel Environment. New York and London: Longman.

Born, Georgina (2002) 'Public Service Broadcasting and Digital Television in the UK: The BBC, Channel 4, and the Politics of Positioning', A paper presented for the RIPE@2002 Conference on Broadcasting and Convergence. Helsinki and Tampere (Finland), 17-19 January.

Collins, Richard & Finn, Adam & McFadyen, Stuart & Hoskins, Colin (2001) 'Public Service Broadcasting Beyond 2000: Is There a Future for Public Service Broadcasting?', Canadian Journal of Communication. 26(1), pp. 3-15.

Eastman, S. T. & Ferguson, D. A. (1997) Broadcasting/Cable Programming Strategies and Practices, 5th ed. Belmont, CA: Wadsworth.

EBU Digital Strategy Group (2001) Media With a Progressive Purpose, Conclusions of the EBU Digital Strategy Group, Part 2: Managing Digital Evolution. Geneva, European Broadcasting Union: 111th Meeting of the Administrative Council, 29-30 November 2001.

Ellis, John (2000a) 'Scheduling: the last creative act in television?', Media, Culture & Society. 22(1), pp. 25-38.

Ellis, John (2000b) Seeing Things: Television in the Age of Uncertainty. London and New York: I.B. Tauris.

Harrison, J. & Woods, L. M. (2001) 'Defining European Public Service Broadcasting', European Journal of Communication. 16(4), pp. 477-504.

Hellman, Heikki (1999) From companions to competitors: the changing broadcasting markets and television programming in Finland. University of Tampere: Acta Universitatis Tamperensis 652.

Hujanen, Taisto (2002) The Power of Schedule: Programme Management in the Transformation of Finnish Public Service Television. Tampere: Tampere University Press.

Küng-Shankleman, Lucy (2000) Inside the BBC and CNN: Managing Media Organizations. London and New York: Routledge.

Kytömäki, Juha & Ruohomaa, Erja (2001) Yleisökertomus 2000 [Audience Report 2000]. Helsinki: YLE.

McDowell, Walter & Batten, Alan (1999) Branding TV: Principles and Practices. Washington: National Association of Broadcasters NAB.

Nissen, Christian S. (2002) 'Towards a strategy for Public Service Broadcasting in an multimedia environment', Invited address for the RIPE@2002 Conference on Broadcasting and Convergence, Helsinki and Tampere (Finland), 17-19 January.

Sampson, Tony & Lugo, Jairo (2002) 'Technological or Ideological Convergence? How the Concepts of Market and Technological Convergence are Displacing Public Service Commitment in the New Communications and Broadcasting Public Policy of the UK', A paper presented for the RIPE@2002 Conference on Broadcasting and Convergence. Helsinki and Tampere (Finland), 17-19 January.

Søndergaard, Henrik (1994) DR i tv-konkurrencens tidsalder [DR in the Era of TV Competition]. Frederiksberg: Samfundslitteratur.

Suomalainen tv-tarjonta 2000 [Finnish TV Supply 2000]. Helsinki: Ministry for Transport and Communication, Publications, 41(2001).

Syvertsen, Trine (1996) Den store TV-krigen, Norsk allmennfjernsyn 1988-96 [The Big TV War, Norwegian Public Service Television in 1988-96]. Bergen-Sandviken: Fagbokforlaget.

Tracey, Michael (1998) The Decline and Fall of Public Service Broadcasting. Oxford, New York: Oxford University Press.

Williams, Raymond (1974) Television: Technology and Cultural Form. Bungay, Suffolk: Fontana/Collins.

Ytreberg, Espen (1999) Allmenkringkastingens autoritet, Endringer i NRK Fjernsynets tekstproduksjon 1987-1994 [The Authority of Public Service Broadcasting, Changes in the Text Production of NRK's Television in 1987-1994]. University of Oslo, Media Studies, Department of Media and Communication.

Ytreberg, Espen (2000) 'Scheduling in Nordic Public Service Television. General Description of an Ongoing Research Project', Nordicom Review. 21(1), pp. 25-34.

Ytreberg, Espen (2002) 'Continuity in Environments: The Evolution of Basic Practices and Dilemmas in Nordic Television Scheduling', European Journal of Communication. 17(3), pp. 283-304.

Gianpietro Mazzoleni is Professor of Sociology of Mass Communication and Political Communication at the University of Milan (Italy). His research interests focus on political communication, mass media, and media policies. He collaborated in various comparative researches in these fields. He has published several works both in Italian and English. His latest publication is the co-editorship of the book The Media and Neo-Populism. A Contemporary Comparative Analysis (Praeger, 2003).He is editor of the Italian journal Comunicazione Politica, and serves the editorial boards of the European Journal of Communication and of Political Communication. He is chairman of the EuroMedia Research Group, and vice-chair of the Political Communication Division of the I.C.A.

Gianpietro Mazzoleni

With the Media, Without the Media: Reasons and Implications of the Electoral Success of Silvio Berlusconi in 2001

'Why Silvio Berlusconi is unfit to lead Italy': With this hostile cover story *The Economist* of 4 May 2001 stepped into Italy's election race in the final critical days of campaign warfare. The outbreak by the magazine inflamed an already hot domestic political climate, providing unexpected ammunition to the *L'Ulivo* coalition, engaged in a strategy of political de-legitimization of its adversary, the Centre-Right front-runner Mr. Silvio Berlusconi. The magazine's thesis was that because of his several judicial troubles ('under investigation for money laundering, complicity in murder, connection with the Mafia, tax evasion and the bribing of politicians, judges, and the tax police'), the candidate Berlusconi was not fit to run one of the world's richest democracies.

The article, however, did not list among the alleged impeding ingredients Berlusconi's control of an exorbitant portion of Italy's media industry. It could not list it for the simple reason that Berlusconi is legitimately in control of all his communication assets: he had been allowed to build his television, advertising and publishing empire by the inability (and unwillingness) of governments and ruling parties to pass anti-trust legislation to govern an orderly transition from the old public service broadcasting monopoly to a liberalization guaranteeing real pluralism of media outlets.

This politician, a media tycoon by definition, Italy's richest man, has succeeded twice in becoming Prime minister and in gaining the voters' trust in his resounding programme to 'change Italy'. Just eight months after his victory in 1994 he beheld the failure of his dream - and of his cabinet, he was defeated in the 1996 general elections, recovered from cancer in 1997, won the 1999 European Elections, made of his 'flash' party - *Forza Italia* - a muscular organization, and routed *L'Ulivo* in 2001, securing a sizable majority in both Chambers. He is indeed a resourceful man, a volcanic personality, restless combatant, absolutely averse to accepting being beaten, of being second to anyone: a leading businessman, he sought to be a leader in the political arena, and nothing less than the leader in government.

This short, opening account of the Berlusconi story suggests the multi-faceted nature of the phenomenon, in which the media variable is just one of the several components.

The Italian Political Stage of Berlusconi's Play

The common wisdom in the aftermath of the 2001 election was that Berlusconi won thanks to his media. In this chapter I shall try to give a picture and attempt an interpretation of the latest electoral success of Silvio Berlusconi that includes other variables in the reasons for his victory. In an article on the 1994 victory I argued that Berlusconi had not won because of his media, yet he could not win without the media (Mazzoleni, 1995). This was still largely true in 2001.

In the Italian political environment of the 1990s the influence of the 'political-media complex' (to borrow Swanson's expression (1992) was all but marginal in determining the climate of opinion, government policies and the electoral strategies of the parties.

In Italy, as in many other Western political contexts, there could be observed most of the trends and patterns - even if with different intensities - that, according to Blumler and Kavanagh (1999), characterise the 'third age' of political communication. Since the early 1980s there has been evidence of a 'professionalization of political advocacy': politicians would increasingly disregard the traditional in-party communication know-how and rely on the expertise and talents of external professionals (Mazzoleni, 1987, 1991). This search by the parties, leaders and candidates for new ways and means to address and capture voters was leading towards a 'virtual re-invention of major parties': not in the sense that the traditional ideological tenets were being abandoned in favour of a more cynical, market-driven political action, but that the actors of the political scene would convert to a more competition-based type of political and especially electoral struggle. The latter trend is perhaps specific to the Italian case and deserves a clarification.

In the so-called 'First Republic' (1947-1993) election campaigns pursued the goal of asserting and confirming the existing identity of the political players engaged in the contest rather than of conquering new consensus. From the 1950s on, the electoral maps revealed a fairly rigid voting dynamic that was seen as paradoxical and labelled by political scientists 'mobility without movement' (Parisi, 1980): the variations in vote outcomes were so insignificant that they never produced an overturning of the existing power balances. This made the Italian political system a fairly stable one, meaning that only a number of parties would share power in government for decades while others would be permanently excluded. The Cold War climate explains most of this Italian political situation. Other reasons are to be found in the unvarying electoral balances of the major political parties (the *DC*'s electoral support averaged thirty per cent, the *PSI*'s ten per cent, and the *PCI*'s twenty-five per cent), and in the rather strong political participation (voting turnout was around ninety per cent in all election contests through the 1990s). However, such stable dynamics generated unending turbulence *within* the governing quarters, to the point of giving birth to an average of one cabinet in every one of the forty-five years of post-war democracy.

Political communication in the 'First Republic' was characterised by a strong control of governing forces over the RAI, the public service broadcasting company, and by a discrete but effective management of the printed media. Italian journalism, with a few notable exceptions, was mostly subservient to the party-political logics on all of the sides of the Right-Centre-Left spectrum. Accordingly, election campaigns would see the media taking sides of their 'political referents' (i.e. parties) with little or no control of the agenda of the electoral debate.

The 1980s started to show signs of decline of the 'old order'. *Vis-à-vis* an increasing secularization of the ideological *raisons-d'être* of political identity and battle, political players realised that consensus should be conquered on other bases: government performance, innovative legislation (such as on civil rights), and by means of new, seductive campaign communication strategies. The political market-place starts to take shape and campaigns become real competitions.

The election campaign of 1983 was a true milestone of the modernization of Italian political and electoral communication: by the mid-1980s, in fact, commercial television had been established as a permanent feature in the Italian media system (Pezzini, 2001). The rhetorical devices of television commercial advertising, swiftly adopted by candidates, took the place of the traditional, emotion-based party propaganda forms. Access to commercial stations, unlike that to public service broadcasting channels, was free and unregulated. Parties and politicians exploited for years these new communication resources. The volume of campaign advertising and of electoral broadcasts in general increased extraordinarily, to the point that election contests would become associated with television-centred campaigning.

It is in those years that campaign practices underwent remarkable change: researchers started to notice the first signs of a process of Americanization, of spectacularization of politics and of campaign communication. The image of parties and candidates started to become paramount in the campaign communications, much at the expense of the traditional predilection for ideological and/or policy issues. All this also represented a change in the traditional temperament of Italian political communication: the marketing mentality prompted a more proselytising outlook in campaign strategies, that is, parties slowly moved from the 'preservation-directed' attitude of the previous decades to a more 'conquest-directed' one, thus anticipating some trends that will be more evident later in the 1990s when the mixed majoritarian-proportional electoral system was introduced.

The critical turning point of Italian politics, and subsequently of Italian political communication, takes place in 1992-1994, when the old party system literally disintegrated under judicial investigations into widespread corruption in the party-funding system. Prominent leaders and former Prime Ministers of the political class who had ruled the country were brought to Court to be interrogated by prosecutors on live TV broadcasts, some were condemned, a few even fled the country. In a context of national drama that symbolically represented a sort of (allegedly short-lived) catharsis, the major governing parties, *DC* and *PSI*, disappeared, some others changed their name and identity. The news media were taken by surprise, and after a disarray *vis-à-vis* the sudden crumbling of the country's leadership, eventually supported the magistrates' actions, providing wide coverage and favourable commentary. Public opinion proved to be on the prosecutors' side; popular participation in the national debate was intense and accompanied the rise of anti-party, anti-politics, protest sentiments within the domestic electorate. Legislators in Parliament sensed the relentless mood of the country and passed in 1993 an audacious electoral reform (from proportionalism to majoritarian) that had never been possible beforehand. Public opinion (through referenda) had blamed the pure proportional system (that allowed dozens of tiny parties to be represented in Parliament) for the weakness of governments and for the endemic corruption.

This dramatic phase has been depicted as one in which a serious political vacuum, a lack of political initiative comes about. A phase that will end with the electoral success of Berlusconi and of his newly founded party *Forza Italia*.

Such political idiosyncrasies of the Italian case in some points reflect patterns that have been observed in other national contexts and stand in the scope of the 'third age' of political communication. One of the major trends is that of commercialization of life-styles that at the same time opened the way to (and was prompted to a certain extent by) 'media populism' and 'popularization' of the news. The phenomena of tabloidization and of trivialization could well be observed also in the Italian media, notably following the introduction (not surprisingly, by Berlusconi himself) of commercial television. Even if it is hard to find empirical evidence, the argument by the philosopher Norberto Bobbio, that Berlusconi's electoral success in 1994 was to be found in two decades of political disengagement diffused by his commercial media, epitomizes the metamorphosis that has occurred in both the media and the political systems.

Political communication scholarship has often highlighted and discussed the general phenomena of 'mediatization' of politics (Mazzoleni and Schulz, 1999) and of its implications in terms of the functioning of democracy, of the personalization of political initiative, of the spectacularization of both the political news and the politicians' communication. All of these trends find plenty of confirming evidence in the Italian context, not only in the most recent years (see Cheles and Sponza, 2001), and are indeed side-scenes of the stage where the Berlusconi play has been - and still is - represented.

From Business to Politics: the Exemplary Story of Silvio Berlusconi

Mr. Silvio Berlusconi became a media mogul late in his life as an entrepreneur. He struck gold in construction and real estate, building satellite cities like Milano 2 and Milano 3, and was very active in financial businesses (Fininvest). Political ambitions were not in his plans in the 1960s, 1970s and 1980s, even if - as most Italian entrepreneurs - he developed close ties with leading politicians and parties, in his case especially with the Socialist Party leader Bettino Craxi.

Following the partial liberalization of broadcasting in the mid '70s, the 'king of bricks' - as he was nicknamed - threw part of his huge financial assets into the commercial television business, creating *Telemilano - Canale 58*, a local channel covering the affluent Milan area. It was 1978 and almost no Italian knew at that time who Silvio Berlusconi was and what was Fininvest. The station, one of the dozens that had popped up in those years of a-regulation was soon distinguished for the power of its transmitters (located in Berlusconi's headquarters in Milano 2) and for the innovatory formats of its programming. It was Berlusconi's introduction to the broadcasting adventure: he personally supervised the making of the programme scheduling, and started head-hunting television professionals at home and abroad. He clearly enjoyed this new experience and enthusiastically decided to dedicate his time and his money to 'building' a completely new edifice: Publitalia '80, a completely revolutionary initiative in the Italian stagnant media market-place of the late 1970s. Publitalia '80 worked as starter motor of the advertising boom of the 1980s, convincing thousands of potential advertisers to pump their money into the new television communication. Most of this enormous flow of new money ended in the company established by Berlusconi, who employed it to buttress the contiguous broadcasting empire that he was building in the same years. In fact, the station *Telemilano* became in 1981 *Canale 5*, a virtually nationwide commercial network of several local stations that Berlusconi cash purchased from Lombardy to Sicily. *Canale 5* is still today Berlusconi's flagship. In the next four years Berlusconi managed to buy up the two other major networks that leading Italian press publishers had established but had almost bankrupt (*Italia 1*, by Rusconi Editore, and *Rete 4*, by Mondadori Editore). Thus, by 1984, Berlusconi, thanks to his own entrepreneurial talent and to his competitors' debacle, became the 'king of commercial television', hence nicknamed 'Mr. Broadcasting' (*Sua Emittenza*).

It was the inception of a formidable monopoly that undermined the state television command of Italian audiences and annihilated any prospect for other private broadcasting entrepreneurs to establish competing businesses.

Canale 5, *Rete 4* and *Italia 1* inundated Italy with a deluge of commercial programming, mostly bought on the US market, with little or no news nor cultural content. The 1980s have been judged by many commentators as the decade of 'going commercial', of rampant consumerism, of the escape from political and civic engagement. Berlusconi's television was later to be blamed as the villain of all this.

The establishment of his monopoly is to be explained in terms of Berlusconi's connections with politicians and governments of those years. Along with the 'far-west' situation in the absence of any regulatory policy of private broadcasting, the well-known friendship between Berlusconi and Bettino Craxi (Prime Minister in 1983-1986) helped Mr. Broadcasting to consolidate his monopoly and even to expand abroad (establishing *La Cinq* in France, thanks to a friend of Craxi - President Mitterrand). Craxi passed a law-decree in 1985 that stopped judicial actions against the commercial networks and which was labelled, by the opposition, 'Berlusconi decree', clearly a favour to his friend.

Berlusconi's growing mogulship in the media domain was not restricted to television, but spread to the newspaper business (he bought *Il Giornale*, an influential but financially troubled daily, edited by the prestigious and controversial journalist - later Berlusconi's foe - Indro Montanelli), and in the early 1990s into book and magazine publishing, taking control of Mondadori, Italy's biggest publishing group. The way he seized Mondadori is a matter of one of the several trials in which Mr. Berlusconi is implicated as defendant, on allegations of bribing judges and other corrupt practices.

The finally approved reform of television broadcasting (the Mammì Law of 1990) came too late to change the state of things that had solidified in the previous years. It failed to dismantle the Fininvest-Rai duopoly and introduced cross-ownership norms easy to circumvent (e.g. Silvio Berlusconi 'sold' *Il Giornale* to his brother Paolo). It legalized the existing order: it was in fact labelled 'carbon-copy law'.

The media power accumulated by Mr. Berlusconi has often been objected to by the parties of the Left, that see it a threat to pluralism, to freedom of access, and to fair competition. The fact that Berlusconi was not personally engaged in the political battlefield at this point, however, to a certain extent would make him appear as a harmless virtual-challenger.

When in January 1994 Mr. Berlusconi announced that he would throw his hat into the political ring, the announcement was like an earthquake, just a little muffled by the other recent, yet much more disastrous earthquake sparked by the judicial wave of so called '*Mani Pulite*' (Clean Hands) investigations that had destroyed the country's old party system.

He inaugurated his entrance into politics with his peculiar style: flamboyant, creative and shrewd. He founded a new party - his personal party. He struck the football fandom's chord by calling it '*Forza Italia*', after the popular incitement to the national team. He launched it by means of an unprecedented barrage of television [his own] advertisements. He positioned his politics in the centre-right, initiating a furious anti-communist campaign.

After barely four months he was premier. From business to politics: his voyage, launched in real estate, continued into the 'fourth estate', concluded in government.

A Unique '*Bouillon de Culture*': the Factors that Helped Berlusconi's Political Odds

The reasons for Berlusconi's comeback in 2001 should be looked for in a series of events, trends occurring in the recent past, and above all in the years in which the *L'Ulivo* coalition governed Italy (1996-2001).

One crucial factor is the electoral system introduced in 1993 that restructured the old map of electoral districts to fit the new majoritarian system. To be true, the Italian one is not a pure majoritarian system, only seventy-five per cent. The remaining quarter is still proportional. However, that reform represented an epochal change in the domestic political arena, as it forced small parties to join coalitions in order to survive, it prompted parties and candidates to turn 'professional' in their campaign communication strategies, it pushed towards a stronger personalization of the coalitions' leaders, it eventually rewarded the winning tickets in the single-member districts.

This new rule of the electoral game did not necessarily advantage Mr. Berlusconi; on the contrary, it helped him in 1994 but it helped also Mr. Romano Prodi in 1996. However, in 2001 Berlusconi cunningly exploited the constraints introduced by the majoritarian rule by succeeding in convincing one of the most irreconcilable political forces, Umberto Bossi's Northern League, to join the *Polo delle Libertà* (*PdL*) coalition. This is indeed the second crucial factor that worked for the electoral success on Election Day. Berlusconi was capable of putting behind himself the past poisoned relations with the League, that in 1994 were responsible for the fall of his cabinet. He clearly saw that he would have not made it in 2001 without the numbers provided by the Northern League - which commanded ten per cent of the national electorate in 1996.

This alliance, that proved to be unexpectedly strong, secured the victory of the *PdL*, in spite of the fact that the League lost more than fifty per cent of its traditional support. Umberto Bossi, who had used vitriolic language with Berlusconi on several occasions before the latter alliance, evidently realized that only a solid association with his former foe could have spared him the dramatic debacle if he had run alone. His party had registered a steady decline in the regional and European elections of 1999: without the alliance with Berlusconi the League would have been wiped out, as it did not reach the minimum threshold of four per cent in 2001. Many commentators have remarked that this knotty party (neo-populist, xenophobic, idiosyncratic) played as the 'pointer on the balance' of Italian political destinies for more than a decade. Said in simple words: Berlusconi won because Bossi was on his ticket in 1994, and Prodi won because Bossi refused to be on Berlusconi's ticket in 1996.

The following Table 1. shows the relevant figures for 1996 and 2001.

Table 1. Outcomes of the Majoritarian and proportional vote 1996 and 2001

	Majoritarian 1996	*Majoritarian 2001*	*Difference*
L'Ulivo	45.3	43.7	-1.6
CdL	40.3		
N. League	10.8		
CdL+N.League	51.1	45.4	-5.7
	Proportional 1996	*Majoritarian 2001*	*Difference*
L'Ulivo	34.7	35.6	.9
Rif. Comunista	8.6	5.0	-3.6
L'Ulivo+R.Com.	43.3	40.6	-3.2
CdL	42.1	45.7	3.6
N. League	10.1	3.9	-6.2
CdL+N. League	52.2	49.6	-2.6

A further factor that secured Berlusconi's success has again little or nothing to do with the communication domain: the many mistakes of his political adversaries. The Centre-Left *L'Ulivo* coalition has been engaged in a relentless self-critique of its own faults since the defeat of 13 May 2001. All of them have been listed, x-rayed, assessed by its leaders and by hundreds of thousands of supporters in public debates, in TV talk shows, in crowded rallies all over the country. *L'Ulivo* is blamed as having been incapable of exploiting its incumbency advantage (Pasquino, 2002), by choosing as the front-runner of the coalition Mr. Rutelli instead of the premier in office Mr. Amato. Mr. Rutelli, even if a popular mayor of the capital city, could not boast any government experience and was not associated with any of the results that the *L'Ulivo* governments had achieved in five years in power. The coalition chose him for his personal qualities: honesty, good dialectics, physical appeal, telegenie, all of them matching the drift to personalization of politics, while not necessarily fitting the profile of a credible candidate to run a country.

Another mistake was the weak capitalization (in terms of communicating to voters) of the undoubted achievements of the *L'Ulivo* governments: especially in the economic domain: e.g. the entrance into the Euro currency system and the restoring of the national economy to health.

But what weighed as the darkest stain on the *L'Ulivo*'s public image and credibility was the fact that in five years in power it had three premiers: Prodi, D'Alema and Amato. Prodi was sacked by an internal conjuration, D'Alema resigned when beaten in the Regional Elections contest, and Amato, not even an MP, was called back from political retirement! Three premiers in five years appeared to many Italian voters a revival of the widely censured practices of the 'First Republic', when the proportional vote allowed the proliferation of tiny and quarrelsome government coalitions that had made Italy gain the Guinness record of forty-seven governments in fifty years! The electoral message coming from this negative record was anything but that of a progressive political force. Their adversary, Mr. Berlusconi, had all the advantage on his side in preaching that he was the man who would 'change Italy'.

One final systemic element has to be taken into account in the assessment of Berlusconi's victory: for the first time in the country's political history, in 2001 Italian voters could decide for the 'alternance', that is, for the rotation of governing forces (Itanes, 2001). Never in the past was this possible: in the 'First Republic' voters supported parties that easily would switch alliances between elections. In 1994, after the fall of the Berlusconi's first cabinet, the legislature continued with another government until 1996. The duration of the *L'Ulivo* coalition for the entire five-year (1996-2001) period of the legislature (no matter if with three cabinets) laid the premise for a 'normal' replacement by a competing political force.

This occurred indeed in May 2001. Overall, it is a sign of a political system that - in spite of its several shortcomings - has in itself the resources to guarantee an orderly democratic process.

'Anointed by God': When Personal Charisma is a Strategic Political Resource

In one of his frequent 'off-the-record' chats, in which he enjoys cracking jokes and entertaining his guests, Silvio Berlusconi declared that he felt 'anointed by God', entrusted with the mighty mission to recast the country's political destiny. Of course this 'sound-bite' hit the news headlines for days, raising hilarious and sarcastic comments from the opposition, echoing as it did the Catholic Church's definition of Mussolini as the 'man sent by Providence' (following the signing of the Lateran Pacts in 1929). It was of course just another Berlusconian quip. Yet, it reflects to some extent what friends and foes acknowledge as Berlusconi's distinctive resource: his personal charisma and his charismatic leadership.

According to Weber, charismatic leaders come forward in times of confusion and distress (Willner, 1984): the first appearance of Berlusconi on the political scene was definitely linked to the huge vacuum that the annihilation of the old political class had produced. His message to the disbanded orphans of the 'First Republic' was the promise of a new pride, a new politics, a new party, a new leader; in other words he presented himself as the leader capable of bringing his fellow citizens out of bewilderment and anguish. Charismatic leaders are distinguished by their unique savvy in sensing popular urges and in responding effectively to them. That message worked powerfully: it explains why Berlusconi and his personal party won such a success in 1994.

His leadership in the centre-right coalition has always been unrivalled: he is 'the' leader by antonomasia. His followers and supporters worship him: no one dares to question or to oppose him, his words and appeals are acknowledged wholeheartedly.

Berlusconi's leadership owes part of its strength to the peculiar climate that has developed in the political arena, and not only in Italy. The reference here is to the process of 'personalization' of politics and of political communication in contemporary democracies. The loosening of the old ideological tenets of political action of traditional party systems has given room to forms of mobilization and government that rely a great deal on the appeal and personal attributes of leaders. This personalization often goes hand in hand with a 'populist' type of political discourse and mobilization (Mény and Surel, 2000).

Berlusconi has the ability to seduce the masses and to touch the hearts of those listening to him in public rallies. In an interview with the *Financial Times* (16 October 2000) he declared: 'Most people know that if the richest man in Italy wants to govern the country, it is not because he wants to get wealthier, but because he wants the complete confidence, the affection, the love and respect of the people.'

In fact Berlusconi in his television appearances addresses directly the 'Italian people' and tries to establish personal contact with each one of them, as he did in the famous live television performance at the closing of the 2001 campaign, when he solemnly signed his 'contract with the Italians' in front of a huge national audience.

In short, Berlusconi's personal charisma is a mix of entrepreneurial talent, Machiavellian savvy, conspicuous narcissism and bewitching charm.

The reference to Berlusconi's 'personal party' is not accidental. A charismatic leader cannot endure long without relying on an organization that ensures the penetration of the leader's message into all corners of society. Berlusconi needed to fabricate a war-machine at his command to accomplish his ambitious goals. He set it up in a few weeks on the blueprint of his marketing firms, backed by an unprecedented communication barrage. *Forza Italia* is the only party not born out of a pre-existing social movement: '[it] is an artificial party, assembled on the basis of a sophisticated analysis of the political market and thanks to an extraordinary entrepreneurial know-how' (Calise, 2000). Unlike the other parties, where power balances and leadership are the outcomes of internal dialectics, *Forza Italia* has a pyramidal organizational structure: the 'natural' leader is Mr. Berlusconi and all decisions are top-down. The leader always initiates the internal debate and the last word is the leader's. For these reasons *Forza Italia* has been labelled as (Berlusconi's) 'personal party', but also 'light' or 'flash' and even 'media' party, with reference to its original flimsy organization, scarce rooted in society (and thus expected to disappear after accomplishing its goals) and its reliance on communication media.

Forza Italia all but disappeared from the political scene after Berlusconi's fall at the end of 1994 and after his defeat in the 1996 elections. But, in spite of the predictions by many critics and commentators, the party consolidated its structure, expanded in a capillary way in the country's social and political ganglions, and improved its communication techniques, becoming a 'muscular' organisation. On the eve of the 2001 general election *Forza Italia* had turned into a 'mass party', a 'people's party' very similar to the (disappeared) traditional big parties, except in the strong business-like nature and flavour of its internal functioning.

This corroboration was made possible thanks to the determination of its leader to carry on the political struggle on the front line for all those years, to hearten his followers and to keep his dream to 'change Italy' alive in his supporters and allies. Through such efficient and disciplined apparatus, Berlusconi was in control of the communication campaign in all the local, regional, European and general elections from 1994 to 2000: he personally instructed his candidates on marketing techniques, provided the party platform, suggested the issues for debate, dissuaded them from portraying their faces instead of his own on posters and leaflets and sold them 'electoral kits' containing gadgets, propaganda material, flags, etc.

Thanks to this organizational strategy, the campaigns of *Forza Italia* candidates were faithful replicas of the leader's message all over the country. The strong image of Berlusconi secured obscure candidates sweeping victories in their constituencies: a phenomenon that has been named 'leaderization' of electoral communication (Mancini and Mazzoleni, 1995). The personal, organizational and political charisma of Silvio Berlusconi produced tangible successes: from 1999 his winning records have formed a crescendo: the European election of that year turned into a plebiscite for Berlusconi. He scored the highest personal vote ever registered in Italy: 3,000,000. The same mix of charismatic ingredients has been the catalyst for his success in 2001.

Tools for Success: Berlusconi's Communication Machine

One current comment in the international press when Berlusconi won his first premiership in 1994 was that he had made a sort of 'media putsch', a '*coup d'état médiatique*', taking for granted that it was thanks to his control of commercial television that he had secured victory for himself and for his centre-right coalition.

A more thoughtful and less prejudiced look at the overall dynamics of that election campaign highlighted a number of systemic factors that - in conjunction with the communication resource - accounted for Berlusconi's success (Mazzoleni, 1995; Statham, 1996).

Nevertheless, Berlusconi has been best known throughout Europe as a media mogul, with assets in almost all communication domains: broadcasting, pay-TV, cinema, advertising, press and publishing. So, it is legitimate to assume that if a mogul of this kind enters politics, he has a big advantage over his adversaries, in terms of financial and strategic resources to be employed in marketing his ideas. This is certainly a well-founded argument by those critics who are concerned about the working of the democratic process in one key country of the European Union. If and when a media mogul comes to power as premier, as in Berlusconi's case, the alarm becomes more intense, because a new risk materialises: the well-known 'conflict of interests' between his public and private roles, the delayed solution of which by legislation has been source of infinite political dispute in Italy, and the cause of a slow tarnishing of Berlusconi's political image, especially abroad.

Silvio Berlusconi is indeed a powerful media magnate, he is the richest man in Italy, the third richest in Europe, with a personal wealth estimated at €15bn: no wonder that such an awesome media battleship causes disarray among the opposition.

He did resort to his powerful financial and communication weaponry to regain power in 2001. There exists no official figure of the whole cost of his campaign, but in general opinion it was enormous, unmatchable by any of his adversaries.

His campaign was planned 'scientifically' in all details, months before the official start. Berlusconi, besides relying on his own long experience, resorted to in-house professionalism, as he had done in 1994, when he engaged his 'advertising salespeople' to disseminate his message. It should be noted, though, that Berlusconi's political activity after his fall has been a perfect demonstration of a 'permanent campaign'. He never stopped rallying voters for his imminent return to power. Together with his closest collaborators, he created the so called 'table for Italy', a board that met every week with him and assured the launching of a campaign machine highly coherent in goals, content and techniques. Great was the use and study of (covert) survey data. In a word, nothing was left to chance.

The attack on his adversaries, who had hired famous American political consultants (like Stanley Greenberg), was launched on two fronts: street posters and television.

Starting six months before Election Day, Berlusconi inundated the country with large posters portraying his (younger) self and carrying catchy promises such as

'Less tax for all', 'Safer cities', or assertions like 'A president-worker to change Italy', 'A president-entrepreneur to launch the great infrastructures', 'A President-friend to help those who can't make it'. It was a clever way to anticipate and to set the agenda of the public pre-electoral debate. Those posters triggered the response of the *L'Ulivo*'s front-runner, Mr Rutelli, who lagged behind in the battle of the opinion polls: he could not but help following Berlusconi's path, producing similar posters with opposing slogans. Berlusconi's posters sparked a bizarre counter-campaign by, mostly, young Internet-fans who circulated on the net hundreds of satirical replications of his posters, creating a wave of ridicule that risked causing his campaign to boomerang. A candidate so familiar with the rules of show business such as Berlusconi could not throw in the towel: he managed to turn this counter-campaign into a chance to enhance his own image, by rewarding the sharpest satire.

The battle of the posters, a sort of revival of the 'old media' through the increasingly important Internet, created the collective imagery of the Italian electorate in the months before the official campaign. It was successful in building a 'favourable climate' for Berlusconi - who continued to outdistance Rutelli in the polls by four points.

However, the television front was by far the hottest of the campaign essentially for three reasons: 1) the exploitation by Berlusconi of his own channels, 2) the anti-Berlusconi flavour of a number of Rai programmes, 3) the strategies for television-centred visibility and legitimization.

To believe that Berlusconi automatically received sympathetic coverage from his channels is plainly naive. His entrepreneurial and political cleverness showed when he decided to carry the news on his channels in the early nineties: he entrusted the most important news outlet (Tg5) to a widely respected journalist and, on the other hand, the other two (Tg4 and *Studio Aperto*) to faithful and even devoted journalists. The result was that, *overall*, his channels guaranteed a balanced coverage of news.

In the 2001 campaign, however, the TV news was not the only resource to rely on for supportive content: several other programmes, such as talk-shows and other minor infotainment shows, were potential spaces for pro-Berlusconi propaganda.

Table 2. - Total 'presence' on TV channels of the two front runners (in minutes) from 10 March to 11 May 2001.

	Rai	Mediaset
Berlusconi	465	1,427
Rutelli	441	887

As Table 2. shows, in the last two months of the campaign, including the last (official) period of thirty days, the total air time occupied by Berlusconi exceeded that of his contender on both public and commercial networks, but the difference was far more evident on his own networks. This is clear evidence that the leader of *Forza Italia* enjoyed preferential treatment by his employees. This imbalance was to a certain extent contained in the last month, when the so called '*par condicio* law', a regulation passed under the Ulivo's government in 2000 - to ensure equality of access - was enforced, which severely inhibited all types of overt and covert political advertising. This interdict undermined only slightly Berlusconi's media strategy, because he had provided an airing for his and *Forza Italia*'s commercials in the months before the start of the ban.

What did undermine to a significant extent his image was the hostile criticism by several adversaries of Mr. Berlusconi, hosted in popular talk shows and satirical programmes aired by channels of RAI. Several prominent representative people of the Left (intellectuals, actors, journalists, writers, etc.) made it clear that they wanted to de-legitimise Berlusconi's candidacy, especially on the basis of criminal charges debated in various courts and trials in the last few years. Because of a fairly balanced distribution of airtime on public channels between the two competitors, it was the tone of certain programmes that irritated Berlusconi and his allies, who often complained about the alleged unfair treatment that the public broadcasting service, paid for by all citizens, reserved for the leader of the Centre-Right. There was also the argument that Berlusconi's candidature had too many worrying shadows that concerned and responsible journalists and citizens needed to investigate.

This dispute was one of the key issues of the entire campaign. The risky policy of the Centre-Left to 'demonise' Berlusconi once more - and thus to provoke a sympathetic response from many voters as had happened in 1994 - warned its leaders against over-exploiting this media-fed anti-Berlusconi sentiment.

Overall, the television campaign was dominated - directly or indirectly, in favour or against - by Berlusconi. Thanks to his know-how as showman and communication wizard, he succeeded in leading the game all the way through. Two tactical decisions were indeed masterful and potentially deadly for his adversary: first, Berlusconi always refused to meet his opponent in a television 'great' debate, thus accomplishing a clear de-legitimation, and second, he kept 'til the very last day a 'coup de théâtre' that concluded his truceless campaign: he appeared on the most popular talk show run by Rai to sign his 'contract with the Italians' in front of the national audience. Through five points he illustrated the goals of his future government: 1) reduction of taxes, 2) defence of citizens against crime, 3) the increase of lowest social pensions to a minimum of 520 € (the psychological lower limit of 1 million lire!), 4) creation of 1 million jobs, 5) launching of the great infrastructures. He solemnly promised that if, at the end of his premiership, four out of five of those commitments had not been accomplished he would withdraw from the next race.

What Impact on Voters?

The question of the impact of the mass media on voters has yet to find a widely shared response by scholarly research. Scepticism seems the most common sentiment among political communication researchers and theorists. As Denis McQuail observes, 'the media are rarely likely to be the only necessary or sufficient cause of an effect, and their relative contribution is extremely hard to assess' (McQuail, 2000, p. 416). Voters react to political television content in several and often contradictory ways: as partisans, as disinterested or angry citizens, as passive spectators, and the like, all processing the communication in quite heterogeneous ways.

If this wisdom is scientifically sound, the immediate implication we can draw from the case of the media campaign by Berlusconi is that we cannot simply infer that he won the 2001 elections because of his command of television communication. This observation corroborates the argument expounded in this chapter that the reasons of his victory are to be sought *also* in non-communication domains.

How to address the 'suspicion' that communication factors have counted a great deal in the political victory of such a powerful media tycoon? The problem again is how we can spot and measure - and so convert into scientific evidence - the working of those factors on voters' outlooks, attitudes and electoral decisions. There is no easy answer to this.

Italian political communication scholars have been engaged since the 1994 Berlusconi success in the effort to come up with a reasonable explanation of the causal link between television and electoral behaviour. Without being convincing.

However, there are signs that some significant evidence can be found, through the measurement of the variable 'channel fidelity'. There has been noted an interesting correlation between constant exposure to Berlusconi's Mediaset channels and voting preference for Forza Italia and its leader, and, vice-versa, a correlation between Rai-fans and the vote for Centre-Left parties and leaders (Testa, Loera and Ricolfi, 2002; Sani and Legnante 2002). However, we face here a further paradox: if this isomorphism is true, it is also a zero-sum effect, that is the impact of Mediaset television in favour of Berlusconi in the 2001 election campaign has been *balanced* by the impact of Rai television in favour of Rutelli. Of course this is going to be a matter of dispute among scholars for years to come. However, two important implications of this paradox are before us: we should look for the 'victory differential' of Berlusconi elsewhere, and, finally, the victory of Berlusconi has added a potential control over public service channels to his personal control of commercial television channels.

The balance that has kept in check his influence on voters might disappear. With what effects on the democratic process nobody can tell.

Conclusion: What are the Implications of the Berlusconi Case?

If it is hard to conjecture about the likely (or unlikely) turn of the quality of democracy in Italy, in spite of certain pessimistic predictions by several apocalyptic critics, it is even harder to project the Berlusconi case onto a wider, supra-national scenario. The political adventure of Silvio Berlusconi epitomises at its best: 1) the *unique* state of Italian politics in the decade 1992-2001, 2) the *unique* situation of the domestic mass media market-place, and 3) the *unique* response of Italian voters to a *unique* political offer.

What is argued here is not that Italy - and its governing Berlusconian majority - is a totally maverick case in the world or even in the EU. There exist several indicators of broader trends that are shared by a good number of political contexts. The mentioned personalization drifts of political leadership and political action are observable in UK, France, Germany and Spain as well, just to mention the largest countries of EU. Similar processes, such as the spectacularization and professionalization of politics, the tabloidization of the news production, the decline of political, ideologies, and the commercialization of the 'public sphere', are 'global' phenomena. As discussed in the previous paragraphs, these are also substantial ingredients of the Berlusconi political adventure. In other words, his successful entry into domestic politics benefited from exogenous factors and international events - such as the end of the Cold War - that also affected other political systems.

However, the uniqueness of the Berlusconi case stands out because of many commonalities, in three domains: the media-politics interaction, the party organization and the political communication strategy.

Mr. Silvio Berlusconi controls a huge media empire: a similar personal asset in liberal democracies is normally viewed as a serious impediment to direct political engagement. Other media tycoons (e.g. Rupert Murdoch) may have political interests to defend or to promote, but it is rare that they step personally into the political arena. In Italy this could and did take place for the reason that no specific legislation inhibited monopolists of the communication industry to seek political power. In post-Fascist history there had never been a case of so much media power in so few hands. Berlusconi succeeded in enlarging his business shielded from obstructive regulations, and often thanks to the support of key political friends. The present idiosyncrasy of Italian democracy has the name of 'conflict of interest', where a media tycoon can also be Prime Minister, in full control of his own commercial broadcast media empire and at the same time exerting powerful influence over the cultural and informational policies of the public broadcasting organization.

The second uniqueness is the 'mission' of Berlusconi's party, *Forza Italia*. He founded it 'in his own image and likeness', mixing corporate schemes with traditional party organization models. The highly centralised, top-down, decision diagram makes the party a secular arm in his own command, promptly adaptable to his (several) policy contortions. The political creed of *Forza Italia* is a blend of neo-libertist, neo-liberal, neo-populist stances that positions it in the moderate, centre-right area of the political spectrum. In spite of the fact that, in comparison to the old parties, *Forza Italia* is ideologically weak and lacking in-house dialectics, it has proved a powerful electoral machine. However, what makes it a unique phenomenon is its nature as a 'personal party', perfectly reflecting the leader's wills and whims, to the point that commentators usually associate its fate with that of its leader.

Finally, the kind of political communication that has developed in Italy since the advent of Berlusconi in the political arena clearly has some features like those described by Blumler and Kavanagh (1999) in the 'third age'. However, looking from the perspective of strategic use of communication devices, from political discourse to electoral marketing, the uniqueness of Berlusconi's communication lies in his personal appeal and charisma. His command of wide popularity among Italian voters is largely due to his capacity to address, entertain and enchant audiences, an aptitude that is, all at once, the result of undoubted personal talents, marketing savvy, and political shrewdness. Ultimately, Berlusconi's communication owes most of its aura to non-political ingredients.

In sum, the rise of Berlusconi's political star has deeply marked Italy's political environment and its international image. However, the early apprehensions of a likely '*coup d'état médiatique*', of a 'media-cracy' that his example would spark in other Western democracies, are definitely lessened by the consideration of the highly idiosyncratic character of the Berlusconi phenomenon. It is a uniqueness even in the Italian media and political systems, it is hardly a model for other contexts. On a closer look at the developments in the political arenas of Europe, there seem to exist no signs of an incipient 'berlusconization' of politics nor of political communication.

References

Blumler, J. G. & Kavanagh, D. (1999) 'The Third Age of Political Communication'. Political Communication. 16(3), pp. 209-230.

Calise, M. (1999) Il partito personale (The personal party). Roma-Bari: Laterza.

Cheles, L. & L. Sponza (Eds.) (2001). The art of persuasion. Political communication in Italy from 1945 to the 1990s. Manchester: Manchester University Press.

Itanes (2001). Perchè ha vinto il centro-destra (Why the Centre-Right has won). Bologna: Il Mulino.

Sani, G. & Legnante, G. (2002). Quanto ha contato la comunicazione politica? (The weight of political communication) in Pasquino, G. (Ed.) Dall'Ulivo al governo Berlusconi. Le elezioni del 13 maggio 2001 e il sistema politico italiano (From L'Ulivo to the Berlusconi government. The general election of 13 May 2001 and the Italian political system). Bologna: Il Mulino.

Mancini, P. & Mazzoleni, G. (Eds.) (1995) I media scendono in campo. La campagna elettorale del 1994 (The media step into the battlefield. The election campaign of 1994). Roma: ERI/Vqpt.

Mazzoleni, G. (1987) 'Media Logic and Party Logic in Campaign Coverage: The Italian Election of 1983'. European Journal of Communication. 11(2), pp. 81-103.

Mazzoleni, G. (1991) 'Emergence of the Candidate and Political Marketing: Television and Election Campaigns in Italy in the 1980s'. Political Communication and Persuasion. 8, pp. 201-212.

Mazzoleni, G. (1995) 'Towards a Videocracy? Italian political communication at a turning point'. European Journal of Communication. 10(3), pp. 291-319.

Mazzoleni, G. & Schulz, W. (1999) 'Mediatization of Politics: A Challenge for Democracy?' Political Communication. 16, pp. 247-261.

McQuail, D. (2000) McQuail's Mass Communication Theory. London: Sage.

Mény, Y. & Surel, Y. (2000). Par le peuple, pour le peuple. Le populisme et les démocraties (By the people, for the people. Populism and democracies). Paris: Fayard.

Parisi, A. (1980) Mobilità senza movimento (Mobility without movement). Bologna: Il Mulino.

Pasquino, G. (Ed.) (2002). Dall'Ulivo al governo Berlusconi. Le elezioni del 13 maggio 2001 e il sistema politico italiano. Bologna: Il Mulino.

Pezzini, I. (2001) 'Advertising politics on television: the party election broadcast'. In L. Cheles & L. Sponza (Eds.), The art of persuasion. Political communication in Italy from 1945 to the 1990s. pp. 180-195, Manchester: Manchester University Press.

Statham, P. (1996) 'Television News and the Public Sphere in Italy'. European Journal of Communication. 11(4), pp. 511-556.

Swanson, D. (1992) 'The political-media complex'. Communication Monographs. 59, pp. 397-400.

Testa, S., Loera, B., Ricolfi, L. (2002) Sorpasso? Il ruolo della televisione nelle elezioni politiche del 2001 (Overtaking? The role of television in the general election of 2001). Comunicazione politica. 3(1), pp. 101-114.

Willner, A. R. (1984). The Spellbinders: Charismatic Political Leadership. New Haven, Conn.: Yale University Press.

Karol Jakubowicz (M.A. 1964, University of Warsaw; Ph.D. 1989, University of Warsaw), is an adviser to the Chairman of the National Broadcasting Council of Poland, the broadcasting regulatory authority, and an international consultant on broadcasting legislation. He has worked as a journalist and executive in the Polish press, radio and television for many years. His academic pursuits have included a teaching post at the University of Warsaw and a Visiting Professorship at the University of Dortmund. His scholarly and other publications work in the field of media studies have been published widely in Poland and internationally.

Karol Jakubowicz

A Square Peg in a Round Hole: The EU's Policy on Public Service Broadcasting

In 1990, the European Commission did not even mention public service broadcasting in a Communication on the Community's audiovisual policy (European Commission, 1990). Soon afterwards, complaints against state aid to PSB (Harrison and Woods, 2001) forced the Commission to tackle the issue. The Commission and other Community authorities have since had to devote a great deal of attention to PSB. The ensuing debate, pitting a cultural perspective on the media against an economic one, and the resolution of that debate so far, illuminate wider issues of the evolution and changing foci of media policy in Europe.

Foreshadowing the 'New Paradigm' of European Media Policy

The EU does claim to have an audiovisual policy (European Commission, 1998), but it is doubtful whether it has a media policy properly so called. According to Michalis (1999, pp. 164-165) the EU has traditionally found it difficult to develop a regulatory regime concerning content and culture, or to adopt European-level measures in regulating content and associated issues (e.g. pluralism, ownership, privacy), an area that has been more contentious and political. Therefore, it 'has primarily utilized telecommunications regulation in regard to broadcasting'. According to another view, the EU's 'media policy' has in fact been an 'industrial policy' (Kaitatzi-Whitlock, 1996, p. 455).

Thus, the EU policy orientation towards the media foreshadowed a major trend in media (or, more broadly, communication) policy development in developed Western countries.

After McQuail (2000, pp. 208-209), we may list three phases of this process:

• 'Emerging media policy' lasting from the end of the nineteenth century to the 1920s, when the main goals were protecting the strategic interests of the government and nation, and to promote the industrial and economic development of new communication systems;

• 'Public service' phase which reached its apex in the 1970s, and was dedicated to the achievement of cultural and social goals (mainly in broadcasting) and to the provision of 'communication welfare', also by ensuring the social responsibility of the print media and limiting the power of monopoly owners of the media. Protection of the public interest and enhancement of democracy were the ultimate goals. State intervention in the media system was seen as justified and necessary to achieve the cultural and social goals of media policy.

• 'New paradigm' of media policy, resulting from internationalization, digitalization and convergence and oriented more to economic goals than to social and political welfare. It concentrates primarily on such issues as continuation of commercial competition and technological innovation, openness and transparency of ownership and control, maximum access for all and choice for consumers. This phase is marked by deregulation and removal of as many constraints to the operation of the media market as possible. This gives rise to a new regulatory model, based on recognizing limitations of government and policy-making, while competition and self-regulation are promoted. Economic mechanisms are increasingly relied upon, since they are considered by proponents of this approach, as 'best suited to the combined tasks of creating equal opportunities for actors and allocating scarce (information and communication) resources in a neutral, transparent and non-paternalist manner' (Van Cuilenburg, 2000, p. 2).

Several factors account for transition from the second to the third phase. One is certainly the political, ideological, and indeed cultural, paradigm shift resulting from the demise of social democracy in its traditional form. The terms of the debate about the future of European communications and the balance of power between the main actors involved have, over the last decade or so, shifted decisively under the impact of two parallel movements: 1) the ascendancy of marketisation policies within both the European Union and its major member countries, and 2) accelerating convergence of the computing, telecommunications and audio-visual industries (Murdock and Golding, 1999).

Policy-makers and regulators accept the de facto commoditization and commercialization of mass media in the hope that this will set the stage for the media's expected contribution to economic and technological growth (Ostergaard, 1998). Accordingly, current developments in television and audiovisual services in Europe are spurred on almost exclusively by commercial motives and private investment. Moreover, the principle of non-commercialism has been effectively transformed into one particular minority value. The old anti-commercial paradigm has almost disappeared (McQuail, 1998). The very notion of the public interest in mass communication is in question (Brants et al., 1998). If Europe is to move forward in its economic and technological development, it is argued, the process must be driven by private entrepreneurs. Commercialism is the engine of change.

The impact of convergence on media regulation and policy goes beyond merely technological issues and extends to social and political issues. As noted by Levin (1999, p. 4), 'the digital age has 'converged' with a time of great structural change in the telecommunications sector. The traditional model of the government owned and operated monopolist phone company is rapidly being replaced by a competitive market-place ... approximately ninety-five per cent of the telecommunications market is now open to competition'. The same, of course, is true of broadcasting.

In this sense, convergence constitutes yet another stage of redefining the media as a sector of the economy, and media policy from a 'cultural' into an 'industrial' one. The stakes are perceived as being very high: 'Reinventing regulatory frameworks in an era of convergence is all about redefining national competitive advantage within a global information economy, the digital economy ... how countries can restructure to participate in the new sources of wealth creation and of economic growth' (Cutler, 1998). They are therefore seen as justifying abandonment of the social and cultural aspects of the media, in favour of economic ones.

The EU has made an important contribution to ushering in the 'new paradigm'. The story of the EU's policy approach to the media can in fact be told precisely in terms of a running conflict between a 'new paradigm' and 'public service' perspective - the only difference being that in the EU the 'new paradigm' is in fact the original paradigm, while the public service perspective has fought an ultimately losing battle to modify it and inject non-market oriented concerns into it. It is in this context that the EU's stand on PSB must be seen.

It was at the height of the public service phase of media policy in Europe that the European Court of Justice concluded in the 1974 Sacchi case that the transmission of television signals involved the Treaty rules on the freedom to provide services, so broadcasting should be classified under Article 86 of the Treaty as a service of 'general [economic] interest'. The Court noted that 'the Italian and German governments have suggested that since television undertakings fulfil a task which concerns the public and is of a cultural and informative nature, they are not 'undertakings' within the meaning of the provisions of the Treaty'. It rejected that argument, however.[1]

Figure 1. depicts the legal basis for this approach in the Treaty and how it has been developed in later EU regulation.

Figure 1. The EU Definition of television as reflected in EU regulation

EJC in 1974: TV is a service 'in the general [economic] interest'	Art. 16 of the Treaty on EU: services in the general economic interest and their role in promoting social and territorial cohesion (public service element, see also Art. 73)
	Art. 86: public undertakings with special or exclusive rights are subject to the rules on competition, must not affect development of trade
	Art. 87: state aid (e.g. licence fees) must not distort competition, trade, be incompatible with common market
	Directive 2000/52/EC amending Directive 80/723/EEC on the transparency of financial relations between Member States and public undertakings (separate accounting of public service and other activities)
	Communication from the Commission – Services of general interest in Europe (COM/2000/0580 final): restrictions of competition and limitations of the freedoms of the Single Market do not exceed what is necessary to guarantee effective fulfilment of the public service mission
	Communication from the Commission on the application of State aid rules to public service broadcasting (2001/C 320/04)

The brief period in 1981-1984 when the Community hoped that media (and television in particular) would be the means by which a European identity and citizenship could be forged was soon over. By 1984/5 the view became that the audiovisual sector was of fundamental importance in completing the internal market and in creating a European common market in production and distribution which could challenge the United States in economies of scale (Prosser, Goldberg, Verhulst, 1998; Collins, 1997; Weymouth, Lamizet, 1997).

Television without Frontiers, Green Paper on the establishment of the common market for broadcasting (European Commission, 1984), the first major EU document on audiovisual policy published in 1984, approached the issue mainly from a legal, economic and technological perspective. In it the European Commission maintained that 'the EEC Treaty applies not only to economic activities but, as a rule, also to all activities carried out for remuneration, regardless of whether they take place in the economic, social, cultural (including in particular information, creative, or artistic activities and entertainment) sporting or any other sphere' (cited in Prosser, Goldberg, Verhulst, 1998). The Green Paper dealt with such issues as freedom of transmission, prohibition of discrimination against foreign broadcasts, programme content (with a view to eliminating differences in laws in Member States which aim to protect the public interest or public order), right of reply, harmonization of rules concerning advertising within Member States, copyright, etc.

The 1990 Communication from the Commission to the Council and Parliament on audiovisual policy (European Commission, 1990, pp. 29-66) listed three 'basic political guidelines' for Community action in the audiovisual field: 1) the overall objective is to strengthen Europe's audiovisual capacity; 2) this requires co-ordinated efforts in the three fields of the audiovisual sector, i.e. the rules of the game (free movement of programmes); the promotion of the programme industries (creation, production, distribution) and mastery of the new technologies (particularly HDTV); and 3) this also requires greater awareness at Community and European level as well as the exploitation of European cultural diversity.

In 1998, the European Commission issued a Communication 'Audiovisual Policy: next steps' (European Commission, 1998c) stressing the need for increased public support *inter alia* at Community level, for strengthening the competitiveness of the European audiovisual industry.

In 1999, the Commission published another yet another Communication on Principles and Guidelines for the Community's Audiovisual Policy in the Digital Age (European Commission, 1999). In formulating its audiovisual policy, the Commission stated, the European Community proceeds according to its particular competence, notably as regards the freedom to provide services and support for the industry.

The EU has pursued an 'integrated communication policy', covering both telecommunications and media institutions (Rollet, 2001, p. 372). Its two main objectives are economic efficiency and general interest, and it was designed to use communications as a major tool to support European integration and the success of the overall economy of the Union, as well as to ensure a smooth transition to the Information Age. Thus, the EU approach has consisted largely in treating media as yet another area in which to promote the general (mostly economic) goals of the organization: 'Because of legitimacy problems,[2] opposition and inability to come up with a compromise, the EU has treated broadcasting as a purely economic industry, largely neglecting its cultural aspects. As a result, there are still issues in the broadcasting sector that have not been dealt with at the European level and arguably this weakens the respective EU policy' (Michalis, 1999, p. 153).

Several broad areas of the EU's media and communications policy can be distinguished:

1. Development of a regulatory framework allowing the realization of an effective single market for broadcasting and protecting competition on that market and aiming at protecting minors from access to harmful audiovisual content;

2. Development of support mechanisms at a European level promoting the

growth of the audiovisual industry and the production and distribution of European audiovisual works, as a way of promoting linguistic and cultural diversity, but also as a tool of boosting the competitiveness of the European production industry;

3. Elaboration of common technical standards to promote integration; preparing the technological and regulatory foundations for the transition of the European audiovisual sector into the digital area; promoting the process of convergence of the media, telecommunications and information technology sectors as a foundation for the emergence of the Information Society;

4. The issue of ownership and the impact of cross-media concentration;

5. The external dimension of the Community's audiovisual policy includes three main elements: the preparation of enlargement of the European Union, the multilateral trade negotiations in the framework of the WTO, and co-operation with third world countries and other international organizations.

Of course, the Maastricht Treaty of 1992 introduced what is now Article 151, giving the organization legal competence to undertake action in the cultural field, and requiring the Community to 'take cultural aspects into account in its action under other provisions of this Treaty'.

And indeed, in 1994, the Think-Tank on the Audiovisual Policy of the European Union argued that the European Union and Member States must preserve their sovereign right to assign to the audiovisual sector the public resources in order to obtain those objectives which cannot be reached by the market alone. It noted a decline of the European audiovisual industry, a sector it regarded as one of strategic interest at the EU level, for both economic and socio-cultural seasons, and argued for an extensive programme of support and assistance to revive it (Report by the Think-Tank ... 1994).

In 1996, the European Parliament adopted a Resolution on the role of public service television in a multi-media society (1996) in which it took a strongly culturalist view of the audiovisual media in general, and public television in particular. It stressed the important cultural role of public service broadcasting and called on the Commission to propose 'adjustments to the Treaty so that the Union can develop a positive policy on PSB recognizing its crucial importance in building national and European citizenship, rather than a policy which is based exclusively on exceptions to provisions on competition and internal market policy'. This, then, was yet another voice in favour of a different policy orientation with regard to a part of the audiovisual industry.

1998 saw the publication of a report by a High-Level Group on Audiovisual Policy *The Digital Age. European Audiovisual Policy* (European Commission, 1998). That group, chaired by Marcelino Oreja, Commissioner for Education and Culture, was deliberately set up to counter the rising deregulatory spirit in the Commission, symbolized by Commissioner Bangemann and his ringing call for transition to the Information Society, to be developed primarily by business interests and free market forces.

The group noted that, despite the many differences between the audiovisual markets of individual Member States, these national markets nevertheless have much in common in terms of social and cultural values and historical experience: 'If we compare this approach with that adopted in the United States, which has one of the largest and the most competitive markets in the world, we see that the starting point for the Europeans was different: namely, that *it has never been assumed in Europe that the broadcasting and audiovisual sector should be treated as an economic subject* only or that the market would per se guarantee a pluralistic service'(European Commission, 1998a, p. 10; emphasis added).

The European approach has traditionally been one of balance. The Group went on recognising the role of the audiovisual media as a societal, democratic, cultural and economic factor, legislators have striven to achieve a balance between conflicting demands. For example, the right to freedom of expression has to be balanced against other rights with regard to matters such as the protection of minors, racial hatred and the right to privacy.

Of equal importance is *a policy of balance with regard to the interests of private broadcasting and public service broadcasting.*

This was thus a deliberate and valiant attempt to articulate a different philosophy of approach from that of the dominant paradigm of EU policy.

However, by then the market-based approach to the media had been firmly established: 'Despite the development of a broader range of policies, implicitly there seems to be a hierarchy of policy within the EC, with the longer established policies and those which provide legal basis for action, such as competition policy [...] taking precedence over less well established areas such as cultural policy' (Harrison and Woods, 2001, p. 478)

The EU's Policy vis-à-vis Public Service Broadcasting

The EBU Digital Strategy Group has found that a possible point of departure for describing public service broadcasting is a combination of three central features or elements in a 'contract', bestowed upon a broadcasting institution by society:

1. Its obligations to society,

2. The regulatory framework required for it to produce and distribute the programming by which it fulfils its obligations, and,

3. The method of financing its activities (Media with a Purpose..., 2002, p. 1).

This provides a convenient framework for identifying strands in the EU approach to public service broadcasting.

In order to facilitate our discussion of the EU's policy on public service broadcasting, let us refer to the various models of PSB now appearing in European debates on the subject, as summed up in Figure 2.

Figure 2. Models of public service broadcasting appearing in the European debate

PSB MODEL	DESCRIPTION
Attrition model	PSB broadcasters should not be allowed to adopt digital technology, develop new channels or services, or move into the Internet, as all of this should be reserved for commercial broadcasters.
Distributed public service	Public service programming can be separated from the organizations performing it today. It can be offered by any broadcaster, mandated (and probably financed) to do so by the regulator.
Monastery model	PSB as a complementary service, making available content commercial broadcasters cannot broadcast profitably.
Classical model	Typical PSB analogue broadcasters of today, mixing quality and popular programming on generalist channels.
Semi-commercial model	PSB broadcasters who rely on advertising revenue to such an extent that it affects their programming policy, forcing them to compete for audiences with commercial broadcasters by means of very similar programming.
Pure PSB digital model	PSB broadcasters are able to launch new DTT channels, but with strictly mission-oriented programming.
Full portfolio	Full gamut of universal and specialized broadcast, digital and on-line services, also of a commercial nature.
'Horses for courses'	Specialized public service broadcasters pursuing different aims (e.g. BBC and Channel 4; or France 2 and France 3).
EPGs with virtual channels	In the convergence/personalization scenario of future media development, when traditional flow channels have disappeared, PSB broadcasters would no longer be needed as programme packagers.

Each of these models is underpinned by a different view of PSB and of its three central features listed above.

The 'attrition' or 'distributed public service' models can clearly be attributed to commercial broadcasters wishing to eliminate public service broadcasters altogether, or at least as competitors on the market.

The 'monastery model' is being pushed both by them *and* by critics of the commercialization of public service broadcasting, nostalgic for the paternalist model of PSB of the past.

The 'full portfolio' model is likely to be adopted by public service broadcasters themselves as their vision of how they should operate in the foreseeable future.

In its draft report (Media with a Purpose, 2002), the Digital Strategy Group of the EBU says that public service broadcasters need to meet the diversified needs of different parts of the audience. They need to become 'full portfolio' content providers, meaning that:

• PSB is empowered and enabled to provide digital free-to-air generalist channel(s) performing the basic public service.

• Free-to-air digital specialised channels, complementing the generalist channel(s), are allowed, serving particular interests or groups, subject to local context and finance.

• Internet portals, web sites, and on-demand services are allowed, offering free public service;

• PSB is empowered to encompass other activities under certain well-defined conditions. These are pay-TV channels, commercial portals, merchandizing, branded goods, publishing, and video on demand. Competition law and fair trading rules must regulate these activities. They are intended to provide additional funding, and to create a virtuous circle of benign effects, which will benefit the core services. These activities should not be detrimental to the core tasks, and should not distort competition for other open market organizations.

Our analysis of the EU's policy *vis-à-vis* public service broadcasting should enable us to decide which of these models has the EU's support. That in turn will be highly indicative of the nature and underlying philosophy of the EU's audiovisual policy.

As Llorens-Maluquer (2002) puts it, EU policy *vis-à-vis* public service broadcasting has turned into a battlefield between the liberal-minded European Commission and Member States 'reluctant to leave their Public Broadcasting to the competition regulation. They claim the existence of a certain type of public television with a position of privilege in a competitive market because of cultural reasons. Therefore, the existence of funding compensation sufficient to develop their mission had to be admitted' (Llorens-Maluquer, 2002, p. 4)

In fact, however, there were more participants in this many-sided tug of war:

• The European Parliament's view of PSB has often been different from that of the Commission. Its already-mentioned Resolution on the role of public service television in a multi-media society (European Parliament, 1996) uses a language to describe PSB, its functions, development prospects and importance for society which public service broadcasters could recognise as their own.[3] Over the years, the European Parliament has generally focused on the general cultural function of PSB.

• The Council and the Commission's DG for Education and Culture have taken a similar approach to that of the Parliament.

• On the other hand, the Competition Directorate General has focused strongly on the organization of broadcasters with PSB obligations, treating them as economic operators subject to normal economic constraints (Harrison, Woods, 2001).

PSB Obligations: What Is It For?

In a 1995 paper (Preparing for the Information Society..., 1995, *passim*), DG IV referred to the fact that the Maastricht Treaty had added a special article (128, later 151) providing an explicit legal basis for EU activities in the field of culture, as well as for state aid policy in the cultural field (87.3.d). On this basis, it acknowledged that 'public service broadcasters have a crucial role to play in the promotion of regional, national and European cultures and the flowering of Europe's audio-visual industries in tomorrow's information society'. Having said that, however, it immediately reverted to its preferred approach and stated:

> [S]ince artists, producers, distributors and indeed all participants in the process of cultural creation and heritage conservation frequently find themselves in competition with each other for audiences, advertisers and outlets, it is as important in this field as in any other that the Commission should ensure that competition is not unduly distorted and that wasteful subsidy races are avoided. Competition policy therefore has a role to play.

A year later, the European Parliament adopted the already mentioned Resolution on the role of public service television in a multi-media society (European Parliament, 1996), alongside the so-called Tongue Report The future of public service television in a multi-channel digital age (Tongue, 1996).

The resolution was clearly meant as a rebuttal to those advancing the 'attrition' or 'monastery' models of public service broadcasting, making the point that since 'the development of new services must be a means of increasing cultural expression and genuine consumer choice [...] public service broadcasters must take a lead in the development of new services and full use of all the new technologies'. Also, that public broadcasters 'must be allowed to broadcast new digital material provided its content is compatible with their remits'.

The resolution made it obvious that 'it would be meaningless to speak of public sector broadcasting only where it is specifically aimed at a particular section of the public or a minority [and] public service programmes should encompass a suitable balance of entertainment, culture, spectacles and education'. Also, that while it is important for PSB to be distinct from commercial broadcasting, 'there will naturally be an overlap in areas of popular programming - sport, comedy, drama, news and current affairs'.

That Resolution and the entire Tongue Report contributed to paving the way to the adoption of Protocol No. 32 to the Amsterdam Treaty of June 1997 on the system of public broadcasting in the Member States. The Protocol recognized that the system of public broadcasting in the Member States is directly related to the democratic, social and cultural needs of each society and to the need to preserve media pluralism. It also recognized the competence of Member States to provide for the funding of public service broadcasting, assuming that such funding is granted to broadcasting organizations for the fulfilment of the public service remit as conferred, defined and organized by each Member State, and that it does not affect trading conditions and competition in the Community.

Following the Protocol's adoption, DG IV sought to develop rules concerning state aid to public service broadcasters, in part by specifying clearly what in its opinion the public service remit really involved.

The view expressed by DG IV in its 'discussion paper' (DG IV, 1998) on the obligations falling within the scope of the public service remit is shown in Figure 3.

Figure 3. Commission: the PSB remit (1998)

Type of Obligations	Description
Obligations imposed on the public service broadcasters and not on other operators.	<ul><li>Specific infrastructure requirements (territorial coverage, technological standards);</li><li>Stricter advertising rules (compared to commercial broadcasters);</li><li>Content obligations.</li></ul>
Additional obligations on provision of services guaranteed to citizens only by public broadcasters.	Commission would accept as a legitimate part of the public service remit such programme obligations as: <ul><li>Information programming;</li><li>Educational programming;</li><li>Cultural programming;</li><li>Programmes with regional scope and/or directed to social and ethnic minorities;</li><li>Fiction, serials, movies – it depends (Bergman – Yes; 'Rambo' – No).</li></ul>

DG IV was of the opinion that programmes falling outside these categories should not benefit of a public service exemption from state aid provisions. Fiction, serials and movies may possibly benefit, depending on the existence of specific obligations, additional to those required by the general legislation and involving specific costs for the broadcaster.

In its paper, DG IV expressed the view that public broadcasters should be fully entitled to engage in commercial activities in competition with private operators, in order to exploit the available assets and to remain competitive in the rapidly changing market-place. It accepted that only efficient PSB broadcasters with the latest technology and a sound financial situation would be able to sustain the increasing pace of competition, while inefficient PSB broadcasters would require ever-increasing State funding to remain on the market: 'Therefore, DG IV believes that public broadcasters should be entitled - *and, indeed, encouraged* - to compete on the market' (DG IV, 1998, p. 12; emphasis in the original), but without distorting competition through state aid.

In short, then, this was a very interesting combination. In DG IV's view, public service broadcasting is there to put on the air a very narrow range of programme types and genres - clearly in line with the 'monastery model' of PSB, and equally clearly in opposition to the views expressed by the European Parliament in its 1996 resolution. Public funding could be earmarked for these genres alone. However, if public service broadcasters wanted to survive in the competitive market-place, DG IV was encouraging them to bring programming down-market, and to engage in commercial activities. In other words, the effects of the application of the 'discussion paper' would have been counterproductive, because it was, to all intents and purposes, proposing a 'semi-commercial model'. If public funding could be spent only on a narrow range of programme types, all the rest would have to be financed from advertising and other commercial revenue. And in order to obtain this revenue, PSB organizations would have to maintain a very high market share, i.e. broadcast very popular programming.

These ideas were rejected with such vehemence (providing evidence of the conflict between Member States and the Commission, referred to by Llorens-Maluquer, 2002) that the 'discussion paper', which had been distributed unofficially to sound out opinion on the subject, was withdrawn.

The High Level Group on Audiovisual Policy expressed the following view of what PSB is for:

> *Quality and diversity must be the basis for public service broadcasting. Public service broadcasting has an important role to play in promoting cultural diversity in each country, in providing educational programming, in objectively informing public opinion, in guaranteeing pluralism and in supplying, democratically and free-of-charge, quality entertainment. It is legitimate for broadcasters entrusted with a public service remit to seek an important audience in order to cater for the needs of all social groups (European Commission, 1998b, p. 26).*

For all its support for the cultural approach to PSB, however, the High Level Group's recommendations were much in line with the traditional European Commission approach:

• Public funds are provided exclusively for public service activities and do not go beyond what is necessary in this respect. Public service activities should be funded mainly from public sources. Member States should provide a clear definition of the public service remit, financial openness should be ensured and where public sector operators engage in purely commercial activities, separate accounts should be kept.

• This should ensure the necessary degree of respect for the principles of free enterprise and competition that private broadcasters need in order to develop their activities.

When the European Commission came to publish its Communication 'Audiovisual Policy: next steps' (European Commission, 1998c), it confined itself to repeating that Member States should define their public service broadcasting mission and should provide for financial transparency as regards commercial services provided by public service broadcasters.

In 1999, a resolution concerning public service broadcasting was adopted by the Council and representatives of the governments of the Member States (Council, 1999).

The Council stressed that the increased diversification of the programmes on offer in the new media environment reinforces the importance of the *comprehensive* mission of public service broadcasters. The resolution also highlighted the important role of PSB media in bringing to the public the benefits of the new audiovisual and information services and the new technologies. In terms reminiscent of the 1996 resolution of the European Parliament, it noted that public service broadcasting must be able to continue to provide a wide range of programming in order to address society as a whole. In this context, the resolution says clearly, it is legitimate for public service broadcasting to seek to reach wide audiences.

The next document issued by the European Commission, i.e. the Communication from the Commission on the application of State aid rules to public service broadcasting (European Commission, 2001), has been described by Coppieters (2002) as 'a breakthrough':

> It recognises a number of principles that the Member States and the Commission were unable to agree and seemed unlikely ever to agree a few years ago. The Commission now recognises the specific character of public service duty in the broadcasting sector. Moreover, the competence of the Member States to define the public service broadcasting remit has been explicitly confirmed, and it is expressly recognised on two occasions that this can be a 'wide definition' through which the broadcaster can offer 'a wide choice of programmes' with a view to 'preserving a certain level of audience'. This means that the Commission no longer confines the public service remit to cultural, educational and news programmes which appeal to only a small segment of the population, but now includes sports and entertainment programmes too. It also stresses that public service broadcasting should benefit from technological developments, and must therefore be capable of providing the population with new, on-line services (Coppieters, 2002, p. 9).

By referring to 'public service' and 'non-public service activities' and by citing examples of what could be meant by both these types of activities (e.g. e-commerce activities could not legitimately be recognized as a public service, which does not mean that PSB broadcasters may not engage in it), the Commission has in effect joined the European Parliament and the Council in accepting the 'full portfolio' model of public service broadcasting. As noted above, this is also the model most likely to be adopted by PSB broadcasters themselves. The Commission's support for it is not really surprising, in that it is in accordance with its long-standing view that public service broadcasters should also operate and compete on the market.

The view of the PSB remit which emerged as a result of this long and tortuous process is shown in Figure 4.

Figure 4. European Council, Council, European Parliament, DG X: the PSB remit

<ul><li>Tongue Report *The Future of public service television in a multi-channel digital age* (1996)</li><li>*Resolution on the role of public service television in a multi-media society* (EP, 1996)</li><li>Amsterdam Protocol</li><li>High Level Group on Audiovisual Policy (1998)</li><li>Resolution concerning PSB, Council and representatives of Member States (Council, 1999).</li></ul>	<ul><li>PSB directly related to the democratic, social and cultural needs of society and media pluralism.</li><li>Comprehensive mission of PSB: wide range of programming in order to address society as a whole.</li><li>Suitable balance of entertainment, culture, spectacles and education; natural overlap with commercial broadcasting in popular genres – sport, comedy, drama, news and current affairs.</li><li>PSB can legitimately seek to reach wide audiences.</li><li>PSB important in promoting new audiovisual and information services and the new technologies.</li></ul>

The PSB Regulatory Framework

In its Communication on the application of state aid rules to public service broadcasting, the Commission came down, to all intents and purposes, in favour of the 'full portfolio model'. The qualitative approach it now embraced is in line with the view expressed by Harrison and Woods (2001, pp. 495-496): 'the genre of particular PSB programmes does not matter provided that the overall balance of programming satisfies the criteria of *quality, diversity, [innovation] and universality of access*. These, after all, are the criteria which many scholars have argued ultimately define PSB' (emphasis added). Price and Verhulst (2001) add that PSB-type objectives also include educational role, impartial news and appeal to minority interests.[4]

All this has important implications for regulatory frameworks in Member States, as does the fact that the Commission accepts that the public service remit might include certain services that are not programmes in the traditional sense, such as on-line information services, to the extent that they are addressing the democratic, social and cultural needs of the society in question.

Regulatory implications can be found in the way the Commission has dealt with some of the complaints lodged by commercial broadcasters seeking to prevent PSB broadcasters from expanding and offering new services, including thematic ones. By rejecting complaints against BBC News 24 and against the Phoenix and Kinderkanal channels, the Commission accepted that PSB broadcasters may legitimately extend their operations beyond the traditional generalist channels, and - as noted above - beyond broadcasting as such.

Another significant regulatory development is the apparent abandonment by the Commission of the 'distributed public service model'. In its 1998 discussion paper

(Application of Articles 90..., 1998, p. 3), DG IV described it as one option available to Member States to provide and finance the public service broadcasting to citizens, whereby different commercial operators could win tenders for the provision of different types of PSB content, and public service broadcasting institutions as such would not be needed at all.

This approach has now apparently been revised. In the Communication on the application of State aid rules to public service broadcasting (European Commission, 2001), the Commission says that 'In order to benefit from the exemption under Article 86(2), the public service remit should be entrusted to one or more undertakings by means of an official act (for example, by legislation, contract or terms of reference)'. The Communication clearly distinguishes between public service and commercial broadcasters, for example when it says that 'clear identification of the activities covered by the public service remit is also important for non-public service operators, so that they can plan their activities'.

Financing PSB

Controversies on this subject rumbled on within the EU for a long time. Article 87 of the Treaty bans 'any aid granted by a Member State or through State resources in any form whatsoever which distorts or threatens to distort competition by favouring certain undertakings or the production of certain goods shall, insofar as it affects trade between Member States', because such aid is 'incompatible with the common market'.

Had television been classified as a cultural institution, it would have been possible to apply to it Article 87(3)(d) which potentially permits aid to promote culture and heritage conservation'. However, that opportunity had been all but lost with the *Sacchi* judgment of the ECJ in 1974.

The first step in resolving this difficulty was the Amsterdam Protocol of 1997, which accepted the Member States' competence to 'provide for the funding of public service broadcasting and insofar as such funding is granted to broadcasting organizations for the fulfilment of the public service remit as conferred, defined and organized by each Member State'. Member States were thus free to determine what sources of financing should open to PSB broadcasters.

A few more years of debates, planning and negotiations were required before the Commission could issue its Communication on the application of State aid rules to public service broadcasting, in which it set out 'the principles to be followed by the Commission in the application of Articles 87 and 86(2), of the EC Treaty to State funding of public service broadcasting'. Though adding public service broadcasting to the list of exceptions from State aid rules had been considered, that was not the solution finally chosen. There was clearly no political will to remove PSB from the field of application of internal market regulations. So, the method finally applied was a relatively low-profile document, interpreting existing norms and regulations and not creating new ones to fit the specific case of PSB.

The Communication accepts explicitly that 'funding schemes can be divided into two broad categories: 'single-funding' (public funds only) and 'dual-funding', comprising a wide range of schemes, where public service broadcasting is financed by different combinations of State funds and revenues from commercial activities, such as the sale of advertising space or programmes. There can be no objection in principle to the choice of a dual financing scheme (combining public funds and advertising revenues) rather than a single funding scheme (solely public funds) as long as competition in the relevant markets (e.g. advertising, acquisition and/or sale of programmes) is not affected to an extent which is contrary to the Community interest.

Member States are free to choose the means of financing public service broadcasting, but the Commission has to verify, under Article 86(2), that the derogation from the normal application of the competition rules for the performance of the service of general economic interest does not affect competition in the common market in a disproportionate manner. This requires:

• a clear and precise definition of the public service remit;

• the formal entrustment of the public service remit to one or more undertakings by means of an official act (legislation, contract or terms of reference);

• and a clear and appropriate separation between public service activities and non-public service activities, where the latter exist.

Separation of accounts between these two spheres is normally already required at national level to ensure transparency and accountability when using public funds. A separation of accounts, if a PSB organization engages in non-public service activities, is necessary to allow the Commission to carry out its proportionality test. It will provide the Commission with a tool for examining alleged cross-subsidization and for defending justified compensation payments for general economic interest tasks. Only on the basis of proper cost and revenue allocation can it be determined whether the public financing is actually limited to the net costs of the public service remit and thus acceptable under Article 86(2) and the Amsterdam Protocol.

In the broadcasting sector, separation of accounts poses no particular problem on the revenue side, but may not be straightforward or, indeed, feasible on the cost side. This is due to the fact that, in the broadcasting sector, Member States may consider the whole programming of the broadcasters as covered by the public service remit, while at the same time allowing for its commercial exploitation. In other words, different activities share the same inputs to a large extent.

For these reasons, the Commission considers that, on the revenue side, broadcasting operators should give a detailed account of the sources and amount of all income accruing from the performance of non-public service activities.

On the expenditure side, costs specific to the non-public service activity should be clearly identified. In addition, whenever the same resources - personnel, equipment, fixed installation etc. - are used to perform public service and non-public service tasks, their costs should be allocated on the basis of the difference in the firm's total costs with and without non-public service activities.

In carrying out the proportionality test, the Commission will start from the consideration that the State funding is normally necessary for the undertaking to carry out its public service tasks. However, in order to satisfy this test, it is necessary that the State aid does not exceed the net costs of the public service mission, taking also into account other direct or indirect revenues derived from the public service mission.

Accordingly, in carrying out the proportionality test, the Commission will consider whether or not any distortion of competition arising from the aid can be justified in terms of the need to perform the public service as defined by the Member State and to provide for its funding. When necessary, the Commission will also take action in the light of other Treaty provisions.

Conclusion

One could say that the EU's policy on public service broadcasting has been *reactive* rather than *pro-active*. The agenda-setting role has been played by opponents of PSB and the EU reacted first by formulating its response to controversies regarding the financing of PSB and later augmented its policy by coming incrementally to the defence of those aspects of public service broadcasting which were challenged by commercial broadcasters.

The European Commission has come a long way: from not even mentioning PSB in 1990, through a decade of ignoring the views of Member States, the European Parliament, the European Council, and the Council, to suddenly changing course and accepting (and quoting at length) everything they had been saying. Llorens-Maluquer (2002, p. 9) comments in this context that 'the PBS issue is a paradigmatic case of the Commission loss of power' *vis-à-vis* Member States and other EU bodies.

Nevertheless, it has not deviated from its main approach of refusing to take a culturalist view and to treat public service broadcasting as a preserve of non-commercial programming. The Commission, and the EU in general, have not heeded the call of the European Parliament in its 1996 resolution for 'adjustments to the Treaty so that the Union can develop a positive policy on PSB recognizing its crucial importance in building national and European citizenship, rather than a policy which is based exclusively on exceptions to provisions on competition and internal market policy'. The Communication 2001 does say that 'public service broadcasting, although having a clear economic relevance, is not comparable to a public service in any other economic sector' (European Commission, 2001, p. 5), but identification of PSB as a special type of undertaking, which is exempt from the application of regulations designed to promote competition in the internal market, is out of the question. So, instead of creating guarantees that PSB could broadcast only pure PSB content, public service broadcasters are seen as those as those who in addition to offering all kinds of other content, *also* provided programming characteristic of their public service remit.

Just like the Amsterdam Protocol before it, so the Communication is a product of a hard-won compromise, an internally contradictory text which was drafted to satisfy conflicting expectations and therefore admits of opposing interpretation. Neither document provides legal certainty for public service broadcasters.

Moreover, no sooner was the Communication published when, literally a week later, the very principle on which it is based was undermined by the European Court of Justice. In its *Ferring* decision of 22 November 2001 it stated that 'only advantages which exceed the necessary cost for ensuring the public service obligations constitute State aid'. Thus, according to a comment by the EBU Legal Department (2002), 'the funding necessary for the fulfilment of the public service remit of a broadcaster should not be qualified as State aid'. Previous to that, in the *Preussen Elektra* decision of 13 March 2001, the European Court of Justice had held that 'only advantages granted directly or indirectly through State resources are to be considered aid within the meaning of Article 92(1) of the EC Treaty'. Consequently, the EBU Legal Department argues, the broadcasting fee paid by viewers and listeners should not simply be qualified as state aid where public broadcasters are the creditors of the fee. In view of these decisions, according to the EBU Legal Department, 'the European Commission will probably have to reconsider its position'. One may presume therefore that the provisions of the Commission Communication on the application of State aid rules to public service broadcasters may need to be changed considerably.

If so, then what has already been a spectacularly unsuccessful effort to develop a policy that would do justice to public service broadcasting will turn into a fiasco. With reference to the abortive debates on EU-wide regulation of media concentration, Kaitatzi-Whitlock (1996, p. 455) has noted that it is impossible to fit 'the political and cultural issue of [media] pluralism on to the economistic [sic] Procrustean bed of the Single European Market'. The same is certainly true of public service broadcasting.

Notes

1   The Court's ruling reads in part: 'In the case of public undertakings and undertakings to which Member States grant special or exclusive rights, Member States shall neither enact nor maintain in force any measure contrary to the rules contained in this Treaty, in particular to those rules provided for in Article 72 and Articles 81 to 89. Undertakings entrusted with the operation of services of general economic interest or having the character of a revenue-producing monopoly shall be subject to the rules contained in this Treaty, in particular to the rules on competition, insofar as the application of such rules does not obstruct the performance, in law or in fact, of the particular tasks assigned to them. The development of trade must not be affected to such an extent as would be contrary to the interests of the Community'. (International Court of Justice, 1974)

2   This has been explained in the following way: 'Under the Treaties, the Community has no independent mandate to shape the area of the media. Rather, the legal bases are 'horizontal', in other words they are designed to achieve general objectives of the Community, especially the completion of the internal market [...] Community policy in the area of the regulation of media content is thus essentially [...] governed and limited by the internal market objective of freedom of movement for goods (including newspapers and magazines, for example) and services (including radio and television broadcasts). Community regulation of content is therefore particularly subject to the requirement of proportionality. It must regulate those matters that are necessary for the completion of the internal market, but may not regulate anything else (Reding, 2002, p. 7).

3   It describes PSB as a fundamental player in the public sphere with a remit to: 'offer a wide range of quality production in all genres to the whole population in their respective Member States, combining both intellectual stimulation and popular entertainment and encompassing the entire range of spectacles, arts and ideas making up the spectrum of cultural life in all its diversity; reflect and support the cultures of Europe's nations and regions through a wealth of original productions; encourage understanding of the non-European cultures and ethnic groups present in the Union, transmitting the notion of shared experience in diversity; set quality standards in popular programmes followed by mass audiences; serve minority interests and cater for all different sections of the population; provide unbiased and fully independent information, both in news coverage and in-depth factual programming, capable of earning the audience's trust and of representing a reference point in the rapidly expanding information market; play a major role in encouraging the public debate that is vital for the proper functioning of democracy and provide a

forum for debate for all groups and organizations in society, to ensure that the general population has access to events of general public interest, including sports events; pioneer innovative programme types, genres and services; encourage audiovisual creation and the expression of new talents particularly by providing broadcasting opportunities for independent producers; lead the way in applying the full potential of new audiovisual technology such as terrestrial and satellite-based digital transmission, audiovisual services and CD-ROM to public policy areas such as education, health and government information; ensure, on the basis of the principle of democratic access to the new media, that where access to new technology is not available to individuals these new services are made readily accessible to the community at large within public institutions and public places.

4   One well-known list of 'those main elements of public service broadcasting as it has evolved in Britain' is as follows: 'Universality: Geographic - broadcasting programmes should be available to the whole population; Universality of Appeal - broadcast programmes should cater for all interests and tastes; Minorities, especially disadvantaged minorities, should receive particular provision; Broadcasters should recognize their special relationship to the sense of national identity and community; Broadcasting should be distanced from all vested interests, and in particular from those of the government of the day; Universality of Payment - one main instrument of broadcasting should be directly funded by the corpus of users; Broadcasting should be structured so as to encourage competition in good programming rather than competition for numbers; The public guidelines for broadcasting should be designed to liberate rather than to restrict the programme makers'. Source: The Public Service Idea..., n.d. The Council of Europe's 4th European Ministerial Conference on Mass Media Policy (Prague, 7-8 December 1994) in its 'Resolution No. 1: The Future of Public Service Broadcasting' listed the following 'Public service requirements': 'public service broadcasters, within the general framework defined for them and without prejudice to more specific public service remits, must have principally the following missions:

• to provide, through their programming, a reference point for all members of the public and a factor for social cohesion and integration of all individuals, groups and communities. In particular, they must reject any cultural, sexual, religious or racial discrimination and any form of social segregation;

• to provide a forum for public discussion in which as broad a spectrum as possible of views and opinions can be expressed;

• to broadcast impartial and independent news, information and comment;

• to develop pluralistic, innovatory and varied programming which meets high ethical and quality standards and not to sacrifice the pursuit of quality to market forces;

• to develop and structure programme schedules and services of interest to a wide public while being attentive to the needs of minority groups;

- to reflect the different philosophical ideas and religious beliefs in society, with the aim of strengthening mutual understanding and tolerance and promoting community relations in pluriethnic and multicultural societies;

- to contribute actively through their programming to a greater appreciation and dissemination of the diversity of national and European cultural heritage;

- to ensure that the programmes offered contain a significant proportion of original productions, especially feature films, drama and other creative works, and to have regard to the need to use independent producers and co-operate with the cinema sector;

- to extend the choice available to viewers and listeners by also offering programme services which are not normally provided by commercial broadcasters. (European Ministerial Conferences... 2000).

References

Brants, Kees, et al., (1998) (Eds.) The Media in Question. Popular Cultures and Public Interests. London: Sage, pp. 18-26.

Collins, Richard (1997) 'Unity in Diversity? The European Single Market in Broadcasting and the Audiovisual 1982-1994' In Stelios Stavridis, Elias Mossalios, Roger Morgan, Howard Machin (Eds.) New Challenges to the European Union: Policies and Policy-Making. Aldershot: Dartmouth Publishing Co., pp. 329-358.

Coppieters, Sandra (2002) The Financing of Public Service Broadcasting. Paper presented during the 94th Ordinary Session of the EBU Legal Committee, Tunis.

Council (1999) 'Resolution of the Council and of the Representatives of the Governments of the Member States, meeting within the Council of 25 January 1999 concerning public service broadcasting' Official Journal of the European Council, C 030, 05/02, p. 1.

Cutler, Terry (1998) Re-inventing Regulation in the Era of Convergence, World Telecommunications Day Forum, Kuala Lumpur, 19 May,

www.cutlerco/com.au/content/speeches/WTD/WTD.html.

DG IV (1998) Application of Articles 90, paragraph 2, 92 and 93 of the EC Treaty in the broadcasting sector. Discussion paper. Brussels.

European Commission (1984) Television Without Frontiers: Green Paper on the establishment of the common market for broadcasting, especially by satellite and cable. COM (84)300. Brussels.

European Commission (1990) The European Community Policy in the Audiovisual Field. Legal and political texts. COM (90)78. Brussels, Luxembourg.

European Commission (1994) Proceedings of the European Audiovisual Conference. Brussels, Luxembourg.

European Commission (1995) Preparing for the information society: Guidelines on state aid for the arts and culture, with particular reference to the audiovisual sector (1995). DG IV Working Document. Brussels.

European Commission (1997) Green Paper on the Convergence of the Telecommunications, Media and Information Technology Sectors, and the Implications for Regulation. Towards An Information Society Approach. Brussels, Luxembourg.

European Commission (1998a) The Digital Age. European Audiovisual Policy. Report from the High-Level Group on Audiovisual Policy. Brussels-Luxembourg.

European Commission (1998b) Proceedings of the European Audiovisual Conference. Brussels, Luxembourg.

European Commission (1998c) Communication from the Commission to the European Parliament and the Council of Ministers 'Audiovisual Policy: next steps'. COM (1998) 446. Brussels, Luxembourg.

European Commission (1999) Communication from the Commission: Principles and Guidelines for the Community's Audiovisual Policy in the Digital Age COM (1999) 657. Brussels.

European Commission (2001) 'Communication from the Commission on the application of State aid rules to public service broadcasting'. Official Journal of the European Communities. C 320, pp. 5-11.

European Court of Justice (1974) Judgment of the Court of 30 April 1974. Giuseppe Sacchi. Case 155-73.

http://europa.eu.int/smartapi/cgi/sga_doc?smartapi!celexplus!prod!CELEXnumdoc&lg=en&numdoc=61973J0155.

European Ministerial Conferences on mass media policy: Texts adopted (2000). DH-MM (2000) 4. Strasbourg, Directorate General of Human Rights, Council of Europe.

European Parliament (1996) 'Resolution on the role of public service television in a multi-media society'. Official Journal of the European Communities. No C 320, October 28.

Harrison, Jackie, Lorna M. Woods (2001) 'Defining European Public Service Broadcasting'. European Journal of Communication. 16(4), pp. 477-504.

Kaitatzi-Whitlock, Sophia (1996) 'Pluralism and Media Concentration in Europe. Media Policy as Industrial Policy'. European Journal of Communication. 11(4), pp. 453-483.

Legal Department (2002) Comments on the Communication from the Commission on the application of State aid rules to public service broadcasting (2001/C 320/04). Geneva: EBU.

Levin, Arthur B. (1999) 'Regulatory challenges in the digital age'. InterMedia. 27(1), pp. 4-7.

Llorens-Maluquer, Caries (2002) The European Union Policy, Pluralism and Public Service Broadcasting. Paper presented at the RIPE@2002 Conference, Helsinki-Tampere.

McQuail, Denis (1998) 'Commercialization and beyond' In Denis McQuail, Karen Siune (Eds.) Media Policy. Convergence, Concentration and Commerce. Euromedia Research Group. London: Sage Publishers, pp. 107-127.

McQuail, Denis (2000) Mass Communication Theory. London: Sage Publications.

Media with a Purpose. Serving the Public in the Digital Era (2002). Part 3: 'The Mission and Financing of Public Service Broadcasting in the Digital Environment' (Draft). Geneva: Digital Strategy Group, EBU.

Michalis, Maria (1999) 'European Union Broadcasting and Telecoms: Towards a Convergent Regulatory Regime?' European Journal of Communication. Vol. 14(2), pp. 147-171.

Murdock, Graham and Peter Golding (1999) 'Common Markets. Corporate Ambitions and Communication Trends in the UK and Europe'. Journal of Media Economics. 12(2), pp. 117-132.

Ostergaard, Bernt Stubbe (1998) 'Convergence: Legislative Dilemmas' In Denis McQuail, Karen Siune (Eds.) Media Policy. Convergence, Concentration and Commerce. London: Sage Publications, pp. 95-96.

Peterson, John, Michael Shackleton (2002) The Institutions of the European Union. Oxford: Oxford University Press.

Price, Monroe E., Stefaan Verhulst (2001) Global Transformations in Public Service Broadcasting. A Comparative and Analytic Approach. Paper presented at a conference on 'Rethinking Public Media in a Transitional Age.' Centre for Media, Culture and History, New York.

Prosser, Tony, David Goldberg and Stefaan Verhulst (1998) EC Media Law and Policy. London: Addison Wesley Longman, 1998.

Reding, Viviane (2002) Speech at the European Voice Conference on 'Television without Frontiers';

http://europa.eu.int/rapid/start/cgi/guesten.ksh?p_action.gettxt=gt&doc=
SPEECH/02/120|0|RAPID&lg=EN&display=

'Resolution of the Council and of the Representatives of the Governments of the Member States, meeting within the Council of 25 January 1999 concerning public service broadcasting' (1999) Official Journal of the European Council C 030, p. 1.

Report by the Think-Tank on the Audiovisual Policy of the European Union (1994). Brussels-Luxembourg: European Communities.

Rollet, Edouard (2001) 'Connecting to the Information Age. A Challenge for the European Union'. Gazette. 63(5), pp. 371-386.

Schlesinger, Philip (1997) 'Building a collective European identity through the media'. The Bulletin. 14(3), September.

Schlesinger, Philip (1997) 'From cultural defence to political cultures: media, politics and collective identity in the European Union'. Media Culture and Society. 19(3), pp. 369-391.

The Public Service Idea in British Broadcasting. Main Principles (n.d.). London: BRU.

Tongue, Carole (1996) The future of public service television in a multi-channel digital age. The Tongue Report, adopted by the European Parliament on 19 September 1996. Illford, Essex: Office of Carole Tongue, MEP.

Van Cuilenburg, Jan (2000) 'Media and Open Societies. An Introduction' In Jan van Cuilenburg, Richard van der Wurff (Eds.) Media and Open Societies. Cultural, Economic and Policy Foundations for Media Openness and Diversity in East and West. Amsterdam: Het Sinhuis, pp. 1-10.

Weymouth, Tony, and Bernard Lamizet (1997) (Eds.) Markets and Myths: Forces for Change in the European Media. London: Addison Wesley Longman.

Index